# How to Do
## *Everything*
### with

# Microsoft®
# Digital Image
# Pro 9

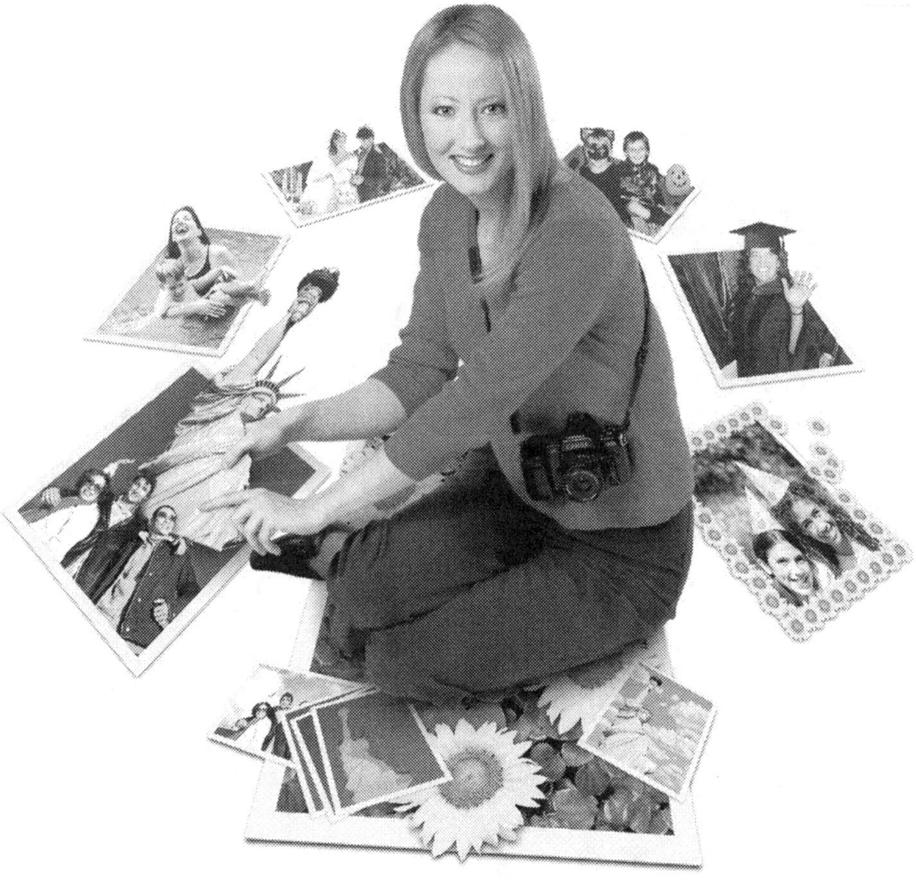

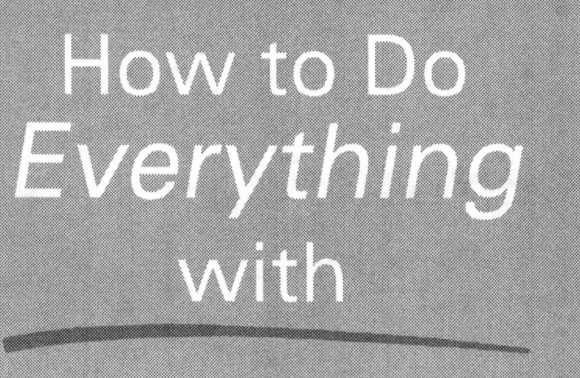

# How to Do *Everything* with

# Microsoft® Digital Image Pro 9

## David Plotkin

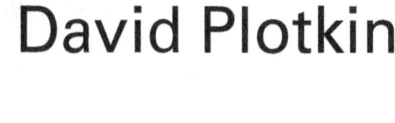

**McGraw-Hill**/Osborne

New York   Chicago   San Francisco   Lisbon
London   Madrid   Mexico City   Milan   New Delhi
San Juan   Seoul   Singapore   Sydney   Toronto

The McGraw·Hill Companies

**McGraw-Hill**/Osborne
2100 Powell Street, 10th Floor
Emeryville, California 94608
U.S.A.

To arrange bulk purchase discounts for sales promotions, premiums, or fund-raisers, please
contact **McGraw-Hill**/Osborne at the above address. For information on translations or
book distributors outside the U.S.A., please see the International Contact Information page
immediately following the index of this book.

**How to Do Everything with Microsoft® Digital Image Pro 9**

1234567890 FGR FGR 019876543

ISBN 0-07-223195-5


| | |
|---|---|
| **Publisher:** | Brandon A. Nordin |
| **Vice President &** | |
| **Associate Publisher:** | Scott Rogers |
| **Acquisitions Editor:** | Katie Conley |
| **Project Editor:** | Julie M. Smith |
| **Acquisitions Coordinator:** | Athena Honore |
| **Technical Editor:** | Bill Bruns |
| **Copy Editor:** | Nancy Rapoport |
| **Proofreader:** | Susie Elkind |
| **Indexer:** | Valerie Perry |
| **Composition:** | Apollo Publishing Services |
| **Series Design:** | Mickey Galicia |
| **Cover Series Design:** | Dodie Shoemaker |
| **Cover Illustration:** | Tom Willis |

This book was composed with Corel VENTURA™ Publisher.

## Dedication

This book is dedicated to the two women in my life who make it all possible. The first is my wife Marisa, who encouraged my writing and picks up the extra load while I am busy with my books. The second is my mother, Nathalie Plotkin. She first encouraged my interest in photography and helped me to set up my first darkroom. She taught me to use a camera as more than just a snapshot machine, and graciously allowed me to use her picture (and my Dad's) throughout this book.

## About the Authors

**David Plotkin** is the Manager of Data Quality for Wells Fargo Consumer Credit Division, and holds a Masters degree in Chemical Engineering from UC Berkeley. He collects business requirements, designs databases, and documents both the data and process of computers systems. He is the author of *How to Do Everything with FrontPage 2003* and *How to Do Everything with Photoshop Elements 2*. He has been a photographer since the age of 12, and has done extensive semi-pro and action photo work. He has his own darkroom and created amp yearbooks long before the days of computers. He has extensive experience with digital photography, including cameras, scanners, printers, and software. David maintains web sites for various non-profit and charitable organizations, and has written several other computer books on database topics and graphics. He lives in Walnut Creek, California with his wife Marisa, a successful writer of children's books.

# Contents at a Glance

# Contents

# Acknowledgments

Many people contribute to a book and this is especially true of a book that includes many photographs. This book would have been much harder to write had it not been for the efforts of the following people:

- My parents, Dr. Norman and Nathalie Plotkin, for allowing me to use them as the subject of many pictures. Most were taken on their 50$^{th}$ wedding anniversary—now *that* is longevity.

- My brother Fred whose likeness appears in many images – and got removed from one of them just because I could!

- My brother Larry. Many of the outdoor scenes—including the famous "floats in the lake" picture—were from Larry's collection, and he graciously allowed me to use them. He is the most artistic of the three of us, and it really shows in his photos.

- My wife Marisa, not only for allowing me to use her portraits, but for putting up with the brutal schedule that goes along with writing a book. Fortunately, she is a writer herself (children's books) so she understands just how hard it is to write a book. And how many women would allow their picture to be published without a trace of makeup and with a giant lizard on their shoulder? Definitely a special lady.

Of course, the other "batch" of people who made this book a reality are the hard-working folks at McGraw-Hill/Osborne. These include my acquisitions editor Katie Conley, and the best tech editor you can hope for—Bill Bruns, who also did pretty much all my other books.

On the production side of the house, Julie Smith did yeoman's duty pulling this all together, and my really excellent copy editor Nancy Rapaport kept everything honest and consistent throughout the book.

# Introduction

The fact that you bought this book—or are considering buying it—means you are ready to join the large number of people who have discovered the wonders of digitally editing their photographs. Whether you get your photos into digital form by using a digital camera, scanning your snapshots or negatives, or having the corner drugstore put them on a CD for you, the wonders of what you can achieve with your photos are only beginning. In front of you is a whole book on how to use a simple, yet powerful, digital editing package. Think of this book as a way to explore this fascinating world.

## What Is this Book About?

Ever-falling prices and increasing quality have made digital photography more and more accessible. Cameras that cost under $1000 now produce images that rival film quality, and even inexpensive cameras produce results you can print at 8 x 10. Color inkjet printers produce beautiful prints on glossy paper, and it is now simple to have your digital images printed at the drugstore or over the internet. Inexpensive scanners produce scans from old prints at high resolution so you work with the images digitally.

And yet, the real opportunity provided by digital photography (beyond seeing your pictures immediately on that tiny screen on the back of the camera) is to fix pictures that are less than perfect. Maybe the exposure was a little off, or a busy background distracts from the main subject. With regular film, you'd need a darkroom, an enlarger, a bunch of nasty chemicals, and considerable expertise (trust me, I know) to correct some of these items. And some—such as a damaged print—you could never fix. And you would definitely have a tough time adding a person to a photograph!

In other words, the real opportunity with digital photography is in the software—software like Microsoft Digital Image Pro 9. You can continue to take film pictures if you wish, but with a scanner or a drugstore digital lab, you can digitize the images —and that is where the fun begins. You don't need the darkroom, enlarger, or the nasty chemicals. What you *still* need is the considerable expertise. And *that* is what this book provides. It teaches you to use Microsoft Digital Image Pro 9 to modify your digital photographs using the power of the built-in tools. With a little care and some hard drive space, nothing you do is irreversible—you can always start over from the original. And you don't have to commit the image to paper (or a coffee mug, mouse pad, etc.) until you are truly satisfied with it.

# How Is this Book Organized?

This book is divided into five parts.

Part I, "Get to Know Digital Image Pro," introduces the various parts of the software, including navigation, the workspace, toolbars, and the task bars. It shows you how to set the software up the way you like, open and save images, get help, use the tutorials, and use the various tools to view images.

Part II, "Make Simple Adjustments to Your Images," teaches you to make general corrections to the overall image, such as adjusting brightness, contrast, and color. It also shows you how to crop an image, use the brushes, sharpen and blur and image, as well as other effects. This section also shows you exactly how to repair old or damaged photographs.

Part III, "Make Changes to Specific Parts of Your Photos," teaches you to select the portion of your photo you want to work with, including all areas of a certain color. Of course, once you have selected an area, you can apply changes limited to just that area, such as a gradient or a blur. This section introduces objects (which live on object layers), which enables you to stack up items without changing the base image. You can apply fills and adjustments (like color or brightness) to objects. You can flip, rotate, skew, distort, emphasize, and make other transformations to selected objects. You can add objects that weren't there, remove objects that were, and even add simple shapes to an image.

Part IV, "Use Filters, Text, and Edges to Go Beyond the Darkroom," introduces filters, powerful tools that can change the look of your image with very little effort. You can add texture, and make the image look like it was created in alternative media (such as watercolors or color pencils). You can add both regular and shaped text to an image, and modify how the text looks, including the font, size, color, and (for shaped text) the overall shape of the text. You can add special edges to an image. These edges are created from small photos or shapes, and you have considerable control over how they look. You can even create frames and mattes, as well as other projects, such as calendars, greeting cards, animations, and assorted gifts such as apparel, mugs, clocks, and mouse pads. You can also make bulk modifications to images in the Minilab.

Part V, "Publishing and Sharing Your Photos," teaches you how to print your images either locally or professionally over the internet. You can print images one at a time or in a layout that combines multiple photos (or multiple copies of the same photo) on a page. You'll learn to prepare your image for transmission via the web or e-mail, and even set up the image to be viewed on a device such a cell phone or a PDA.

## Who Is this Book Written For?

This book is primarily written for people who want to learn how to use Digital Image Pro 9 to manipulate and produce results from digital photographs. This book does not assume you are an expert photographer, but it focuses on the software and does not teach you to become an accomplished photographer. It assume you know how to either create digital photos or convert film images/slides/negatives to digital form. It presents information in a logical, step-by-step format, so you can read the book through to learn what Digital Image Pro 9 can do – and then refer to it later as you need to refresh your memory on a particular technique.

So, enjoy the experience! There is nothing quite like taking a so-so photo and turning it into a work of art. Working with digital photos and Digital Image Pro 9 is fun and rewarding. And the first time you restore a damaged (and possibly irreplaceable) photo for someone, you'll know the real feeling of satisfaction.

# Get to Know Digital Image Pro

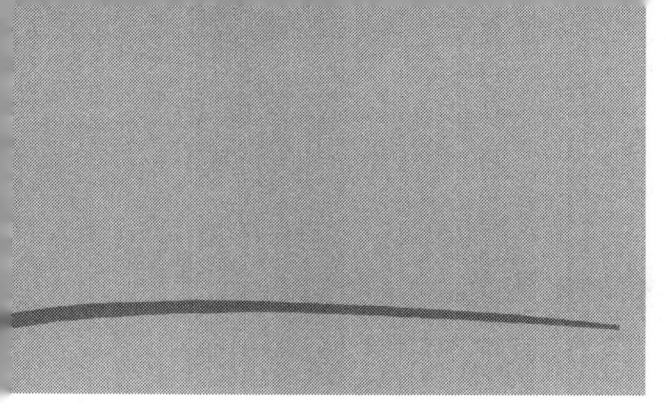

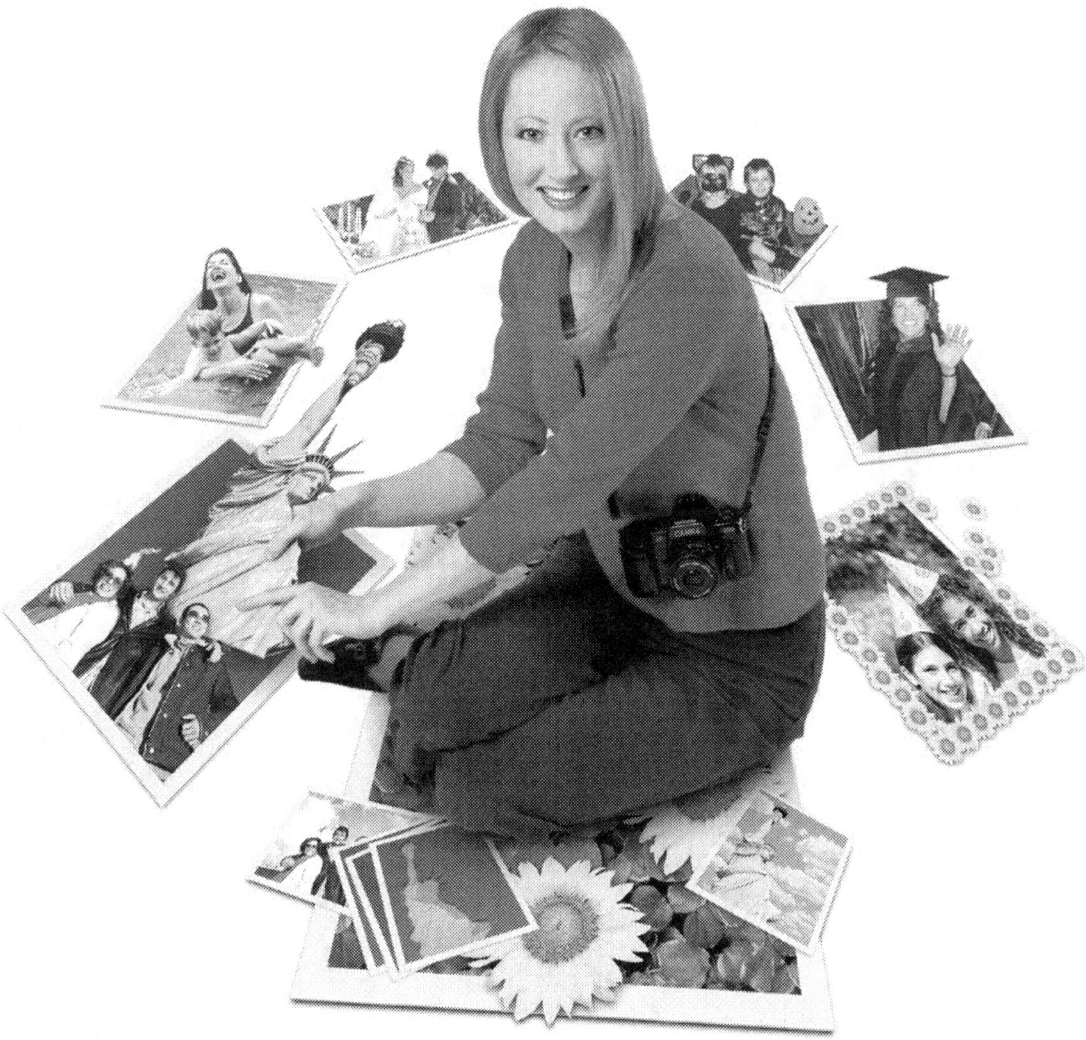

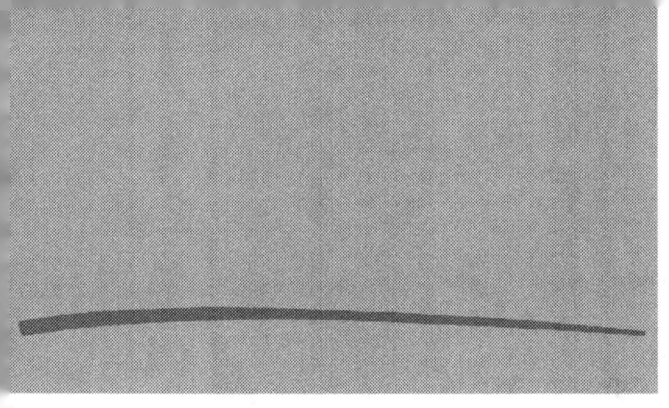

# Navigate in Digital Image Pro

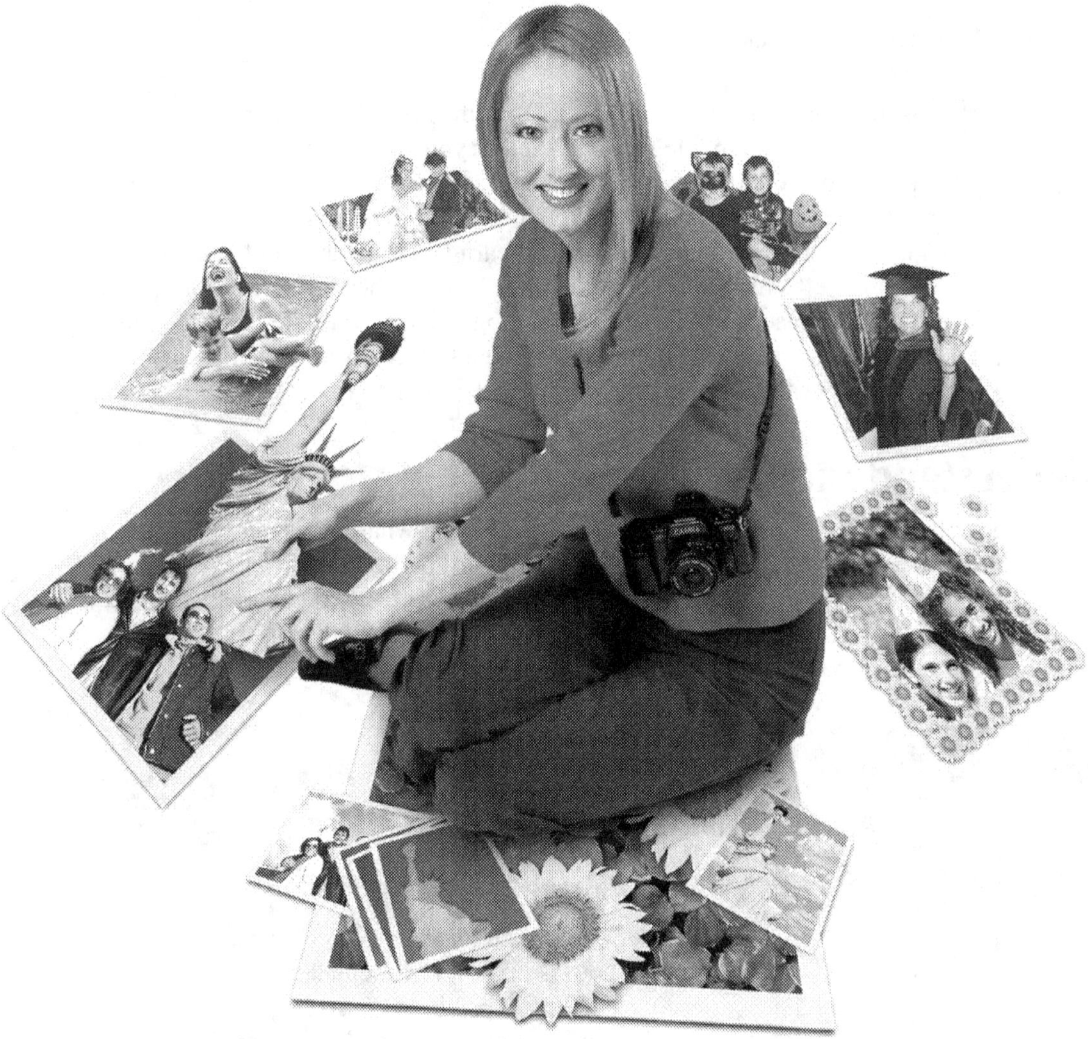

## How to…

- ■ Configure the interface
- ■ View and work with the zoom and pan controls
- ■ Position the rulers
- ■ Get help from the program
- ■ Use the Tour and instructional videos
- ■ Undo your mistakes

Microsoft Digital Image Pro is designed specifically to help you clean up and modify your digital photographs. Whether you create your photos by using a digital camera, or by shooting film and then scanning the prints or negatives into your computer, Digital Pro enables you to customize the results.

As with any software program, you must learn your way around the interface if you hope to use it effectively. The Digital Image Pro interface is relatively simple, leaving you lots of space to work on your photographs. Nevertheless, a little time spent understanding what the various parts of the interface do and how to customize the interface to your liking will help you be more productive.

# Understand the Interface

Figure 1-1 displays the Digital Image Pro interface in what I consider to be the most efficient configuration. As described in the following sections, the Digital Image Pro interface provides a space to work on your image (the workspace), a set of tools (the two toolbars as well as the zoom and selection controls), a list of the open files (Files palette), and the "stack" of objects you are working with (Stack).

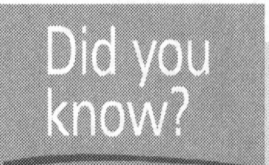

## Change Your View

You can turn the Files palette, Stack, Pan palette, and Common Tasks list on and off using the View menu. The entries in the View menu are toggles— selecting an item that is unchecked makes it visible in the workspace and adds a checkmark to the item. Selecting an item that is checked (and therefore visible in the workspace) hides that item and clears the checkmark.

Toolbar          Selection tools                Zoom controls   Pan Palette button

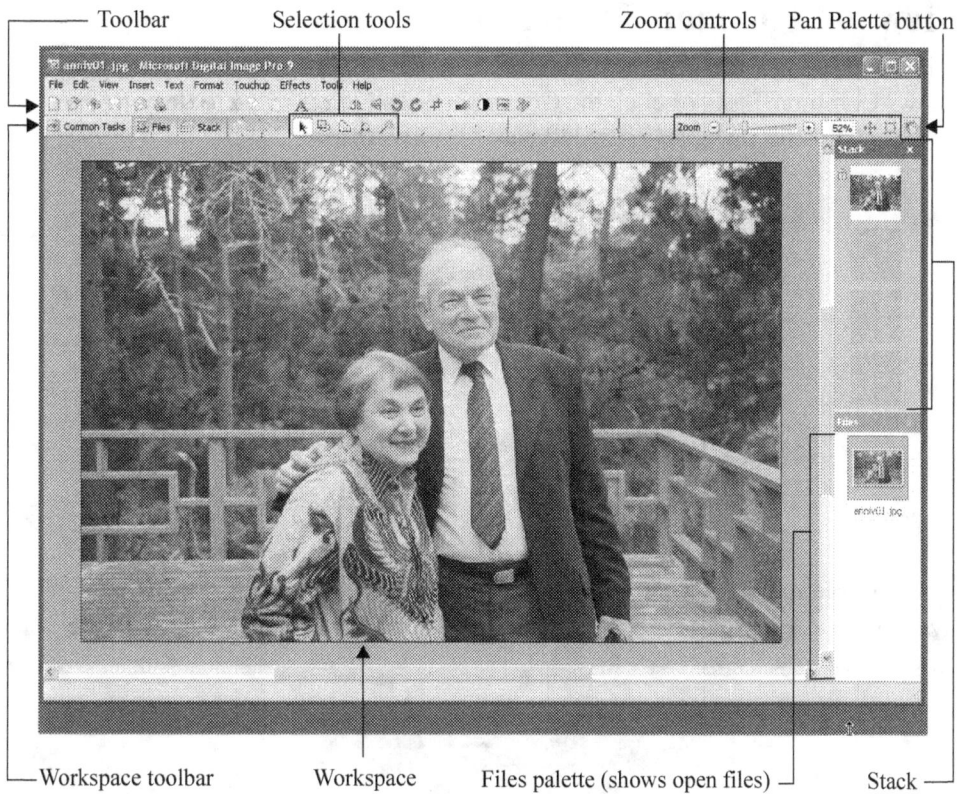

Workspace toolbar          Workspace          Files palette (shows open files)          Stack

You can configure the interface to your liking.

## View the Workspace

The workspace is the entire screen below the toolbars. This area is where you open an image to work on it, as discussed in Chapter 3. Your open image shares the workspace with any of the items (such as the Files palette, Stack, and Common Tasks list) that you have open. You can have multiple image files open in Digital Image Pro, but you can see only one image a time in the workspace. To switch to another image, you must select the image in the Files palette by clicking it.

NOTE
*Your screen may look different from what is pictured in Figure 1-1, especially if your monitor is configured to display a different resolution from the one in the figure (1,024 x 768). Higher resolutions give you more room to work on an image because the Files palette and Stack (and any other items you have open) are smaller and thus take up less of your workspace.*

## View the Common Tasks List

Digital Image Pro provides the *Common Tasks List*. To activate the list, choose View | Common Tasks or click the Common Tasks button in the toolbar. When activated, this list appears on the left side of the workspace.

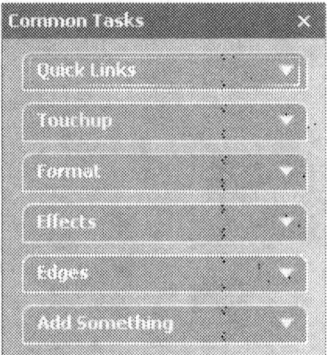

The Common Tasks List displays a set of tool categories. To see the options available under a category, click the category name, as I've done here with the Effects category.

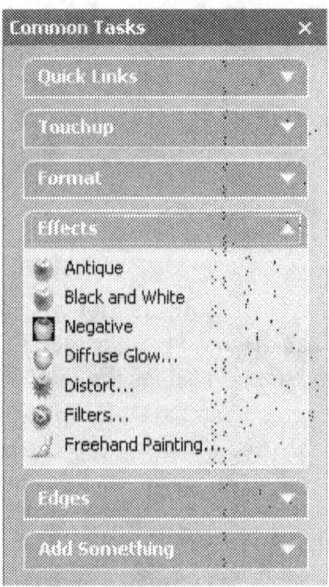

To close a category list, simply click the category title again.

> **TIP**  *The Common Tasks List takes up a LOT of room on the screen, and all the options in the list are duplicated in the menus. Thus, there is really no good reason to keep the list open. To close it, either click the x in the upper-right corner, click the Common Tasks button in the toolbar, or select View | Common Tasks.*

## View the Files Palette

As mentioned earlier, you can open multiple files in Digital Image Pro. Each open file is displayed in the Files palette as a thumbnail. To view a file in the workspace, click the thumbnail for that file in the Files palette. By default, the Files palette and the Stack are docked against the right side of the workspace (as shown previously in Figure 1-1). You can adjust the split between the Stack and the Files palette by moving the mouse to the top of the Files palette title bar (it becomes a two-headed arrow), holding down the left mouse button, and dragging the Files palette title bar up or down.

To hide or display the Files palette, click the Files button in the toolbar or choose View | Files. You can also hide the Files palette by clicking the x in the upper-right corner of the Files palette.

You can undock the Files palette from the right side of the screen, turning it into a regular window that you can move and resize.

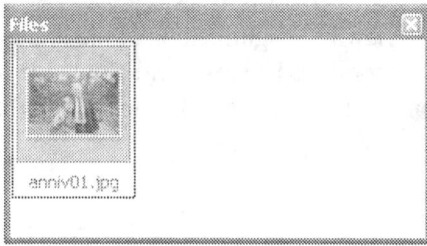

To undock the Files palette, choose View | Dock | Files. To dock the Files palette again, select View | Dock | Files again (it is a toggle).

## View the Stack

You can add objects to an image, such as shapes, text, portions of other images that you have copied and pasted, and much more. Each object sits on its own layer. As you'll find out in Chapters 8, 9, and 10, you can rearrange the stacking order of the objects. All the objects in the selected image are displayed in the Stack. The object at the top of the Stack is "highest" in the stacking order, and you can click and drag objects to change the stacking order. If the object displays a small lock icon next to it, it means (can you guess?) that the object is locked and you cannot perform normal operations (such as moving, sizing, and rotating) on the object. To lock an object in the stack, choose Lock from the shortcut menu. To unlock an object, choose Unlock from the shortcut menu.

To hide or display the Stack, click the Stack button in the toolbar or choose View | Stack. You can also hide the Stack by clicking the x in the upper-right corner of the Stack.

As with the Files palette, you can undock the Stack to turn it into a regular window. Unlike the Files area, however, you cannot make the Stack window any wider than its default width; you can only make the Stack window taller or shorter.

## View the Toolbars

There are two toolbars at the top of the screen. The lower one is called the *workspace toolbar* and houses buttons to turn on and off the Common Tasks bar, Files palette, and the Stack. It also houses the Selection tools (discussed in Chapter 8) and the zoom/magnification tools (discussed later in this chapter).

The upper toolbar, known simply as the *toolbar* (see Figure 1-2), displays a set of common tools you can activate with a single click. This toolbar cannot be hidden or moved, so learn to live with it!

## View and Work with the Zoom Controls

The zoom controls set the viewing magnification of the image, and are located at the right end of the workspace toolbar. The text field alongside the + button displays the current magnification. You can change the zoom in the following ways:

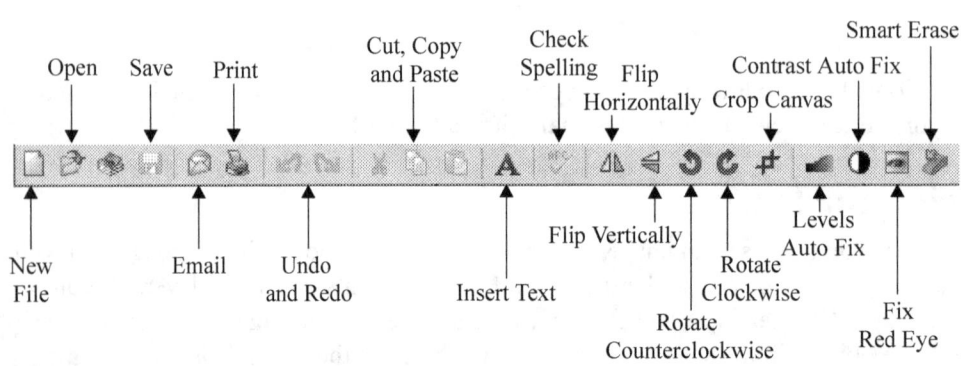

Use the toolbar tools to choose a command quickly.

1

- **Click the - or + buttons**   Clicking the - or + buttons changes the magnifications (either down or up) by standard increments. For example, if the image is currently displayed at 25 percent, clicking the + button changes the magnification to 50 percent, and clicking it again changes the magnification to 67 percent. You get the same effect by selecting View | Zoom Out or View | Zoom In.

- **Drag the slider**   Drag the slider to the right (towards the + button) to increase the magnification; drag the slider to the left (towards the - button) to decrease the magnification.

- **Type a magnification value into the text field**   Select the text field and type a value into the field. You cannot type a percent symbol, but if you accidentally erase the percent symbol, simply type a number and press ENTER and the percent symbol is automatically inserted.

- **Zoom to whole page**   Click the Zoom to Whole Page button (just to the right of the text field) to automatically choose the highest magnification for which your image is entirely visible in the workspace.

- **Zoom to selection**   Click the Zoom to Selection button (just to the right of the Zoom to Whole Page button) to automatically choose the highest magnification for which the selected section of the image fills the workspace. For example, here I selected the subject's face and clicked the Zoom to Selection button.

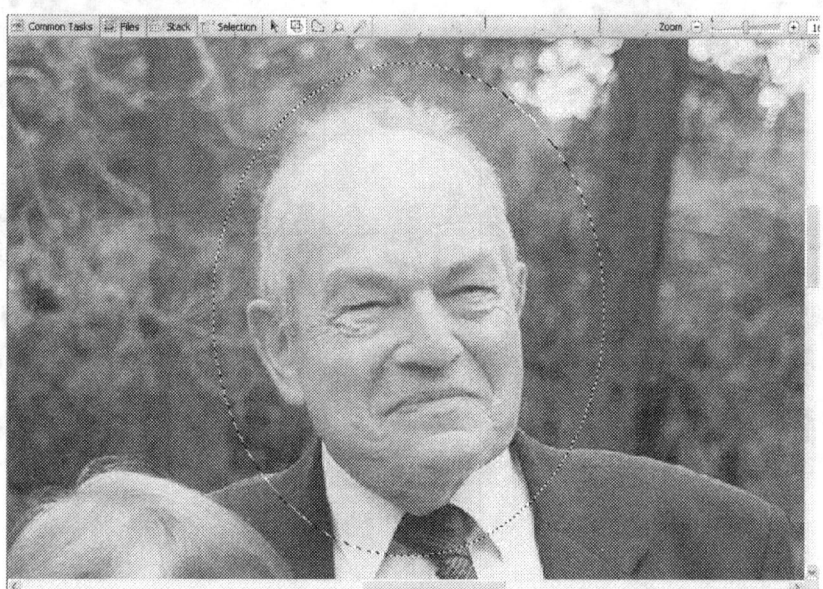

■ **Select a magnification from the menu**   You can select a magnification from the View | Zoom submenu. Options include standard magnifications, zooming to the whole page, zooming to the page width, and zooming to the selected object.

> **TIP**   *If you have a mouse with a scroll wheel, you can quickly change the magnification. Roll the scroll wheel forward to increase the zoom; roll it backwards to decrease the zoom.*

## Work with the Pan Controls

If your image is too big to fit into the workspace at the magnification you need, you may need to move the image around to make various parts of it visible. This is called *panning*. One way to pan the image is to use the horizontal and vertical scroll bars. However, a more precise way to pan is to turn on the Pan palette by either selecting View | Pan or clicking the Pan Palette button at the right end of the lower toolbar. The Pan palette is a window that displays the entire workspace in miniature.

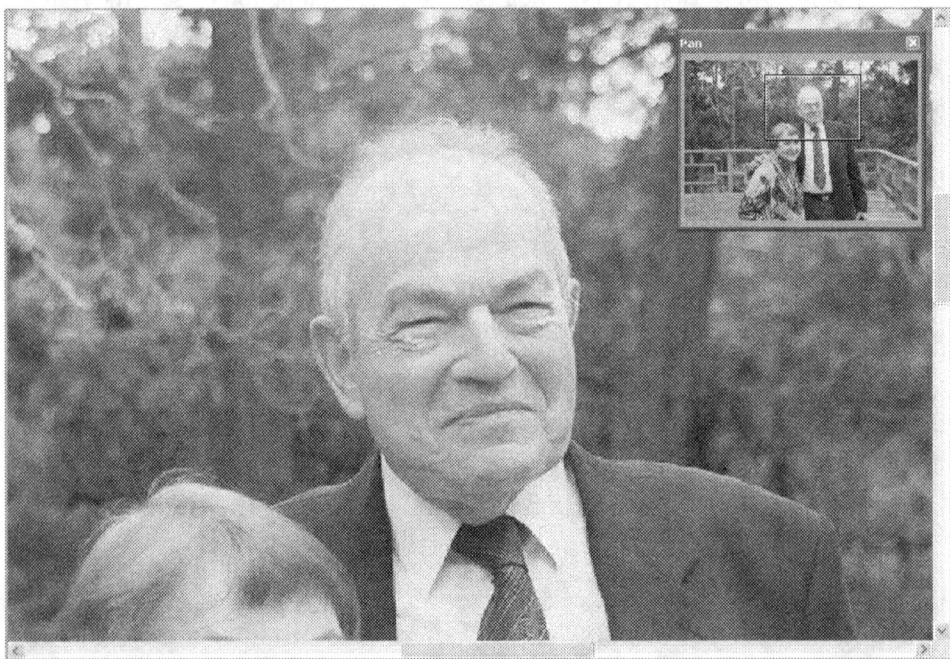

To pan the image and make an area visible in the workspace, click the rectangle in the Pan palette (which represents the visible portion of the image) and drag the rectangle to display the area you want to see.

> **NOTE** *You can size the Pan palette window just like any other window—by clicking and dragging one of the window borders. This is handy for increasing the size of the workspace representation so that you can see more of the details in the Pan palette window.*

## Position the Rulers

When you need to do precise work on an image, it can be very helpful to have rulers available. For example, say you want to add an edge to an image (as discussed in Chapter 11). To position the edge exactly and ensure that it is the right width, turn on the rulers by selecting View | Rulers. There are two rulers: one across the top of the screen, the other down the left side.

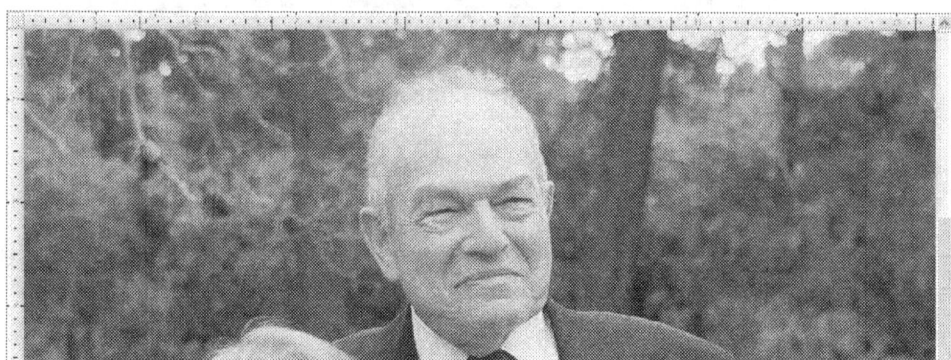

You can position the top ruler by clicking and dragging it up and down. To position the left-side ruler, click and drag it left or right. You can also click at the triangle where the two rulers intersect and drag them both at the same time.

As you move the mouse around the workspace, lines in the ruler show the location of the mouse in relation to the rule measurements. Thus, you can position the mouse precisely.

> **NOTE** *The rulers are calibrated in inches, millimeters, or centimeters. To select the unit of measure, choose Tools | Options and make the selection from the Units of measure drop-down list.*

## Get Started with the Startup Window

When you first run Digital Image Pro, it displays the Startup window.

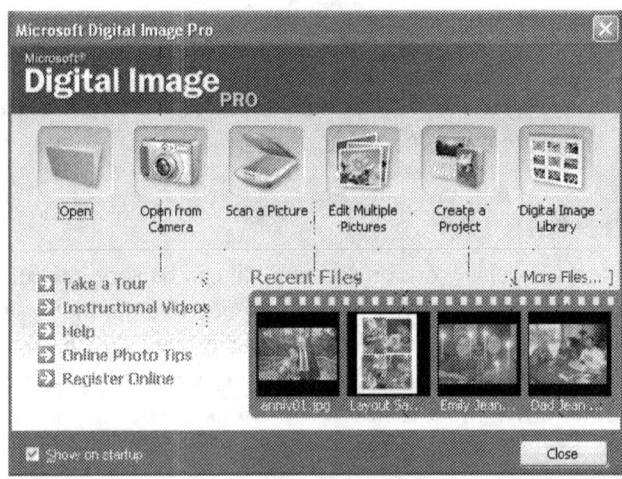

This window enables you to get to work quickly by offering the most common options you need to begin working in the application. These options include the following:

- **Open a file**    Click the Open icon to choose a file to open from the File Browser (discussed in Chapter 3).

- **Download files from a digital camera**    Click the Open From Camera icon to import pictures directly from a digital camera.

- **Scan a Picture**    If you have a scanner connected to your computer, click the Scan a Picture icon to begin the process of scanning a picture directly into Digital Image Pro.

- **Edit Multiple Pictures**    Clicking this icon launches the *Mini Lab*, discussed in Chapter 14. The Mini Lab enables you to apply corrections to a whole set of pictures at once.

- **Create a Project**    Clicking this icon begins the process of creating a *project*, such as a photo album, business cards, calendars, cards, flyers, labels, postcards, and online gifts. Projects are discussed in more detail in Chapter 13.

■ **Digital Image Library**   Clicking this icon opens the Digital Image Library, an application that helps you catalog and view your images. This application is part of the Digital Image Suite. If you purchased just Digital Image Pro, then this menu option is not available.

■ **Choose a recent file**   A list of thumbnails for recently opened files is available at the bottom of the Startup window. To open one of these files, simply click the thumbnail. You can also click [More Files…] to choose a file from the File Browser.

■ **Get help or tips**   Choose an option to take a tour, watch an instructional video, or open the online help from the list at the left side of the Startup window. These options are covered in more detail later in this chapter.

■ **Get Online Photo Tips**   If you are connected to the Internet, clicking this option connects to MSN Photos, a resource for photo tips, as well as new product announcements about digital cameras.

> NOTE   *If you don't want to see the Startup window each time you run Digital Image Pro, clear the Show On Startup checkbox. Alternatively, to display the Startup window at any time, choose File | Startup window.*

# Obtain Help from Digital Image Pro

Digital Image Pro has many ways to help you master its tools and options. These methods include the Windows Help facility, as well as a variety of tutorials and instructional videos to help you learn your way around. Of course, there is also this book…

## Get Help from the Main Help Facility

Your first line of defense is the Windows Help facility. Digital Image Pro includes extensive help, including contents, an index of keywords, a search facility, and a list of help topics that you have designated as your favorites. To access Help, choose Help | Microsoft Digital Image Pro Help.

> TIP   *If you're new to digital photography, check out the Tutorials section of the Contents tab in the Help facility. The four tutorials walk you through subjects such as Basic Photo Touchup, Advanced Photo Editing, and (my favorite) Retouching a Portrait. There are only three tutorials if you didn't purchase Digital Image Suite.*

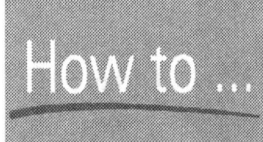 **Maximize Your Workspace**

Because the workspace is where you do all your editing, you will want to maximize this area to give yourself more room to work. Here are some steps you can take to make the most of your workspace:

- **Close any open palettes**   By default, Digital Image Pro displays the Files palette and the Stack, and these take up some room. If you need the space, close these areas by clicking the x in the upper-right corner of the area.

- **Close the Common Tasks list**   This huge bar runs down the left side of your screen, and duplicates commands that are easily found in the menus. Get rid of it!

- **Set your desktop resolution to the highest value you can**   You may be able to increase the resolution of your Windows desktop. This makes everything appear smaller on your monitor, but enables you to display more items in Digital Image Pro (as well as any other applications). If your graphics card and monitor support it, you can increase the resolution to 1024 x 768 (good for a 15-inch monitor), 1280 x 1024 (good for a 17-inch monitor), or even higher (for 19-inch and larger monitors). To change the resolution of your desktop, right-click the desktop and choose Properties from the shortcut menu. Choose Settings from the Display Properties dialog box, and then choose the resolution you want from the Screen Area section of the dialog box.

- **Upgrade your hardware**   If you are serious about doing digital photography, you may wish to consider upgrading your monitor and graphics card, especially if you can't use the resolution you'd like to. seventeen-inch monitors can be purchased for about $100, and larger monitors (nineteen-inch and 20-inch) can be purchased for around $400 (sometimes less). An upgraded graphics card can not only provide increased resolution, but better performance as well. The graphics card is often the bottleneck when rendering digital images. After adding more memory, replacing your graphics card is the wisest investment you can make.

## View the Tour

A quick way to get familiar with the capabilities of Digital Image Pro is to take the Tour. To do so, select Help | Take a Tour. This opens the Tour dialog box.

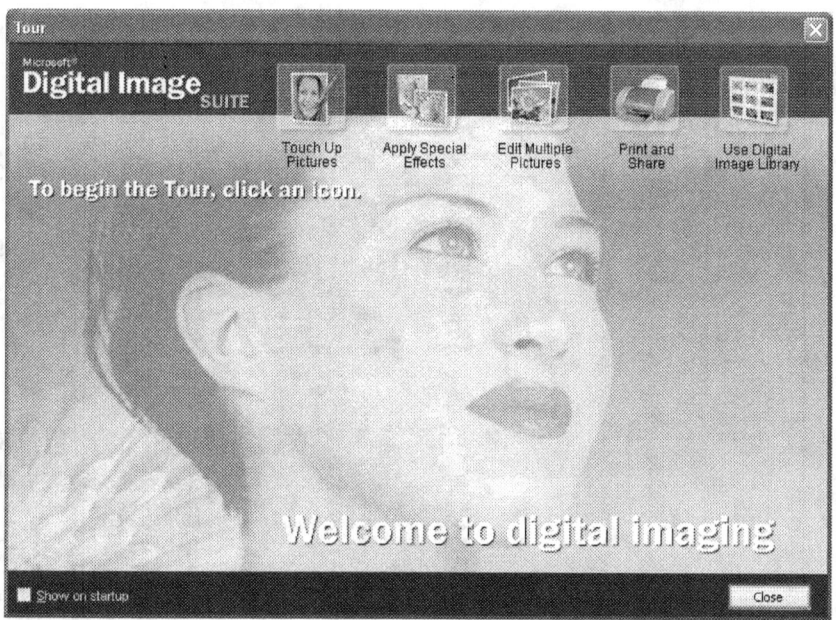

Clicking one of the icons across the top of the dialog box displays a list of related items down the left side of the dialog box. For example, choosing the Touch Up Pictures icon provides choices for Focusing tools, lighting, removing imperfections, straightening a picture, cropping, and using the selection tools. Selecting one of these options displays an animated explanation of what the item does. If you want more detail, you can click a hyperlink that takes you to the Help facility and opens the appropriate content for you to read.

## Use the Instructional Videos

Choosing Help | Instructional Videos opens the main Help facility with the Instructional Videos section selected.

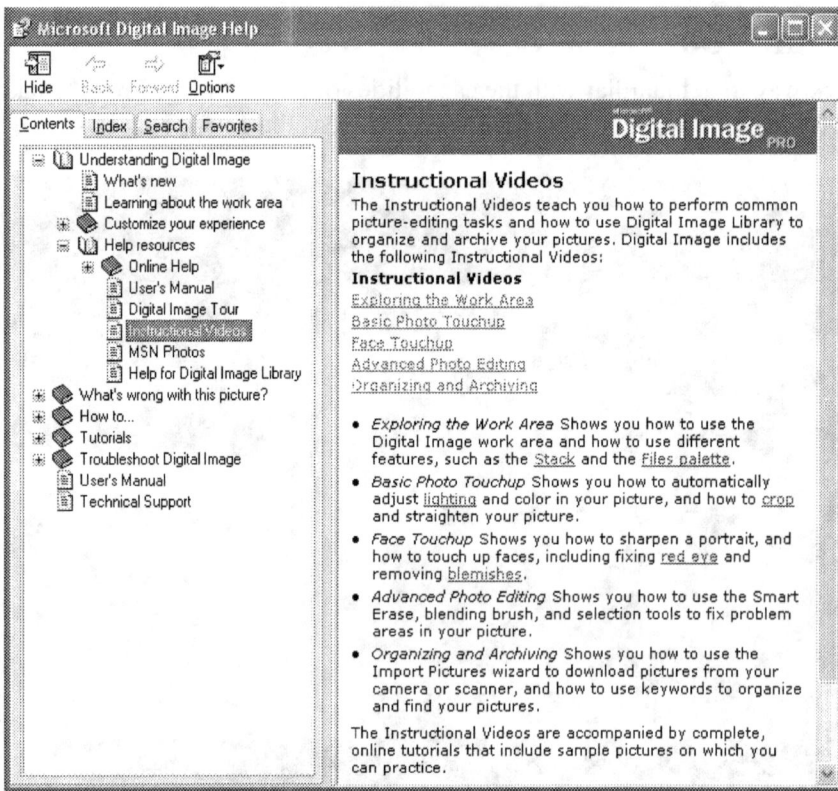

The Help dialog box explains which instructional videos are available, and enables you to select the video you'd like to see. The instructional videos show a reduced version of the Digital Image Pro application, and combines actual use of the tool with voice narration to explain the concepts. Here is an example of the Basic Photo Touchup instructional video.

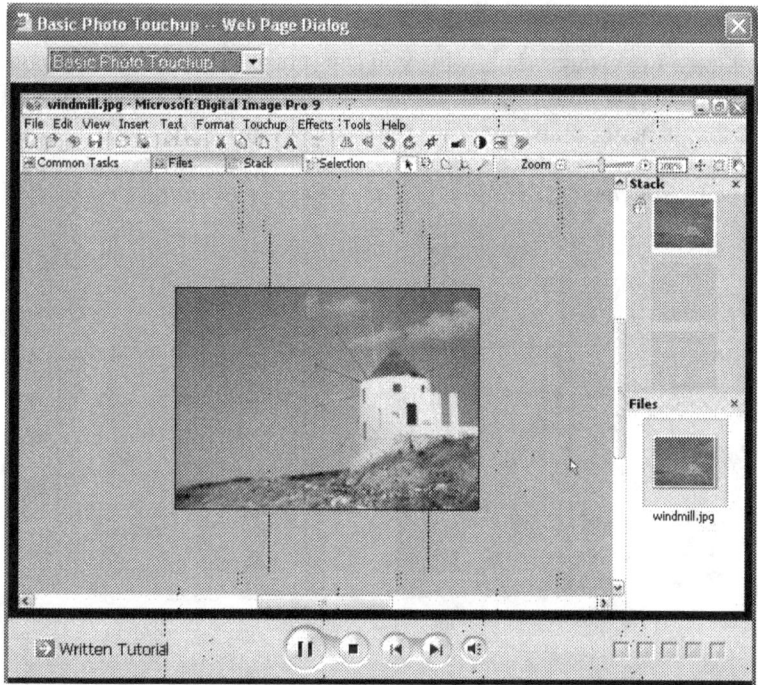

Of course, nothing is ever quite as easy as it looks in a video, but at least you can see the tool in action and have some idea of which tools to choose for which task.

# Correct Mistakes You've Made

It's pretty easy to get carried away with all the wonderful tools and effects in Digital Image Pro. Fortunately, there are a number of ways you can return to an earlier version of your work if you find that you don't care for the results. The options are as follows:

■ **Cancel a step**    As you'll see, many of the tools walk you through a process of customizing the image, showing you what the image looks like each step of the way. At any point, you can click the Cancel button and undo all the effects you've applied in that tool.

■ **Undo your work**    Clicking Edit | Undo steps you back to the previous state of the image. You can continue to click Edit | Undo to step back to a point where you want to start working with the image again.

- **Save your work**   You should always save a copy of your image before making a big change. That way, you can return to that earlier version simply by reloading it from the file. Of course, you'll lose your intermediate work, but that is better than wrecking the image completely.

TIP    *Always, always, ALWAYS keep a copy of your original, unmodified image, just in case...*

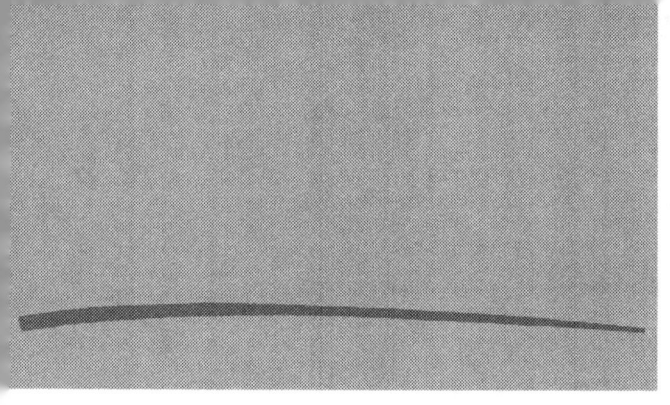

# Configure Digital Image Pro

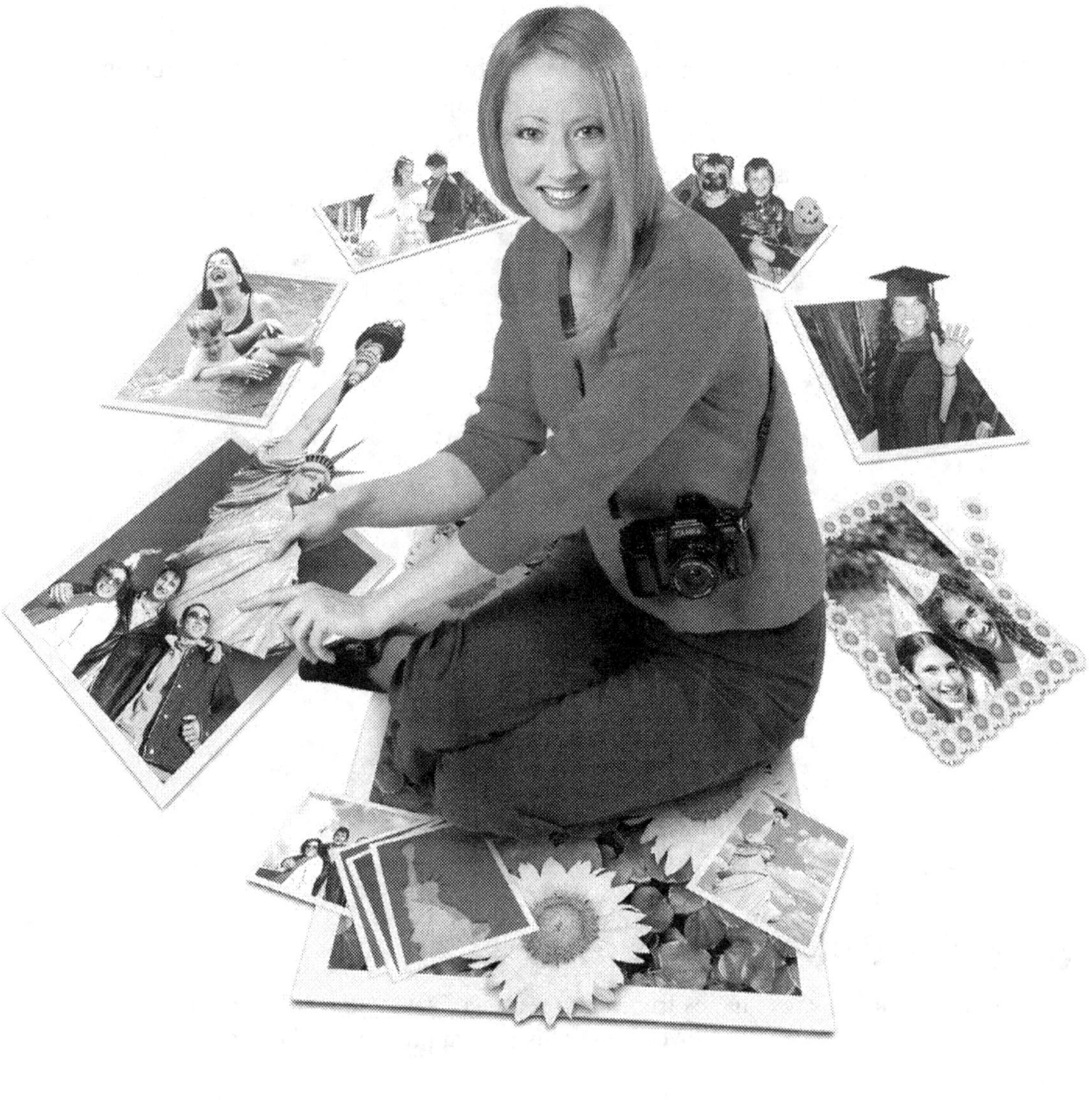

## How to...

- Set the image options
- Set the scanner and camera options
- Configure plug-ins
- Reset all messages
- Adjust the default image resolution and size

There are a number of options you can set in Digital Image Pro so that the program defaults to the settings you use the most. By adjusting these settings, you don't have to remember to modify them each time you use a feature (such as e-mailing a picture) that depends on the options.

To modify the options, select Tools | Options to open the Options dialog box.

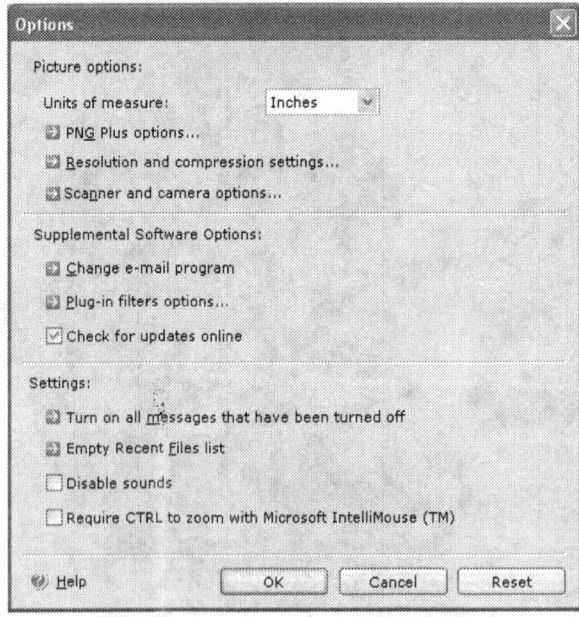

# Adjust the PNG Plus Options

Although you can save images from Digital Image Pro in many different formats, the "native" format is called *PNG Plus*. This format preserves all of your brush settings, objects, stack layers, and so forth, but can only be read by Digital Image Pro and several other products in the Microsoft Picture It! family of products.

Digital Image Pro also saves a version of the image as a PNG file inside the PNG Plus file. While this embedded format discards some information (such as stack layer information), it can be read by many other graphics programs and Internet Explorer. When you try to open a PNG Plus file with some other program, the program finds the embedded PNG file and opens that instead. The embedded PNG file is typically saved at the same size as the image in the PNG Plus file, which can considerably increase the size of the PNG Plus file.

**NOTE**  *Because the stack layer information is discarded in the PNG format file, it is referred to as flattened PNG file by Digital Image Pro.*

If you don't need a full-size, flattened version of the image for use in another program, you can reduce the size of the embedded PNG file, which also reduces the overall size of the PNG Plus file. To change the size, click PNG Plus options in the Options dialog box to open the PNG Plus Options dialog box.

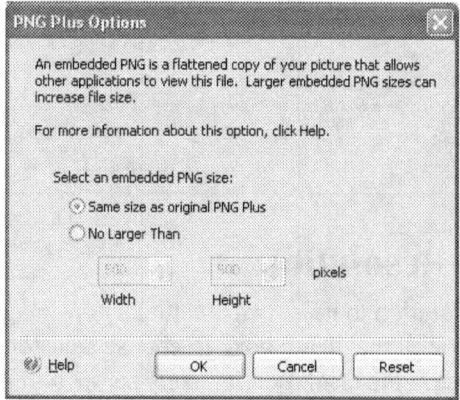

This dialog box provides two options. The first is just to leave the embedded PNG file at the same size as the PNG Plus image. The second option enables you to set the maximum height and width of the embedded file in pixels. To specify the maximum size, choose the No Larger Than option, and specify the maximum width and height by either typing a number into the Width and Height fields, or using the associated *spinners* (up/down arrows to the right of each field).

# Adjust the Resolution and Compression Options

The resolution and compression options enable you to set the default resolution when creating a new image, as well as the default compression level used when saving an image. To adjust the resolution and compression options, click Resolution and Compression Settings in the Options dialog box to open the Image Options dialog box.

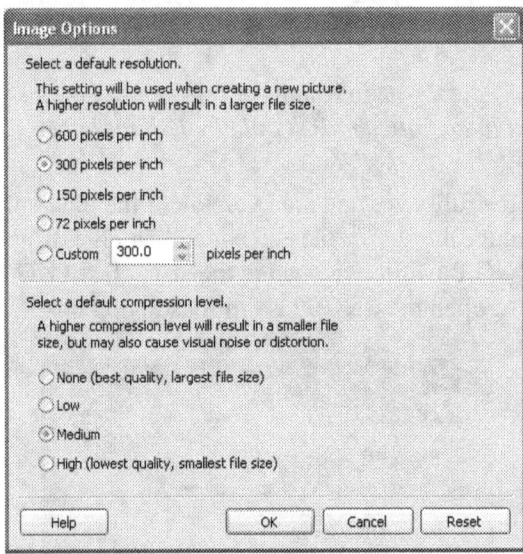

## Set the Default Resolution

To choose a default resolution to use when creating a new image, choose one of the options in the top portion of the dialog box. To choose a custom resolution, click the Custom option and specify the resolution in pixels per inch in the text field.

## Set the Compression Level

Image files can become quite large, so one of the ways to reduce the file size is to use compression. But unlike *lossless* compression (such as zipping a file), image compression usually results in some degradation in the quality of the image (called *lossy* compression). As with so many other things, there is a trade-off: high compression leads to smaller file sizes, but more degradation in image quality. Less compression results in larger files, but more of the image quality is preserved. The lower portion of the Image Options dialog box enables you to set the default compression level to use when you save a file or convert a file to PNG format. Simply pick one of the options.

## How to ... Pick a Reasonable Resolution

You may be tempted to pick a very high resolution for your new images, thinking that the higher the resolution, the better the quality of the output. But picking a very high resolution can make your output files really huge. For example, doubling the resolution (from, say, 300 pixels per inch to 600 pixels per inch) quadruples the size of the output file because you are doubling both the height and width. As it turns out, beyond a certain point, higher resolution does *not* lead to higher quality output.

The resolution you should choose depends on what you want to do with the final result. If you simply intend to post the image on your web site, choose 72 pixels per inch. Because most monitors actually display images at this resolution, all you have to do is build (or resize) the image to the actual size you want at 72 pixels per inch. If you choose a higher resolution, the image will be displayed at a larger size than you anticipated. For example, if you choose 150 pixels per inch, the image will be roughly twice as large (both in height and width) as you intended because the monitor will display all 150 pixels in each inch at 72 pixels per inch—thus doubling the size. You can, of course, scale the image down in a web page that you are building. But that is a really bad idea because the web page still has to download the entire image file, which will take four times as long (remember the rule about resolution and file size!) as it would have if you had just sized the image correctly in the first place.

If you intend to print your image, set the resolution at 300 pixels per inch. Trust me on this one—setting the resolution higher does not increase the quality of the printed image, except in a very few cases for very high-quality professional printers. For today's inkjet and dye sublimation printers (including the so-called "photo printers"), 300 pixels per inch is plenty. You may be wondering why this is so, when that inkjet printer advertises printer resolutions much higher than 300 pixels per inch. This is because *printer* resolution and *image* resolution are unrelated. The printer resolution states how finely the printer can place dots of color on paper, and higher is better. But the printer uses each pixel in the image to place many dots on the paper to accurately simulate the color and intensity of the image pixel. When the image resolution exceeds 300 pixels per inch, the printer driver discards the excess information because it can't use it.

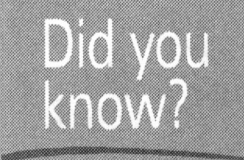

## Degradation

Digital Image Pro does not apply compression to the native PNG Plus format. Thus, if you intend to work on the image multiple times, you should leave it in the PNG Plus format until you are done, and then convert it to PNG or some other format because image degradation is cumulative. That is, if you open an image, work on it, and then save it, a certain amount of degradation occurs if you use compression. The next time you open the image, this same cycle happens again, resulting in further degradation.

# Set the Scanner and Camera Options

Digital Image Pro can accept direct input from both digital cameras and scanners (provided you have installed the necessary drivers). To set the options for capturing images from a camera or scanner, choose Scanner and Camera Options from the Options dialog box to open the Scanner and Camera Options dialog box.

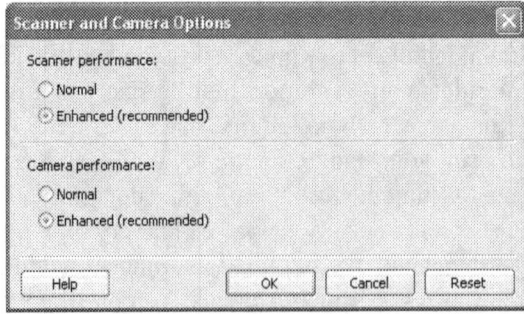

Both the Scanner and Camera performance offer only two choices: Normal and Enhanced. The Enhanced mode uses computer memory to download the image from the device, and is thus generally faster than Normal mode, which does not use memory. However, if you find yourself running out of memory due to a really big image, you may wish to switch to Normal mode because Digital Image Pro can crash if you run out of memory (trust me on this one).

> TIP
>
> *How do you know when you are running out of memory? One simple way to tell is to notice whether your computer hard drive starts up when you execute a command in Digital Image Pro. This indicates that memory is low because the computer is having to place part of the image information on the hard drive (called spooling). This also slows the program WAY down, so if it happens a lot, you may wish to investigate adding more memory to your computer.*

# Change Your E-mail Program

One way to send an image to someone else is to e-mail it, as discussed in Chapter 15. If you have multiple e-mail programs on your computer, you can click Change E-Mail Program in the Options dialog box to open the Send Options dialog box and choose which e-mail program you want to use.

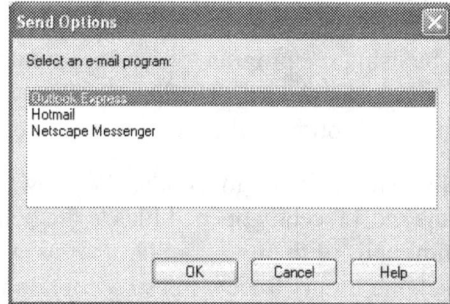

Simply pick the e-mail program you want to use from this dialog box. When you e-mail a picture from within Digital Image Pro, the selected e-mail program will be used.

# Set Plug-In Filter Options

The functionality of Digital Image Pro can be extended by separate programs called *plug-ins*. These are sold by third-party companies, and are often advertised as "Photoshop-compatible plug-ins" because they were originally developed for users of Adobe Photoshop. However, Digital Image Pro can also use "Photoshop-compatible plug-ins," and you may wish to purchase some if you often need to perform a function that is not included (or is very difficult or tedious) in Digital Image Pro. Once you install plug-ins, you must specify where Digital Image Pro is to look for them. To do so, click the Plug-In Filters options from the Options dialog box. This opens a simple dialog box in which you can select (or browse for) the folder that contains your plug-ins.

# Check for Updates Online

Microsoft posts bug fixes and updates for Digital Image Pro on the Internet. If you want the program to automatically look for these updates and offer to download and install them, check the Check for Updates Online checkbox.

# Adjust the Settings

The bottom section of the Options dialog box enables you to make changes to various program settings. These setting are as follows:

- **Turn on all messages that have been turned off**    As you work with Digital Image Pro, it may display warnings and informational messages in small dialog boxes. Many of these dialog boxes have a checkbox that you can select if you don't want to see that message again (they can get pretty annoying). However, if you haven't used the program for a while, or a new user is going to be using the program on your computer, you may wish to turn these messages back on. To do so, click the Turn On All Messages That Have Been Turned Off option in the Options dialog box.

- **Empty recent file list**    As with most other Windows programs, Digital Image Pro lists the most recently opened files at the bottom of the File menu and displays thumbnails of them in the Startup dialog box. If you wish to clear this list, click the Empty Recent Files List option in the Options dialog box. This also clears the list of recent files in the Startup window.

- **Disable sounds**    Click this option if you don't want Digital Image Pro to give you audio feedback for your commands.

- **Require CTRL to zoom with Microsoft Intellimouse**    As mentioned in Chapter 1, you can zoom in and out of an image using the scroll wheel on a mouse. However, if you would rather use the scroll wheel to scroll the workspace window up and down (the normal way a scroll wheel works), click the Require CTRL to Zoom With Microsoft Intellimouse option. If you do, you'll need to hold down the CTRL key while moving the scroll wheel in order to change the image magnifications.

NOTE    *Zooming with the scroll wheel works with most scroll wheel-equipped mice, not just the Microsoft Intellimouse.*

# Get Your Images into Digital Image Pro

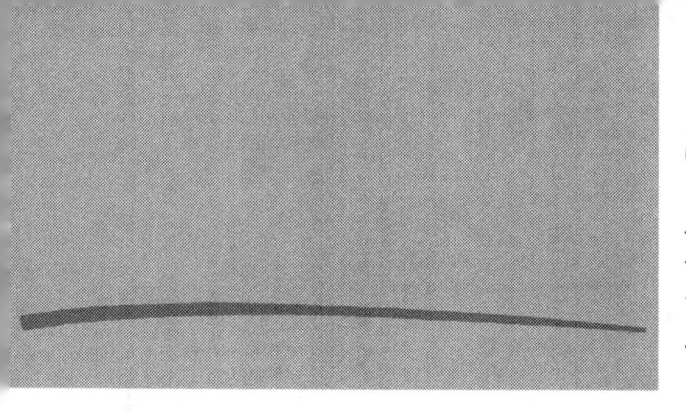

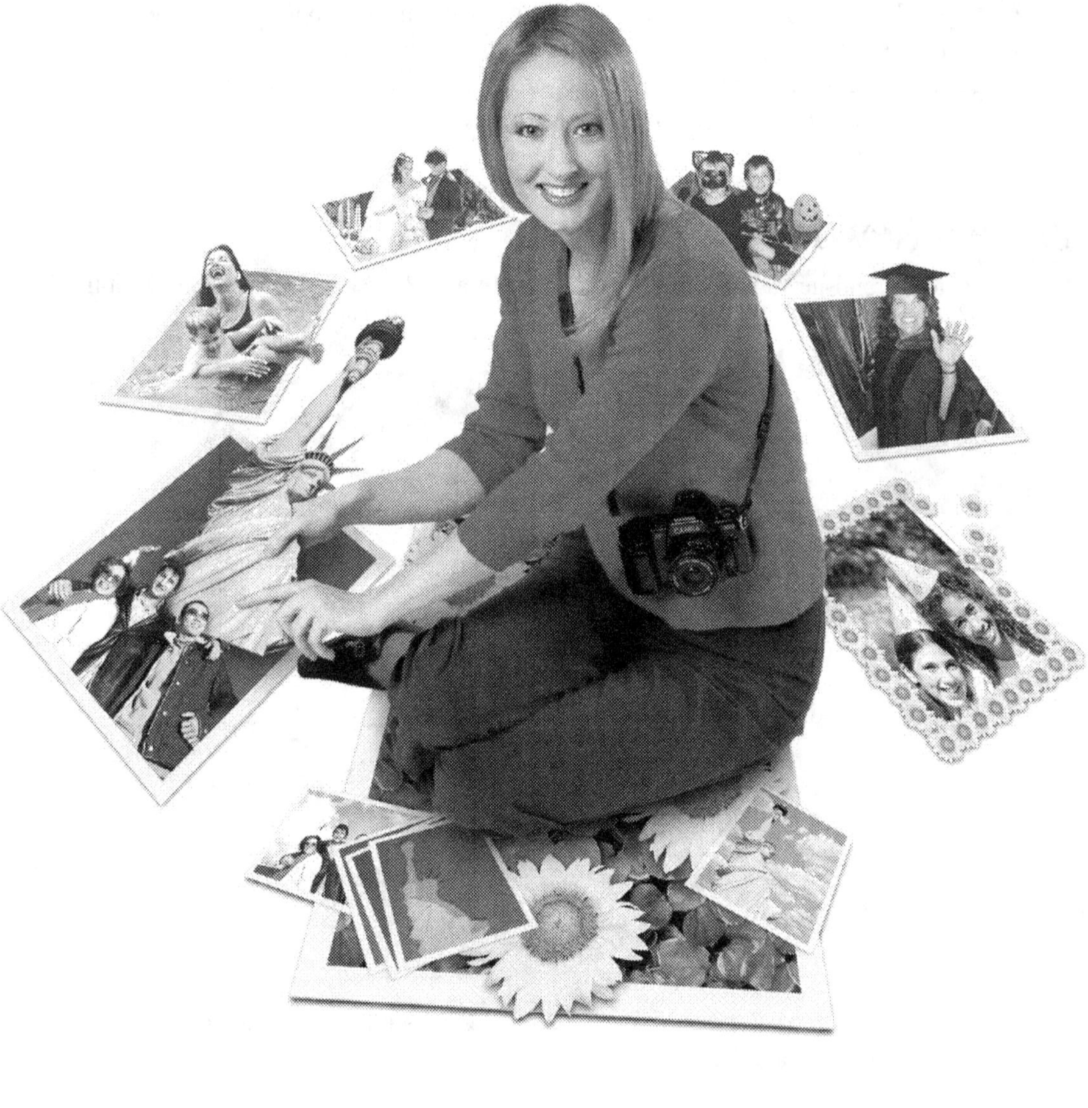

## How to...

- Create new images
- Open existing files in a variety of ways
- Work with file thumbnails
- Save a file in any format

Digital Image Pro is a program for working with images, so the first thing you will need to know is how to get images into the program. You can create an image "from scratch," open an image file, or import a file from an external source, such as a digital camera. Of course, when you are done working on the image, you'll need to save the result.

# Create a New Image

To create a brand-new empty image in Digital Image Pro, select File | New. Digital Image Pro displays the New task bar on the left side of the screen.

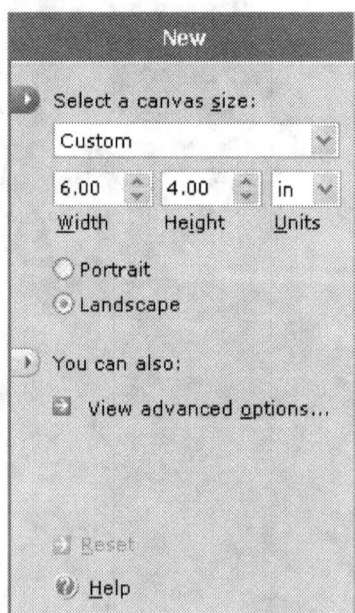

Fill out each of the fields in the task bar as described in the following sections, and click Done to create the new image.

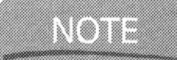 *You can also create a new file by choosing the New button in the toolbar. This creates a new image with the default settings.*

## Choose the Canvas Size

You have two ways to select the initial size of the canvas on which you'll create the image. The first way is to choose a size from the Select A Canvas Size drop-down list. The list includes common photographic sizes, as well as other useful options, such as business cards and CD inserts.

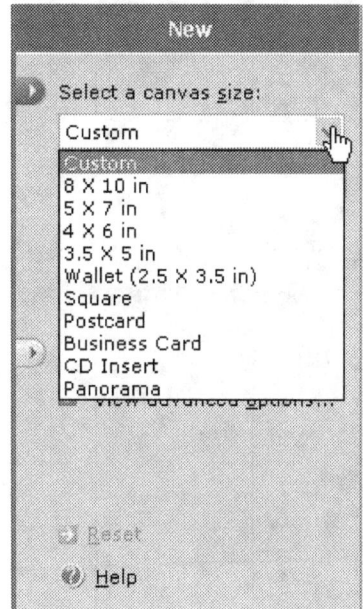

The second way is to type values into the Width and Height fields (or use the field spinners). You can set the unit of measure by selecting it from the Units drop-down list.

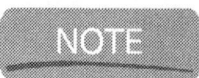 *Units of measure include inches (in), centimeters (cm), millimeters (mm), and pixels (pxl).*

## Set the Image Orientation

There are two orientation options in the New task bar: *Portrait* and *Landscape*. The portrait orientation is tall and narrow, while the landscape orientation is short and wide.

## Set the Image Resolution

The New task bar only allows you to set the new image size; the resolution is automatically set to the value you specified in the Options dialog box (see Chapter 2). If you wish, however, you can adjust the resolution for the new image yourself. To do so, click View Advanced Options in the New task bar to open the Resize Image task bar.

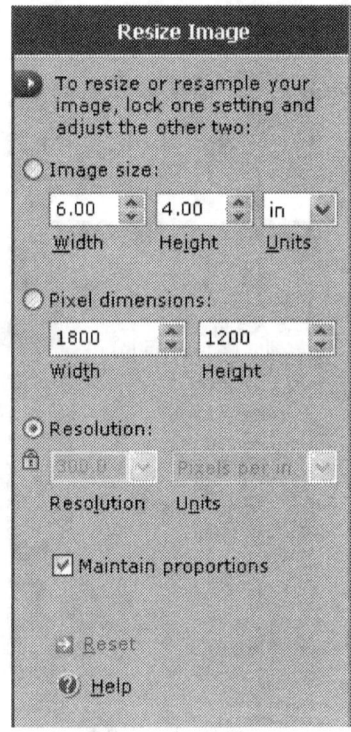

The Resize Image task bar displays three quantities: the Image Size (discussed previously), the total Pixel Dimensions of the image (which is just the image size multiplied by the resolution), and the Resolution. You can lock any one of these quantities by clicking the radio button alongside the item, and then adjust the other two. The locked quantity will automatically adjust to match. For example, if you lock Pixel Dimensions, you can change Image Size and Resolution.

If you lock Resolution, the Maintain Proportions checkbox becomes available. Selecting this checkbox maintains the ratio of the height to width of the image, while clearing this checkbox enables you to set the height and width independently. For example, say your image size is 6 inches (width) by 4 inches (height). With the checkbox selected, changing the width to 9 inches automatically changes the height to 6 inches.

NOTE    *Clicking the Done or the Cancel button in the Resize Image task bar returns you to the New task bar; you'll need to click Done again to actually create the image.*

# Open a File Using the File Browser

3

You can open a file from any drive attached to your system or network: your internal hard drive, external hard drive, floppy disk (remember those?), Zip, CD-ROM, DVD, or even one those little USB memory drives.

To open a file in Digital Image Pro, select File | Open to view the File Browser, shown in Figure 3-1.

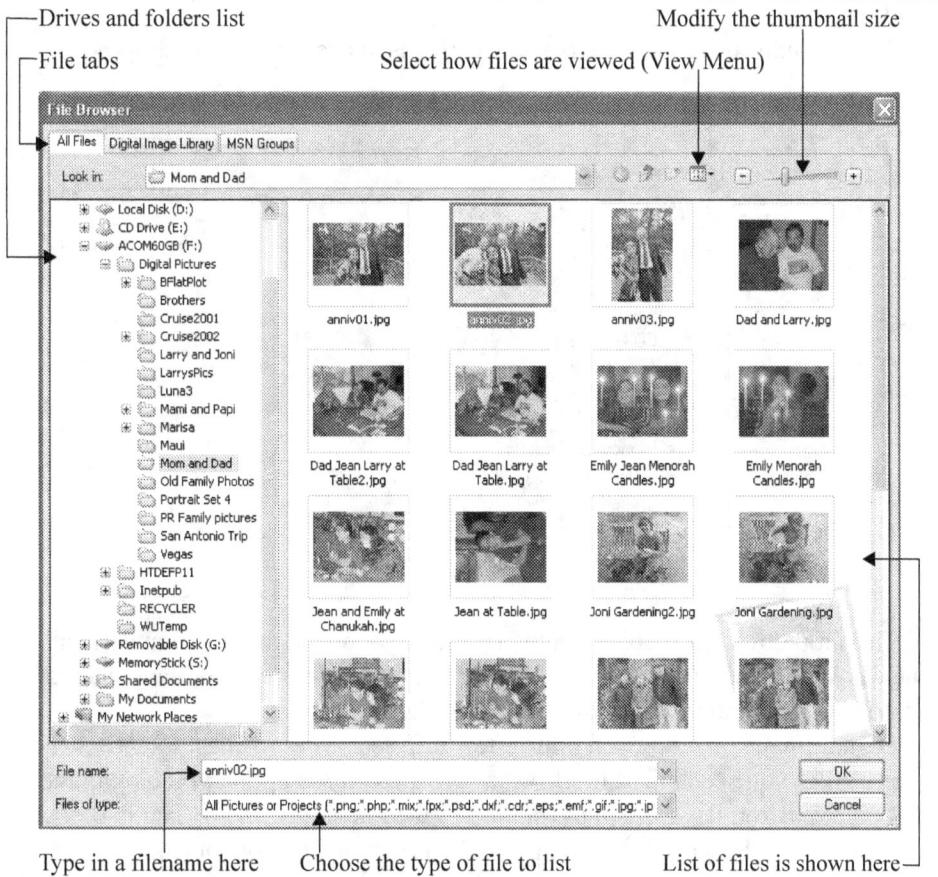

Choose an image from a hard drive, the network, or MSN Groups with the File Browser.

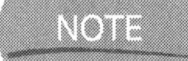 *The File Browser has three tabs—All Files (covered here), Digital Image Library, and MSN Groups. Digital Image Library is a separate product, which you may or may not own. MSN Groups is a special area on the Microsoft Network (MSN) where you can store photographs. This will be covered in the section "Get a Picture from MSN Groups" later in this chapter.*

## View Your Drives and Files

The File Browser contains two tools for navigating to the location of your images. The first is the drives and folders list on the left side of the File Browser. This area works just like Windows Explorer. You can expand the contents of a drive or folder (if any) by clicking on the small + sign alongside the drive or folder. The contents of the selected drive or folder are displayed in the file list on the right side of the File Browser.

The second way to navigate to a destination is to use the Look In drop-down list.

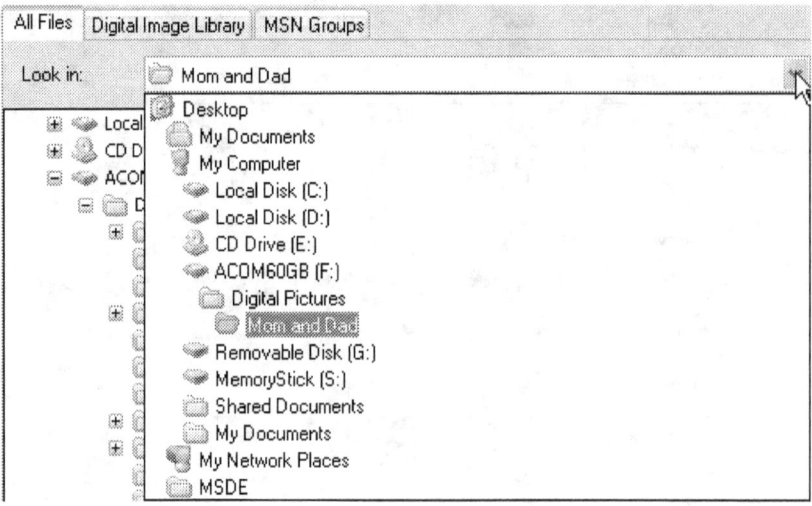

This drop-down list enables you to pick a drive or one of the common destinations (such as My Documents or My Network Places). Once you do so, the contents of the drive or destination are displayed in the file list.

Digital Image Pro can open quite a few different types of files. Exactly which types of files you see in the File Browser depends on the option you pick in the Files Of Type drop-down list at the bottom of the File Browser. For example, if you only want to see JPEG format files, pick JPEG Interchange Format from the list.

 *If you want to see every type of file that Digital Image Pro can open, choose the first option in the list: All Pictures or Projects.*

## Set the File Display

As with Windows Explorer, you can choose to view the list of files as Thumbnails, Details, or a List. To make your choice, click the View Menu icon (just to the left of the scroll control) and make your choice from the list. If you select the Details view, you can see the name, image dimensions, size, when the picture was taken, and when the file was last modified.

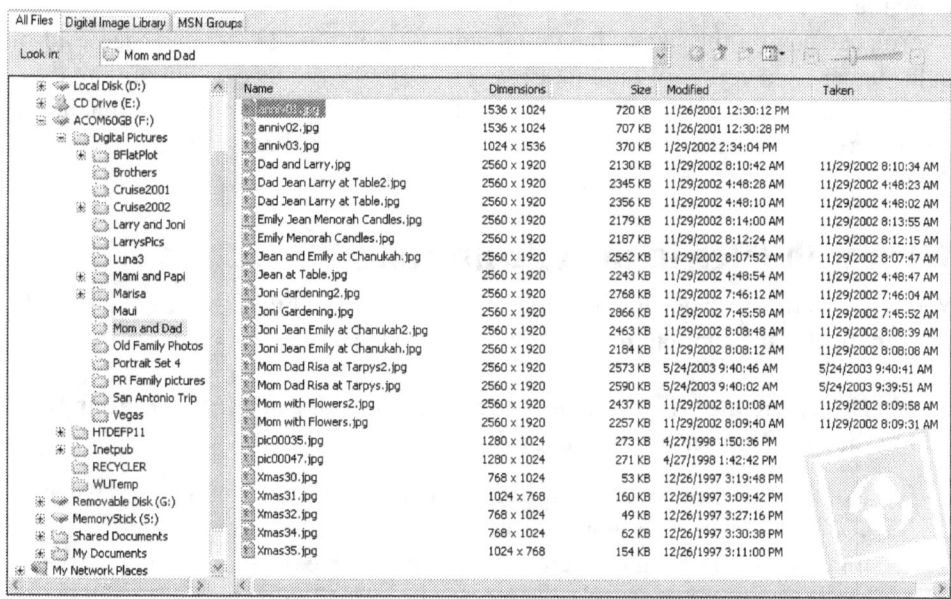

You can sort the list by any of these quantities (the default is to sort by name). To change the sort order, click one of the headings. Clicking a heading the first time sorts the list ascending (lowest at the top); clicking the heading a second time sorts the list descending (lowest at the bottom). A small arrow in the heading points in the sort direction (up for ascending, down for descending).

NOTE *The information in the Taken column comes from a special area in a JPEG image file. This column is populated only if the image originated in a digital camera that is capable of writing to this special area, and if the image was a JPEG file (many cameras can save images in other formats besides JPEG). Otherwise, the Taken column is blank.*

A somewhat more useful file display is the thumbnail option. This represents each file as a miniature version of the images. Although it takes a few moments to generate the thumbnails when you first access an image folder, the results are worth it—you can actually tell what the picture contains! The thumbnail view was used in Figure 3-1.

You can control the size of the thumbnails by using the Thumbnail Size control in the upper-right corner of the File Browser. Click the minus (–) sign or drag the slider to the left to decrease the size of the thumbnails and see more thumbnails on the screen. Click the plus (+) sign or drag the slider to the right to increase the thumbnail size and see more of the detail of each picture.

## Work with Files in the File Browser

You can perform some useful operations on the files in the File Browser. Right-click a file to display the shortcut menu, from which you can:

- **Delete the file**    If you no longer need a file, you can delete it right from the File Browser by choosing Delete.

- **Rotate the thumbnail**    Depending on how you held your camera when you took a picture or how you placed an item into a scanner, some of your images may be lying on their side. You can rotate the thumbnail (and the attached image) so that it is displayed properly. To do so, choose either Rotate Clockwise or Rotate Counterclockwise.

- **Rename the file**    To change the name of the file, choose Rename. This makes the filename editable; simply type in the new name. You can also change the name by choosing Properties from the shortcut menu to open the Properties dialog box, and then typing a new name into the field at the top of the dialog box.

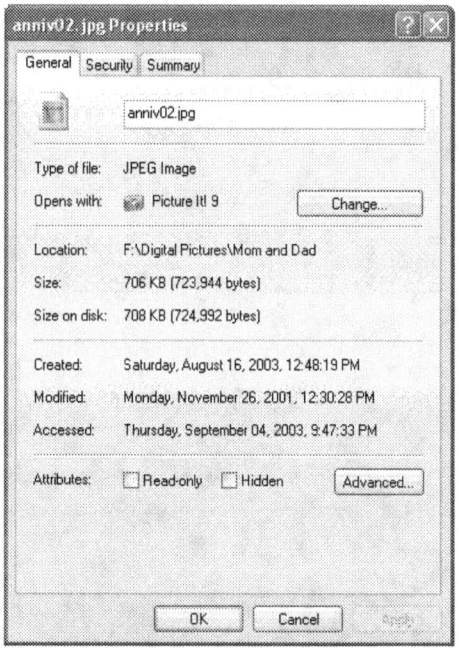

CAUTION    *When renaming, be careful not to change the file extension or you won't be able to open the file.*

■ **Cut, copy, or paste the file**    Use Cut or Copy to place the entire file on the Clipboard so you can paste it into another file as an object (see Chapter 8).

## Set the File Summary Properties

As mentioned earlier, JPEG images (the most common type of digital photo format) have a special area for saving information about the file (called "metadata"). While some of this metadata is read-only (such as the date when the picture was taken, the exposure information, original size, and so on), you can add some of your own metadata to the image. To do so, choose Properties from the shortcut menu in the File Browser, and click the Summary tab.

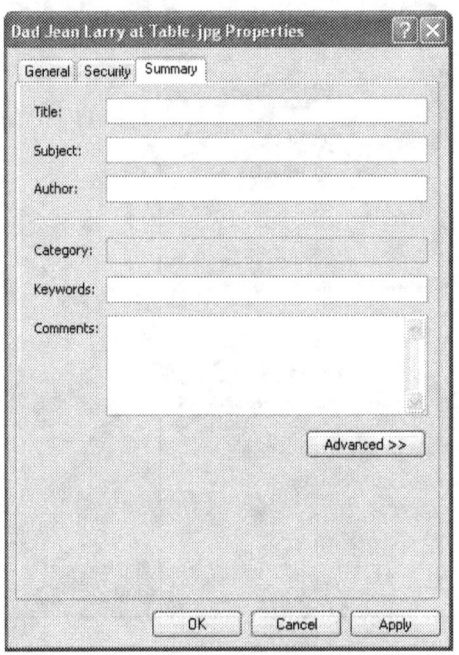

Type the title, subject, author, keywords, and comments into the dialog box. When you click OK or Apply, the metadata is saved into the file. To add multiple keywords, separate them with a comma.

NOTE    *Saving metadata into the file does not change the Modified date and time for the image.*

To view a complete summary of all the image metadata, click Advanced>>. This displays all the camera-recorded information, which you cannot modify.

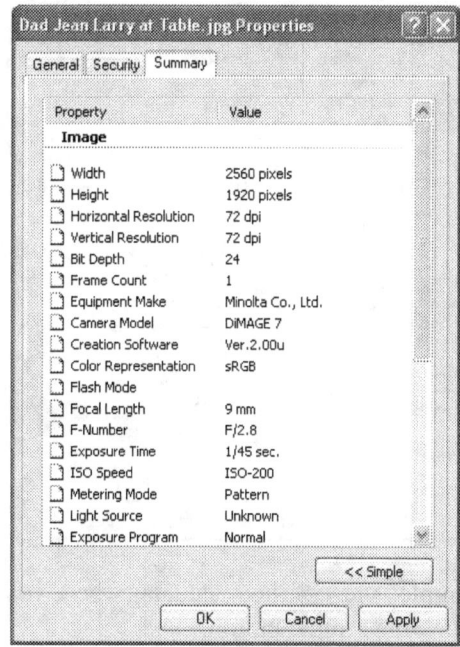

If you scroll the Properties dialog box to the bottom, you'll find the enterable metadata (title, subject, and so on). To modify this metadata from the Advanced view, click the item you want to change to make it editable, type in your changes, and click OK or Apply to save the changes.

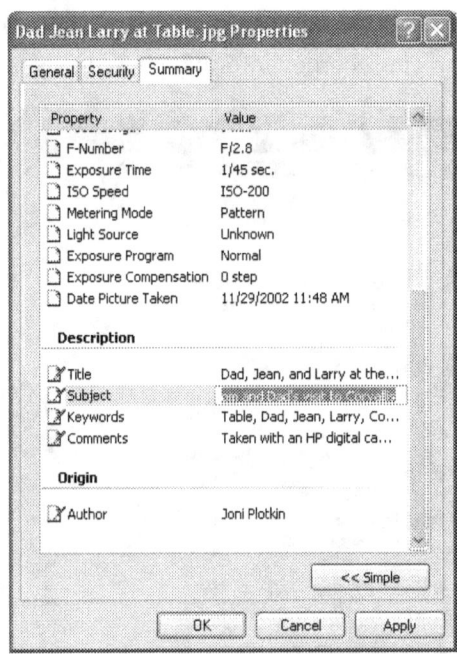

To return to the "simple" view of the metadata (where you see only the enterable metadata), click the Simple button.

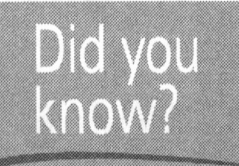

## Heavy Rotation

You can rotate multiple thumbnails at the same time. To do so, select all the thumbnails you want to rotate before applying the rotation command. One way to select multiple thumbnails is to click the first thumbnail, hold down the CTRL key, and click the rest of thumbnails. If you accidentally include a thumbnail you didn't want, simply click it again (with the CTRL key still held down).

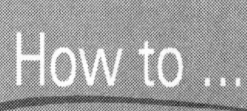 **Control Which Program Opens a File**

Sometimes, you may not want Digital Image Pro to be the program you use to open a particular type of file when you double-click that type of file in Windows Explorer. For example, if you use only GIF files for animations, you may wish to open GIF files in your animation program. To change the program you use to open a particular type of image, right-click a file of that type (such as a file ending in .gif) in the File Browser and choose Properties to open the Properties dialog box. Click the Change button to open the Open With dialog box.

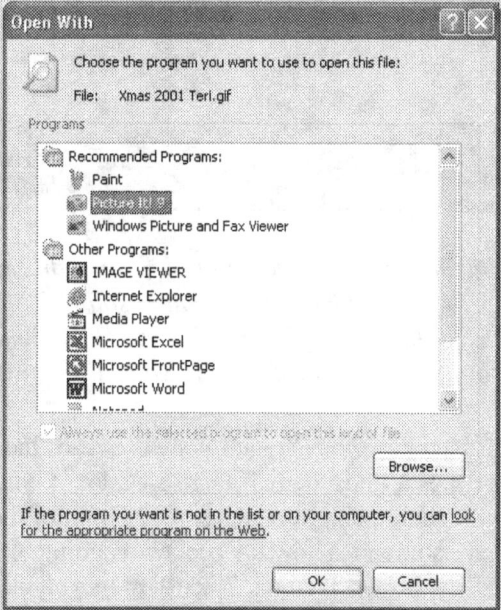

Choose the program you want to use to open files of that type and click OK. From now on, whenever you try to open a file of that type in Windows Explorer, it will open in the selected application (provided, of course, that the application is actually capable of opening that type of file!). If the program you want to use to open the file does not appear in the dialog box, you can try to locate it yourself by clicking the Browse button, selecting the program from the resulting dialog box, and clicking Open.

# Use the Import Pictures Wizard

The Import Pictures Wizard walks you through the process of importing pictures from any storage device (including CD-ROM drives) connected externally to your machine. To start the Import Pictures Wizard, choose File | Import Pictures to open the Select Device dialog box.

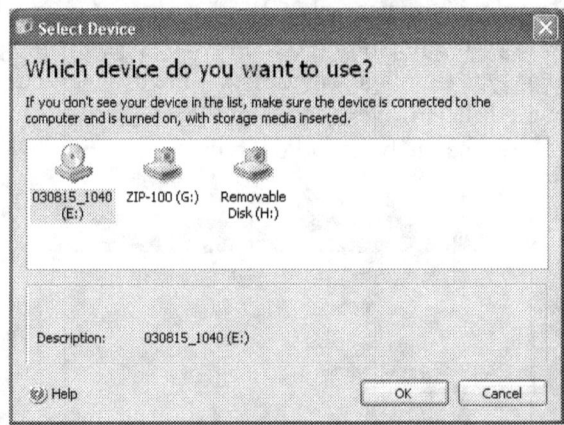

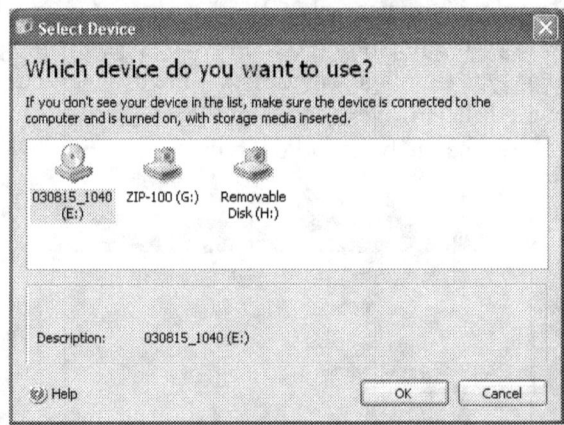

**NOTE**    *The Import Pictures Wizard is less useful if you didn't purchase Microsoft Digital Image Suite 9, which includes Microsoft Digital Image Library 9 in addition to Digital Image Pro. If you only have Digital Image Pro, the Import Pictures Wizard only allows you to save your files to disk.*

Choose the device and click OK. Digital Image Pro reads the data on the device and catalogs the image files it finds there. If there are a lot of image files, this process can take a while, but the dialog box keeps a running count of the number of images it has found so you have some idea how the process is going. Once the cataloging process has completed, the Import Pictures Wizard offers you the option to copy the images to your computer and catalog them into Digital Image Library, or, catalog the files in place (for mass-storage devices such as CDs and DVDs).

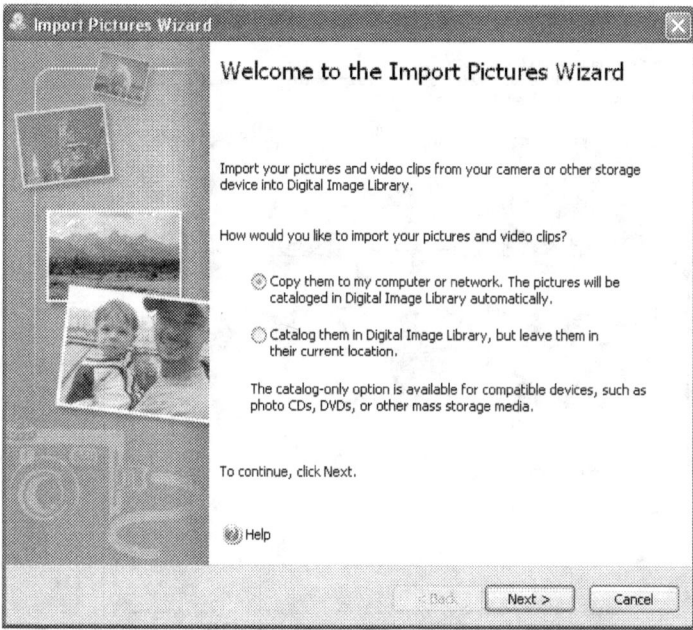

**NOTE** *For devices that use removable media (such as CD-ROM drives and Zip drives), the Select Device dialog box only shows devices that contain media. For example, if the CD-ROM drive does not contain a disc, it won't be visible in the Select Device dialog box.*

## Copy the Pictures from a Device

If you choose to copy the images, the next dialog box shows you the thumbnails of the images and enables you to choose the ones you want to copy. You can use standard Windows techniques (such as Shift-click and Ctrl-click) to make multiple selections.

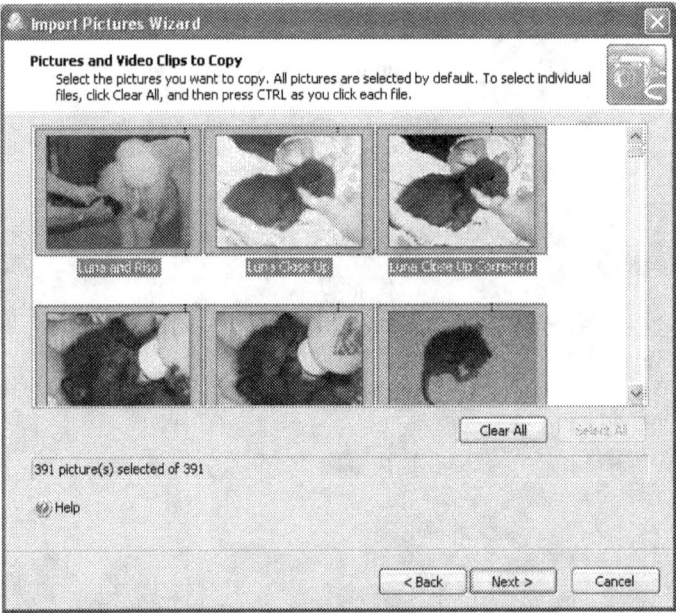

Click Next to continue. The next dialog box enables you to name the group of pictures to import and choose a destination for the pictures. If you wish, you can rename the picture files using the group name. This discards the existing picture filenames and renames the files using the group name you specified and a sequence number.

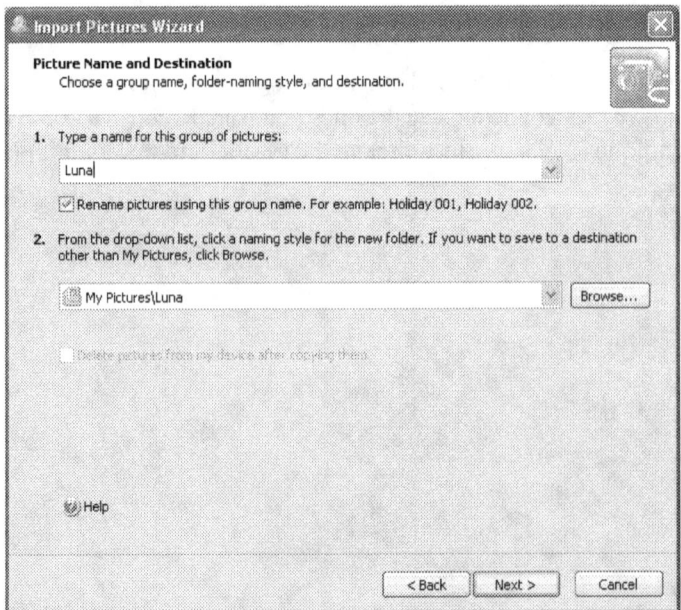

Click Next> to continue. The pictures are imported and Microsoft Digital Image Library 9 opens to display the pictures in their new destination.

## Catalog the Pictures in Their Current Location

If you choose to catalog the pictures in their current location (such as on a CD), the Import Pictures Wizard catalogs all the pictures found *without* giving you a chance to specify the ones you want to include in the catalog. On a CD-ROM with a lot of files (such as the Digital Image Pro disk 1), this can take *quite* a while, so be patient while the job completes. Once it does, the thumbnails are displayed in Microsoft Digital Image Library 9.

## Get a Picture from a Digital Camera

If you own a compatible digital camera, you can connect it to your computer and import pictures from the memory media directly from the camera—no need to remove the card or use a card reader. To do so, choose File | Get Picture From | Digital Camera. This opens the Digital Camera task bar.

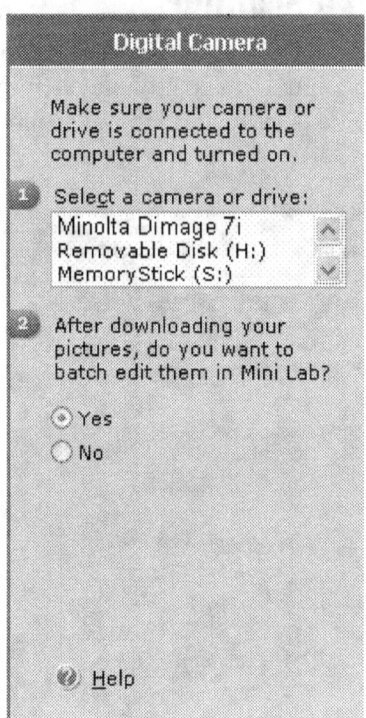

Select your camera from the scrolling list near the top of the task bar, and choose whether you want to edit the imported pictures in the Mini Lab by clicking either Yes or No. Then click Download to continue.

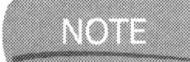 *The Mini Lab is a special tool that enables you to make changes to multiple images at once. For example, if all your images need to have their contrast adjusted, you can adjust them all in one shot in the Mini Lab. This feature is covered in Chapter 14.*

Digital Image Pro catalogs the files in the digital camera (or any other device you might have picked from the list), and presents them in the File Browser. Select the files you want and click OK to open the files in Digital Image Pro (and list them in the Files palette).

 *To save the files on your hard drive, open each file in Digital Image Pro, and then use File | Save As to choose a new destination to save the file.*

## Get a Picture from a Scanner

If you have a flatbed or slide/negative scanner connected to your computer, you can scan an image directly into Digital Image Pro (and then save it to your hard drive). To scan an image, choose File | Get Picture From | Scanner. This opens the Scan Picture task bar.

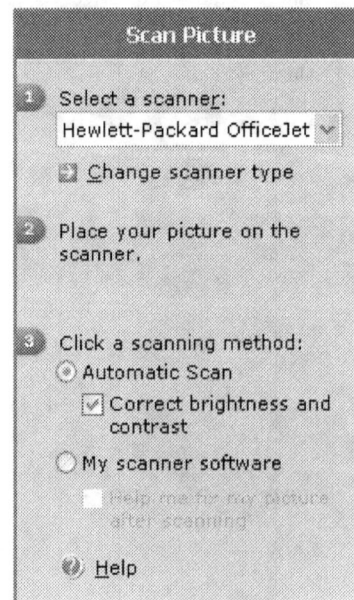

If you have more than one scanner, select the scanner you want to use from the Select A Scanner drop-down list.

TIP *The first time you use a particular scanner, you may wish to click the Change Scanner Type hyperlink and check to make sure that Digital Image Pro has identified the type of scanner correctly. There are two choices—flatbed scanner and "Other." The "Other" choice is used for handheld and sheet-fed scanners, as well as digital cameras.*

The next step is to select the scanning method. The two methods are:

■ **Automatic Scan** When you use automatic scan, Digital Image Pro simply scans the picture. If you wish, you can select the checkbox to correct brightness and contrast, although you can do this yourself manually once the image has been scanned.

■ **My Scanner Software** If you select My Scanner Software, Digital Image Pro opens the scanner software you should already be familiar with, and you can use those facilities to produce the scan. However, instead of saving the image to disk (as you would normally), the scan goes straight into Digital Image Pro. If you select the Help Me Fix My Picture After Scanning checkbox, Digital Image Pro presents a new version of the Scan Picture task bar, which enables you to apply three different corrections: Straighten, Crop, and Levels auto fix, all discussed in Chapter 4.

TIP *Select My Scanner Software if you need to change the scan resolution because the Automatic Scan option does not allow you to change this very important parameter.*

## Get a Picture from the Gallery

Digital Image Pro comes with a huge collection of clip art and pictures, called the "Gallery." During the install, you had the choice whether to load the Gallery pictures onto your hard drive or leave them on the CD-ROM. To use a picture from the Gallery, select File | Get Picture From | Gallery. This opens the Gallery task bar, showing the Browse tab.

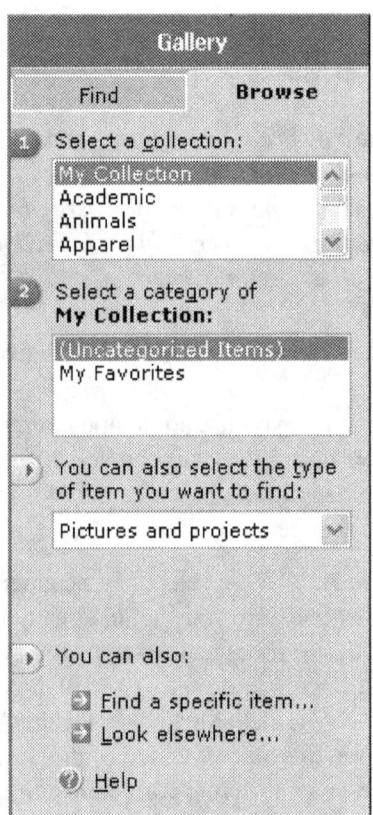

The Gallery is broken up into "collections." To choose a collection, select it from the Select A Collection scrolling list near the top of the task bar. Next, choose a category from the Select A Category Of scrolling list. Thumbnails that match the collection and category appear in the main area of the Gallery window, as shown in Figure 3-2.

## Open a Gallery Picture Using the Thumbnail

To open an image, right-click the image and choose Open from the shortcut menu. If Digital Image Pro needs one of the CD-ROMs to retrieve the image, it will display

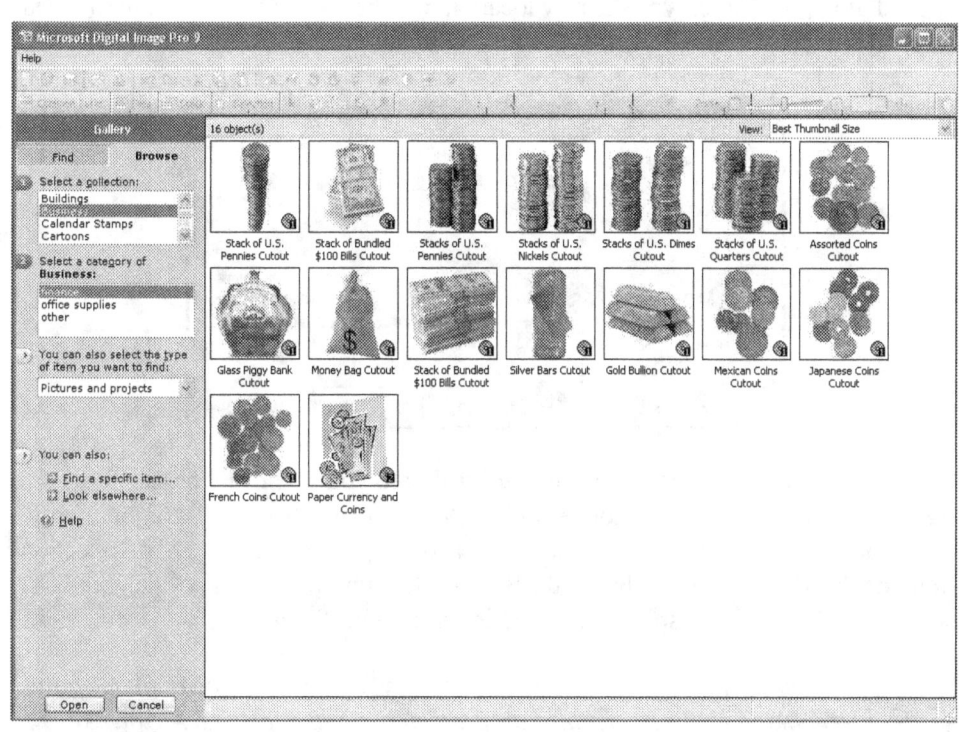

Find and use images from the Gallery with the Gallery window.

a dialog box telling you to place the correct CD-ROM in the drive. Once you have done so, click OK to load the image.

> **TIP**    *The number of the CD-ROM containing the image (either 1 or 2) appears in the lower-right corner of the thumbnail.*

If you manually copy some of the Gallery files to your hard drive, you don't have to put the CD-ROM in the drive. From the dialog box that prompts you to insert the correct CD-ROM, click the Options button to open the Advanced Options section of the dialog box. Either type the new location into the "I Moved This Item To" field or use the Browse button to locate the image on your hard drive.

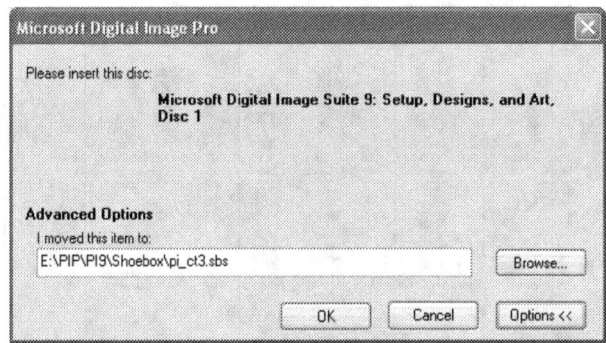

You can add any of the images in the Gallery to your list of favorites. To do so, right-click on an image and choose Add To My Favorites from the shortcut menu. Once you have added images to your list of favorites, you can choose My Collection from the Select A Collection list, and My Favorites from the Select A Category list, and Digital Image Pro displays thumbnails for all your favorites.

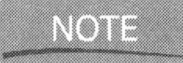 *You can further fine-tune your selection by picking the type of image you are looking for from the third drop-down list in the task bar: "You Can Also Select The Type Of Item You Want To Find." Options include Pictures and Projects, Pictures (clip art and photographs), Photographs, and many other choices.*

## Find a Picture in the Gallery

If you can't find the picture you are looking for in the Browse tab, click the Find tab or choose "Find A Specific Item" in the Browse tab. Either of these actions opens the Find tab, where you can search for the image you are looking for.

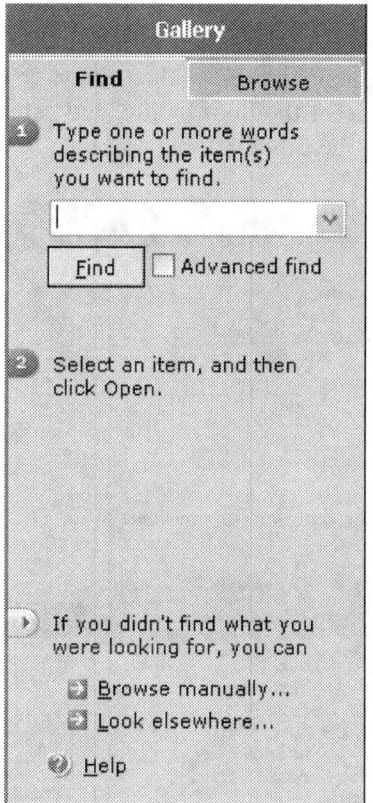

Finding an image is pretty simple—just type the keyword you are looking for into the field at the top of the task bar and click Find. In a few moments, thumbnails are displayed for all the images in the Gallery that match your search criteria. You can then pick the thumbnail you want and open the image.

You can also fine-tune your search. To do so, select the Advanced Find checkbox. In addition to the keyword(s) you type in, you can specify the date range for the files you are looking for (start date, end date, or both) and the type of item (as described in the previous Note). Then click the Find button to execute the search.

### Adjust the Properties of a Gallery Image

You can change the properties of images in the gallery. To do so, select one or more thumbnails, right click one of the thumbnails, and select Properties from the shortcut menu. This opens the Edit Gallery task bar.

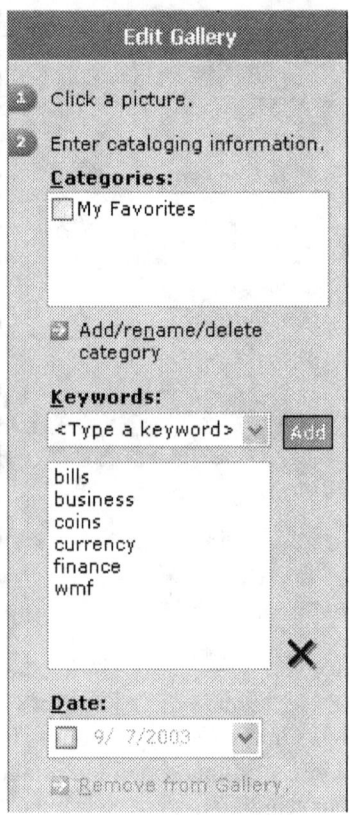

To customize an image, click the image in the workspace and make the following changes:

- **Add the image to a new category** To add the image to your list of favorites, select the My Favorites checkbox in the Categories list. To add the image to any of the other user-defined categories that appear in the list, select the checkbox alongside the category name. To remove the image from a user-defined category, clear the checkbox for that category. Note that the user-defined categories don't appear until you create them, as discussed later in this chapter.

- **Add keywords to the image**   To add a keyword to an image, click the Keywords field and type in the new keyword. Then click the Add button to add the keyword to the scrolling list of keywords located just below the Keyword field.

- **Remove keywords from the image**   To remove one or more keywords from the image, select the keyword(s) in the scrolling list of keywords and select the X button at the lower-right corner of the scrolling list.

Click Apply to apply the changes before moving to another image. If you don't click Apply, Digital Image Pro prompts you as to whether you want to apply the changes. Click Yes to apply the changes or No to cancel the changes.

## Add, Rename, or Delete a Gallery Category

You can add, rename, and delete your own categories. When you add categories, they show up in the Select A Category Of My Collection scrolling list (item 2) of the Gallery task bar. To get started, click Add/Rename/Delete Category in the Edit Gallery task bar. This opens the Add, Rename, or Delete a Category dialog box.

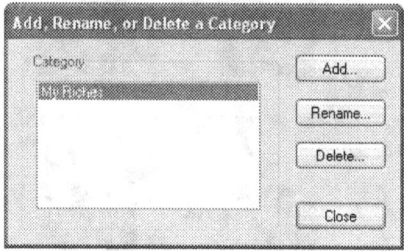

From this dialog box, you can do the following:

- **Add a category**   To add a category, click the Add button, type in the name of the new category, and click OK to create the category.

- **Rename a category**   To rename a category, select the category and click the Rename button. Type in the replacement name and click OK to change the name of the category.

■ **Delete a category**   To delete a category, select the category and click Delete. If the warning appears, click Yes to confirm the deletion and remove the category. The category is removed from the list in the Add, Rename, or Delete a Category dialog box and from the list of Categories in the Edit Gallery task bar.

When you are done modifying categories, click the Close button to close the Add, Rename, or Delete a Category dialog box and return to the Edit Gallery task bar.

## Get a Picture from MSN Groups

If you have a .Net passport (such as yourname@hotmail.com), you can retrieve pictures stored in an MSN (Microsoft Network) group. To do so, select File | Open to open the File Browser and click the MSN Groups tab. This prompts you for your .Net Passport sign-in name and password. Fill these in and click OK.

At this point, the File Browser dialog box displays a list of the MSN groups you are a member of on the left. Click a group that contains photos and the File Browser displays the images on the right side of the dialog box.

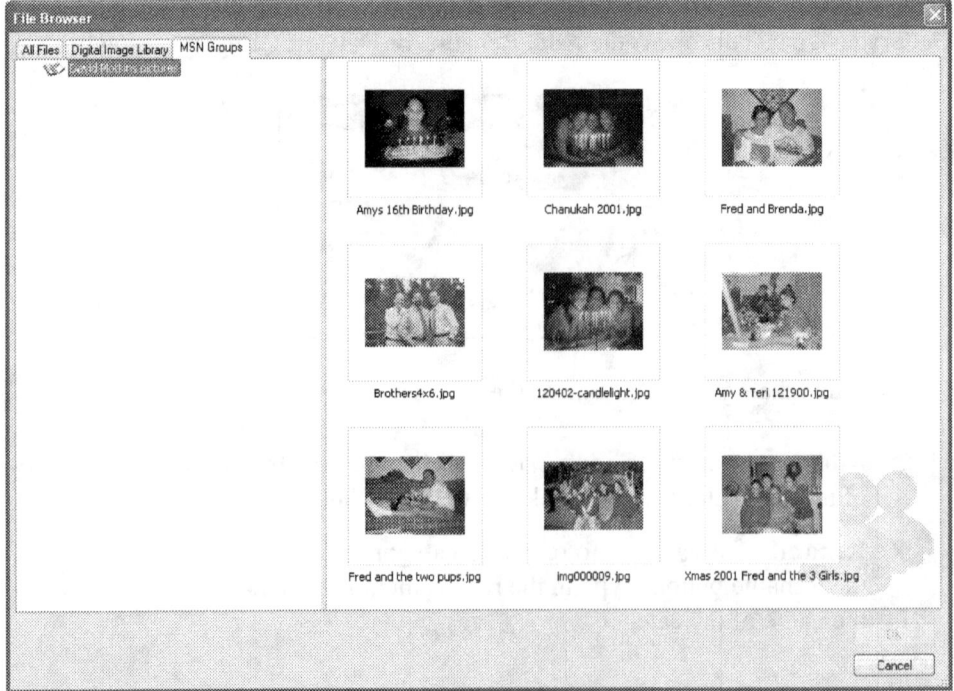

Choose one or more of the files you want to work with and click OK to download them and open them in Digital Image Pro.

## 3

> NOTE    *Once you have made changes to the images, you can save them to your hard drive—but you cannot save them directly back to the MSN group. To move the modified images to MSN, you'll have to upload them using the photo upload utility provided by MSN.*

# Save a File in Any Format

Once you've opened an image in Digital Image Pro and made some modifications, you'll want to save it. Digital Image Pro can save a file in quite a few common formats, including:

- **Digital Image Pro's native format**   The Digital Image Pro native file format (called PNG Plus) uses the .png extension. It is ideal for works in progress, as it can contain any type of information Digital Image Pro needs, and it doesn't compress the file (the way JPEG does) with resulting loss of information. In addition, the PNG Plus format does not flatten the objects in the Stack (see Chapter 8) when you save the file. Flattening collapses the various layers into the image and makes them permanent. With PNG Plus, you can go back and work with the Stack object layers later. All other file formats flatten the file when they save it, so you can't go back later and remove an object from the Stack.

- **JPEG**   JPEG (indicated by a file extension of .jpg or .jpeg) is the file type of choice for storing photographs for the Web. JPEGs can be opened and displayed by any browser. They are compressed as they are saved, so some information can be lost. However, by setting the compression parameters during the save (as described later in this chapter), you can balance the resulting file size with the quality of the image. Higher compression ratios degrade the image more, but can reduce the size of the file considerably. High-quality JPEGs take up less room than other good photo file types, such as TIFF files. However, because JPEGs lose information each time you save them, it is best to work on images in some other file format (such as PNG Plus), and then convert the finished product to a JPEG when you're done. You should keep a copy of the PNG Plus file in case you need to apply further changes.

■ **GIF** A GIF file (indicated by a file extension of .gif) is a good choice for clip art and other images that don't require more than the 256 colors possible with a GIF file. You can store photos in GIF format, but the smooth color gradations may be lost due to the limited number of colors available. GIF files are compressed, but unlike JPEG files, they do not lose information when compressed.

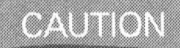

*GIF files can also be used to create animations. However, Digital Image Pro cannot handle animated GIFs. If you open an animated GIF and then save it again, the resulting file contains only the first frame of the animation.*

■ **TIFF** TIFF files (indicated by the file extension .tif or .tiff) are also a good choice for storing photographs. These files can be really huge, but unlike JPEGs, information is not lost when you save a TIFF file. You can apply lossless compression to a TIFF file as well (either LZW or RLE). Browsers cannot read TIFFs (except with special plug-ins), but many graphics programs and office applications *can* use TIFFs.

■ **BMP** Windows Bitmap files (indicated by the file extension .bmp) are pretty simple—even when compressed, they can get very large. Some very simple graphics programs may only be able to read bitmap files, so you might have to save a file using this format to allow someone else to see it. In general, however, other file formats are better choices.

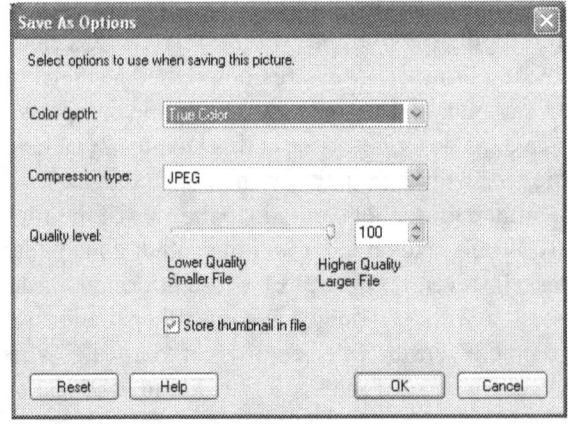

The Save As Options dialog box provides configuration options that vary slightly for the different file types.

The next few sections explain what you need to know about the most common digital photo formats to decide which format to use. Each of the file types uses the same Save As Options dialog box (see Figure 3-3); however, some options are unavailable for some file types.

**NOTE**  *Saving files for specialized purposes—such as for Windows wallpaper or for the Web—is covered in Chapter 15.*

To save a file for the first time, choose File | Save As to open the Save As dialog box.

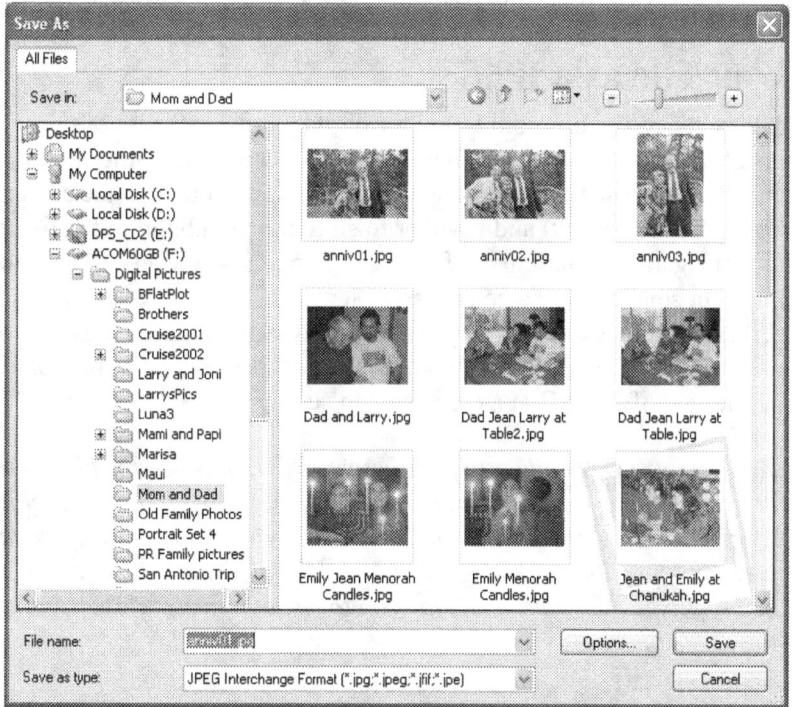

You can also choose File | Save a Copy As, which works the same way, except that is provides a default filename that includes the phrase "Copy of." Most of the listed formats have options you can set. To specify the options, click the Options button.

**NOTE**  *After you save a file for the first time, choosing File | Save simply resaves the file using the same filename.*

## Save Your File in Digital Image Pro Native Format

As mentioned earlier, Digital Image Pro uses PNG Plus as its native format. You can only specify the color depth in the Options dialog box; all other "options" are fixed.

The Color Depth drop-down list offers two options:

- **True Color**   Saves the image with its entire original palette, even if your computer was not set to display all colors present in the image.

- **Palette**   Saves the image using only those colors that can be displayed on your computer. This option does reduce the size of the file, but it also (typically) removes colors from the image, which can degrade it.

## Save Your File as a JPEG

JPEG files are the most commonly used for digital photos because of the smooth gradations of color possible. JPEG files have considerable flexibility in how they are saved, but unfortunately, Digital Image Pro only allows you to set the compression level (ranging from 1 to 100) and whether to store the thumbnail in the file (which makes displaying a thumbnail much faster). A compression level of 1 produces a low-quality (but smaller) file; a compression level of 100 produces a high-quality (but larger) file. The file size can vary considerably depending on the compression. An example file I was using resulted in a file size of 80K at a compression setting of 1 and a file size of 1.1 MB at a compression setting of 100.

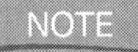 *You cannot save the file as a progressive JPEG, in which the file opens first at low resolution, and is then redrawn at increasingly higher resolution as the file contents are downloaded. Progressive JPEGs are nice because the person viewing the file can get an idea of the file contents before the file has been fully downloaded (and move on to something else if they don't wish to see the image).*

## Save Your File as a GIF

When you save your files as a GIF, there are no options you can set. The fixed choices set the color depth to the palette (but only 256 colors are saved) and the compression to LZW, the standard GIF compression scheme.

## Save Your File as a TIFF

When you save your files as a TIFF, you can choose between no compression, LZW (recommended), or RLE. No other options are available because the color depth is fixed at true color.

# Make Simple Adjustments to Your Images

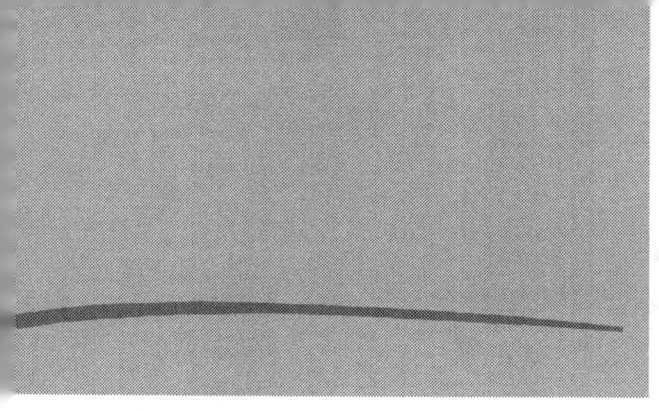

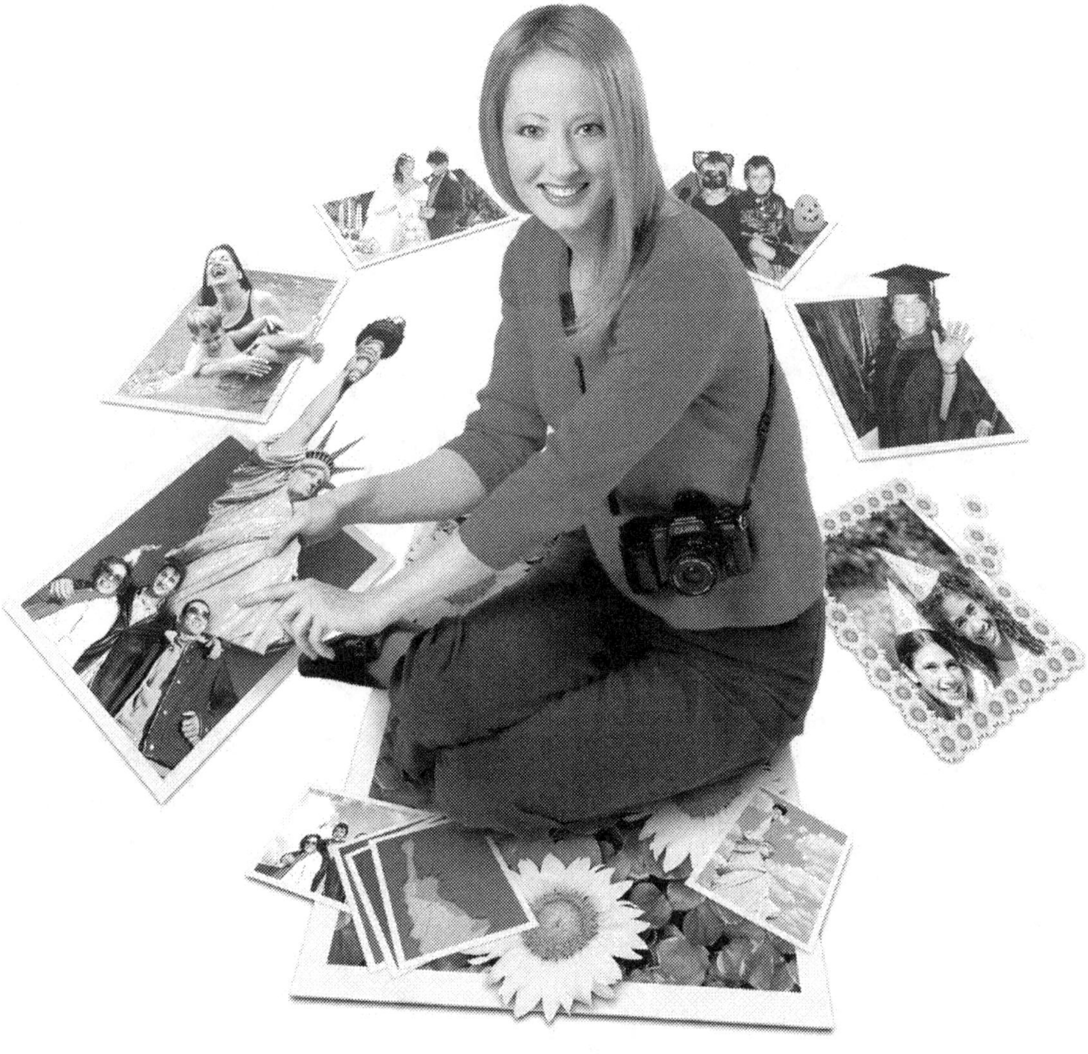

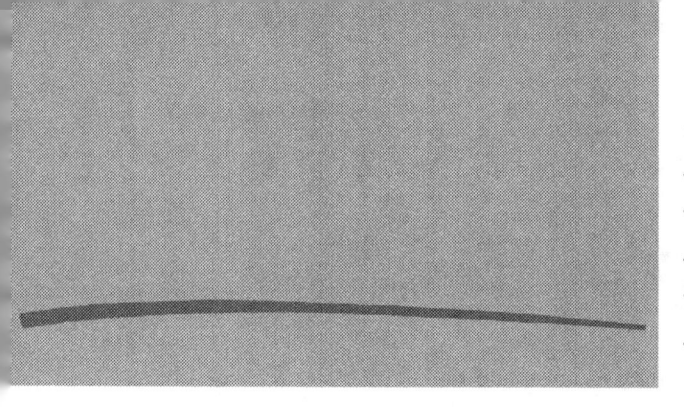

# Make General Fixes to an Entire Image

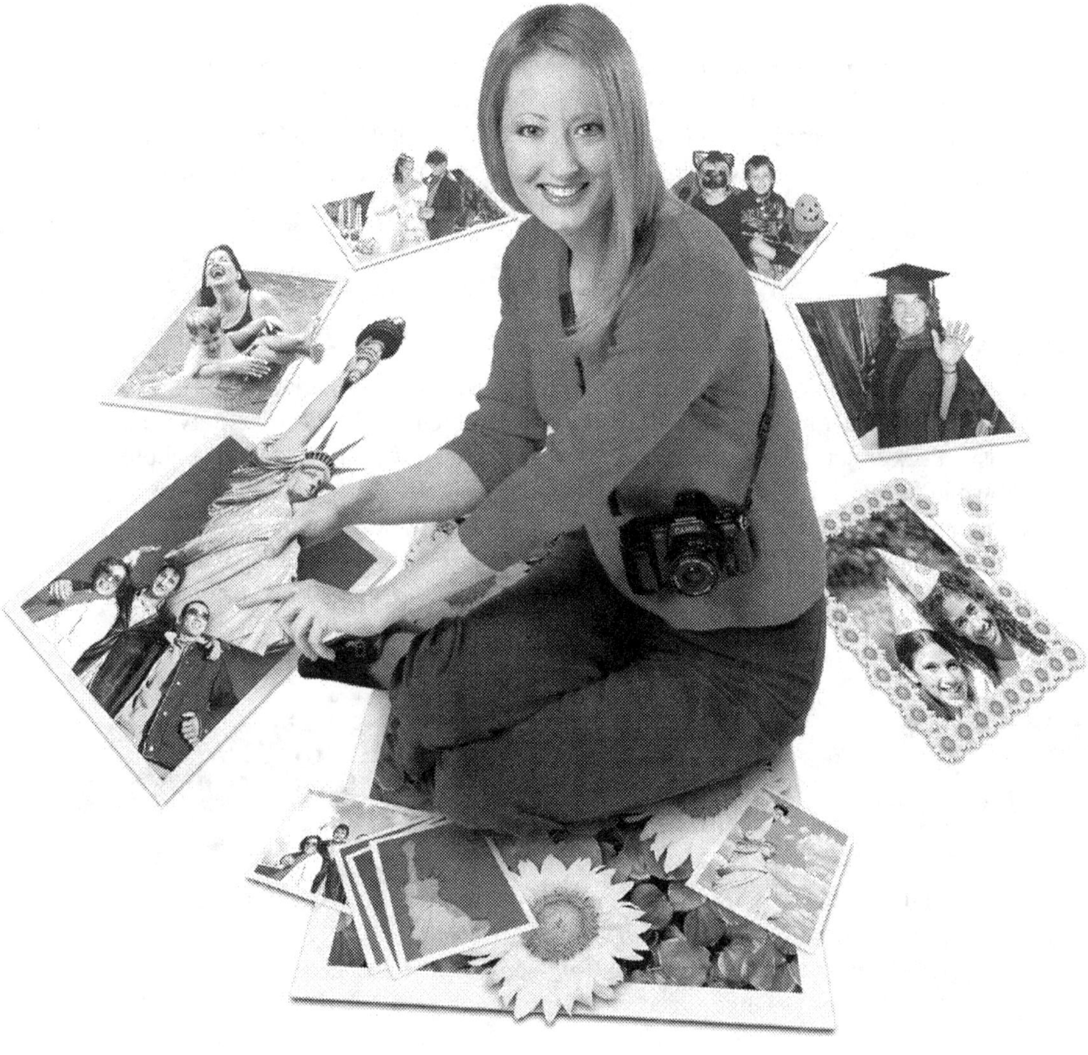

## How to...

- Crop an image to change its size

- Make automatic corrections to contrast, color, and brightness

- Use flash and backlighting to correct lighting problems

- Adjust color, contrast, and brightness manually

- Rotate and flip images

Digital Image Pro provides tools that make it easy to apply changes to an entire image. Of course, as we'll see later in this book, many of these tools can also be applied to a selected portion of an image as well. Digital Image Pro does a pretty good job of diagnosing problems with an image and applying a fix automatically, but you will often need to make manual corrections yourself when the automatic fixes don't get the picture quite right.

# Crop the Image to Remove Unneeded Portions

Pictures often include large areas that take away from the overall effect. For example, your main subject may be well off to the side of the picture, or there may be a "busy" background that detracts from your subject. An example of such a photo is shown in Figure 4-1. Editing a picture to remove unwanted areas is called *cropping*. Cropping an image to remove part of it is even more possible with today's high-megapixel cameras because even if you throw away some of the image, enough pixels are often left that the remaining part of the picture can still be printed. For

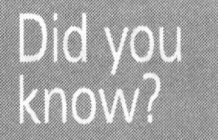

## The Dangers of Digital Zoom

Cropping part of the image and throwing it away is exactly what a digital camera does when you use the "digital zoom" feature. Because you are far better off performing this operation in Digital Image Pro on your computer (where you have a great deal of control over exactly what gets cropped), you should never use digital zoom on your camera.

4

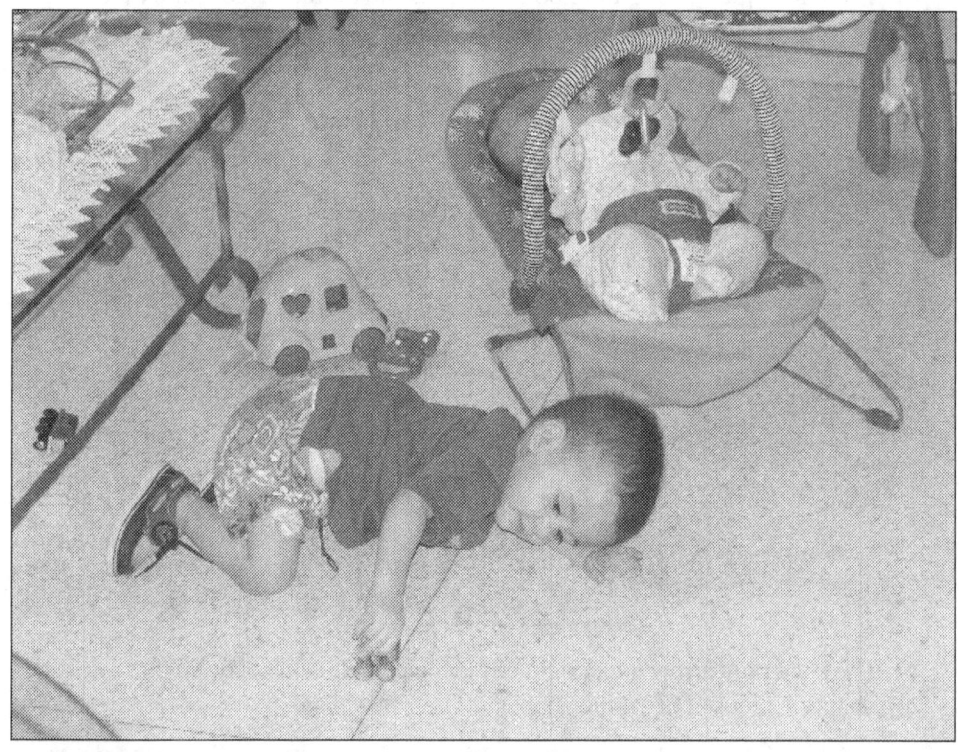

The background takes away from the impact of the photo.

example, I cropped away all but about 20 percent of an image I took with my 5 megapixel Minolta, yet I was able to get a very good 4 x 6 print from what remained.

## Crop an Image to a Selection

The quickest way to crop an image is to choose a selection tool, select the area of the image you want to keep, and choose Format | Crop | Canvas to Selection. Digital Image Pro discards everything outside the selected portion of the picture. This can provide some really unique effects. The fine points of making selections are covered in Chapter 8, but you can experiment with cropping to a selection by using the following steps:

1. Open an image file you want to crop.

2. Choose the Marquee selection tool (the one at the left end of the selection tools).

3. If the Marquee Tool dialog box is not visible on the screen, click the Selection button in the workspace toolbar.

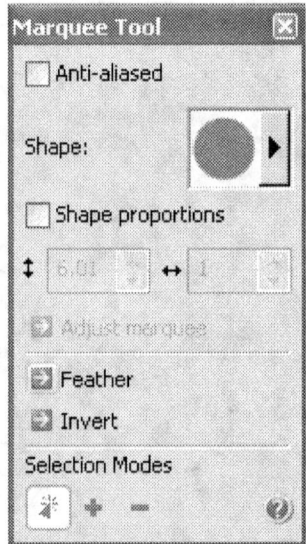

4. Click the right arrow to the right of the Shape field to display a list of available shapes. Choose one of the shapes in the list.

5. Click and drag in the image to make a selection.

6. Select Format | Crop | Canvas to Selection to create the crop.

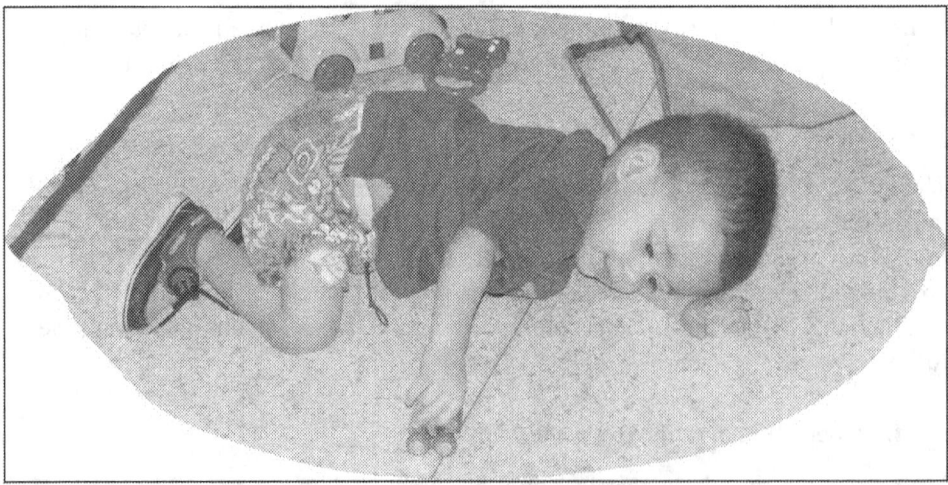

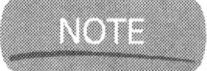 *If the selection shape you chose is not a rectangle, Digital Image Pro sets the size of the image to the rectangle that will fit the selection. However, all areas of the image that fell outside the selected area will be white.*

## Crop an Image with the Crop Tool

To crop an image with the Crop tool, display the image and choose Format | Crop | Canvas. This opens the Crop task bar and overlays the image with a light white mask to make it easier to see the area that will be cropped (see Figure 4-2).

The first step in cropping an image is to set the *proportion* (or ratio) of the height to the width of the cropped picture. Click the Select a Proportion drop-down list to view a list of available proportions (including *Custom*, which lets you set any ratio you want).

**4**

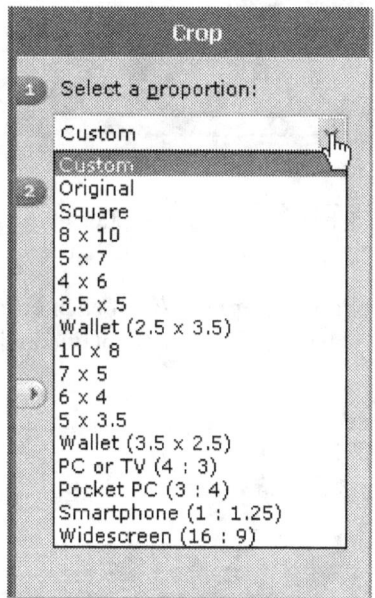

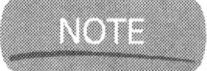 *When you first set a proportion, nothing changes visibly because you haven't specified the size of the cropped image.*

The next step is to set the size of the image. The easiest way to do that is to move the mouse pointer to the upper-left corner of the area, hold down the left mouse button, and drag to the lower-right corner. When you are done, Digital Image Pro displays the selected area by removing the light white mask. It also outlines the

Choose a proportion for your cropped picture

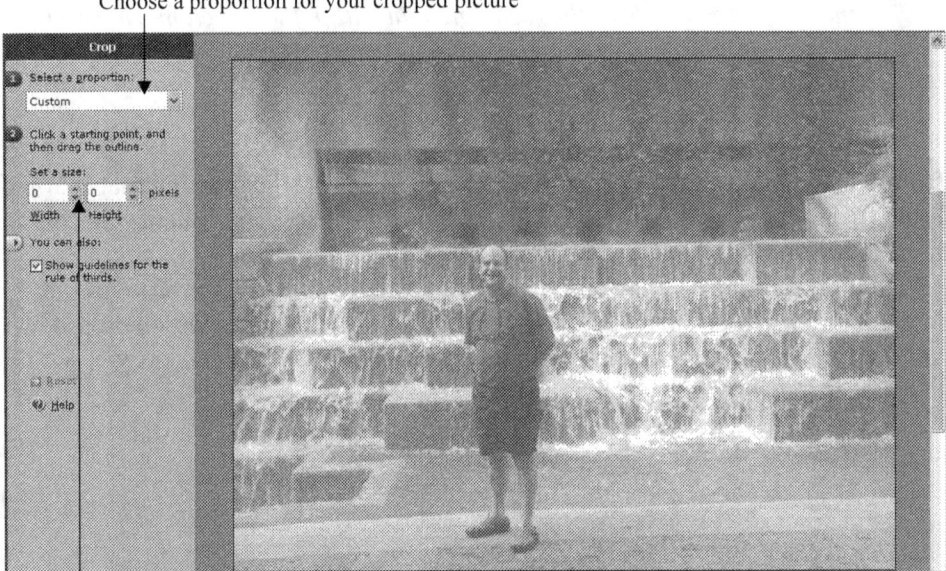

Set the size of the cropped image

The Crop task bar shows you the options for cropping an image.

cropped area and places yellow *sizing handles* at each corner and in the middle of each side. The proportions you set earlier are maintained when you select a cropped area this way.

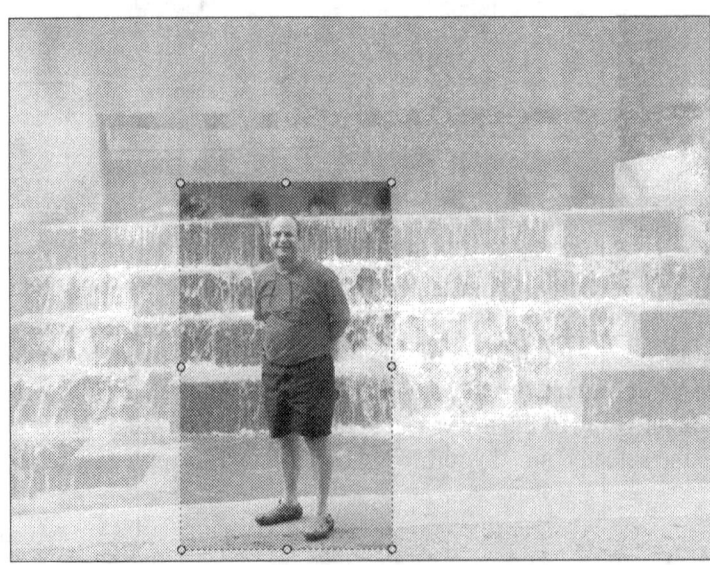

Once you've specified the cropped area, you can click one of the yellow sizing handles and drag to adjust the cropped image size. Here are your options for resizing the cropped area using the mouse:

■ **Click and drag a corner sizing handle**    Clicking and dragging a corner sizing handle changes the size of the cropped image while maintaining the ratio of height to width. Thus, the value in the Select a Proportion drop-down list does not change.

■ **Click and drag a top or bottom side center sizing handle**    Clicking and dragging one of these sizing handles makes the cropped image taller or shorter. The ratio of height to width is not maintained, so the value in the Select a Proportion drop-down list switches to *Custom*.

■ **Click and drag a left or right side center sizing handle**    Clicking and dragging one of these sizing handles makes the cropped image wider or narrower. The ratio of height to width is not maintained, so the value in the Select a Proportion drop-down list switches to Custom.

■ **Click inside the selected area and drag**    Clicking and dragging inside the selected area moves the cropping area without changing the proportion or size.

You can also use the Width and Height fields to set the cropped image size. Simply type in a value or use the spinners. These fields do not preserve the proportions, so the value in the Select a Proportion drop-down list switches to Custom. Click the Done button at the bottom of the taskbar to crop the image.

# Resize the Canvas

If you find that the "canvas" that holds your image is the wrong size, you can adjust the size, making it either larger or smaller, and changing the orientation (landscape/ portrait). Resizing the canvas to make it smaller gives the same effect as cropping the image. However, cropping gives you more control over the result, and is the better way to reduce the size of the image canvas.

Making the canvas larger can certainly be useful. For example, say you want to paste several images together into a panoramic, or add a frame around the edge. In both cases, you need to make the canvas bigger to allow extra room for these operations.

To resize the canvas, select Format | Resize Canvas to open the Resize Canvas task bar.

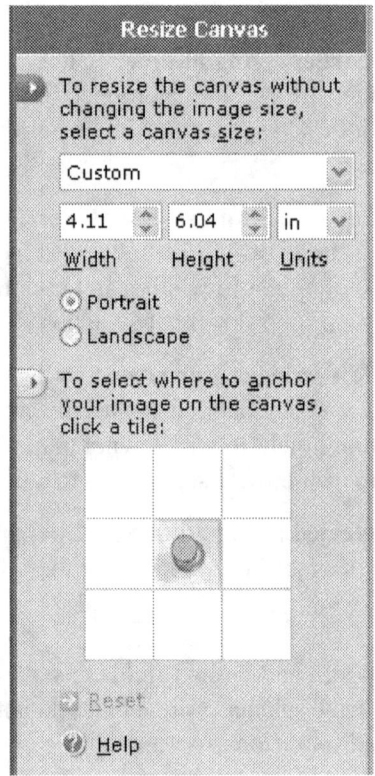

As with cropping, the first step in resizing the canvas is to set the *proportion* (or ratio) of the height to the width of the canvas. Use the drop-down list at the top of the task bar to view a list of available proportions (including Custom, which lets you set any ratio you want).

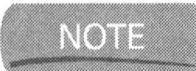 *You can also skip setting the proportions and simply set the canvas size, as described next.*

The next step is to set the size using the Width and Height fields. If you set a proportion, directly changing the field sizes returns the proportion setting to Custom. If you shrink the canvas, Digital Image Pro displays the cropped canvas the same way it shows a cropped image—by showing a light white mask. If you increase the size of the canvas, it shows the extra area around the edges in white.

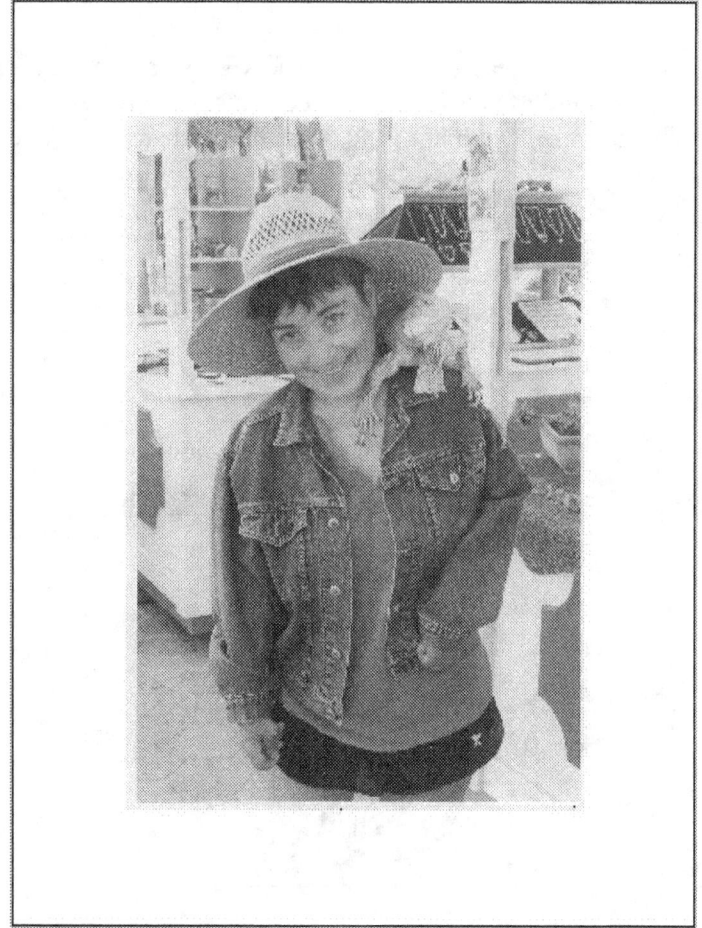

4

Choose either the Portrait or the Landscape option to set the orientation. The last step allows you to anchor your image to the canvas as the canvas size grows. You use the tool in the middle of the task bar that shows a grid and a pushpin. Essentially, you place the pushpin in the quadrant where you want to anchor your image. For example, in the last illustration, the pushpin was located in the center (the default) so the canvas is enlarged evenly on all sides. However, if you move

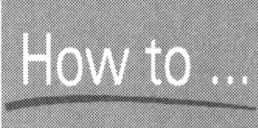

# Use the Rule of Thirds

Near the center of the Crop task bar, there is a checkbox labeled "Show Guidelines For the Rule of Thirds." If you select the checkbox, the crop mask changes to show three intermediate length lines and three intermediate width lines.

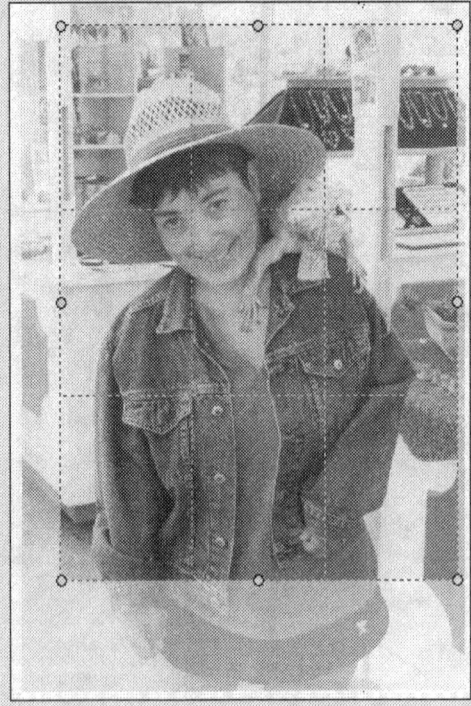

These lines give you guidance in using an old photographic adage called "the rule of thirds." Basically, the rule of thirds states that (contrary to what many think) your main subject should *not* be centered in the frame. Instead, you'll get a much more interesting picture if you split the length and width of the picture into three equal parts (represented by the lines in the cropped image), and position your main subject at the intersection of two of the lines.

As with so many other things photographic, following the rule of thirds is a matter of taste. Many people prefer to have their main subject centered. However, as you can see from the preceding illustration, it does look more interesting when the two main subjects (my wife and her iguana) are both placed on a "rule of thirds" vertex.

the pushpin to the upper-left corner, the image is anchored to the upper-left corner of the canvas, and the new area is added to the right side and below the image.

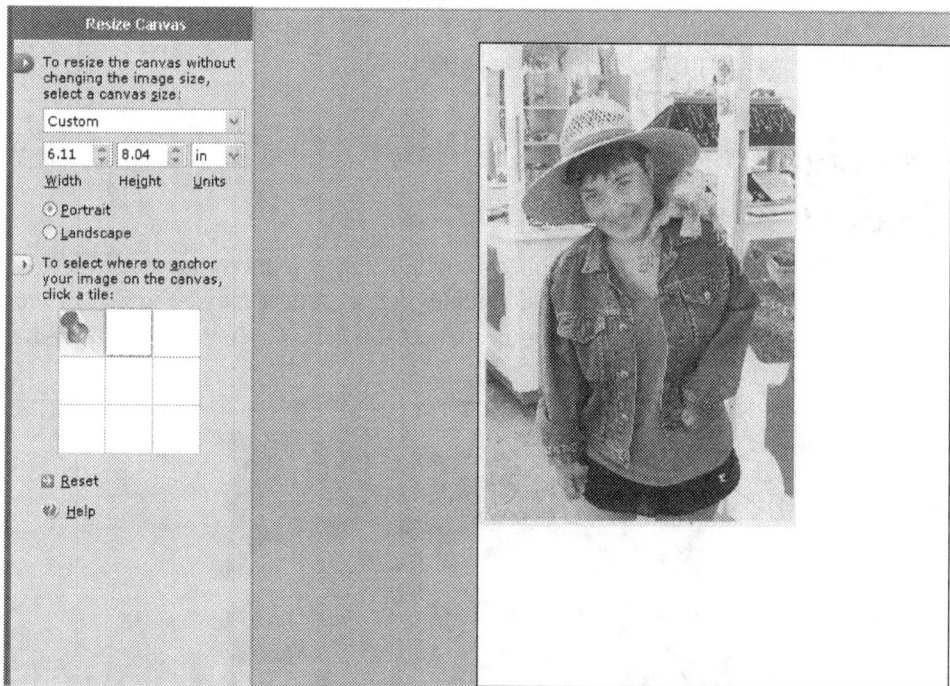

NOTE    *You can also resize the image by selecting Format | Resize Image. This enables you to change image size using all the options (Height, Width, Pixel Dimensions, and Resolutions) when creating a new image, as discussed in Chapter 3. When you resize an image this way, Digital Image Pro rescales the image to fit the new dimensions. This may degrade the picture quality, especially if you are enlarging the image, because Digital Image Pro has to insert new pixels to make the image larger.*

# Let Digital Image Pro Correct Your Pictures

One of the nicest features of Digital Image Pro is its capability to make many corrections automatically—analyzing the errors in your pictures and correcting them with little or no input from you. This is especially helpful when you are first getting started and aren't sure exactly what is wrong with an image. As you get more practiced with Digital Image Pro, you'll probably find yourself using these automatic tools less and less, but they are very handy when you are just getting started and aren't quite sure how to fix your pictures.

Using the two auto-fix features is very simple. To automatically adjust the contrast (which enhances the contrast without changing the color balance), choose Touchup | Contrast Auto Fix. To automatically adjust the levels (which balances the light and dark areas of the image), choose Touchup | Levels Auto Fix. Levels are described in more detail later in this chapter.

# Correct Lighting with Add Flash and Reduce Backlighting

Using "fill flash" is an old photographer's trick. When you photograph a subject against a bright background, the exposure meter on the camera may be fooled by the background and exposes for it, leaving the subject too dark, as shown in Figure 4-3.

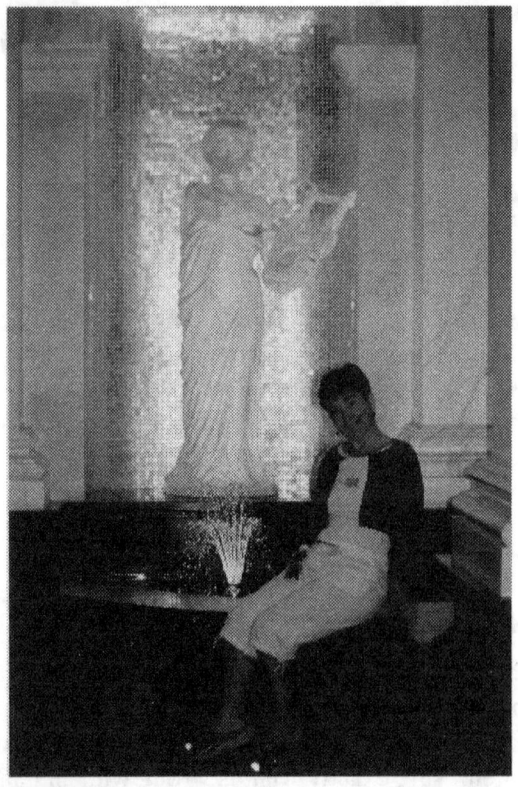

When the background is bright, the face of the subject is underexposed and left in deep shade.

To brighten the subject, the photographer turns on the camera's flash and forces it to fire. The flash "fills in" the dark area, hence the name "fill flash." Of course, up until now, there was no way to correct the problem after the fact. But Digital Image Pro fixes that with its fill flash facility. This nifty tool selectively lightens dark areas of the photograph, as shown in Figure 4-4.

Another lighting issue concerns "backlighting." The main subject may be properly exposed, but the area behind the subject may be "blown out" (overexposed), with a resulting loss in detail (see Figure 4-5). You could darken the whole picture, but then the main subject will be too dark. Instead, Microsoft Digital Image Pro allows you to selectively adjust the backlighting to correct this, as shown in Figure 4-6.

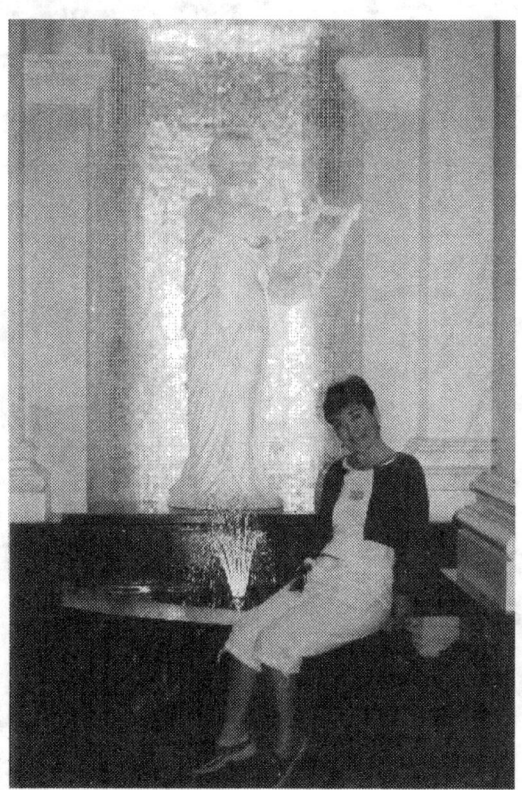

After using fill flash, the ruined photo was rescued!

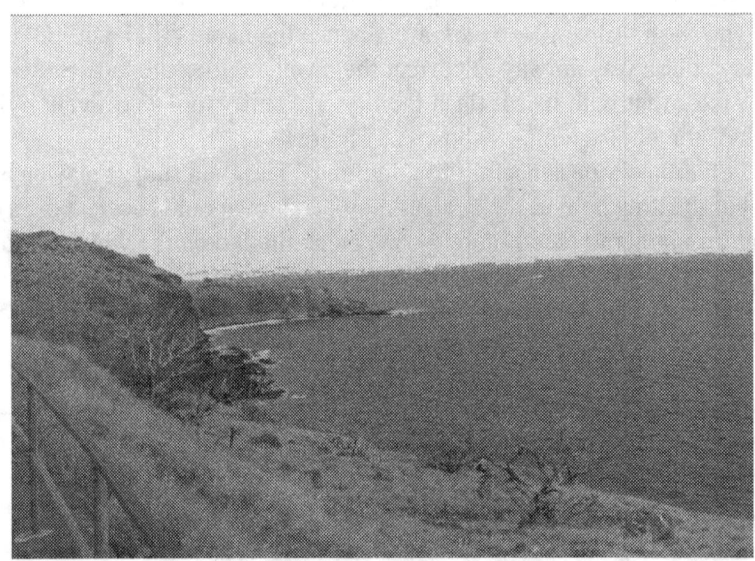

The backlighting of this image hides interesting patterns in the sky.

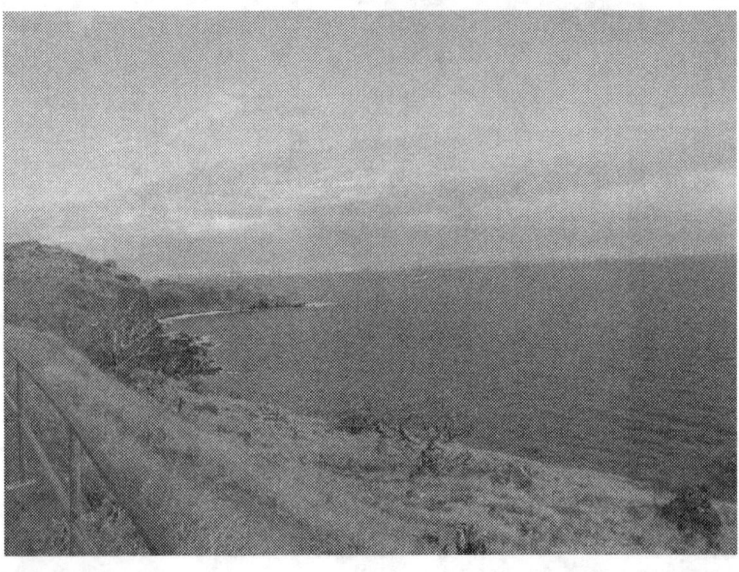

By "turning down" the backlighting, the sky becomes much more interesting.

To correct lighting problems, select Touchup | Adjust Lighting to open the Adjust Lighting task bar.

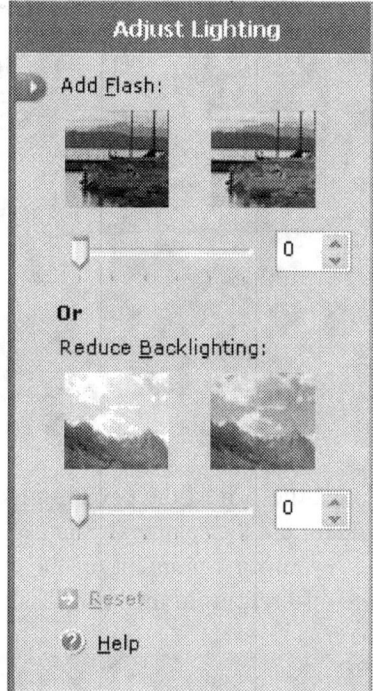

To add fill flash, click the Add Flash slider and drag it to the right to lighten the dark areas. Alternatively, you can set the value in the Add Flash field by typing in a value or using the spinner.

To reduce backlighting, click the Reduce Backlighting slider and drag it to the right to darken the light areas. Alternatively, you can set the value in the Reduce Backlighting field by typing in a value or using the spinner.

# Sharpen a Photo to Fix the Focus

You can fix a photo that is slightly blurred or out of focus to make it look more sharply focused. Digital Image Pro has two different sharpening tools: a fairly simple one that is good for quick fixes, and the more complex Unsharp Mask tool, which enables you to exercise a great deal of control over the amount and type of sharpening applied to the image.

To quickly sharpen an image, choose Touchup | Sharpen or Blur to open the Sharpen or Blur task bar.

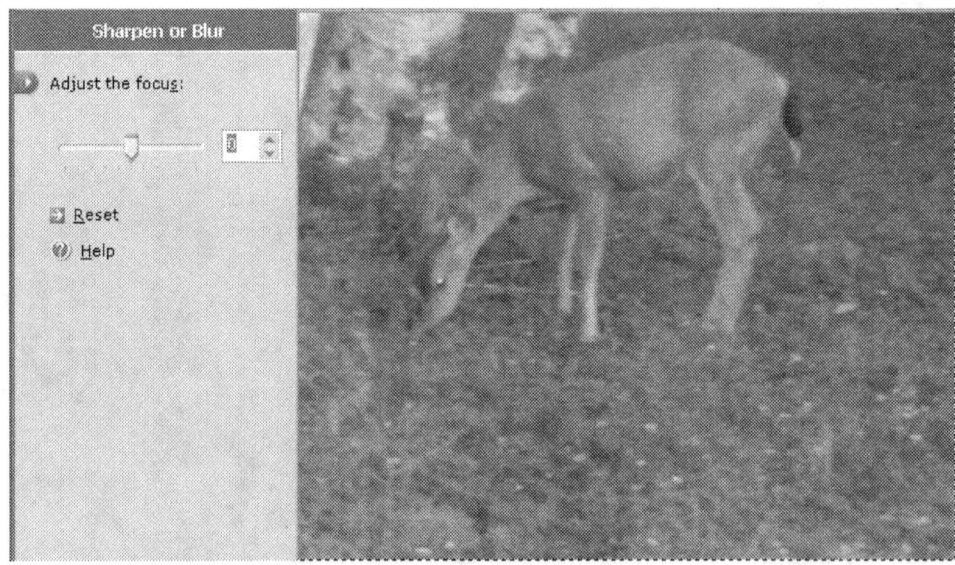

To sharpen the image, click the Adjust the Focus slider and drag it to the right, or type a number into the field (or use the spinners). Sharpening an image is processor-intensive, so you may have to wait for a moment for the effect to be applied. The sharpened image looks quite different from the "soft focus" original.

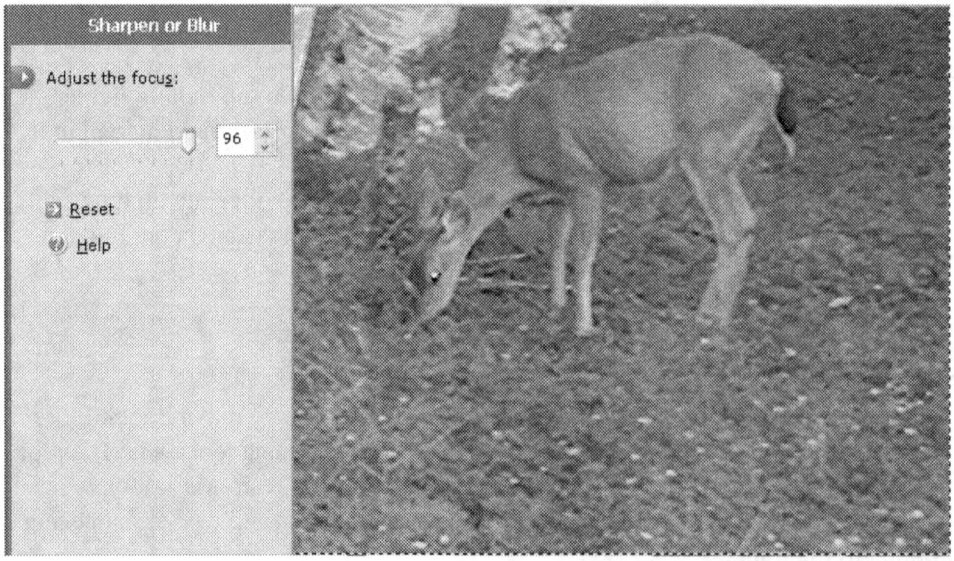

NOTE  *You can also drag the slider to the left (or type a negative number into the field) to blur the image. However, as you'll see in Chapter 8, blurring is usually something that works much more effectively on a selected area, rather than the entire image.*

The Sharpen or Blur tool works fairly well, but allows you little control of how the image is sharpened. To exercise more control, choose Touchup | Unsharp Mask. Despite its name, this tool actually helps you sharpen an image.

---

**Unsharp Mask**

1  To automatically sharpen the picture, click:

☐ Sharpen
☐ Sharpen more
☐ Sharpen a portrait

2  Fine-tune the sharpness:

Edge Width

[slider]  0.0

Pixels

Contrast

[slider]  0%

Noise Reduction Threshold

[slider]  0

☐ Reset
② Help

---

The Unsharp Mask tool works by detecting high-contrast edges in your image, and sharpening (increasing the contrast) of only those edges. This avoids "sharpening" areas that don't need it. You control the three parameters of the Unsharp Mask tool using either the sliders or the fields. The three parameters are as follows:

■ **Edge Width**   This determines the number of pixels surrounding edge pixels that are sharpened. I recommend an edge width of between 1 and 2 pixels.

Lesser amounts sharpen only the edge pixel itself, whereas a larger number sharpens a wider band of pixels. Taken to the extreme, this has the same effect as just sharpening the entire image.

- **Contrast**    This value determines how much to increase the contrast of the detected pixels. Amounts between 150 and 200 percent usually work best.

- **Noise Reduction Threshold**    This determines how different the contrast of the pixels must be from the surrounding area before they are considered "edge pixels." A value of between 2 and 20 works well. Lower values detect every color change as an edge; very high values fail to find edges at all.

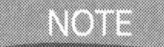 *You can automatically sharpen a picture by picking one of the three listed in section 1 of the Unsharp Mask task bar. Each choice applies a set of parameters to the Edge Width, Contrast, and Threshold. The Sharpen a Portrait option applies a softer focus by applying a narrower edge and higher degree of contrast (Threshold) before a pixel is considered an edge pixel.*

# Make Color Corrections for Yourself

As you get more experienced with Digital Image Pro, you'll find yourself wanting to exercise a very fine degree of control over color, brightness, and contrast adjustments. This is primarily because the "exactly right" adjustment is very much a matter of personal preference, and the automatic adjustments may not apply corrections the way you want.

Fortunately, Digital Image Pro sports a number of controls that enable you to fiddle with color corrections to your heart's content. These controls include Hue and Saturation, Tint, Brightness and Contrast, and Levels.

## Understand the Color Wheel

A color wheel (see Figure 4-7) will help you understand how to make adjustments to colors in an image. As you can see from the figure, each color has an opposite, or complementary color, which is indicated on the color wheel by the lines connecting different colors. For example, the complementary color of green is magenta (they are at opposite ends of the same line).

## Adjust the Tint

You can adjust the tint of the colors in a photograph by selecting Touchup | Adjust Tint to open the Adjust Tint task bar.

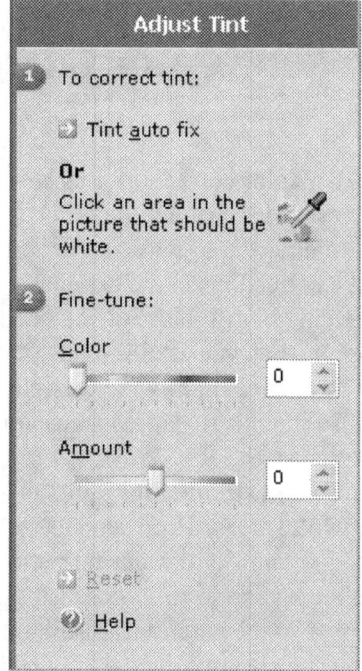

To change the tint of a particular color, choose the color by moving the Color slider. The colors vary from red at the far left end of the Color slider to magenta at the far right. Essentially, as you move the slider you are moving around the color wheel.

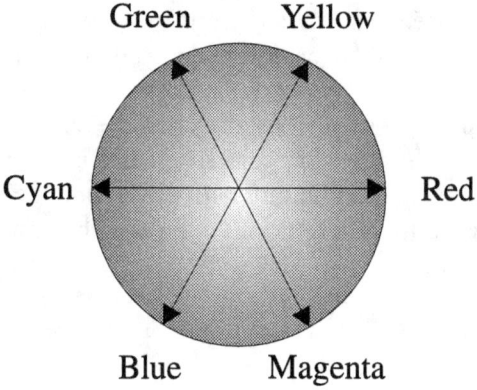

A color wheel shows the relationship between related colors.

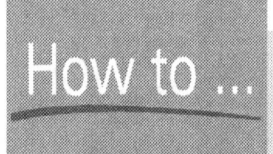 **Plan Your Color Corrections**

To get the best results from a color correction, it is best to make the corrections in a certain order. The correct order enables you to focus on what is important, as well as more easily see the results of making the corrections to the image.

The first step is to make corrections in the extreme areas of the image—the deep shadows and the extreme highlights. For the deep shadow areas, you'll want to lighten and bring up whatever details are available; you may also need to increase the color saturation and slightly increase the contrast. The contrast adjustment is tricky because it tends to darken areas you just took great pains to lighten!

Making adjustments in the extreme highlights enables you to take the "edge" off specular (pure white) areas. These tend to get introduced either from reflection (from your flash, or snow and water reflections) or high-intensity light sources (car headlights, and so forth). There isn't much you can do with these except tone them down so they aren't as distracting because these areas have lost all detail. With other bright areas (sky, bright water reflections, overexposed faces), you can decrease the brightness and increase the color saturation and contrast.

After you have modified the extremes of the image, focus your attention on the midranges. Adjusting the extremes will have modified the midranges somewhat, but additional adjustments may be necessary to get them just right. You should focus on getting the brightness and contrast corrected because the next step is to adjust the overall color balance of the image, which is most visible in the midranges. This step removes color casts (where white shows up as another color, such as light green) and over- and under-saturated colors.

The last step in making a correction is to sharpen the image using the Unsharp mask or Sharpen or Blur. By correcting the extremes, overall color balance, and overall contrast *first*, the edge sharpening is more effective, and you avoid introducing false color and moiré patterns around the edges. This step also helps to correct softness in the focus introduced by previous steps (due to *resampling* of the image).

## Did you know?

## Beware of Resampling

*Resampling* is the process of re-analyzing the contents of the image when making color corrections. Resampling, however carefully done, can introduce subtle errors in the image. This is most apparent when saving JPEG files, but it occurs at other times, too. The effects of resampling are most apparent around the edges in the image, which is why you should sharpen your image as the last step.

When you select a color from the Color slider (or field), the Amount slider changes. On the right side of the Amount slider, Digital Image Pro displays the color you selected, increasing in intensity as you move right. The left side of the Amount slider shows the decreasing intensity of the selected color by displaying the complementary color in increasing intensity. To add more of the selected color, move the Amount slider to the right; to remove some of the selected color, move the Amount slider to the left.

Probably the most useful task you can accomplish with the Adjust Tint tool is to correct *color cast*. *Color cast* is a situation in which the entire tonal range of the photograph has too much of one color. "Warm" photographs tend to have a reddish cast; "cold" photographs tend to have a bluish cast. Color casts usually occur because the film was not balanced for the type of light you were using. For example, a daylight-balanced film (most films are daylight-balanced) will show a greenish color cast when shooting under fluorescent or mercury vapor lights. For digital cameras, a color cast can occur if the automatic white balance is fooled by the lighting conditions. You will usually notice a color cast in photos that have large areas that should be white, but instead have faint (and sometimes not so faint) overtones of the cast color.

To correct a color cast with Digital Image Pro, move the mouse pointer over the image (where it turns into an eyedropper) and click an area that should be white. From there, Digital Image Pro takes over and adjusts the overall tint of the photograph by the same amount it had to adjust the indicated area to make it white. This usually works pretty well.

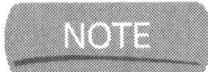 *Because the difference between the "before" and "after" photos for correcting color casts is impossible to see in the black and white images in this book, I've included an example in the color insert section.*

## Adjust Hue and Saturation

Digital Image Pro provides the Hue and Saturation task bar (select Touchup | Hue and Saturation) to adjust the color (hue), purity of color (saturation), and brightness of the image.

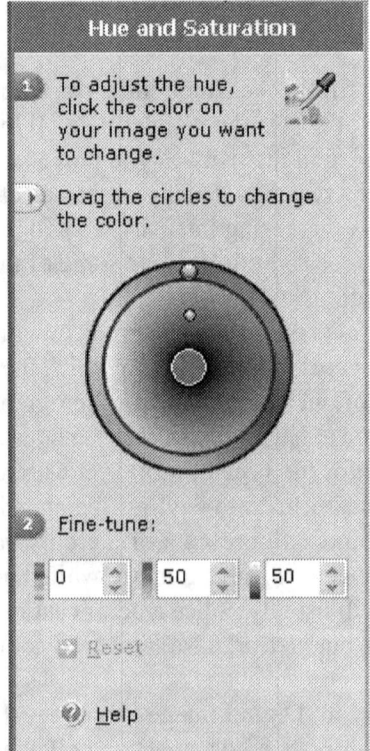

NOTE *Your selections in the Hue and Saturation task bar affect all the colors in the image so, in general, they are not particularly useful when applied to the whole picture unless you are looking for psychedelic effects (but hey, it's your picture). However, as you'll see in Chapter 8, you can select a single portion of a picture (such as a white shirt) and change its hue and saturation to good effect.*

To adjust the hue, saturation, and brightness, use the following steps:

1. If you wish, move the mouse over the image and click to set the starting color you want to work with.. This step isn't really necessary because the color adjustments apply equally to all the colors in the image. However, if there is a particular color (such as a blue jacket) that you want to ensure ends up as a particular color, select that color before adjusting the hue in the next step.

2. Click the yellow circle along the outer rim of the color wheel and drag it around the perimeter of the circle. This sets the color that will be substituted for the original color (from step 1), and adjusts all the other colors in the image by the same amount.

3. Click the blue circle in the inner circle of the color wheel and drag it to the right to increase the color saturation. Drag it to the left to decrease the saturation.

**TIP** *If you drag the blue circle all the way to the left (decreasing color saturation to the minimum), you have just converted the image to black and white!*

4. Drag the blue circle closer to the center to decrease the image lightness. Drag the blue circle closer to the perimeter to increase the lightness.

You can fine-tune your choices by using the three fields in the Fine-tune section (2) of the Hue and Saturation task bar. You can specify a value for these fields between 0 and 100. The three fields are (from left to right): Hue, Color Saturation, and Brightness. The Brightness field is useful if you just need to lighten the entire picture by a bit.

**TIP** *To create a black and white photo, it is much easier to set the Saturation field to 0 than to try and drag the blue circle all the way to the left side of the color wheel.*

## Convert the Image to Black and White

You can easily convert a color image to black and white by selecting Effects | Black and White. For a more "old time" look, you can also use Effects | Antique, which results in a photo approximating the old tintypes you see in museums.

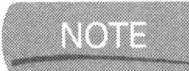 *You can also convert your image to a negative by selecting Effects | Negative. I just can't figure out why you'd want to.*

## Adjust the Brightness and Contrast

One of the most common problems with photographs is over or under exposure. Take, for example, the photograph in Figure 4-8. It is washed out, with much detail apparently lost. But with Digital Image Pro's Brightness and Contrast tool, you can fix this problem, as well as problems with photos that are too dark.

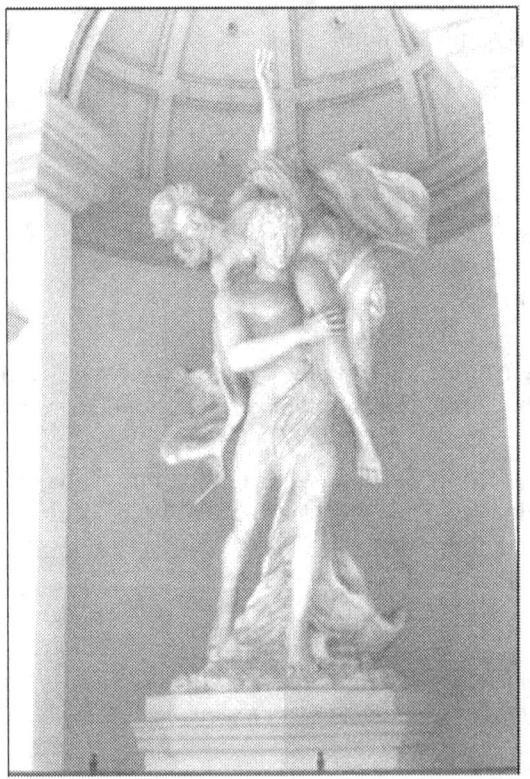

You can fix a photo that is overexposed, like this one.

To access the Brightness and Contrast task bar, select Touchup | Brightness and Contrast.

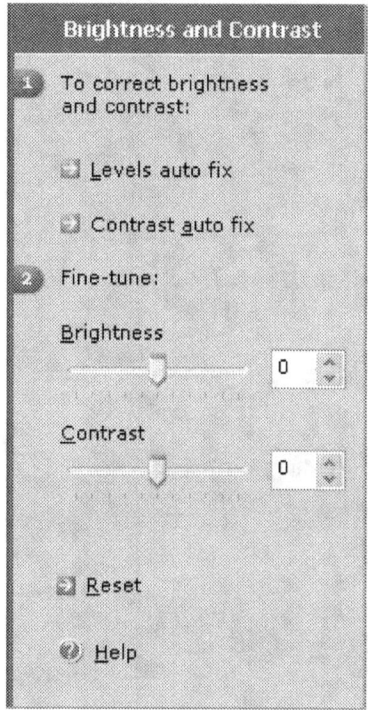

Use the Brightness and Contrast sliders to increase (move the sliders right) or decrease (move the sliders left) the brightness and contrast. You can also type a value into the fields or use the spinners to set the value between –100 and 100.

## Correct Your Photo with the Adjust Levels Control

The Adjust Levels task bar (see Figure 4-9) enables you to adjust the brightness and contrast for an image. However, unlike the Brightness and Contrast task bar described earlier, the Adjust Levels task bar enables you to adjust the brightness and contrast not only for the image as a whole, but for each of the primary colors (red, green, or blue) individually. In addition, you can make adjustments that apply only to the shadows, the highlights, or the midtones. To open the Adjust Levels task bar, select Touchup | Adjust Levels.

Histogram ─────────

Set the color channel
affected here ─────────

Set the input levels
for shadows, midtones,
and highlights

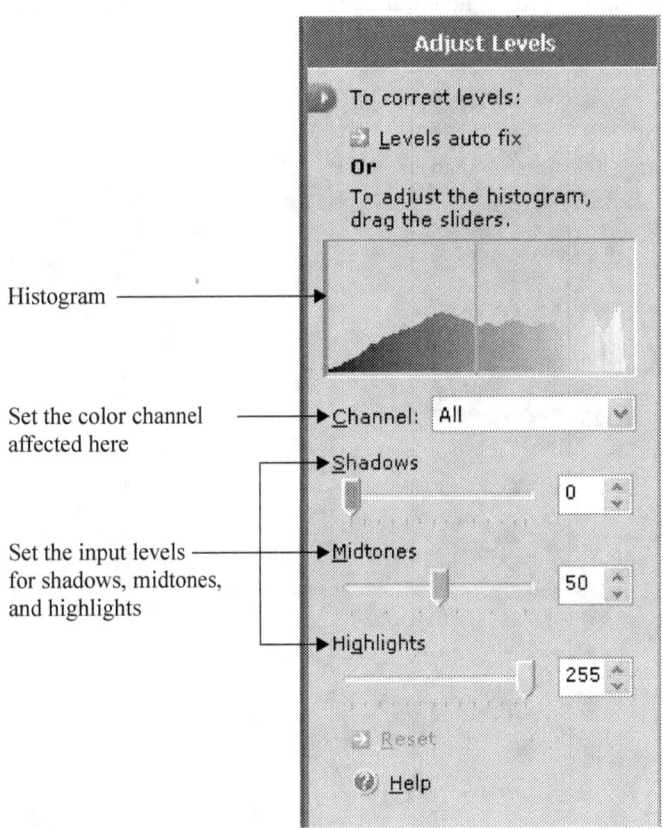

Change the brightness of an image for individual colors and brightness
ranges.

The histogram shows the distribution of color for the image. If you select All
from the Channel drop-down list (as shown in the last figure), the histogram displays
the overall brightness of the image. If you select one of the primary colors, the
histogram displays the distribution of the brightness of that color.

To adjust the tonal range of the image, use either the sliders (Shadows, Midtones,
and Highlights) or the associated fields. You can also drag the three bars in the
histogram itself. The entire tonal range stretches from a value of 0 at the low end
to 255 at the high end. Adjusting the sliders does the following:

■ **Adjust the Highlights**   The maximum highlight (white point) is controlled
by the value in the Highlights field or the Highlights slider control. Setting

the value of this field (or dragging the control to set the value) to a number less than 255 resets all pixels in the image that had a value greater than the new value of the Highlights field equal to pure white (255), and remaps the remaining pixels so that the color balance is unaffected. The overall affect is to increase the tonal range (contrast) at the high end of the image, and the image appears to lighten because pixels are being mapped to higher values.

4

■ **Adjust the Shadows**   The minimum shadow (black point) is controlled by the value in the Shadows field or the Shadows slider control. Setting the value of this field (or dragging the control to set the value) to a number greater than 0 resets all pixels in the image that had a value less than the new value of the Shadows field equal to pure black (0) and remaps the remaining pixels so that the color balance is unaffected. The overall effect is to increase the tonal range (contrast) at the low end of the image, and the image appears to darken because pixels are being mapped to lower values.

■ **Adjust the midtones**   The midtones are controlled by the value in the Midtones field or the Midtones slider control. To darken the midtones, type in a higher number or drag the slider to the right. To lighten the midtones, type in a lower number or drag the slider to the left. Note that these corrections do not change either the white point or the black point.

The typical way to adjust the Levels for an image is to drag the Highlights *down* to the point where a significant number of bright pixels appear in the histogram. Likewise, you would drag the Shadows up to the point where a significant number of dark pixels appear in the histogram. For example, the following is the histogram of an image that contains virtually no pixels in the very bright range:

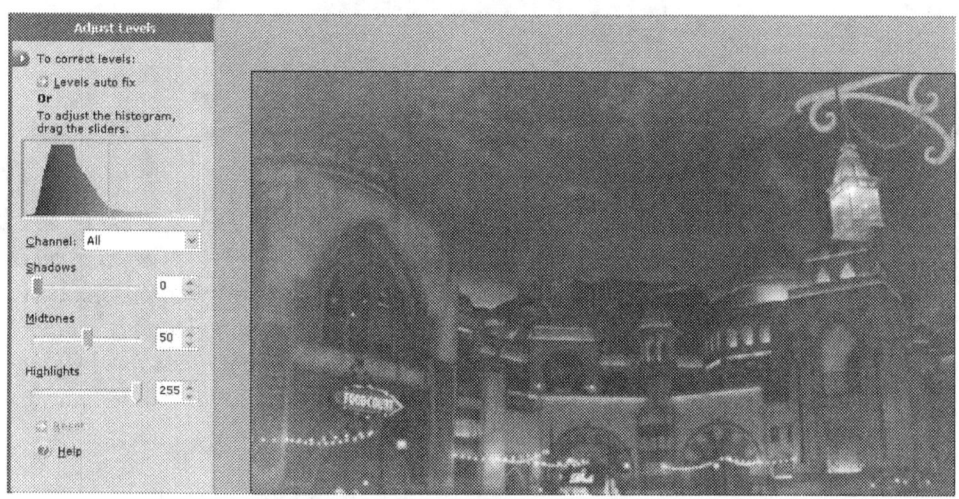

By dragging the Highlight slider down to the point where the histogram shows bright pixels occurring, the brightest pixels that *do* exist are mapped to white; the rest of the pixels are remapped proportionately, increasing the tonal range. You can do the same at the Shadow end of the range as well.

If you accept the changes you just made (click OK), and then reopen the Levels dialog box, you'll find that the tonal range has been adjusted so that pixels now stretch across the entire range:

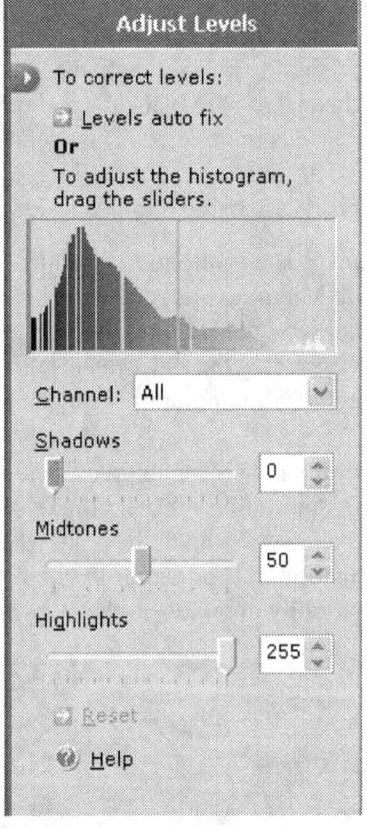

It is easy to overdo the adjustments to the Input levels. For example, if you drag the white level slider down past the point where a lot of bright pixels appear in the histogram, you'll lose all details in those bright areas because all the bright pixels above the value of the slider are mapped to pure white. You can also lose details in the shadows by dragging the black level slider up past the point where a significant number of pixels appear at the dark end of the histogram.

# Rotate and Flip Images

If your image didn't end up quite with the orientation you expected, you can easily fix that with Digital Image Pro. For example, you might have scanned an image crooked, or even upside down. Not to worry, you can deal with these sorts of problems with just a few mouse clicks.

## Rotate the Canvas

**4**

If you turned your camera to take the picture (resulting in an image lying on its side) or scanned an image upside down, you can adjust the orientation of the image by selecting Format | Rotate Canvas to open the Rotate task bar.

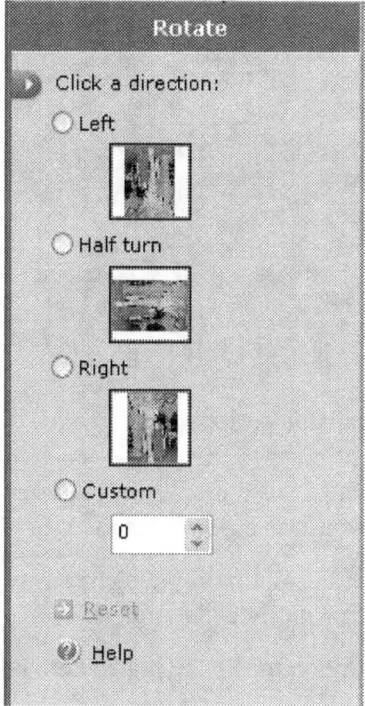

Choose the Left or Right option to turn an image that is lying on its side. Choose the Half Turn option to flip the image over.

You can also rotate the canvas by an arbitrary amount by selecting the Custom option and typing a value into the field (or using the spinners). Valid values are from 0 to 180 (rotate the image clockwise) and from 0 to –180 (rotate the image counterclockwise).

## Flip the Canvas

You can flip an image to correct for scanning errors. To flip the canvas, choose
Format | Flip | Canvas to open the Flip task bar.

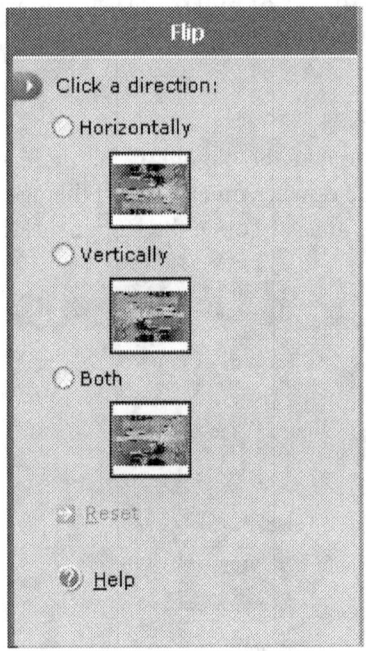

Choose one of three available options:

- **Horizontally**    Choose this option if the picture is reversed left to right.
  This can happen if you scan a negative and place it in the scanner backwards.

- **Vertically**    Choose this option if the picture is upside down. This is a
  common occurrence with flatbed scanners.

- **Both**    Select this option to flip the image both horizontally and vertically
  at the same time.

When you select one of the options, Digital Image Pro immediately flips the large image so you can preview the result. As with most other task bars, you can return the image to its original state by clicking Reset.

## Straighten the Picture

One of the more common ways to get images into Digital Image Pro is to scan them. If the scan comes out slightly crooked, you could end up with a skewed photo.

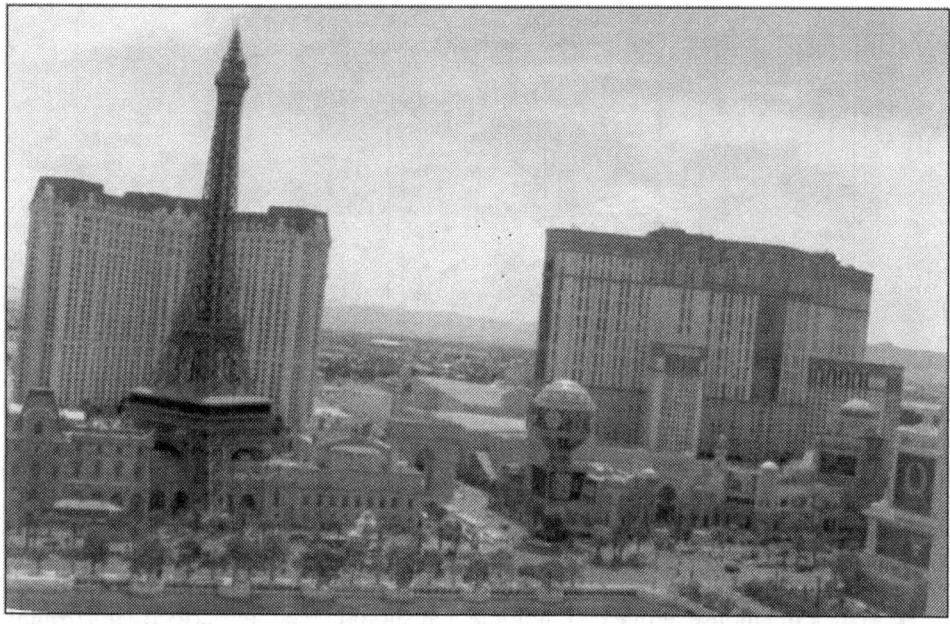

To fix this problem, choose Format | Straighten Picture | Canvas to open the Straighten Picture task bar.

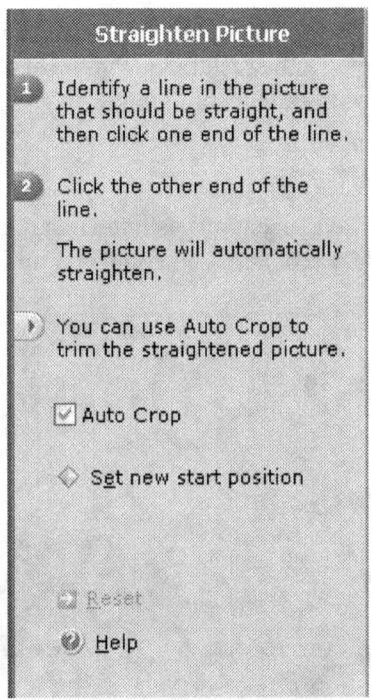

The onscreen instructions in Digital Image Pro are confusing because they refer to selecting a line "that should be straight." The problem with this is that even in skewed images, the lines are still straight—they are just not going in the right direction. To straighten the picture, use the following steps:

1. Click the mouse at one end of a line that should be either perfectly horizontal or perfectly vertical. Good lines to use are the horizon (if it is visible), the edge of a counter, or the corner of a building.

2. Move the mouse pointer to the other end of the line and click again. Digital Image Pro automatically straightens the picture and shows you which portions of the picture no longer fit on the canvas by using the cropping mask.

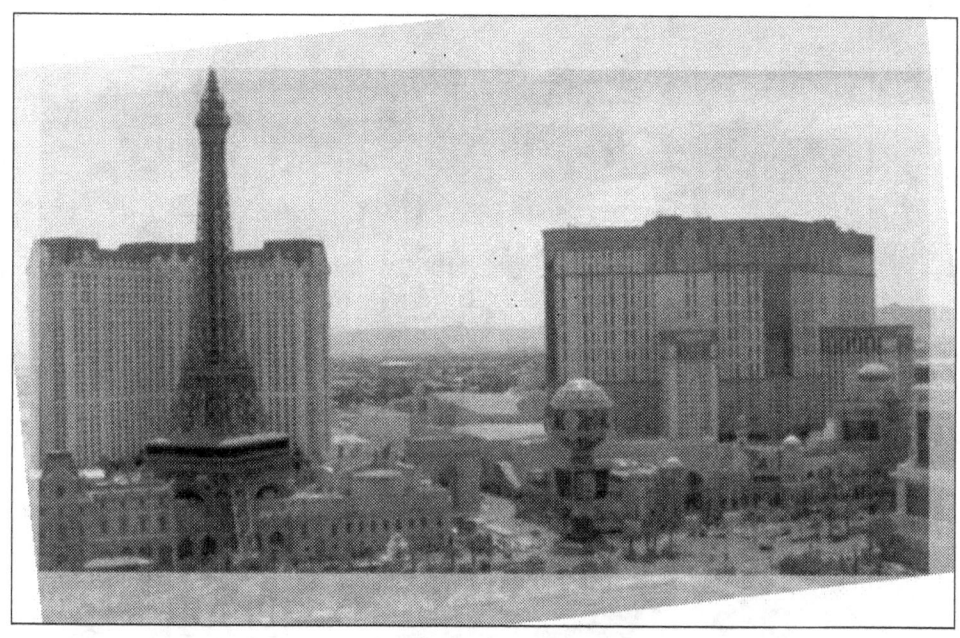

**3.** Click Done to finish the job. If you selected the Auto Crop checkbox, Digital Image Pro automatically discards the portions of the image that no longer fit on the canvas. If you *don't* select the Auto Crop checkbox, you'll need to remove those portions yourself with the cropping tool.

TIP    *If you want to keep your entire image, expand the canvas (adding blank space all around the edges of the image) prior to straightening the picture. To expand the size of the canvas, select Format | Resize Canvas. Of course, if you do this, you'll need to figure out how to deal with the uneven white space that appears. Add a frame (see Chapter 11) perhaps?*

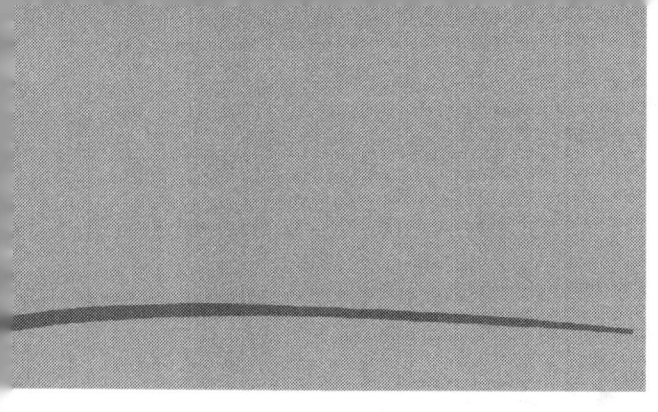

# Customize and Use the Paint Tools

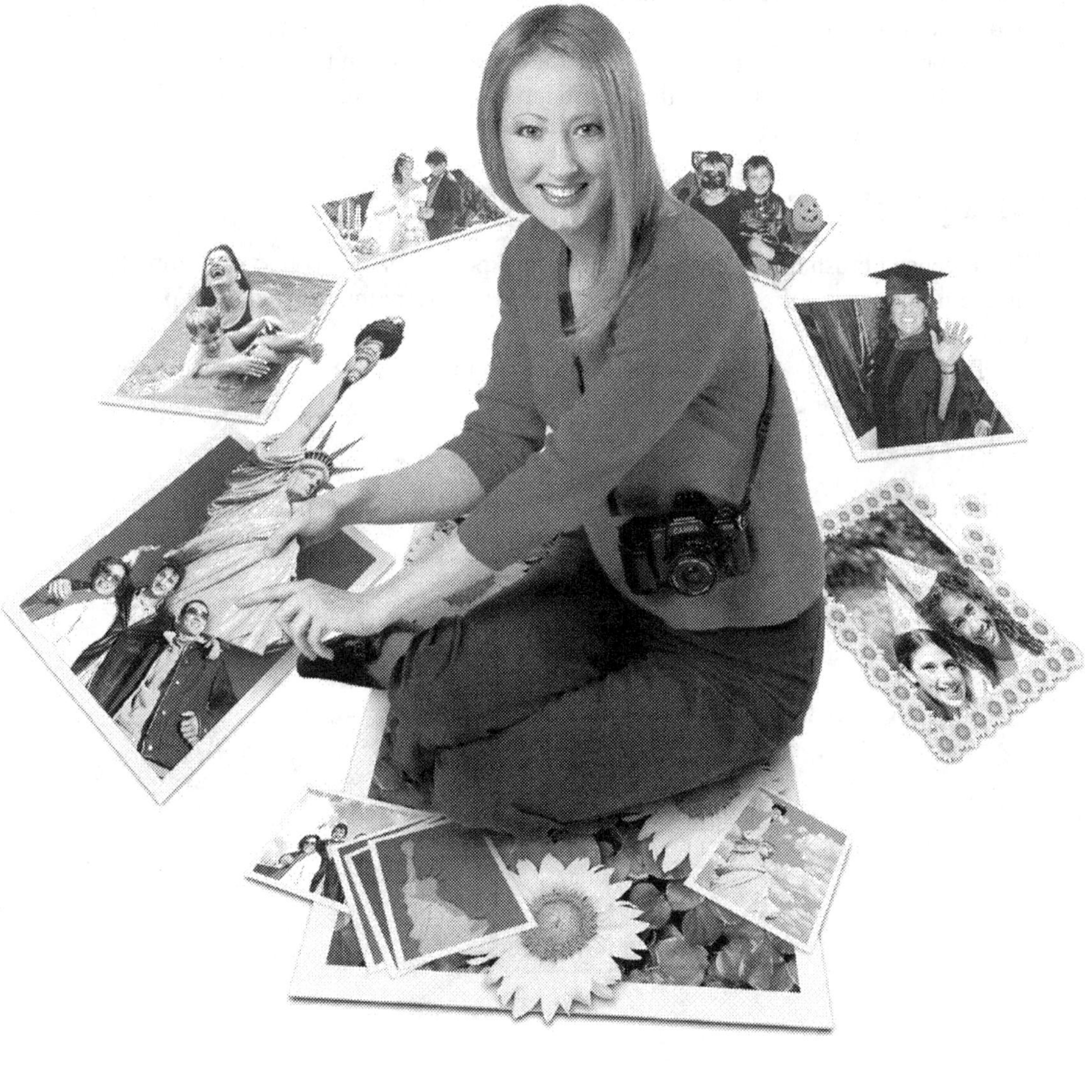

## How to…

- Choose a paint color and brush size
- Choose and configure the brush tools
- Customize your image with Photo Stroke, Art Stroke, and Stamps

You can paint directly on your image to "spice it up." Your painting tools include a Freehand brush (paint anything you want), brushes that paint with small photographs or art, and a brush that "paints" on the picture using pre-built stamps. All the brushes add an object layer to the image and paint on that separate layer, so if you change your mind about the modifications, you can simply delete the layer (as described in Chapter 8).

# Paint with the Freehand Brush

The Freehand brush does just what you might expect—enables you to paint directly on the image, using the color and brush you want. To paint, you set your paint parameters, and then click and drag the image.

To start working with the freehand brush, choose Effects | Paint Brush | Freehand to open the Freehand Painting task bar.

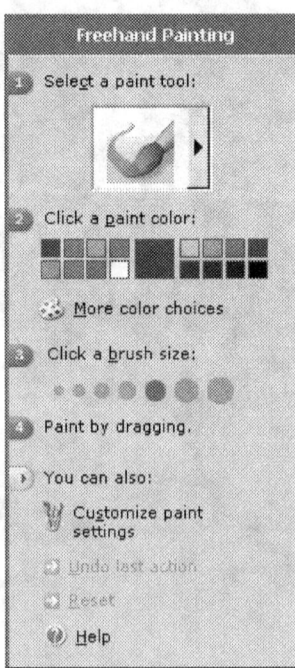

## Pick a Paint Tool

The first step in getting ready to paint on an image is to pick the paint tool you want. To do so, click the right arrow in the Select a Paint Tool field.

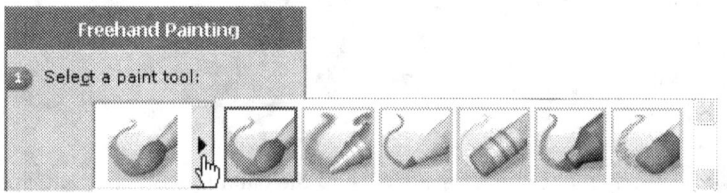

5

Figure 5-1 shows a sample of each of these tools against a patterned background. Each paint type is on a separate layer on the stack.

The following paint tools are available:

- **Paint Brush**   The Paint Brush draws a solid line with slight feathering at the edges. At a transparency setting of 0 (see "Customize the Paint Settings" later in this chapter), it is almost completely opaque.

- **Airbrush**   The Airbrush tool sprays on the selected color over the background. Even at a transparency setting of 0, a great deal of the background shows through. The intensity of the color is greater at the center of the stroke than at the edges. Airbrushing over the same area again builds up the amount of color and decreases the amount of background that shows through.

> TIP   *The Airbrush is good for modifying the color of specific items, such as whitening teeth in a portrait.*

- **Pencil**   The Pencil draws a solid line with sharp edges. It is completely opaque at the transparency setting of 0.

- **Eraser**   The Eraser removes paint applied by any of the other tools. The color you use for the Eraser does not matter.

- **Highlighter**   Much like the Airbrush, the Highlighter applies a transparent color through which you can see the background, and reapplying the Highlighter darkens the color and makes it more opaque. Unlike the Airbrush, however, the color intensity of the Highlighter is even across the width of the stroke.

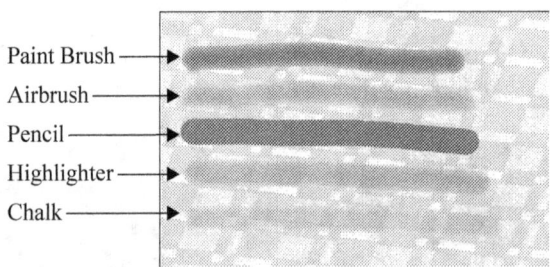

Paint Brush
Airbrush
Pencil
Highlighter
Chalk

Study the results of using each of the paint tools. They were applied with the default brush shape and a transparency of 0.

■ **Chalk**    The Chalk tool applies a light, partially transparent color to the image. As with real chalk, the edges of the stroke are slightly jagged and uneven.

## Pick a Painting Color and Brush Size

To choose a paint color, you can either click one of the color squares under Click a Paint Color, or click More Color Choices. Clicking More Color Choices opens the Custom Color task bar, which displays the Color wheel and Fine-tune fields. These work identically to the controls for Hue and Saturation, described in Chapter 4.

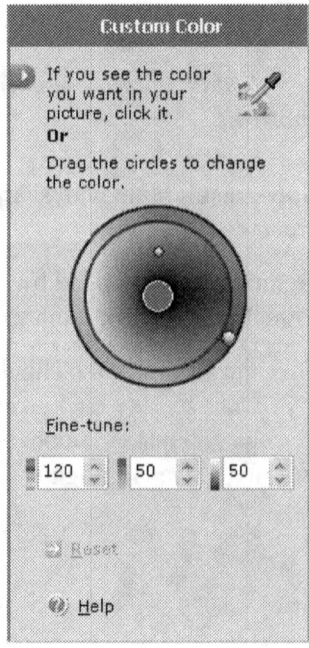

As with the Hue and Saturation controls, you can move the mouse pointer over the image, where it turns into an eye dropper. Clicking a color in the image chooses that color for the brush.

Choose the brush size you want to use by clicking one of the circles under Click a Brush Size. It can be difficult to get exactly the right size, but these are the only options available.

## Customize the Paint Settings

If the default brush shape and transparency aren't quite right, you can click Customize Paint Settings to open a new task bar whose label reflects the currently selected paint tool.

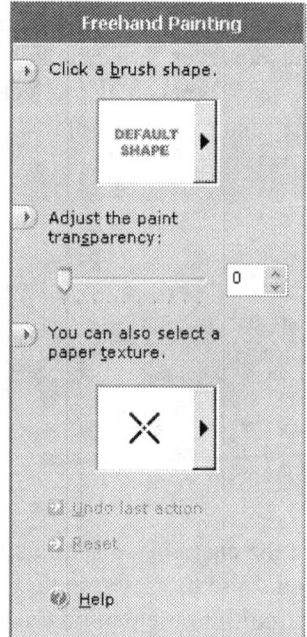

From this task bar, you can do the following:

■ **Choose another brush shape**   To select another brush shape, click the right arrow in the Click a Brush Shape box. Select the brush shape you want to use.

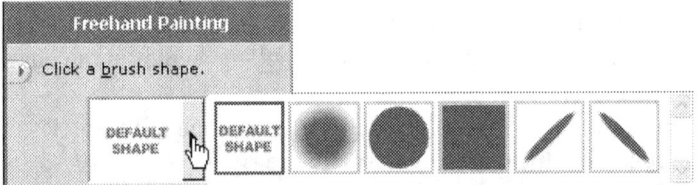

- **Set the transparency** To adjust the paint transparency, click and drag the Adjust the Paint Transparency slider (or use the field). Dragging the slider to the right increases the value of the transparency, which makes the paint less opaque and allows more of the background to show through. As described previously, a transparency of 0 does not necessarily mean that the paint is completely opaque.

- **Select the paper texture** Under normal circumstances, your paint applies smoothly on the image. However, you can choose a "paper texture" from the last box in the task bar ("You can also select a paper texture"). When you paint with a texture, that texture is applied along with the color, as shown here:

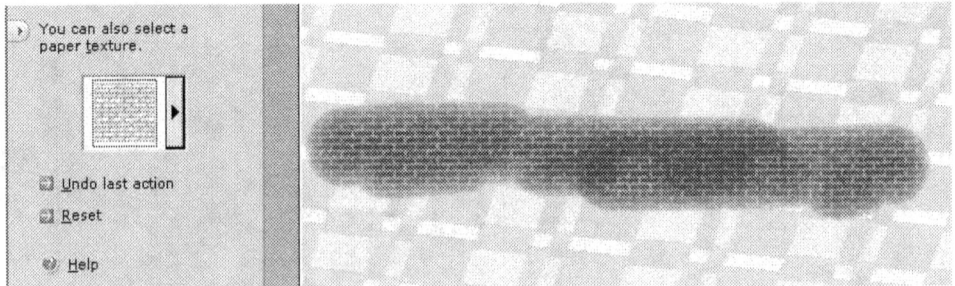

When you're done picking the customized settings, click the back arrow (<) at the bottom of the task bar to return to the painting task bar. Or, click Cancel to discard your settings and *then* return to the painting task bar.

# Paint with the Photo Stroke Tool

The Photo Stroke tool enables you to "paint" on your image with simple, pre-built photographs, such as the chili peppers shown next.

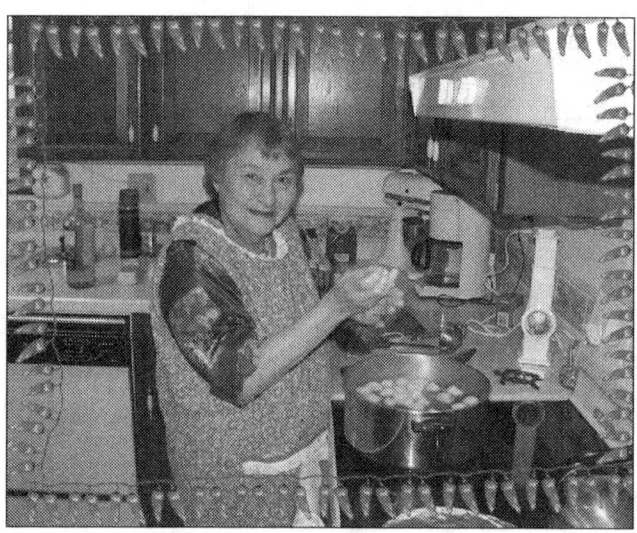

To paint with the Photo Stroke tool, choose Effects | Paint | Photo Stroke to open the Photo Stroke Painting task bar.

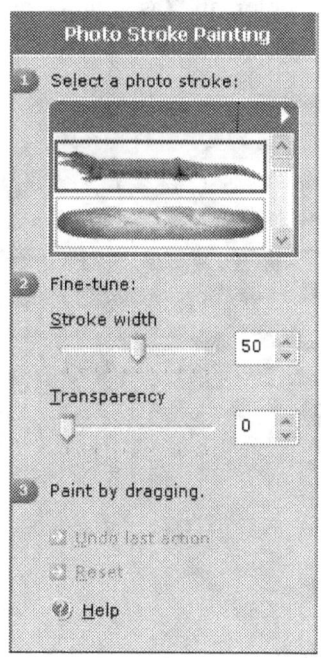

Use the following steps:

1.  Use the scrolling list under Select a Photo Stroke to pick the photo you want to paint with. Simply scroll through the list and click the item you want.

2.  Set the Stroke width by using the Stroke Width slider or the adjacent field. The stroke width can vary from 1 (a very fine line) to 100.

3.  Set the stroke transparency by using the Transparency slider or adjacent field. A transparency of 0 is completely opaque, while a transparency of 100 is invisible.

4.  Paint with the selected parameters by clicking and dragging the image.

## Paint with the Art Stroke

The Art Stroke tool enables you to "paint" on your image with artistic patterns. To paint with the Art Stroke tool, choose Effects | Paint | Art Stroke to open the Art Stroke task bar. The Art Stroke tool works pretty much like the Photo Stroke tool, except that you need to pick a color, and (as with the airbrush), a transparency of 0 is *not* completely opaque. Here is a sample of the art stroke patterns available:

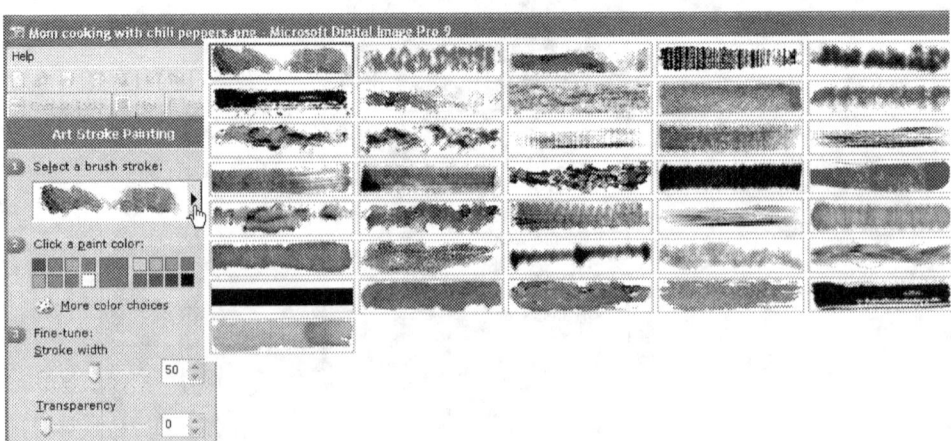

## Paint with Stamps

You can "paint" with pre-built shapes called stamps. These are handy for edges, as well as adding missing items to an image. For example, in Figure 5-2 I've added a set of prize ribbons to an image.

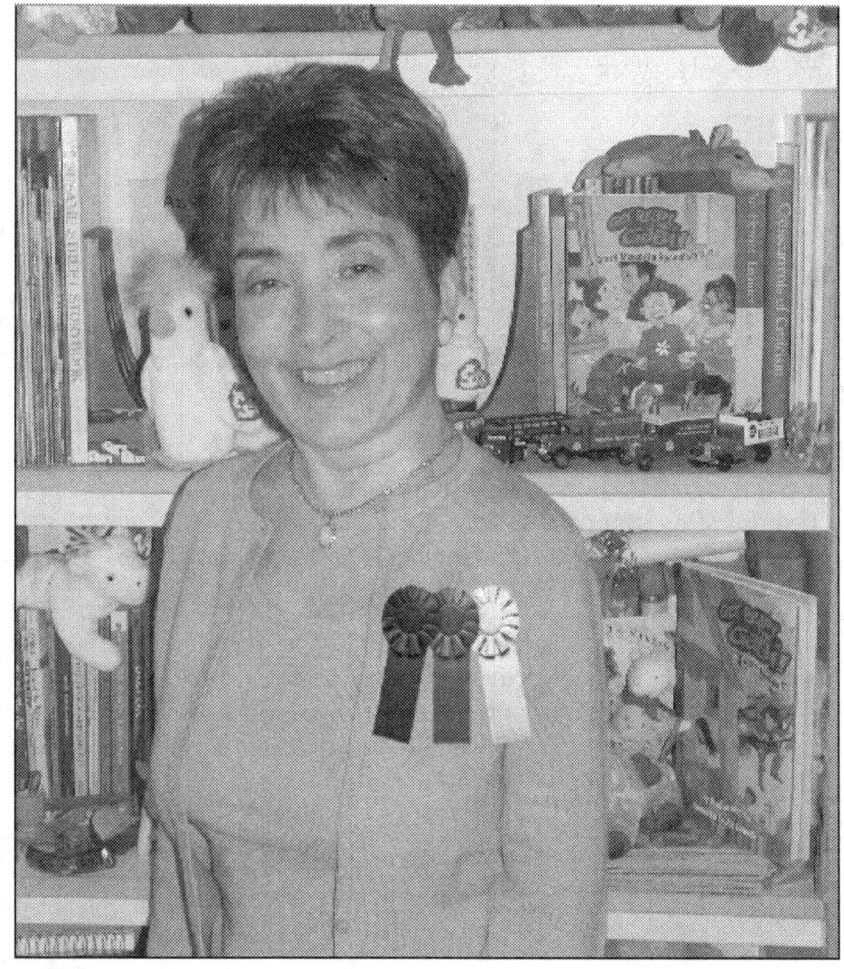

You can stamp shapes onto an image with the Stamps paint brush.

To get started painting with stamps, choose Effect | Paint Brush | Stamps to open the Stamps task bar (visible in Figure 5-2).

## Set the Stamping Style

Digital Image Pro provides three distinct stamping styles (and an eraser, which erases any stamps). Samples of the styles are visible in Figure 5-3. The three styles are

■ **Stamps**   This is the basic stamping style. When you click and drag to draw with the Stamps style, the stamps touch at the edges and may overlap a bit.

The Stamps style uses miniature images, such as the prize ribbons we saw in Figure 5-2. When you use this style and select a stamp (Select a Stamp in the task bar), you can choose from these stamps:

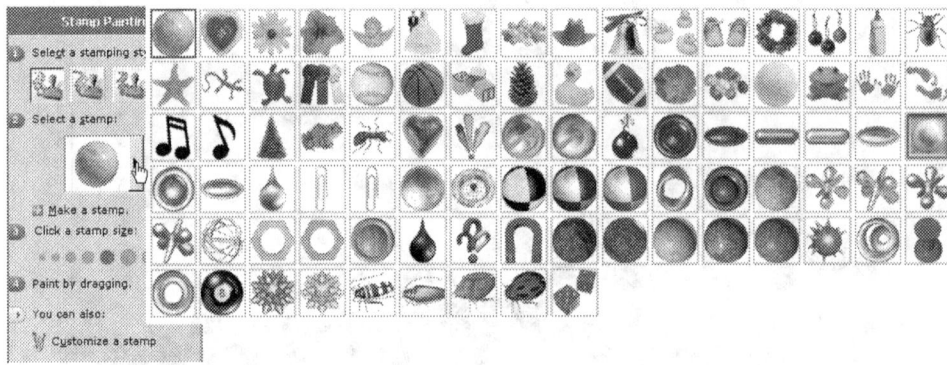

- ■ **Overlapping Stamps**   As the name implies, this style causes the stamps to overlap when you click and drag to draw the stamps. This style also uses miniature images.

- ■ **Shapes**   Unlike the other two styles, the Shapes stamping style uses simple, one-color shapes. Although these are not as complex as the miniature images, you can control the color of the shape stamps (which you cannot do with the miniature images). When you use this style and select a stamp, you can choose from these stamps:

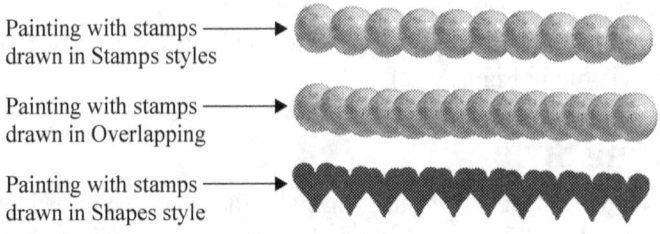

Painting with stamps drawn in Stamps styles

Painting with stamps drawn in Overlapping

Painting with stamps drawn in Shapes style

Using different stamp styles provides three very different effects.

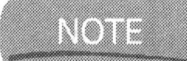 *When you add stamps (of any style) to an image, they are placed on their own object layer and show up in the Stack as a separate layer. As described in Chapter 8, you can move, rotate, resize, and skew the stamp layer to further customize the effect.*

## Choose and Customize a Stamp

The next step is to choose the stamp you want to use from the Select a Stamp box in the task bar. The list of available stamps varies depending on the stamping style you selected, as mentioned in the last section. All you need to do now is pick the stamp size, and click and drag to paint with the selected stamp.

If you wish, you can customize the stamp further by clicking Customize a Stamp. This displays the Stamp Painting task bar.

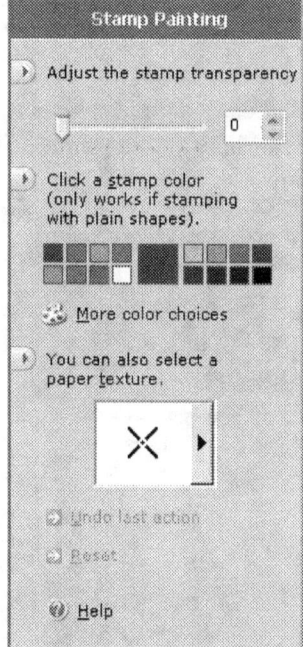

Using this task bar, you can:

■ Adjust the stamp transparency by dragging the slider or entering a value between 0 and 100 in the associated field.

■ Click a stamp color to set the color of the stamp. This only affects the stamp if you are using the Shapes stamping style. You can also click More Color

Choices to display the Custom Color task bar. Here you can set the color using the color wheel, fine-tune fields, or choose a color from an image by clicking the image with the mouse cursor (which looks like an eye-dropper).

■   Select a paper texture. This texture is applied to the stamps used by all three stamping styles.

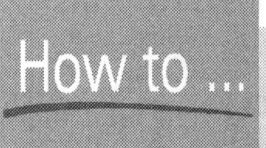 **Build Your Own Stamps**

If the available graphics for the Stamps and Overlapping Stamps styles don't quite meet your needs, you can make your own stamp. To do so, you need the image from which you'll create the stamp. Simple images that contain a single object work best as stamps; otherwise, they can get too "busy."

To build your stamp, click Make a Stamp in the Stamp Painting task bar. This opens the Custom Stamp task bar.

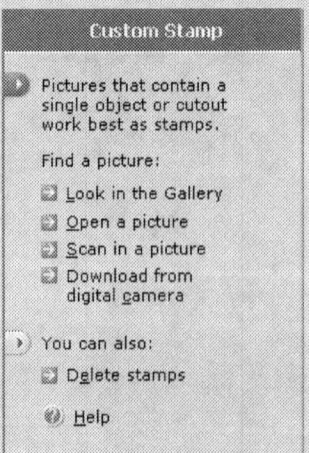

Choose one of the options for locating the file you want to convert to a stamp (such as Open a Picture). Locate the file you want and click OK.

The image is converted to a stamp and added to the end of the list of stamps available for the Stamp and Overlapping Stamp style.

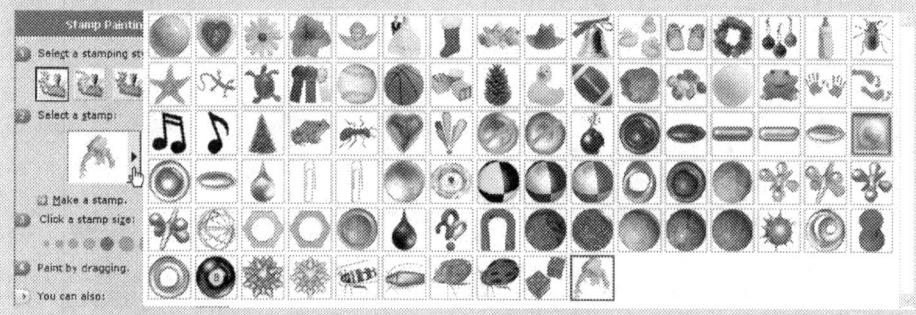

**NOTE**  *You can actually create a new stamp for the Shape style, but it is just a filled shape (usually just a colored rectangle if you used a rectangular photo). Thus, it is not very interesting to do this.*

You can delete any of the stamps, although I don't recommend deleting the stamps provided with Digital Image Pro. To delete a stamp, click Delete Stamps in the Custom Stamps task bar. This opens the Delete Stamps dialog box, from which you can select a stamp and then click Delete Selected Stamp.

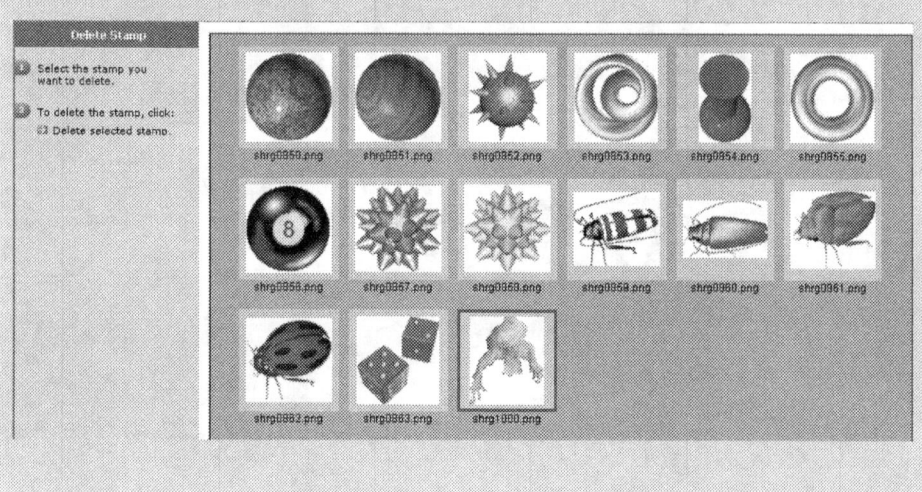

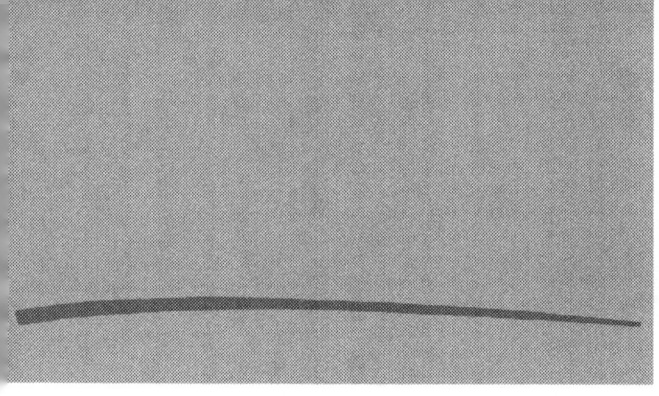

# Touch Up
# Your Photo

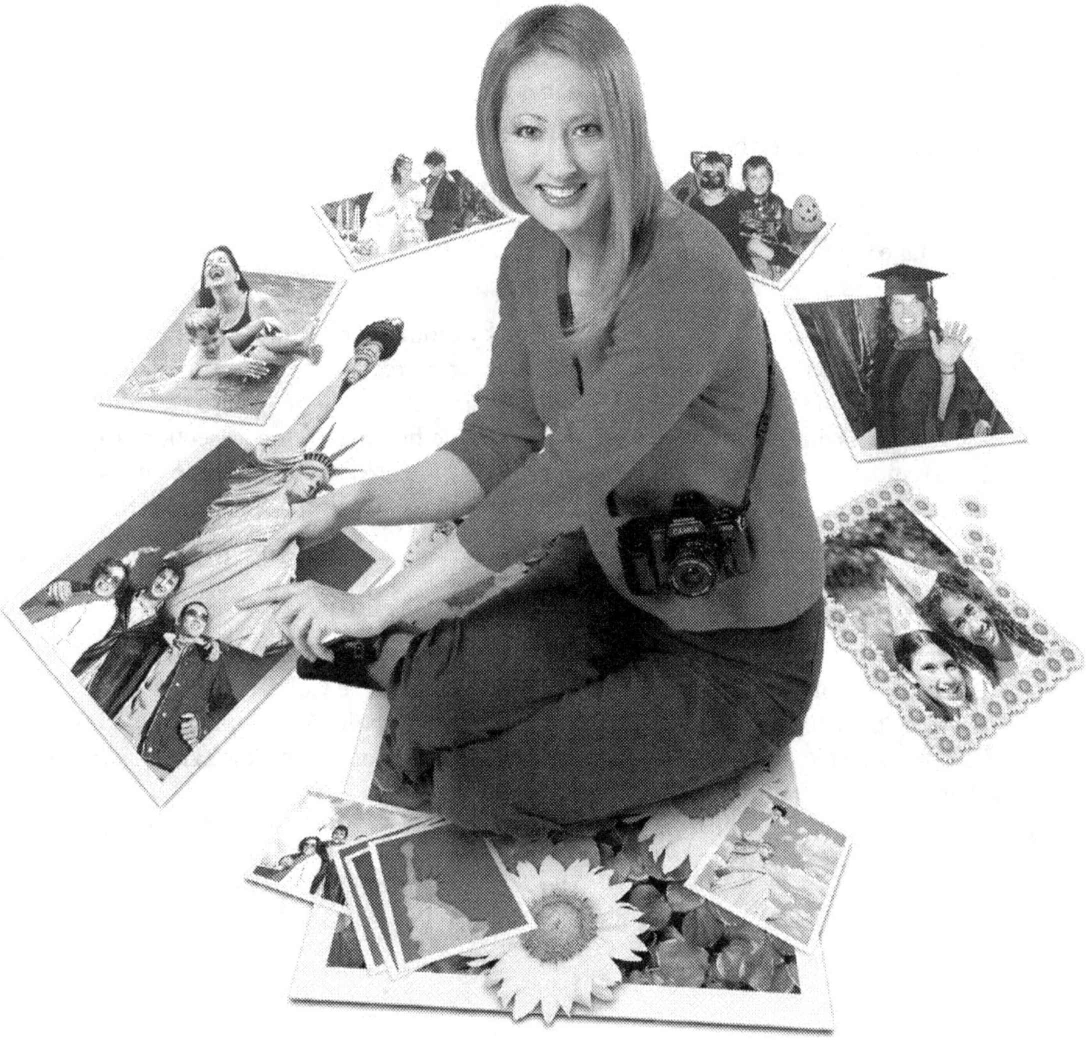

## How to...

- Apply color or tint with brushes

- Blend textures to hide flaws

- Distort the photo with the Distortion brush

- Remove red eye

- Lighten or burn in an area with the Dodge & Burn Brush

- Automatically repair an old photo

- Remove wrinkles, dust, and scratches

- Remove spots or blemishes

- Erase unwanted objects with Smart Erase

- Make repairs by cloning an area of the photo

Once you have corrected the overall image by cropping and adjusting the color, brightness, and contrast, the next step is to make corrections to specific portions of the image, leaving the balance of the image unchanged. Digital Image Pro provides a variety of tools that enable you to apply color, hide blemishes, repair sections of a photo, remove red eye, and darken or lighten specific areas of an image. You can even clone another part of the image (or a different image) to hide an imperfection.

# Colorize a Photo with the Colorize Brush

You've probably seen those old black and white photos that have been hand-colored. You can achieve this same effect in Digital Image Pro with the Colorize Brush. You can also use the Colorize brush to change the colors of a color photograph as well.

To colorize a picture, select Effects | Colorize Brush to open the Colorize Brush task bar.

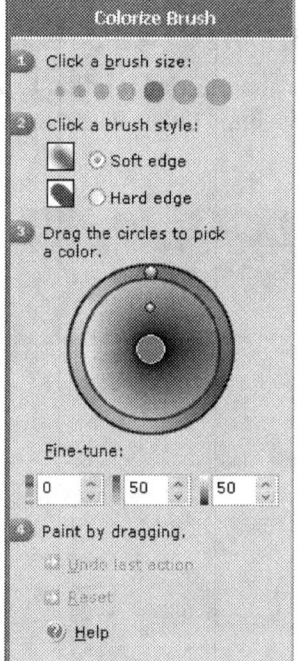

Use the following steps to colorize your photo:

1. Pick the brush size by clicking one of the Click a Brush Size circles.

2. Choose either a Soft Edge or a Hard Edge brush by choosing the appropriate option under Click a Brush Style.

3. Set the color you want to use by dragging the yellow and blue circles in the color wheel or by using the Fine-tune fields, as described in Chapter 4.

4. Click and drag on the image to paint.

The amount of color applied to the image depends on the brightness (the far right Fine-tune field). If the brightness is high, a lot of color is applied; if the brightness is low, very little color is applied. This gives you quite a bit of control over the amount of colorizing you do.

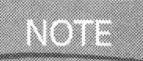 *It is impossible to show what colorizing looks like using the black and white images in this book, so check out the color insert for an example.*

# Change a Photo's Tint with the Tint Brush

You can re-tint the colors in a photo (or add tinting to a black and white image) with the Tint brush. Select Touchup | Other Photo Repair | Tint Brush to open the Tint Brush task bar.

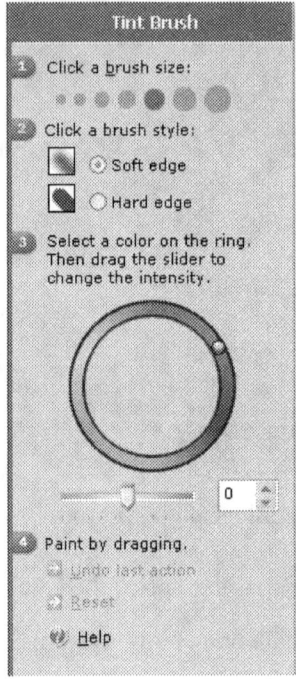

To use the Tint brush, pick a brush size and either a soft edge or a hard edge. To choose your tint, drag the yellow circle around the perimeter of the color wheel to select a color, and then drag the slider to choose the intensity of that color (or use the associated field). When you click and drag to apply the tint, Digital Image Pro modifies the existing color by adding the specified tint to it.

# Blend Away Blemishes with the Blending Brush

Digital Image Pro's Blending brush makes it possible to fix imperfections in photographs. It is especially useful in removing blemishes and wrinkles, as well as those dark circles under the eye. Figure 6-1 shows a picture of my wife during our

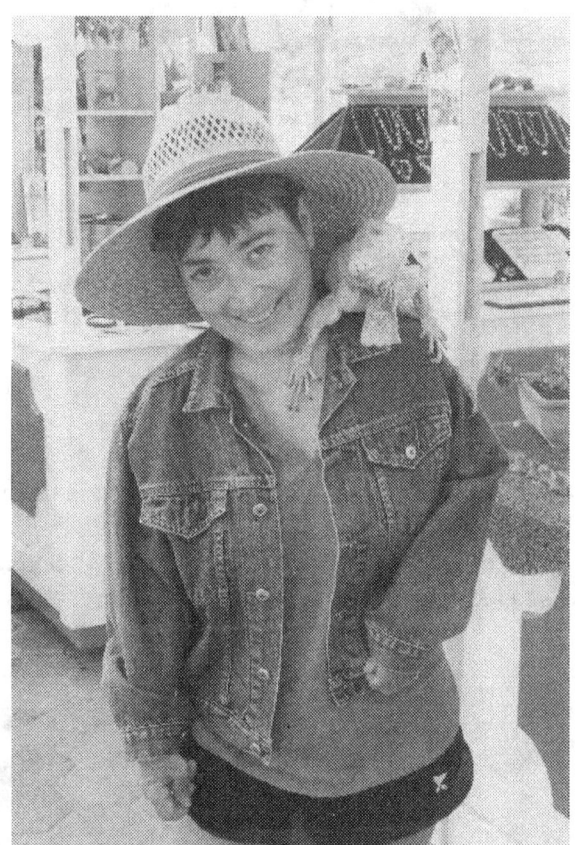

We won't be able to get this shot again, but it sure needs some fixing!

last cruise. We were exploring Curacao all day, and we were hot and tired. But as we were returning to the ship, we encountered a fellow who had this large iguana. For $5, he perched him on my wife's shoulder, and I snapped the picture. As you can see, there are lots of nonideal things about the photo, but all of them are fixable with Digital Image Pro, and the result was an irreplaceable memento of that trip.

To use the Blending brush, choose Touchup | Blending Brush to open the Blending Brush task bar.

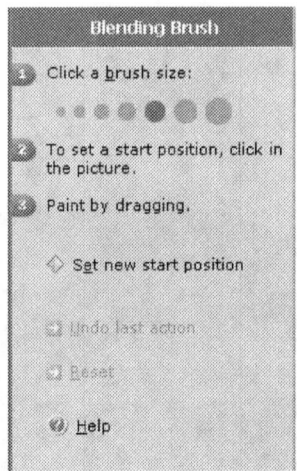

To use the Blending brush, select a brush size and click in the picture to set the *start position*. This is the position that will serve as the source from which the texture and color is taken and blended into the area in which you are painting. Digital Image Pro displays a cross to indicate the start position (see Figure 6-2). Click and drag

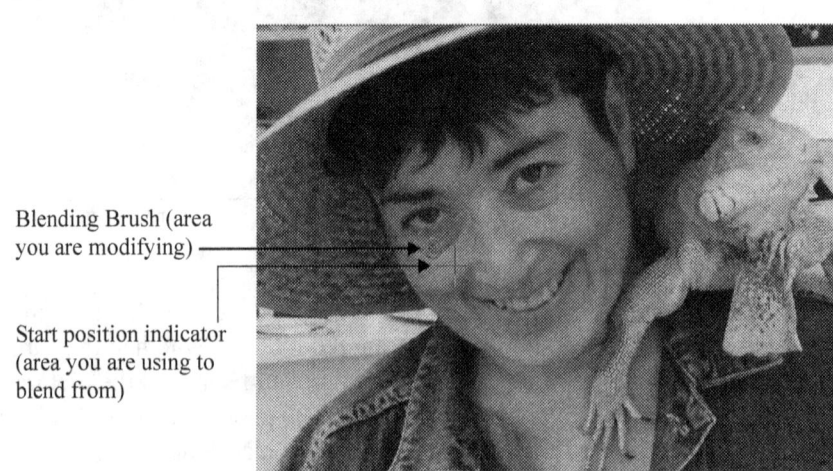

The start position indicator (cross) and the Blending Brush are both visible while you are blending.

the mouse to "paint" (actually, to blend) the source texture into the area where you are painting. As you paint (moving the brush), the start position (indicated by the cross) moves as well. This prevents you from blending only from a single point, which would look very fake. Instead, you blend from an area the same size as the area that you are painting.

As you paint, you may find that the cross (starting point) is moving into an area from which you don't want to blend. In that case, you'll have to reset the start point. To do so, click Set New Start Position. You can then click the image to respecify the start position and begin blending again.

And how well does this work? Look under her eyes, and you be the judge!

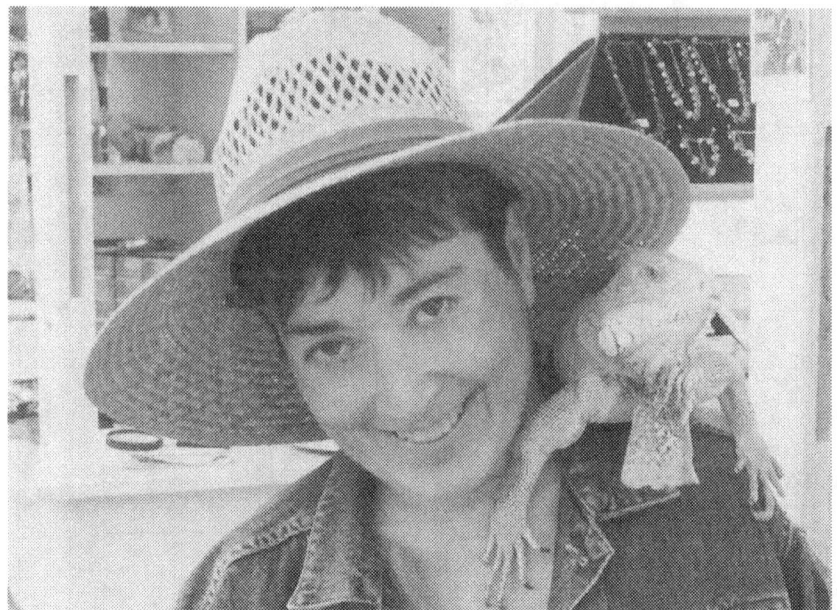

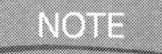 *You could try fixing the problem areas with the Clone brush (described later in this chapter), but if you clone the cheek area to hide the area under the eyes, it ends up looking very fake. The Blending brush works much better.*

# Apply Distortion to a Photo

You can apply all sorts of fun effects to a photo by distorting limited portions of it. And in at least one case, you can even do something useful to fix problems with the photo! To use the Distortion brush, select Effects | Distortion Brush to open the Distortion Brush task bar.

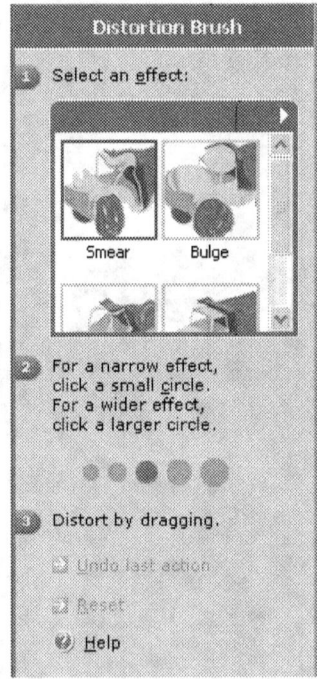

Digital Image Pro provides three different distort effects. They are:

■ **Smear** This effect isn't too useful for digital photos. With it, you can "push" the image ahead of your brush, distorting it into, well, a smear.

■ **Bulge** This effect causes whatever is inside the brush to bulge out. Believe it or not, this can be useful to fix squinting eyes, because it can make them appear to be open wider than they are. Just apply it with restraint or people will wonder why your relatives are so bug-eyed. I applied this effect to my wife's eyes. I guess maybe I overdid it (but don't tell her).

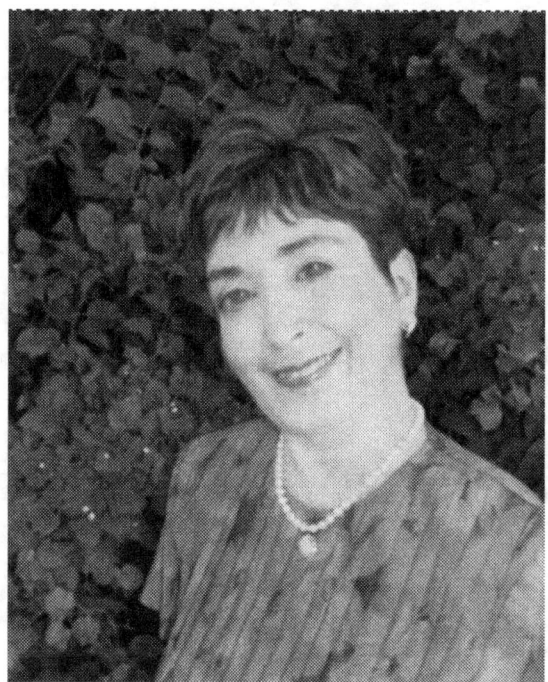

- **Shrink**   This effect causes anything inside the brush to shrink. This can be useful to make background items less noticeable—but it only works well if the item is on a plain surface; otherwise, you'll notice the distortion.

There is also an Erase effect, which reverses any distortions you have applied. To use the Erase effect, position the brush over a distorted area and click. Each time you click, part of the distortion is removed, until it is all gone. You can also click and drag the Erase effect over a wider area.

# Lighten or Burn-in an Area with the Dodge and Burn Brush

If an area of a photograph is underexposed—and therefore prints too dark—a photographer can try to fix this in the darkroom. Because the underexposed area of the negative is too light, too much light from the enlarger reaches the photo paper. To correct this situation, the photographer needs to block some of that light. In the darkroom, this is accomplished by attaching a piece of opaque material (usually cardboard) to a stick, and holding it over the photo paper during the printing cycle

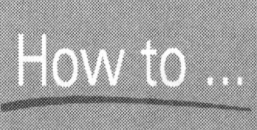 **Remove Red Eye**

Many photos of people and animals (especially dogs and cats) display "red eye," as shown here.

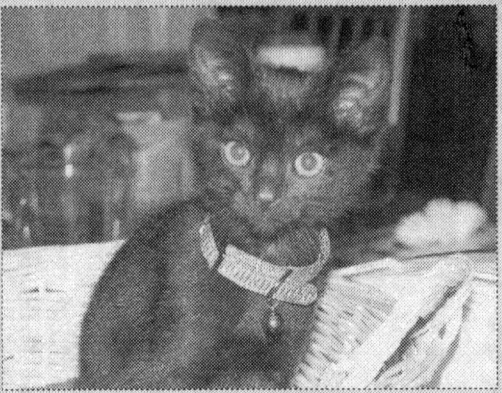

Red eye occurs when you use a flash on your camera, and the flash is situated too close to the camera lens. The light from the flash bounces off the back of the eye, causing the center of the eye (which should normally be brown or blue) to glow red. This effect is more pronounced in people with blue eyes, and it is also more pronounced when conditions are dark—which is exactly when you need to use your flash!

Digital Image Pro has a special tool to remove red eye. Select Touchup | Fix Red Eye to open the Fix Red Eye task bar.

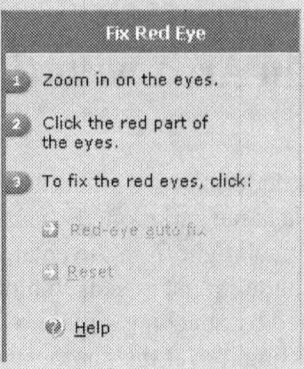

To fix red eye, zoom in on the eyes so you can see the red area well. Then, click in the red part of the eye and choose Red-eye Auto Fix. If any red eye remains, repeat the operation, once again clicking in the red portion of the eye. And that, as they say, takes care of that.

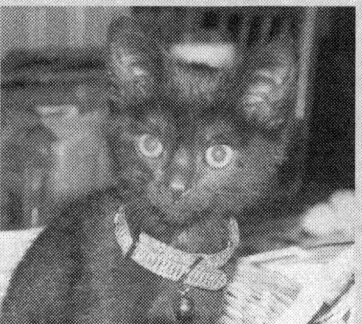

> NOTE    *The difference between the picture of the kitten with red eye and without is very subtle and hard to see in the black and white images. To see a better example, check the color insert of this book.*

to block the light. To avoid having a very noticeable white area on the paper, the photographer moves this tool around to feather the effect. This is called *dodging*. Figure 6-3 shows an example of an image that needs some dodging applied.

Another photographer's trick is to *burn in* an area that was overexposed. The overexposed area of the negative gets too dark, so not enough light passes through the negative and the print is too light in that area. To fix this in the darkroom, a photographer applies a trick similar to dodging. First, the photographer exposes the photo paper for the properly exposed portion of the negative. Next, the photographer re-exposes the paper, holding back light from everywhere except the area that needs to be *burned in*.

6

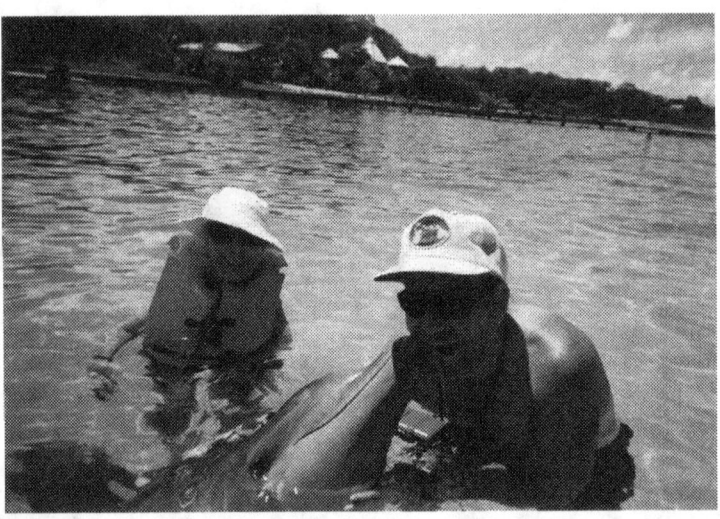

Areas of this image are too dark, so detail is lost in the shadows.

Digital Image Pro provides tools to simulate both these effects. To use them, choose Touchup | Other Photo Repair | Dodge and Burn Brush. This opens the Dodge and Burn Brush task bar.

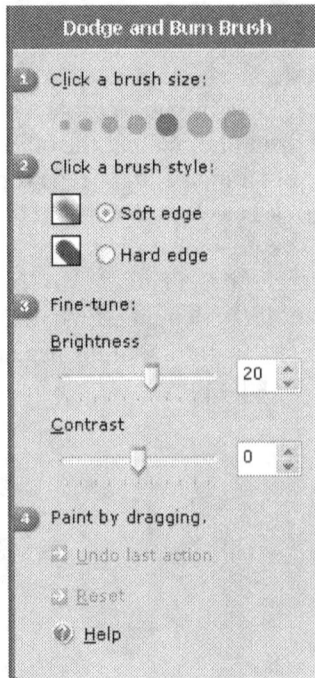

To use the Dodge and Burn Brush, choose a brush size and select either a soft edge brush or a hard edge brush. To simulate *dodging* (lightening an area), set the Brightness value to a positive value by dragging the Brightness slider or using the associated field. To simulate *burning-in* (making an area darker), set the Brightness value to a negative value. To actually apply the effect, click and drag across the affected area. Each time you release the mouse button and then click and drag again over an area, the effect is reapplied, brightening or darkening the area further. Figure 6-4 shows the same image as Figure 6-3 after the dodging correction was applied.

**TIP** *I recommend using a soft edge brush, and leaving the contrast set fairly low. Too high a contrast makes the burned-in area too noticeable. And go easy—you usually don't need a lot of dodging or burn-in, and these effects become noticeable if you use too much.*

6

A really excellent use for the Burn tool is apparent in Figure 6-5. The bald areas of the men's heads are overexposed compared to the rest of the photo. A quick pass with the Burn tool over those shiny scalps results in Figure 6-6, which is much better!

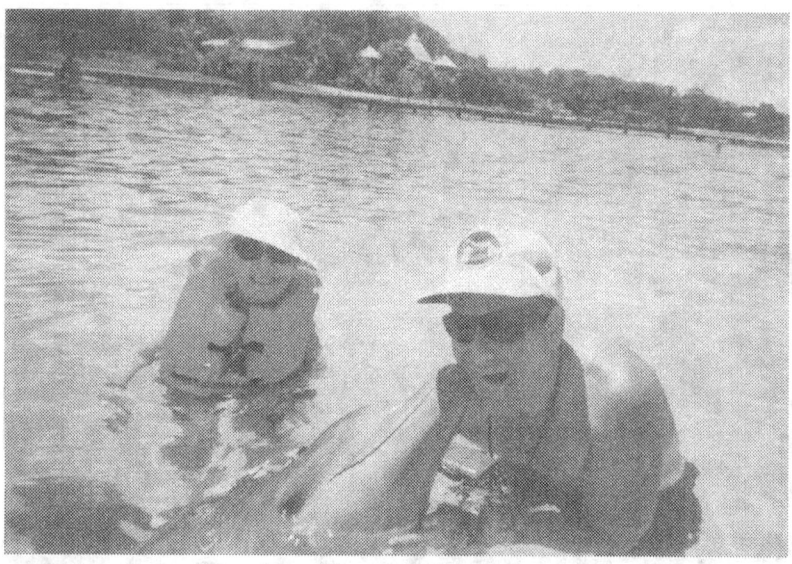

You can see the faces in the shadows much better now.

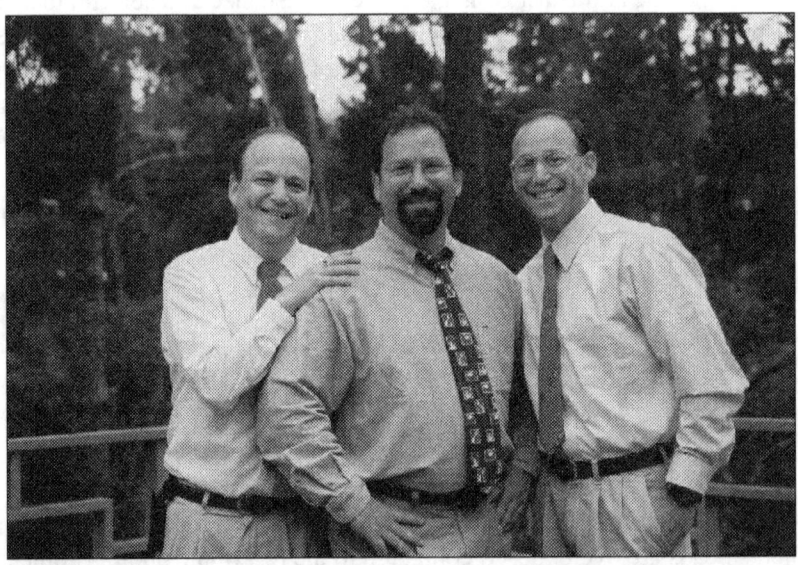

That shiny area where there should be hair can ruin a picture.

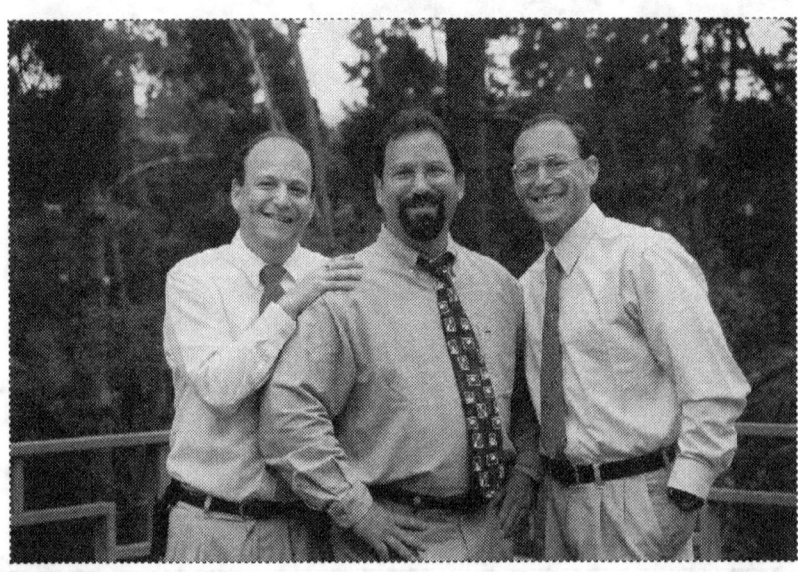

Now we are not being blinded by that reflection from the bald spots.

## Fix an Old Photo Automatically

Old photos tend to fade, getting lighter and losing contrast and sharpness with age, especially if they have not been well cared for. Figure 6-7 shows such a photo.

Digital Image Pro does a pretty fair job at automatically correcting the fading and loss of contrast with the Restore Old Picture tool (select Touchup | Other Photo Repair | Restore Old Picture).

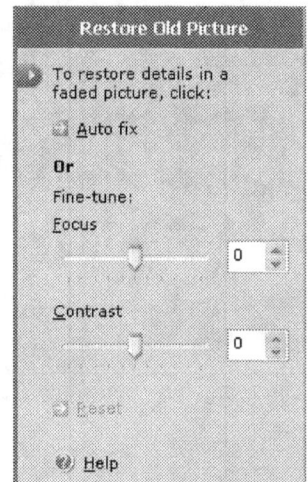

You can choose to try Auto Fix, or adjust the Focus slider (and its associated field) and the Contrast slider (and its associated field) yourself. Figure 6-8 shows the old photo after some adjustments in Digital Image Pro. Notice that Fix Old Photo does not correct dust and scratches—that is coming up in the next few sections.

## Remove Dust from a Photo

Photos—especially old ones—often have small spots. These might be dust, or (in the case of digital photos or scanned photos) digital "noise" introduced by the camera or scanner. This noise is most noticeable in large, dark areas. Fortunately, it is easiest to fix when located there.

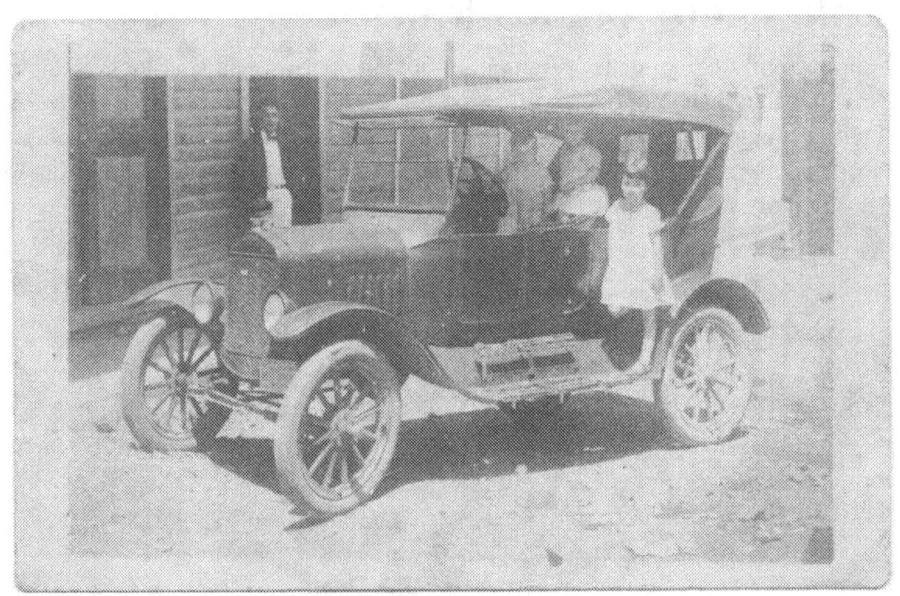

Old photos are charming, but often show their age!

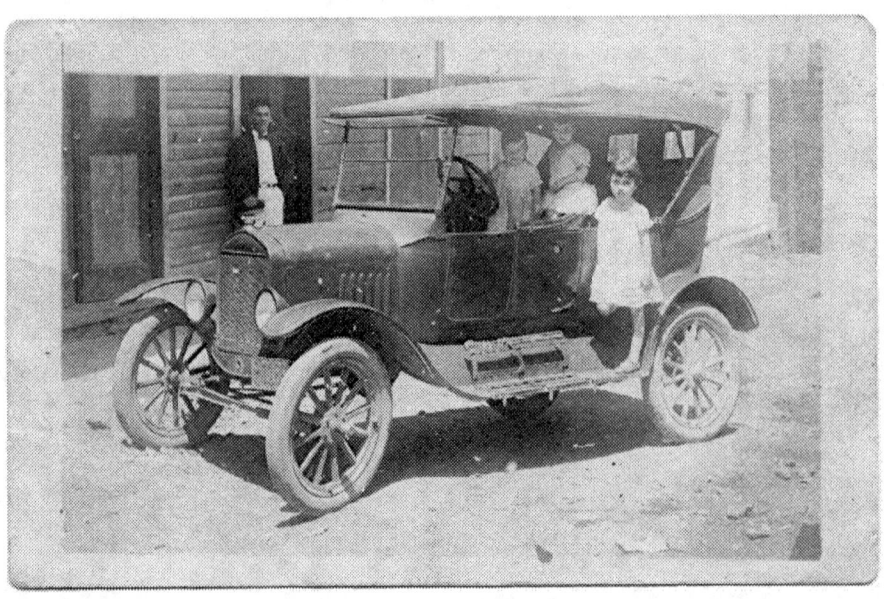

The picture looks much better now, although it still has some flaws.

Digital Image Pro provides the Remove Dust tool (select Touchup | Other Photo Repair | Remove Dust).

This tool is simple to use, but somewhat limited. Click one of the circles and wait while your photo is "dusted." The tool can remove a small amount of dust or noise by using the smallest circle. However, clicking the larger circles leads to an unusable result, because the tools works by softening the focus, and too much softening leads to a major loss of detail.

# Remove Spots and Blemishes

You can remove skin imperfections using Digital Image Pro's Remove Spots or Blemishes tool. You can also use this tool to remove scan noise and dust spots one by one. This is obviously more tedious than using the Remove Dust tool—but you have a lot more control over the result. To begin, select Touchup | Remove Spots or Blemishes to open the Remove Spots or Blemishes task bar.

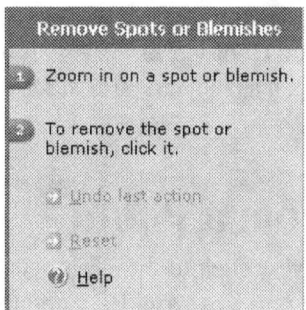

To remove a spot or blemish (or dust spot), zoom in on the spot and click it.

This tool works by creating a square pattern that averages the area around the blemish. This square pattern can be quite noticeable if the skin texture has a distinct pattern, because this pattern is obliterated in the square area. You can see several of these patterns above and to the left of the nose (and they are much more noticeable in the color version of this picture).

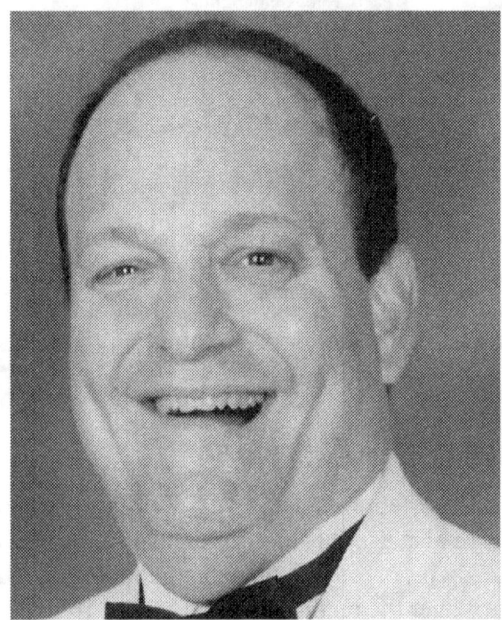

Thus, it is often better to either blend a similar area in with the Blending Brush, or use the Clone brush (covered later in this chapter) to carefully "paint over" the blemish. On the other hand, this tool works very well when the spot is surrounded by fairly featureless areas—such as the dark area surrounding a spot created by dust or scan noise.

# Remove Wrinkles from a Photo

Digital Image Pro contains a very slick tool for removing wrinkles. Unlike the Spots and Blemishes tool, the result removes wrinkles without leaving a noticeable result. To remove wrinkles from a photo, select Touchup | Other Photo Repair | Remove Wrinkles to open the Remove Wrinkles task bar.

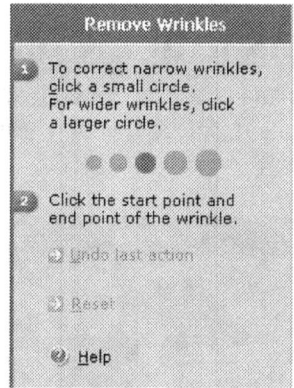

Pick a brush size depending on how wide the wrinkle is. Then, click at one end of the wrinkle, move the mouse to the other end of the wrinkle, and click again. The wrinkle disappears! As you move the mouse to the far end of the wrinkle, Digital Image Pro draws a rectangle that shows what area will be affected by the tool. The larger the brush size you picked, the wider the rectangle.

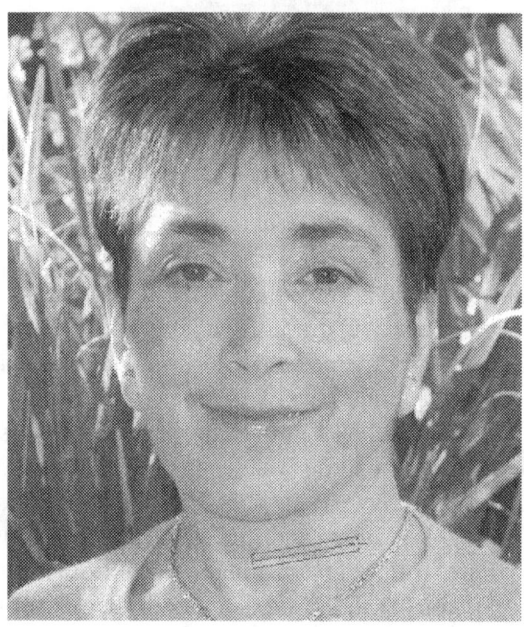

TIP   *If the wrinkle is curved, correct it in short segments.*

# Erase Unwanted Items with the Smart Erase Tool

Digital Image Pro has a quick and easy way to remove items from a photograph—the Smart Erase tool. To activate it, select Touchup | Smart Erase to open the Smart Erase task bar.

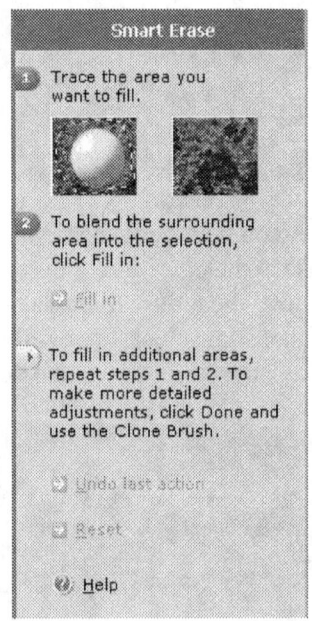

In essence, you indicate the object you want to remove, and the program analyzes the surrounding area and uses that information to fill in the hole where the item was. To specify the area to remove, draw a line around the object. Just click at the starting point, and move the mouse around the outline, clicking at each point that the line needs to change direction. When you're done, click back at the starting point to finish the shape. Then click Fill In in the Smart Erase task bar. Again, how well this works depends very much on what is around the item. If the background is fairly featureless or doesn't have a sharply-defined pattern, this tool works pretty well, as shown in Figure 6-9 (before) and Figure 6-10 (after). But it doesn't do as good a job when there are distinct features in close proximity to the item you are removing. For example, this tool does not do a good job of removing one person from a group photo.

NOTE    *Even when the Smart Erase tool doesn't work very well, it is (in general) easier to clean up the result with the Clone tool than it would have been to do the whole job with the Clone tool.*

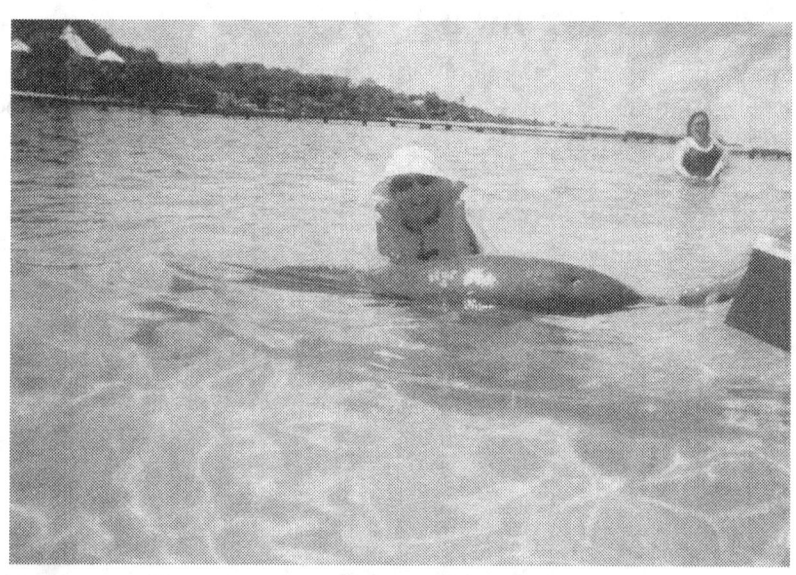

This photo contains a stranger that needs removing.

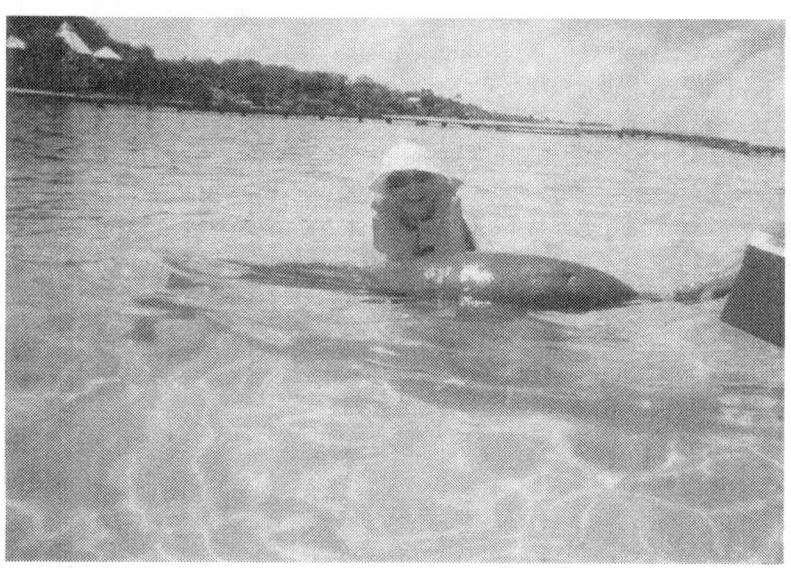

And now it is gone, making the photo much more attractive.

# Remove Scratches from a Photo

The Remove Scratches tool can remove scratches from an abused photo. To use this tool, select Touchup | Other Photo Repair | Remove Scratches to open the Remove Scratches task bar.

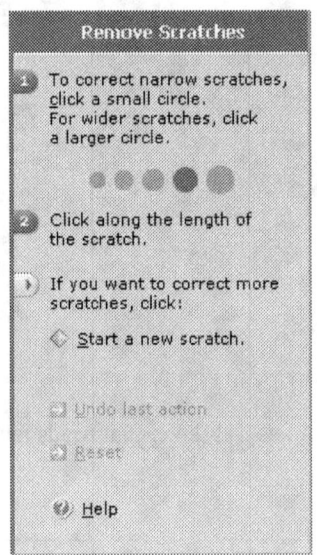

The Remove Scratches tool is simple to use—just pick a brush size, click at the beginning of the scratch, and click again at the end of the scratch. Digital Image Pro then uses the adjacent information to "fill in" the scratch. After each section is repaired, you can continue clicking along the length of the scratch—Digital Image Pro will correct the area starting with the end of the previous section and ending with the location where you last clicked. To start a new scratch, click Start a New Scratch.

Here is an old wedding photo that was damaged when it was bent. You can see the scratch running down the middle of the photo.

Scratch in photo

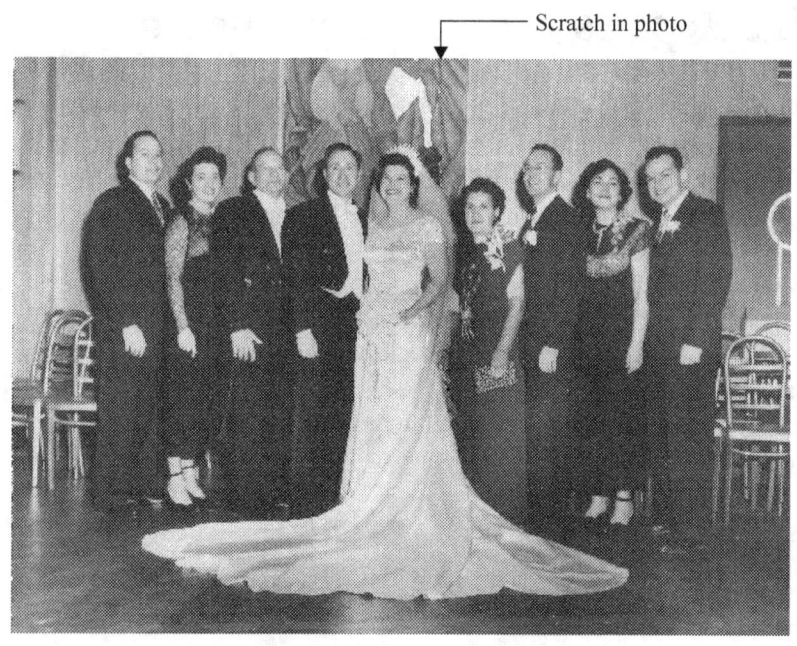

6

And here is that same photo after I applied Remove Scratches.

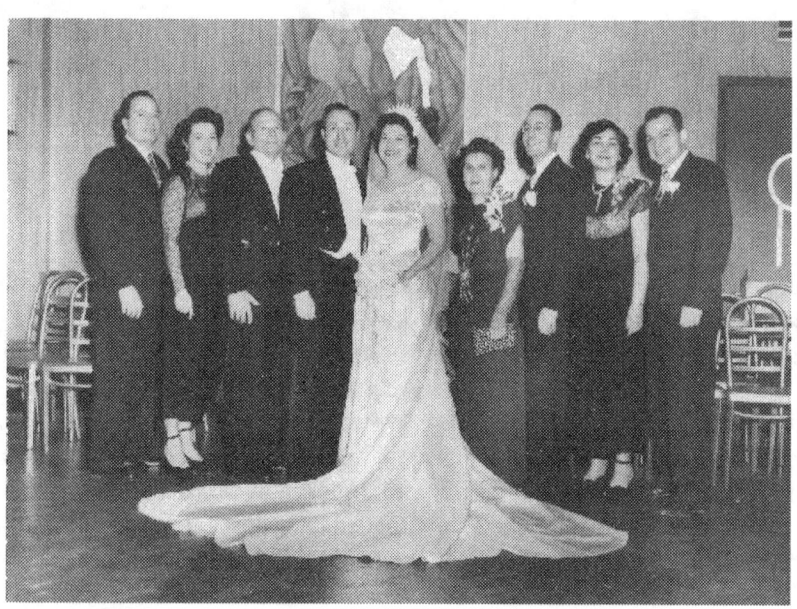

# Make Fine Repairs with the Clone Brush

Digital Image Pro's Clone Brush enables you to clean up many problems that are beyond the capabilities of Smart Erase, the Blending Brush, Remove Spots or Blemishes, Remove Wrinkles, Remove Scratches, and Remove Dust. Essentially, this tool enables you to clone a particular part of an image to hide a blemish, repair a damaged area of a photo, clean up scan noise, or remove an item from a photo altogether. The Clone Brush gives you tremendous control over both the source (from where you paint) and the target (what you are painting over). However, unlike all the other tools mentioned, there is nothing "automatic" about the Clone Brush—you must do all the work yourself, and quality results demand a steady hand and some patience.

To use the Clone brush, select Touchup | Clone Brush to open the Clone Brush task bar.

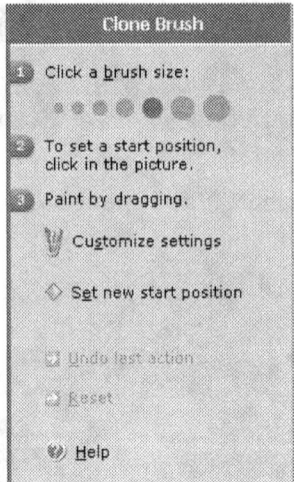

Using the Clone Brush is similar to using the Blending Brush: choose a brush size, set the start position, and click and drag to paint. As with the Blending Brush (see Figure 6-2), the Clone brush displays a cross to indicate the start position, and this indicator moves as you paint.

Figure 6-11 shows a good example of where you might use the Clone Stamp tool. This old photo has fingerprints marring the background over my Aunt Claire's head and on my father's face. To fix the wall, I picked a similar pattern from another section of the wall, and then clicked and dragged over the fingerprint. To fix the face, I used a nearby section of face as the clone source. Figure 6-12 shows the result.

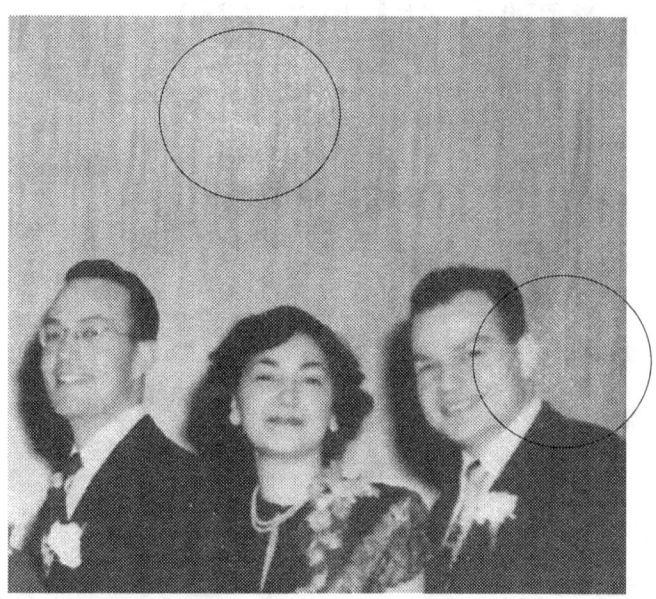

A fingerprint would be difficult to remove with Digital Image Pro's automatic tools.

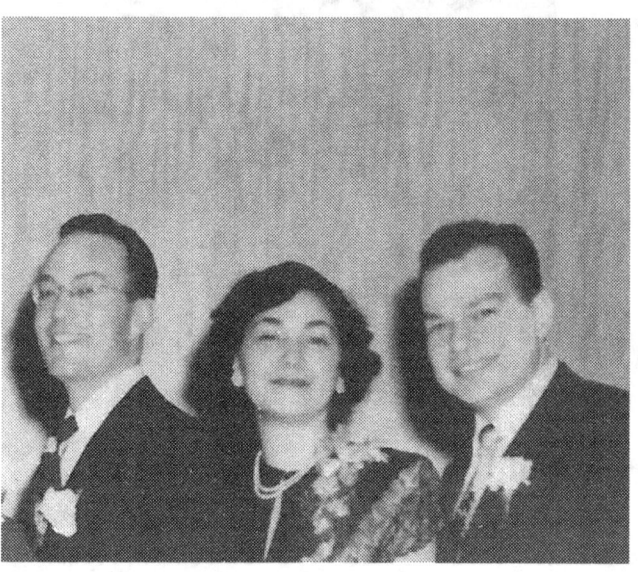

But the Clone Brush makes quick work of it!

## Fix Scan Noise with the Clone Brush

Another excellent use of the Clone Brush is to remove dust and scan noise. This section of the photograph had a lot of scan noise introduced when I scanned it at high resolution:

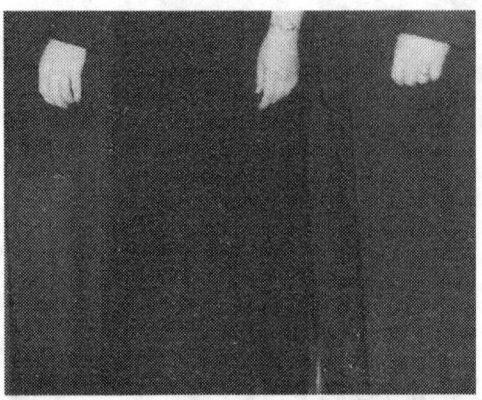

All I needed to do was pick a start point in the black area, and clone over the spots. Voilá!

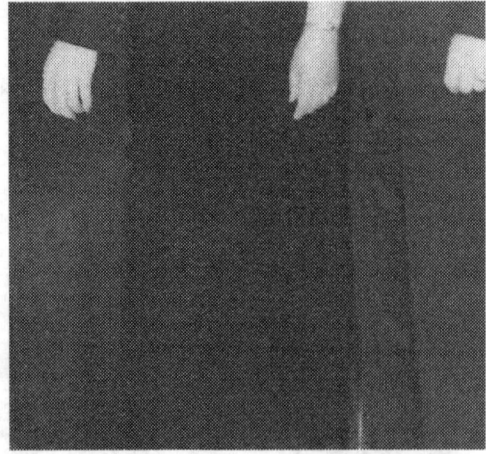

## Repair an Old Photo with the Clone Brush

Recently, my mother-in-law found an ancient photo of my wife's aunts and uncles in a drawer. It was badly deteriorated, as you can see from Figure 6-13. There are

6

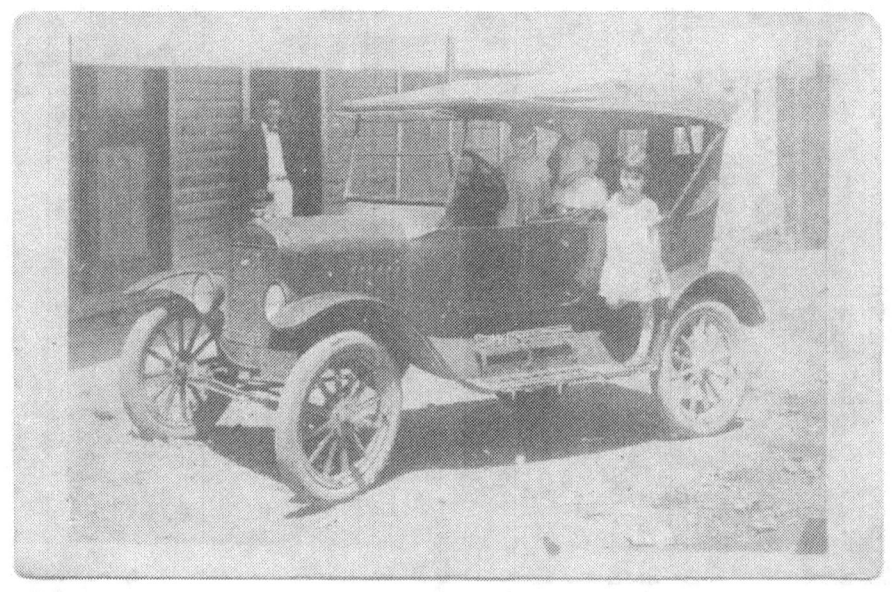

Even a photo in bad shape—as this one is—is repairable

creases, missing flecks of emulsion (the photo coating that contains the image information), and portions are faded. Still, there is enough information to attempt a repair.

The main job was to fill in the missing pieces using the Clone Brush. I had to exercise care to choose areas that were the same color as the missing flecks. Fortunately, because the photo is not in color, it was easy to find another area of the photo that matches. I had to reproduce a missing section of the wooden wall alongside my wife's grandfather (standing in the background) and rebuild his face (that tested my artistry!). Finally, I adjusted the brightness and contrast of selected portions of the image, especially the dirt areas around the car and girls' dresses. You can see the result in Figure 6-14.

NOTE     *To limit the corrections to brightness and contrast to a specific section, I had to select that section using the Selection tools, described in Chapter 7.*

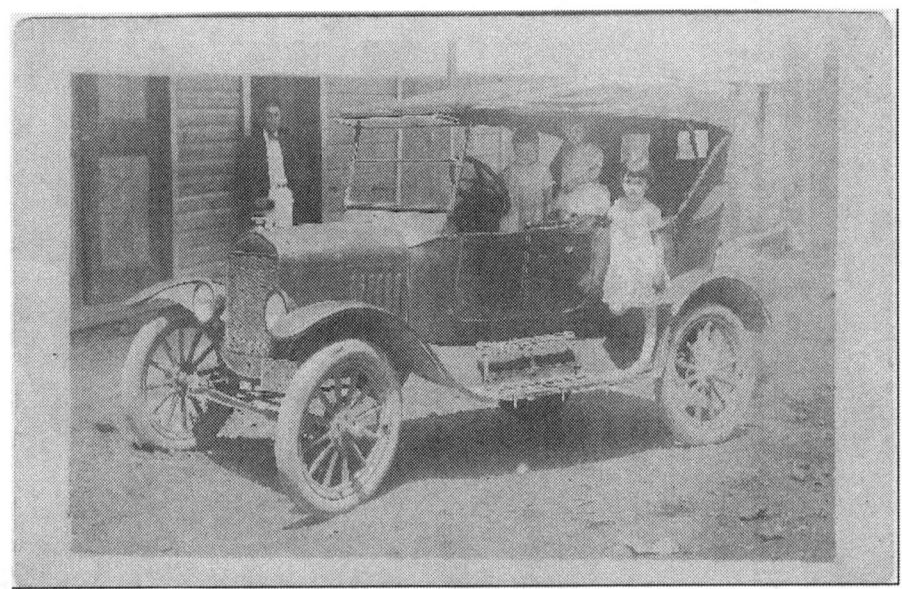

After about six hours of working on the photo, it is in much better shape.

## Remove an Object with the Clone Brush

The Clone Brush can do more than just clean up an image—it can remove objects from the image altogether! The photo on the left side of Figure 6-15 was taken at my parents' fiftieth wedding anniversary. A few seconds later, I took the photo on

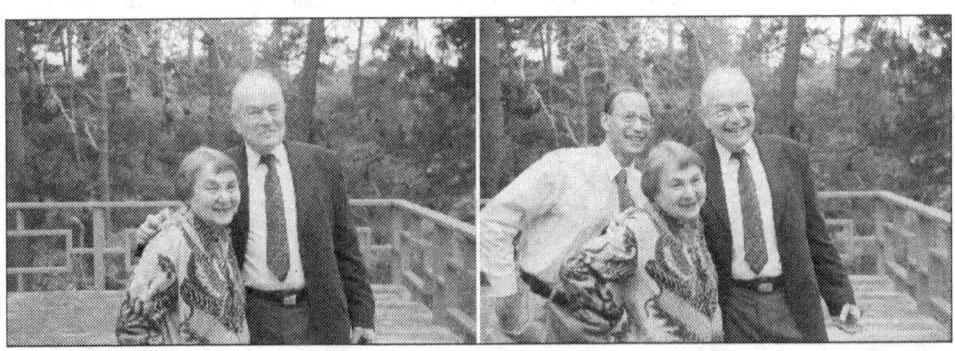

Using the background from the left photo as the Clone Brush start point, I can correct the right photo to remove my brother.

the right. However, just as I was snapping the shot, my brother jumped into the picture. Unfortunately, I like my parents' expressions better in the right-hand picture, and the Clone Brush enables me to remove my errant brother from that picture.

The trick is that the two photos were taken just seconds apart, and have identical backgrounds. Essentially, I can clone a portion of the background in the left photo to paint over my brother in the right photo. In order to do this, I'll have to use selections, objects, and layers. These are fully described in Chapters 7 and 8, but you can follow along here even though we haven't covered that topic yet.

> **TIP** *Sometimes, two pictures can have different brightness and color even when they were taken at the same time because of sloppy commercial printing. Thus, you may have to make some corrections to one of the photos to make the exposures in the two photos as identical as possible before cloning a portion of one image to another.*

To remove my brother from the right-hand photo, I followed these steps:

1. I opened the left photo (the one without my brother). Using the Marquee selection tool, I clicked and dragged to highlight the background section to the left of my parents. I then copied this selection to the Clipboard (Edit | Copy).

2. I then opened the right-hand photo (the one *with* my brother), and pasted the copied section into that picture. This created a new layer, containing the pasted section. I dragged this layer off the canvas to the left side. These steps were necessary because Digital Image Pro does not let you display two photos in the workspace at once, so you can't use one photo as the start point for the Clone brush while painting on another photo.

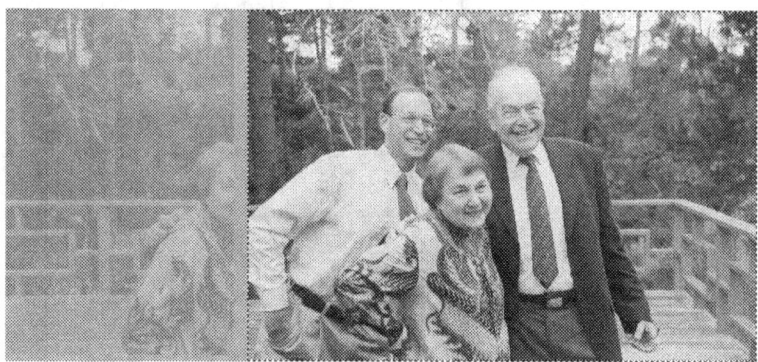

3. In the Stack, I clicked the new layer (it should be at the top of the Stack). I then selected Touchup | Clone Brush to open the Clone Brush task bar.

4. I zoomed in until I could just see the new layer and the section of the photo I was going to replace.

5. Moving the cross over the new layer, I clicked to pick the starting point. It is extremely important that the start point be a point that is recognizable (a specific feature in the image) in order to properly execute the next step. In this case, I chose one of the stumps sticking out of the tree in the center of the layer.

6. I moved the Clone Brush over the main image and clicked exactly the same feature of the tree that I had picked as the start point in the layer.

7. I then began to paint by clicking and dragging with the mouse, replacing my brother with the background from the layer:

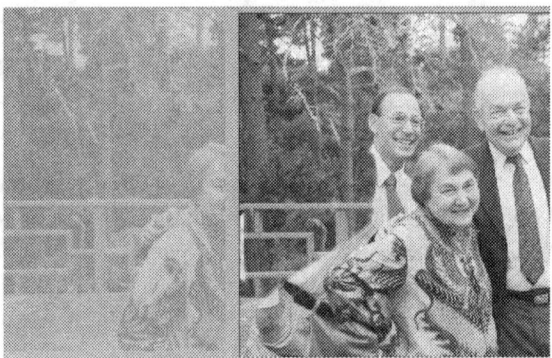

8. I did a little cleanup around the edges and clicked Done. This left me with the result you see here.

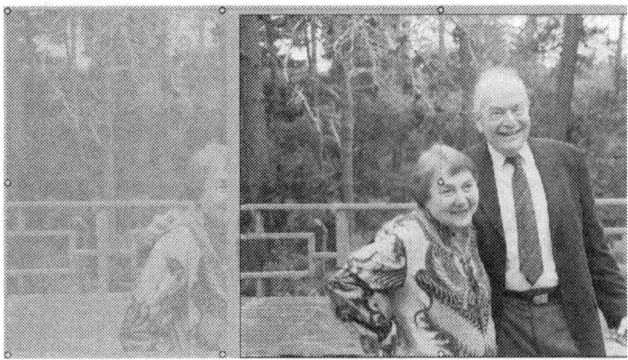

*Notice something interesting—the layer has expanded to include the area I cloned. That is, the original image is actually unmodified—if I drag the layer out of the way, you'll see my brother still there! But we're about to fix that.*

9.  To get rid of the portion of the original layer that we used as the clone source, make sure the layer is still selected and select Format | Crop | Selected Object.

10. Click and drag an area that coincides only with the image, leaving out the original part of the layer that we pasted in and dragged to the left of the image.

11. Click Done to remove all of the layer that does not overlap the image.

12. Select the top layer in the Stack. Hold down the CTRL key and click the second layer (the original image). Then right-click either layer in the Stack and choose Flatten Selected Objects to collapse the layer into the original image, leaving the final result:

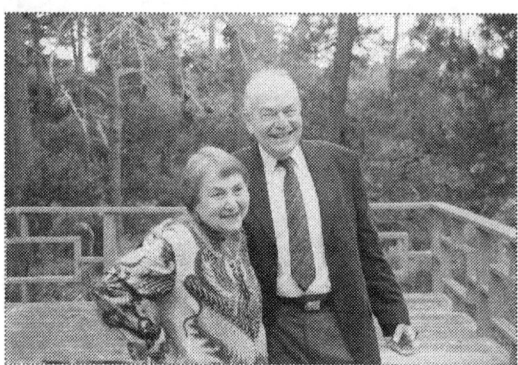

6

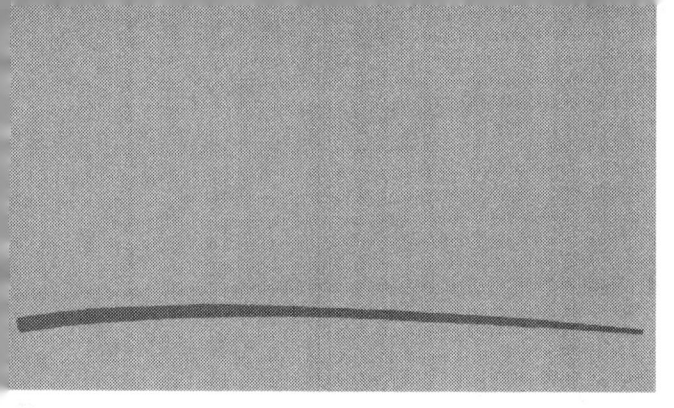

# Make Selections
# and Apply Changes

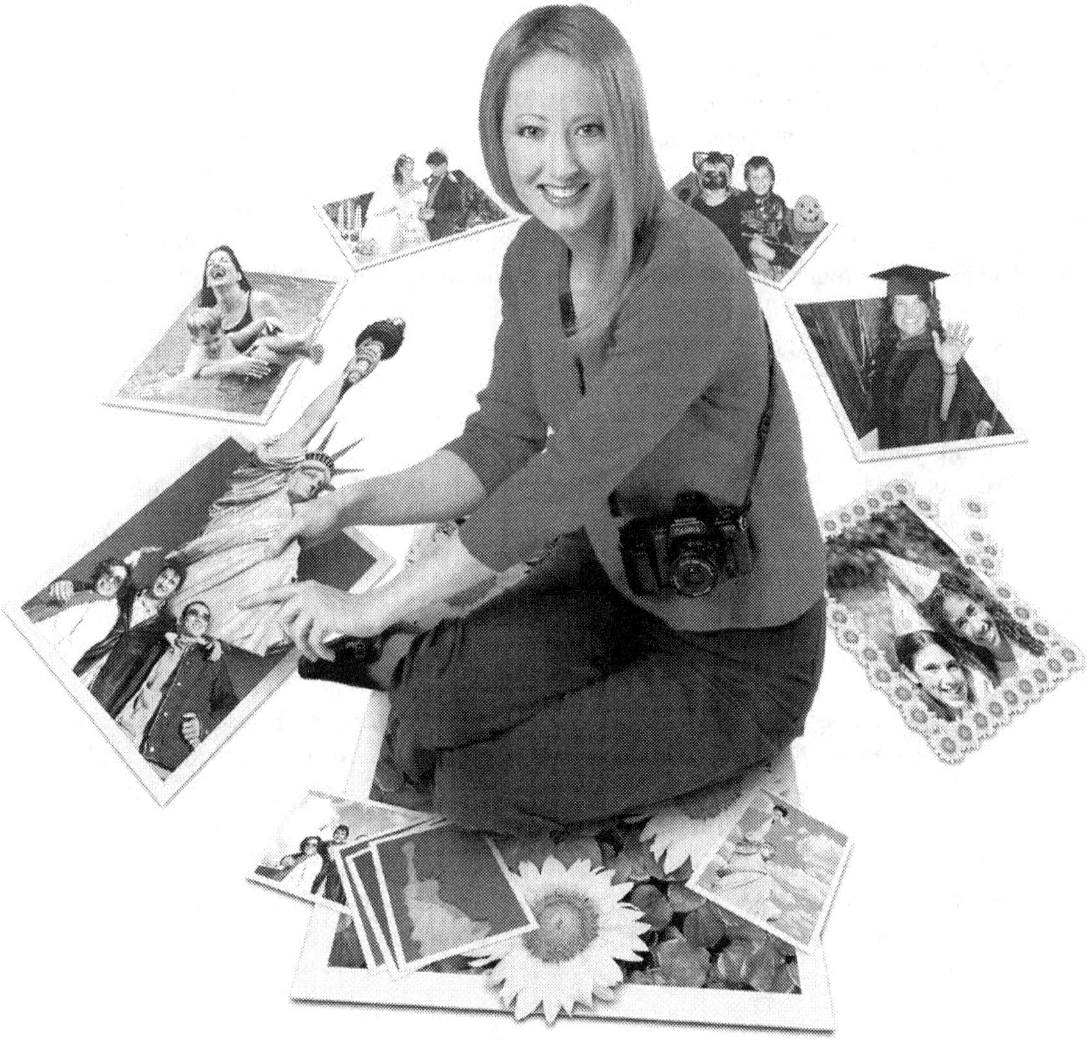

## How to...

- Make freehand selections
- Make selections by finding edges
- Select all items of a certain color
- Make selection of a certain shape
- Apply changes to just the selected areas

You've looked at tools that allow you to apply a correction to an entire photo—such as adjusting the color, brightness, and contrast. You've also looked at tools for applying "touchups," such as burning, dodging, cloning an area, removing scratches, and removing wrinkles. However, many photos have problems that can only be solved by applying corrections to a specific area—and leaving the rest of the image alone. For example, a landscape might have the correct exposure for the field in the foreground, but the ocean and sky in the background may be overexposed, losing interesting details. The image shown in Figure 7-1 has exactly this problem. If you adjust the image to show the details in the background, the foreground area comes out too dark.

To correct a problem such the one shown in Figure 7-1 (and a whole range of similar problems), you need to apply a brightness correction to just the background. To do so, you must select just the problem area before applying the fix. When you select an area in Digital Image Pro, any work you do from that point on occurs only in the selected area.

> **NOTE**  *It is important to remember that Digital Image Pro applies your corrections only to a selected area. It is quite disconcerting to choose one of the brush tools and start "painting" on your image—only to find that nothing is happening! If you discover that your changes don't seem to be working, choose the Object tool (the arrow at the left end of the selection tools) and click in the image to deselect your selection.*

Digital Image Pro provides several selection tools so you can pick the area you want to work on. You can configure these tools to change how they behave. You can modify the selection by adding to it or subtracting from it until you have exactly the area you want.

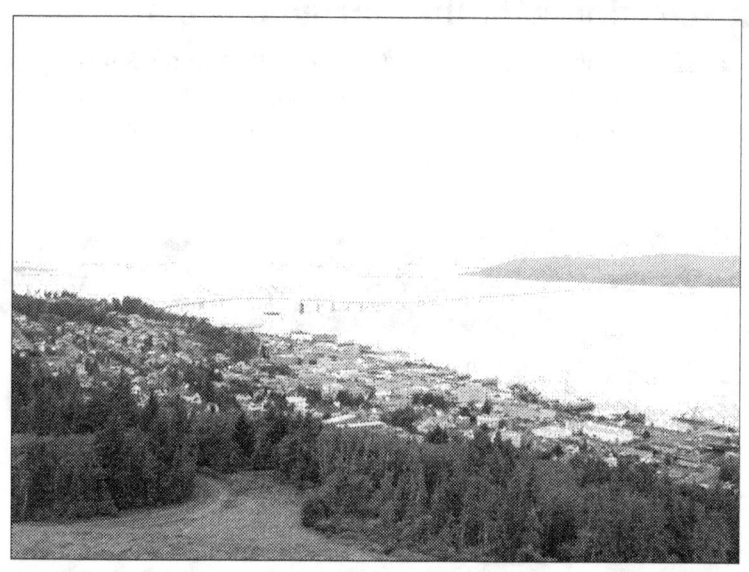

There is no easy way to make an overall correction to this photo so that both the foreground and background are correctly exposed.

Once you have the area selected, you can apply corrections to that area. Technically, you can use *any* tool in a selected area, but there are a number of tools we will cover in this chapter that really make sense to use only in a selected area.

## Make a Selection with the Selection Tools

Digital Image Pro provides five different types of selection tools: the Object Tool, the Marquee, the Freehand tool, the Magic Wand, and the Edge Finder. They are located in the center of the workspace toolbar, in that order. The Object Tool is used to deselect any selection by clicking the image after you've made a selection. You can also use the Object Tool to choose an object (see Chapter 8) by clicking the object in the Stack area.

NOTE  *Once you choose a selection tool (except for the Object tool), you can modify how the tool behaves using a special dialog box. If the dialog box does not appear automatically when you choose a selection tool, click the Selection button in the workspace toolbar.*

# Make a Selection with the Marquee Tools

The Marquee Tools enable you to make a selection that corresponds to a particular shape. The most commonly used shapes are rectangles and circles or ovals, but a huge variety of shapes are actually available. To see the available shapes, click the Shape box in the Marquee Tool dialog box:

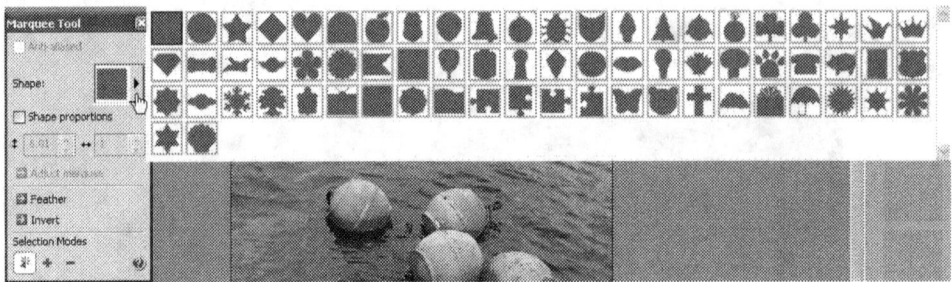

Creating a selection with the Marquee Tool is simple—just click and drag, starting from the upper-left corner of the selection area. To subtly smooth the edges of the selection, select the Anti-aliased checkbox (which is also available for the Freehand and Edge Finder tools).

You can enforce a ratio of height to width for the selection by selecting the Shape Proportions checkbox, and then setting values in the left (height) and right (width) fields. When you click and drag the Marquee, the resulting shape will be limited to these proportions.

If you decide that the selected shape isn't quite the right size or in the right position, you can adjust it before you do anything else. Click Adjust Marquee in the Marquee Tool dialog box to display a sizing rectangle around the selection. From here, you can:

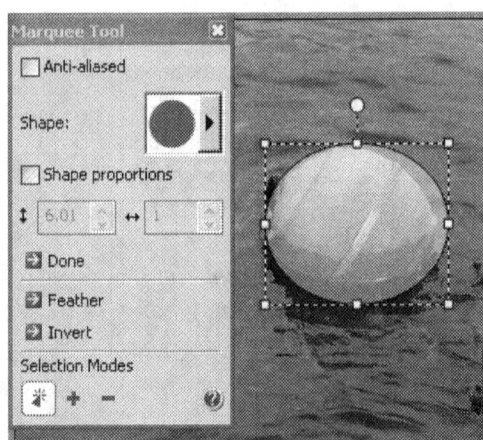

- ■ **Resize the Marquee**    To resize the Marquee, click and drag the sizing handles at the corners and on the sides of the sizing rectangle.

- ■ **Rotate the Marquee**    To rotate the Marquee, click and drag the rotation handle (just above the center of the top of the rectangle).

- ■ **Move the Marquee**    To move the Marquee, click inside the sizing rectangle and drag the rectangle (which moves the included selection).

Click done when you are finished modifying the marquee shape.

## Draw a Selection with the Freehand Tool

The Freehand Tool is just what it sounds like: you can draw a selection freehand.
To do so, choose the Freehand Tool and click at the starting point for your selection.
To draw completely freehand, simply hold down the left mouse button and drag to
outline the selected area. To complete the selection, move the mouse over the starting
point (it turns into a black square) and release the left mouse button. Alternatively,
you can double-click, which draws a straight line from the current mouse position
back to the starting point.

   The Freehand Tool offers another drawing option if the area you want to select
consists mostly of straight edges. Click at the starting point, and then move the mouse
to a new position and click again. Digital Image Pro draws a straight line between
the points. You can continue moving the mouse and clicking to draw more straight
lines. To finish the selection, click the start point or double-click anywhere.

**TIP**   *You can also combine the two techniques using "move and click" to create
straight lines, and "click and drag" to outline nonlinear sections.*

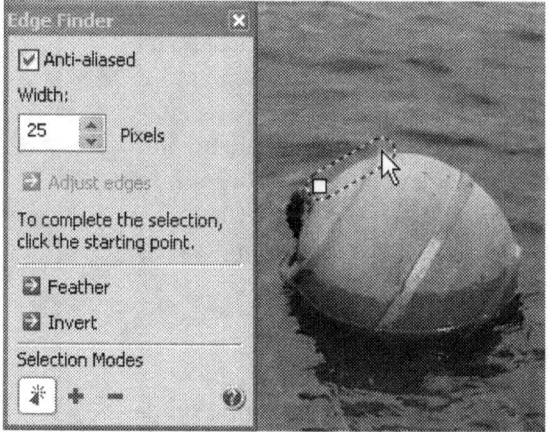

## Create a Selection with the Edge Finder

The Edge Finder (as its name implies)
finds edges in the image—areas where
there is a strong change in contrast or
color. To use the Edge Finder, select it
and click at an edge. Move the mouse
along the edge, and Digital Image Pro
draws an oval, the width of which
depends on the Width (in pixels) you
set in the Edge Finder dialog box.

   Click the mouse to draw the selection
along the edge. Continue moving and
clicking to select the entire object. To finish, move the mouse back over the
starting point and click, or double-click, to draw a straight line from the last point
back to the starting point.

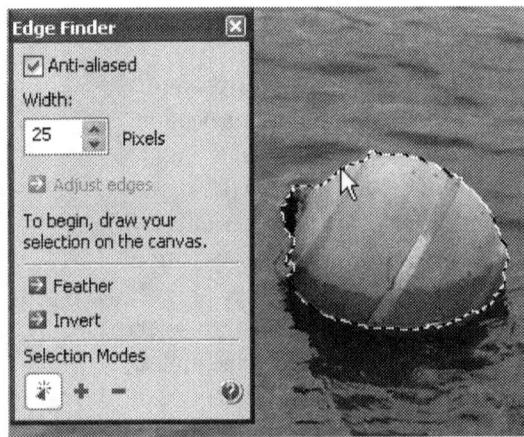

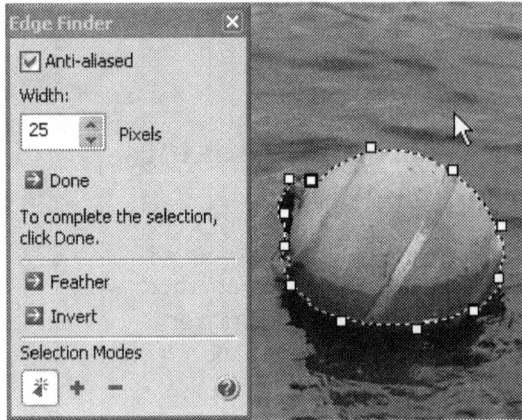

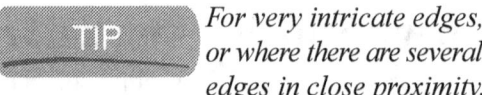

*For very intricate edges, or where there are several edges in close proximity, set the Width to a small number of pixels. This requires you to be more precise in positioning your mouse, but enables you to get exactly the edge you want.*

Finding edges can be a tricky business, so you may find that you need to adjust the result. To do so, click Adjust Edges in the Edge Finder dialog box. Digital Image Pro displays the selection with a series of adjustment points along the edge.

To move an adjustment point, move the mouse over it (it turns into a black dot). Click the point and drag it to its new location, resetting the edges on both sides. If you need to adjust the edge at a location where there is no adjustment point, move the mouse over the selection until it turns into a cross with a small plus sign. Click the edge to add an adjustment point at that location, and then move the point as just described. When you're finished adjusting the edge, click Done in the Edge Finder dialog box.

## Create a Selection with the Magic Wand

The last selection tool is *Magic Wand*, which enables you to select areas of a similar color. This can be handy for adding color to a white shirt or changing the background of a portrait. To use the Magic Wand, select it and click the area that has the color you want to select, as shown in Figure 7-2. There are two special controls in the Magic Wand dialog box:

- ■ **Contiguous** If you select the Contiguous checkbox, only areas that are contiguous to the selection point are included in the selection. That is, areas of the selected color that do not touch the selected area are *not* selected.

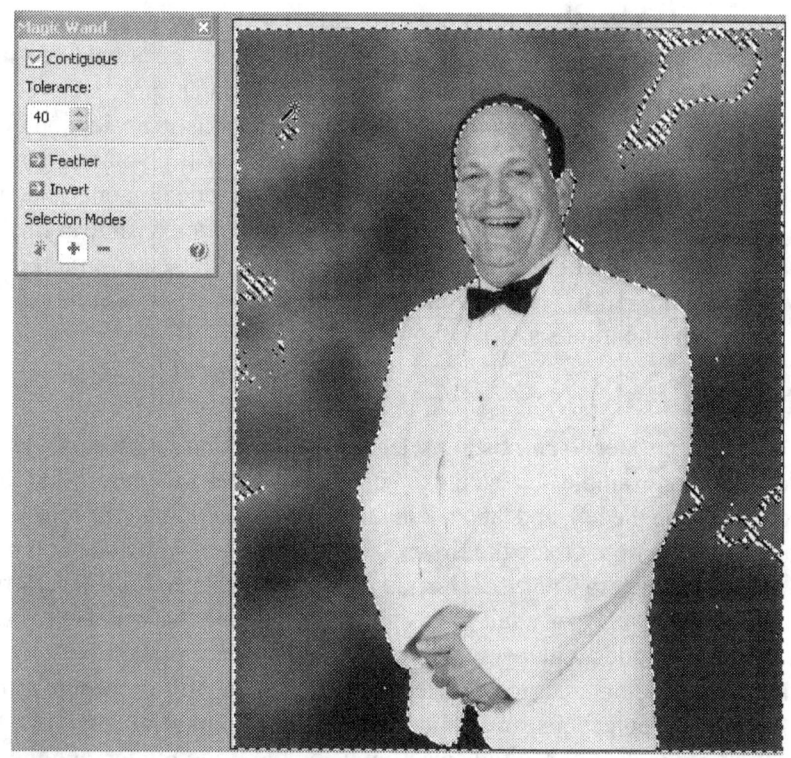

Selecting an area of a given color (or range of colors) is easy with the Magic Wand selection tool.

Clearing the Contiguous checkbox selects all areas of the image that have the selected color.

■ **Tolerance**   The Tolerance field determines how similar to the selected color a pixel has to be before it is included in the selection. If you want to select a broad area (such as the background of a portrait) and find that isolated sections are not selected, try increasing the value of the Tolerance. Alternately, if you discover that Digital Image Pro is selecting too much, try reducing the Tolerance.

NOTE   *You can also add areas to or subtract areas from your selection, using the tools discussed in the next section, "Modify a Selection."*

## Modify a Selection

It can be difficult to select the exact area you want in one try. For example, you might want to select two areas that are not adjacent so you can later apply a correction. Or, you might need to add a small area at the edge of an existing selection because the Edge Finder missed that area. Or (as described previously), you might need to use a wider range of color for the Magic Wand than is practical in one selection.

The key to modifying selections is in the *Selection Modes*, visible at the bottom of the various selection tool dialog boxes. The Selection Modes (from left to right) are New Selection, Add to Current Selection (the plus sign), and Subtract from Current Selection (the minus sign).

## Add to a Selection

When you add a new area to an existing selection, the resulting selected area includes both selections. For example, I created two nonadjacent areas in Figure 7-3 by first selecting the area on the left, and then adding the area on the right to the selection.

To add to a selection, create the first selection using the New Selection mode. Then switch to the Add to Current Selection mode and create additional selections. The mouse cursor displays a small plus sign (+) to indicate that you are in Add to Current Selection mode. When you are done, both areas are part of the selection. You can continue adding areas to the selection by following this procedure as many times as you like. You can also switch between the different selection tools; for example, you can make your initial selection using the Edge Finder, and then add to that selection with the Freehand Tool.

TIP    *Instead of choosing the Add to Current Selection mode from the dialog box, you can hold down the* SHIFT *key while creating the second selected area. When you press the* SHIFT *key, the mouse cursor displays a small plus sign (+) to denote that you are adding to the selected area.*

### Subtract from a Selection

When you subtract an area from an existing selection, the resulting area does not include any overlap between the second selection and the original selection. This can be handy if your initial selection included too much information, which often happens with the Magic Wand. It is even more handy when you need to "cut out" an area before applying a correction. For example, Figure 7-4 displays a section of roof that needs to be darkened and color-enhanced, but I don't want to apply these

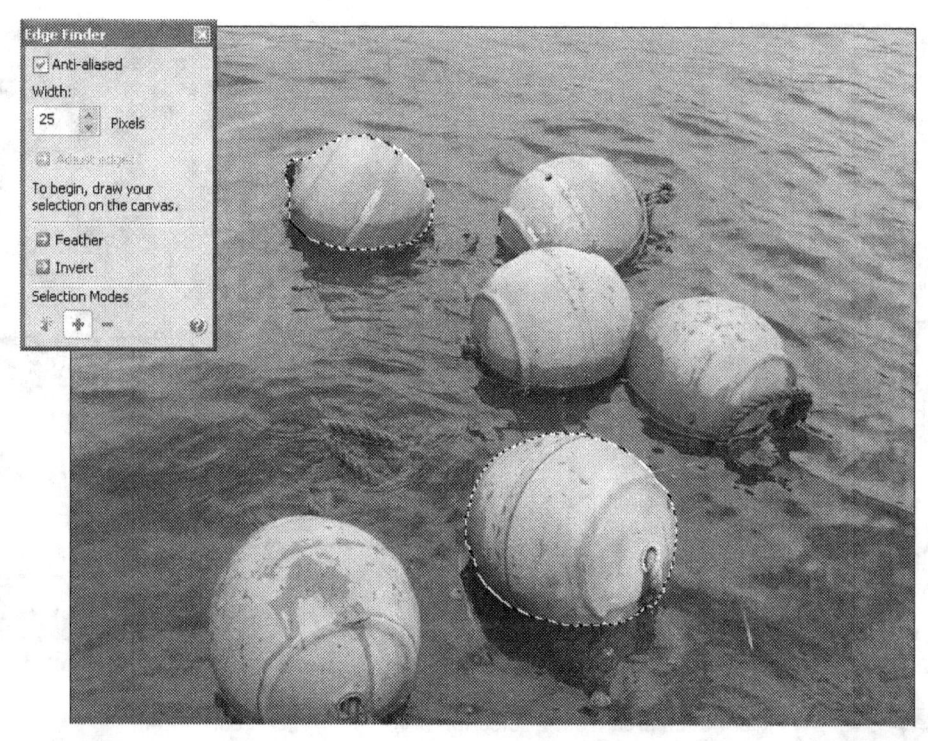

Create a selection from two nonadjacent areas by adding the second area to the first.

same effects to the dark skylight. So, I just selected the entire roof with the Edge Finder, and then subtracted out the skylight area (again using the Edge Finder).

When you switch to the Subtract from Current Selection mode, the mouse cursor displays a small minus sign (–) to indicate that you are in that mode. As with adding to a selection, you can repeat subtractions and switch selection tools, fine-tuning your selection until you have exactly what you want.

TIP *Instead of choosing the Subtract from Current Selection mode from the dialog box, you can hold down the* ALT *key while creating the second selected area. When you press the* ALT *key, the mouse cursor displays a small minus sign (–) to denote that you are subtracting from the selected area.*

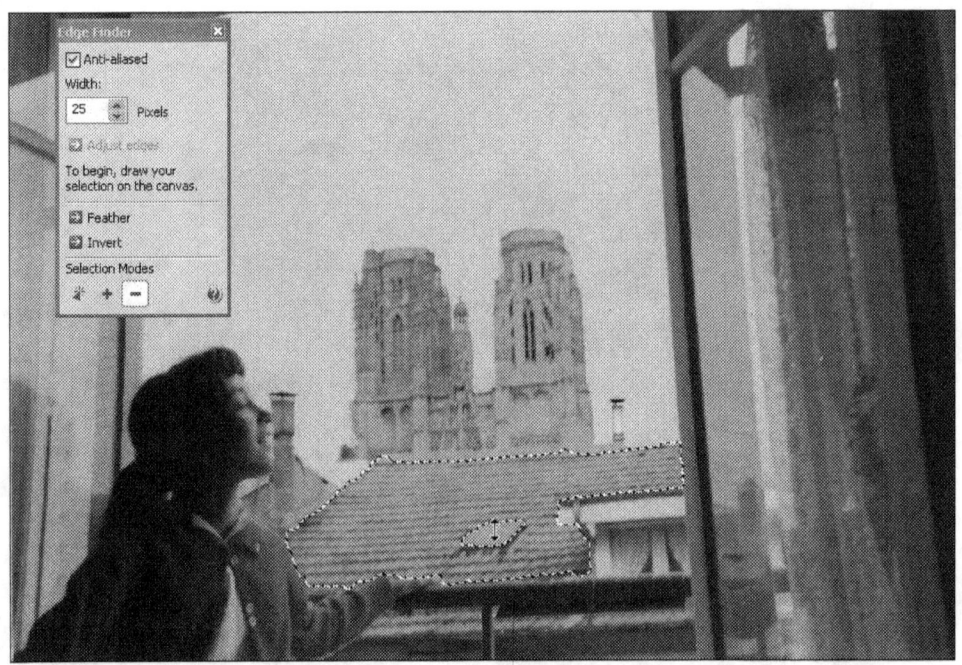

Cut out an area from a selection before applying a correction.

## Invert the Selection

It can often be easier to select what you *don't* want from an image than to select what you *do* want. For example, as mentioned earlier in this chapter, it is quite simple to use the Magic Wand to select a single-color background in a studio portrait. Once you have made this sort of selection, it is easy to invert the selection so that everything *except* what you originally selected becomes the new selection. Thus, in this example, the subjects of the photo become the new selection, leaving out the background. You could then copy them and paste them into another image (as discussed in Chapter 8), perhaps to give them a different background.

To invert your selection, simply click Invert in the selection tool dialog box.

7

# How to ... Feather a Selection

One of the reasons you may want to select a portion of an image is to copy it and paste it into another image or into another portion of the same image (see Chapter 8). Photoshop Elements provides the Feather option to soften the edges of the selection so that the border of the selected area is not as jarring when you paste it.

Feathering blurs the edges of the selected areas, and is available for all selection tools except for the Magic Wand. The effect of feathering is to introduce more and more transparency into the selected image as you move closer to the edge. To use feathering, click the Feather option in the selection tool dialog box to open the Feather Selection dialog box. The only option in this dialog box is the amount of feathering. Enter a value or use the spinner to set a value in the field, and then click OK. As you increase the amount of feathering, the transparency effect starts farther and farther away from the edge. You can't actually see the effect of the feathering unless you copy the selected area (choose Edit | Copy) and then paste the selected area (choose Edit | Paste). The effect is clearly visible here, where I've copied a section of an image and pasted it into a new, empty document with lots of feathering.

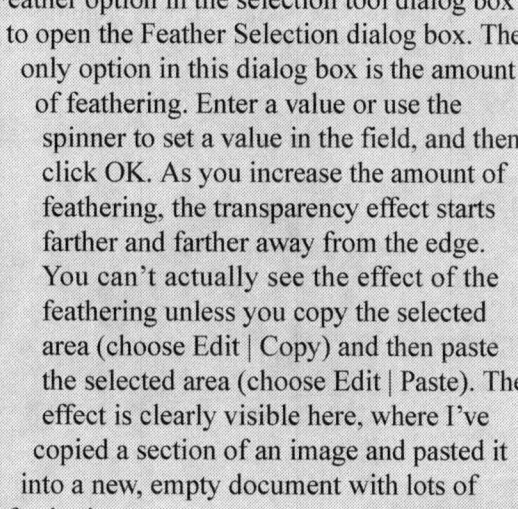

# Make Adjustments to Selected Areas of an Image

Now that you understand how to create selections and limit your work to just the selected area(s), you can explore some of the more advanced corrections that Digital Image Pro makes possible. These corrections make the most sense when applied to a limited area, rather than to a whole image (although you *can* apply them to the whole image if you want).

## Change the Color of a Selected Area

Changing the color of an item can be useful. For example, a white shirt in a group photo might stand out too much, taking your attention from the main subjects. To correct this situation, follow these steps:

1. Select the item you want to change. I selected the light-color shirt that was jarring to the eye. I actually made the selection in two steps. The first step selected the entire shirt, including the tie. I then changed to the Subtract from Current Selection mode and selected just the tie, removing it from the selection, as shown in Figure 7-5.

2. Choose Touchup | Hue and Saturation to open the Hue and Saturation task bar.

3. Adjust the hue, saturation, and brightness to change the color of the offending item (the shirt, in this case). Figure 7-6 shows the less-jarring result.

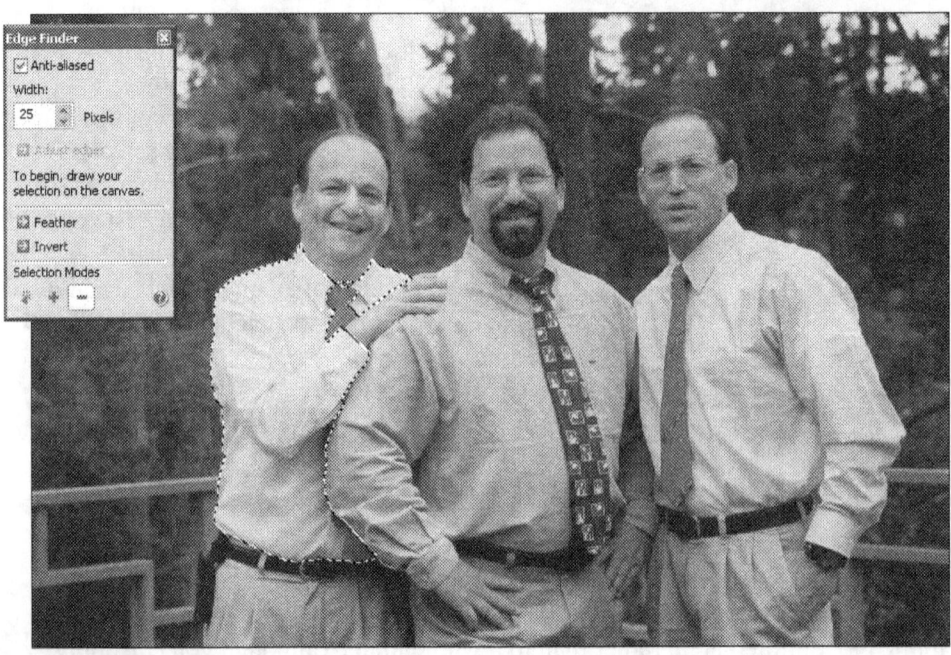

The item I want to change is now selected.

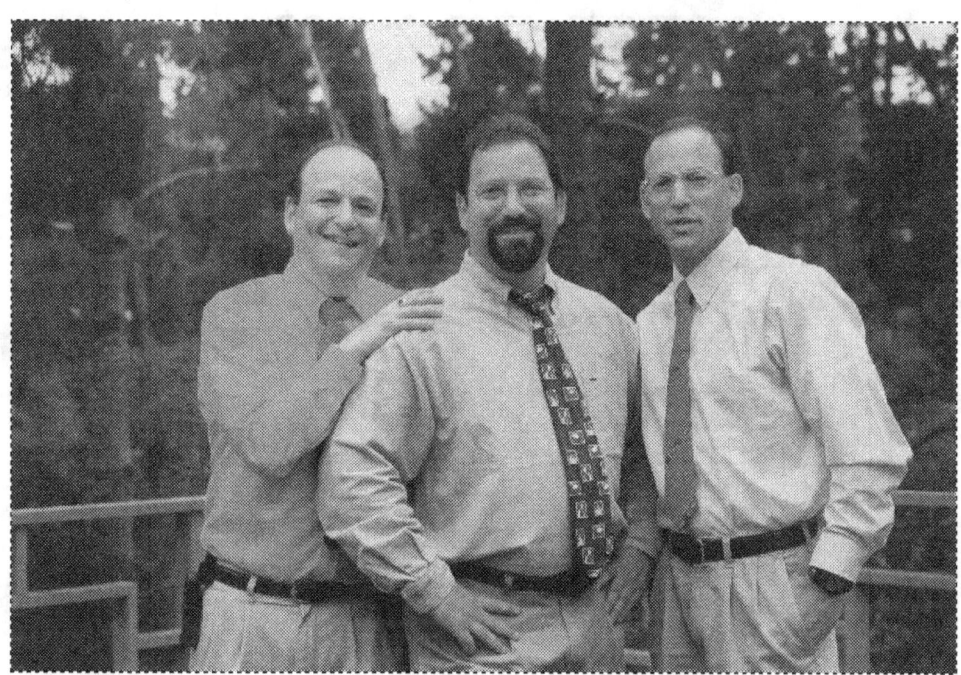

7

Your eye doesn't automatically gravitate toward my bright-white shirt any more.

## Use Brightness/Contrast to Fix an Area

It is not unusual for a section of a photo to need drastic changes to make the photo more pleasing. For example, Figure 7-7 shows an image that is in pretty good shape, except for a couple of flowers near the right edge of the image that caught the flash, leaving that portion of the photo severely overexposed. The bright white area overpowers the rest of the picture. You could crop this section out, but this bunch of flowers in the foreground gives the picture depth, and removing them would be a shame. Further, because you can see some details in the flower petals, the damage is repairable.

To correct the image, follow these steps:

1. Select the portion of the image you want to correct. I actually selected the first white area of the flowers only, and added the second white area to it, leaving me with just the two white areas to work on. Either the Edge Finder or the Magic Wand (set a low tolerance) work fine for making this selection.

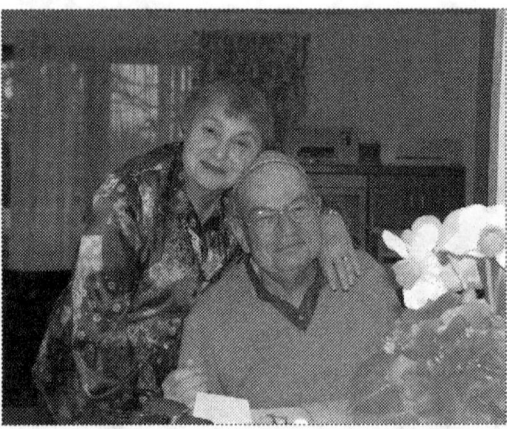

A picture with interest and depth—and a really ugly flash reflection

**2.** Choose Touchup | Brightness and Contrast to open the Brightness and Contrast task bar.

**3.** Reduce the brightness to take the edge off the white flare, and bump up the contrast a bit to bring out the details in the petals. The result is visible in Figure 7-8.

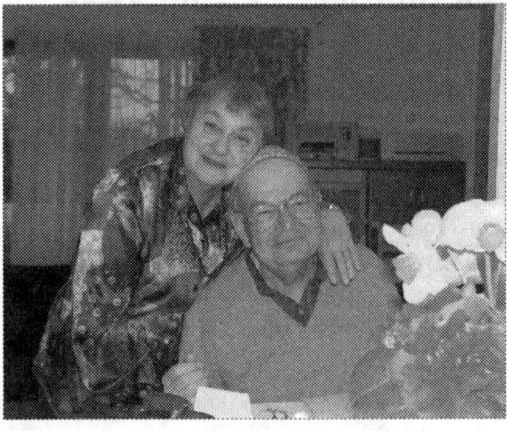

The reduction in intensity of the white makes this a better picture.

# Blur the Background of an Image

When an entire photograph is in sharp focus, a busy background can distract the eye from the main subject. To combat this effect, you can blur the background, leaving the main subject sharply focused. To accomplish this, we will use the *Gaussian Blur* function. Follow these steps:

1. Open an image and select the main subject. In this example, I got good results using the Edge Finder and making some small adjustments to the edges.

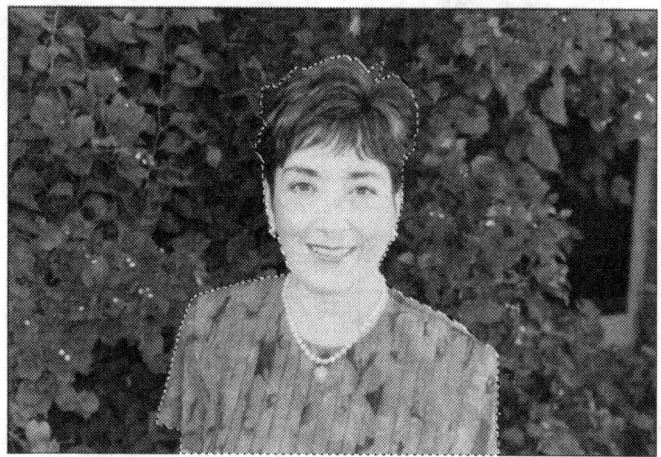

2. Invert the selection so that everything *except* the main subject is selected by choosing Invert in the selection tool dialog box.

3. Select Touchup | Gaussian Blur to open the Gaussian Blur task bar.

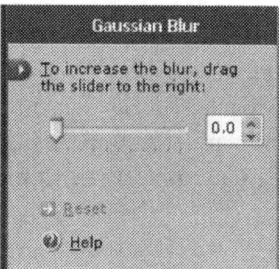

4. Use the slider to set the amount of blur and click Done to blur the background, leaving only the subject in sharp focus.

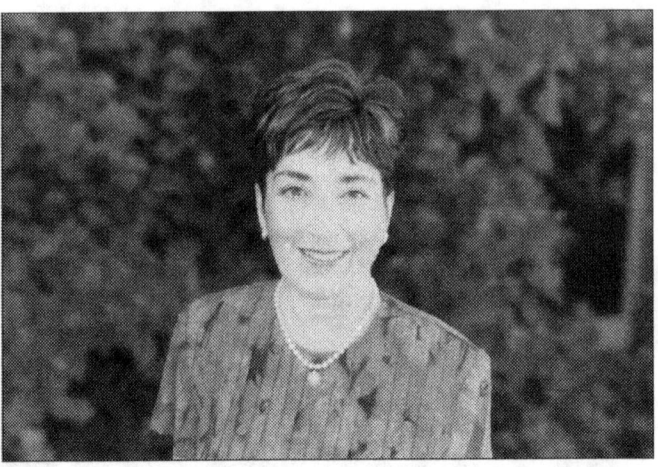

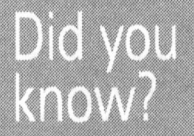

NOTE    *You could also use the Sharpen or Blur function (select Touchup | Sharpen or Blur) if you wish. But Gaussian Blur gives an effect that less obviously shouts "the background was blurred!"*

## Sharpen a Selected Area

The automatic focus on a camera—especially digital cameras—can be fooled. For example, Figure 7-9 shows a photo of a black kitten. She is so dark that the camera focused on another object in the frame (one that was *not* important), leaving the

## Did you know?    About Gaussian Blur

Gaussian Blur quickly blurs a selection by an adjustable amount (use the slider in the Gaussian Blur task bar). You can select the radius, which determines how far the filter searches from a pixel to find dissimilar pixels to blur. The amount of applied blur falls off as you move away from a sharp edge according to a bell-shaped curve.

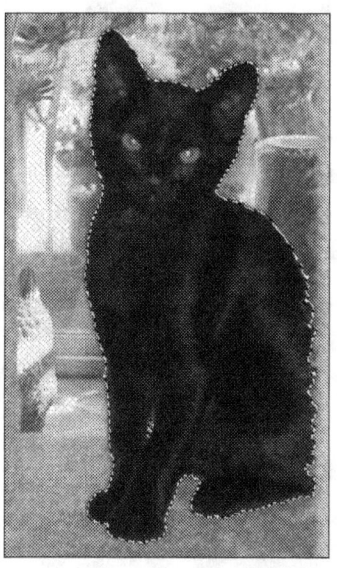

If the main subject is a little soft, you can fix it by adjusting the focus on just the main subject.

kitten slightly out of focus. To fix this situation, we want to sharpen up just the kitten. Adding sharpness to the overall picture is not a good idea because you are introducing extra contrast into the background.

To correct the focus problem, use the following steps:

1. Select the main subject in the image. In this case, the Magic Wand with a high tolerance worked pretty well, although I had to fill in a couple of small missed spots (like the eyes).

2. Select Touchup | Unsharp Mask to open the Unsharp Mask task bar.

3. Set the Edge Width, Contrast, and Noise Reduction Threshold. In this case, I set the Edge Width to 3.8, the Contrast to 44 %, and the Noise Reduction Threshold to 42.

4. Click Done to sharpen the focus on just the main subject.

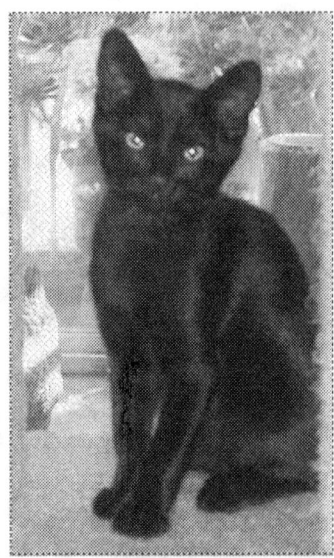

# Make Changes Specific to Parts of Your Photos

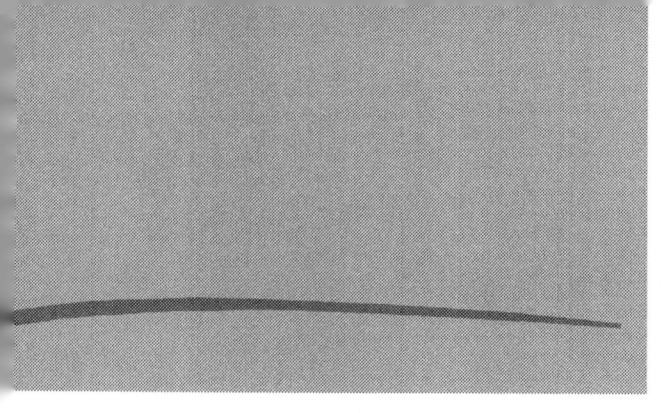

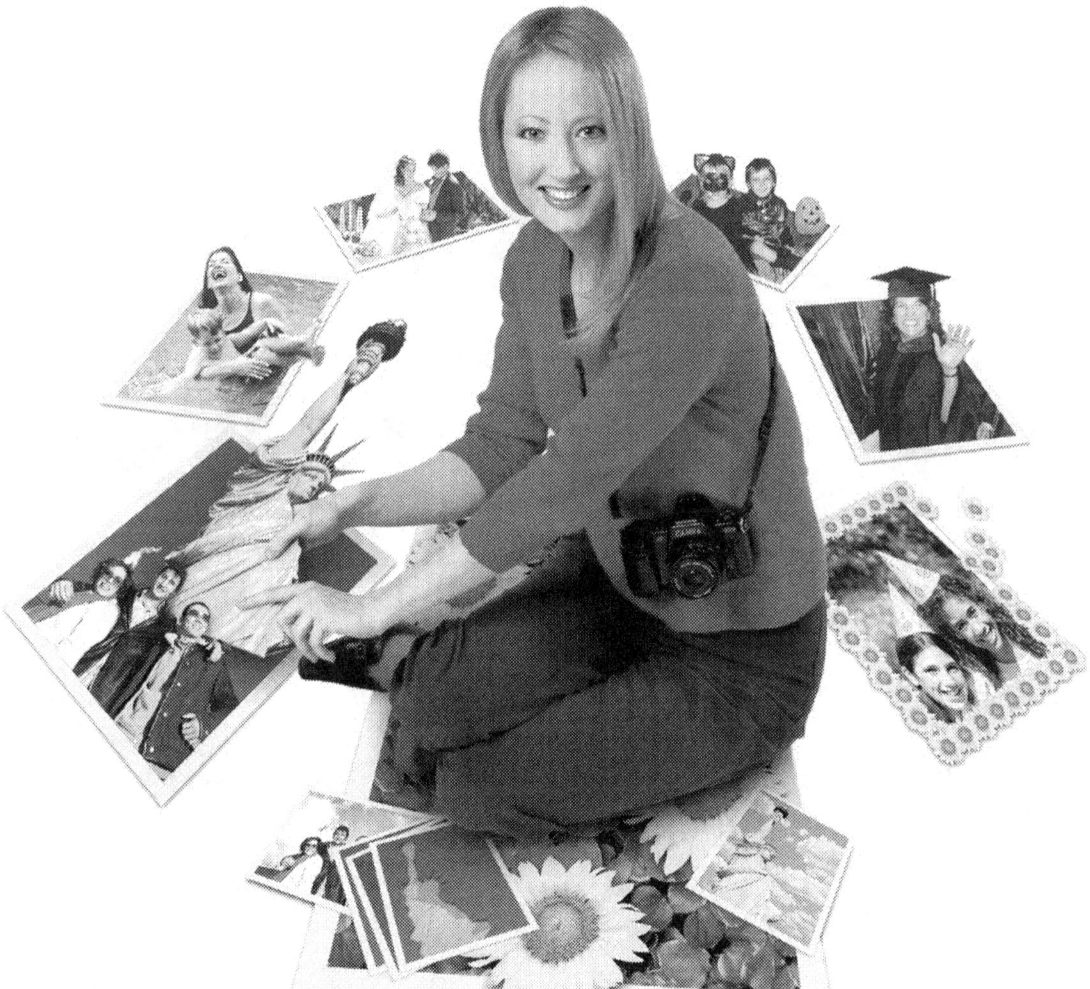

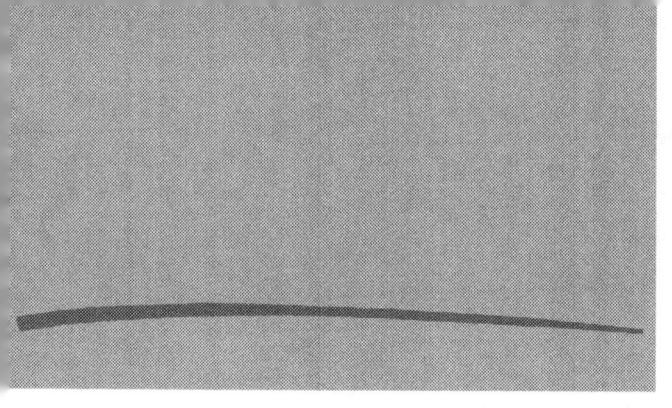

# Work with Objects and Layers

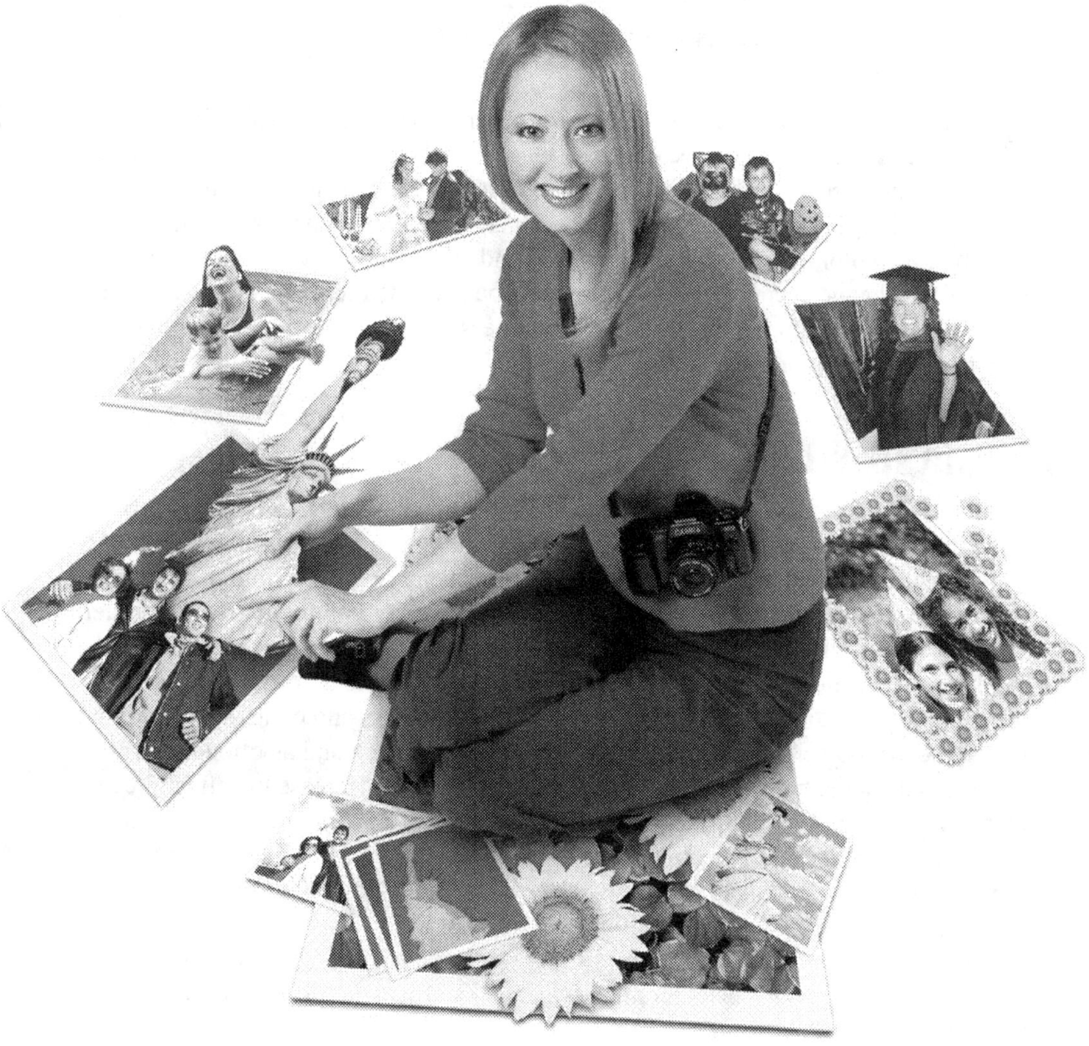

## How to...

- Create objects
- Move, size, and rotate objects
- Change the object stacking order
- Adjust the color and transparency of an object
- Add a shadow to an object
- Use objects and layers to add items to a photo

When you first bring an image into Digital Image Pro, it consists of a single layer—the image you see on the screen. With the exception of an example in Chapter 7, up to this point in the book I have been making changes to this single layer—touching it up with the brush tools, changing the brightness and contrast, adjusting the color, sharpening and blurring, and so on. Provided you don't undo a change, the change becomes permanent when you save the file. For example, if you select the sky in an image, decrease the brightness, and save the result, you have no way to return to the original state of the image.

# Understand What Layers Can Do

Digital Image Pro's layers (which are visible in the Stack) enable you to add objects to an image—each on its own layer—and make changes to the objects without changing the base image. Each layer and the objects it contains is an independent part of the picture, and you can make adjustments to a layer without affecting other layers or the original image (which I will now refer to as the *background*). In my example, I can select the sky, and copy and paste it (creating a layer containing just the sky portion of the image). I can then apply a brightness and contrast correction to just the sky object. I can fine-tune the correction as much and as often as I want, and even adjust the transparency of the layer to increase or decrease the effect. I can then save the file as a PNG Plus file (Digital Image Pro's native format), and the next time I open the file, the object and its layer are still there, ready for me to use. Finally, at any time, I can simply delete the object and its layer—leaving me with the unchanged original image, ready for me to try again.

Figure 8-1 shows the image I am discussing. Note that the Stack shows two layers—the background (original image) and a sky object on a layer for the brightness/contrast adjustment.

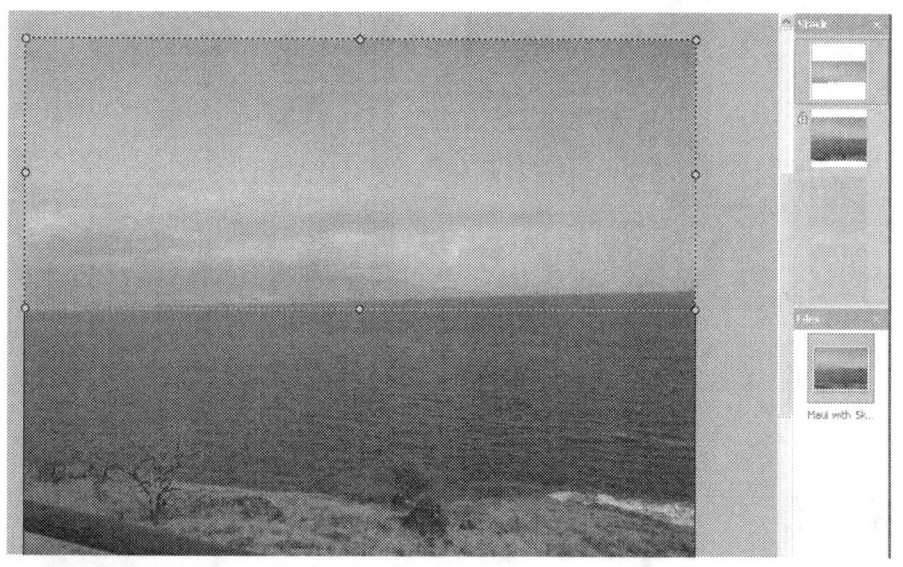

A landscape with the sky adjusted using a layer.

A good way to think about layers is as sheets of clear plastic, stacked on top of each other. You can see "down" through a layer anywhere there is no object on that layer. Likewise, you can see through an object if you set it to be partially transparent. This is illustrated by Figure 8-2, where the objects present on various layers stack up to form the entire image. You can change the stacking order to change the composition.

# Use the Stack

The Stack (see Figure 8-3) is your "control panel" for working with objects and layers. You can do much of what you need to do with layers using the Stack, including deleting layers (and the objects on them), rearranging the stacking order, and locking and unlocking layers.

## Lock or Unlock a Layer

Under normal circumstances, you perform many actions on a layer and its object(s), including moving, resizing, and rotating the object. If you lock the layer, however, Digital Image Pro prevents you from performing these actions, effectively locking the layer in place. Oddly, locking a layer does not prevent you from deleting it, nor

8

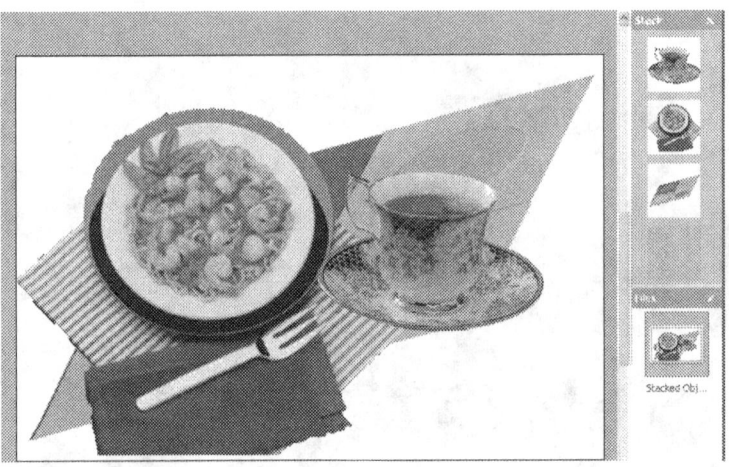

The overall image is a combination of the objects on all layers.

does it prevent you from changing the stacking order. To lock a layer, right-click the layer in the Stack or the object in the image, and choose Lock from the shortcut menu. To unlock the layer, choose Unlock from the shortcut menu. A small lock icon (visible in Figure 8-3) indicates that the layer is locked.

Click a layer in the stack to select that layer (and its object)

Lock icon

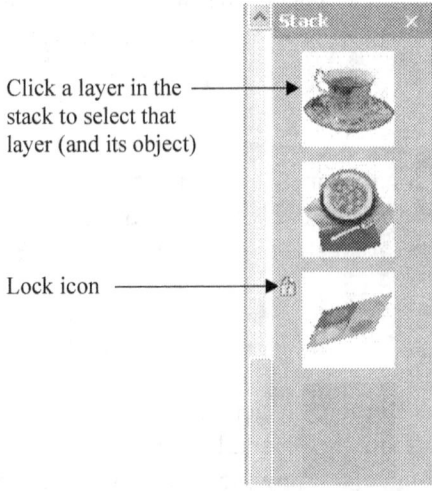

Use the Stack to work with objects and layers.

## Change the Layer and Object Stacking Order

As mentioned earlier, the order of the objects and layers is important. For example, here is an image that contains two objects (on separate layers). Initially, the photo object is placed above the frame object. You can see how that looks in both the workspace and the Stack in Figure 8-4.

We can rearrange the stacking order of the two layers. If, for example, you position the frame layer above the photo layer, you can immediately see the difference, as in Figure 8-5. The frame now hides part of the photo.

The easiest way to change the stacking order of the layers is to click and drag a layer in the Stack. As you drag the layer, a red line appears in the Stack, indicating where the dragged layer will appear when you release the mouse button.

You can also change the stacking order using the Move Forward or Backward menu item, which is available in the Object shortcut menu, Stack shortcut menu, or

8

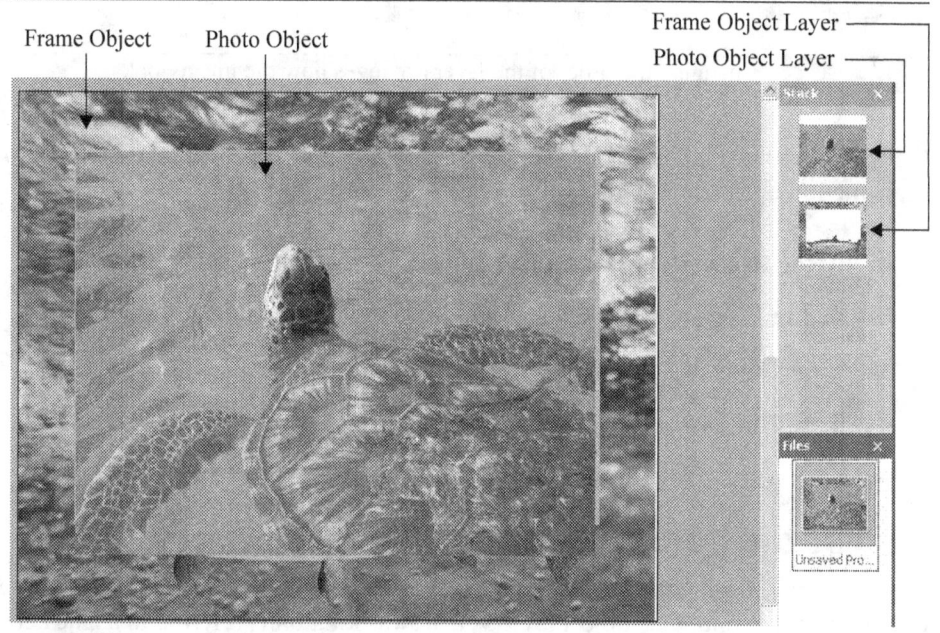

The arrangement of objects in the Stack matches the stacking order in the main workspace.

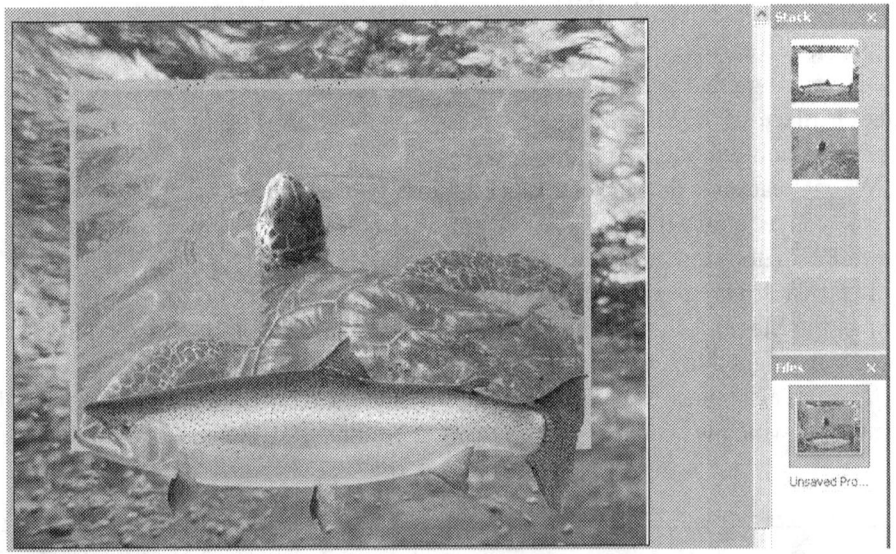

Changing the order of the layers changes how the image looks.

the Format menu. Choose the layer you want to move up or down, and then one of these menu items:

- **Bring to Front**   Makes the selected layer the top-most layer.
- **Send to Back**   Makes the selected layer the bottom-most layer.
- **Bring Forward**   Moves the selected layer up one layer in the stacking order.
- **Send Backward**   Moves the selected layer down one layer in the stacking order.

## Choose the Object Layer to Work On

You can apply the actions in the Format, Touchup, and Effects menus on only one object layer at a time—the object layer you are working on is referred to as the active layer. The easiest way to choose the active layer is to click it in the Stack. The active layer is highlighted in the Stack. In addition, the object corresponding to the active layer shows its sizing and rotation handles.

Another way to select an object layer is to click the object in the image. When you click the object, the layer that contains the object automatically becomes the active layer.

## Delete an Object Layer

If you find you no longer need an object (and the layer it is on), you can choose Delete from the object shortcut menu (right-click the object), or the layer shortcut menu (right-click the layer in the Stack). You can also select either the object in the image or the layer in the Stack and press the DELETE key or choose Edit | Delete.

# Create Object Layers

There are several ways to create object layers in Digital Image Pro: copy and paste an object, insert a picture, insert a shape, and add text. I discuss inserting a shape in Chapter 9, and adding text in Chapter 10.

## Paste to Create an Object Layer

Whenever you copy something and paste it, Digital Image Pro creates a layer for that pasted object. It doesn't matter if the source of the copy was another image or the same image. Further, a new layer is created for each pasted object, even if you paste the same object several times. For example, here I copied one of these floats and pasted it back into the original image three times—and you can see from the Stack that I have three additional layers.

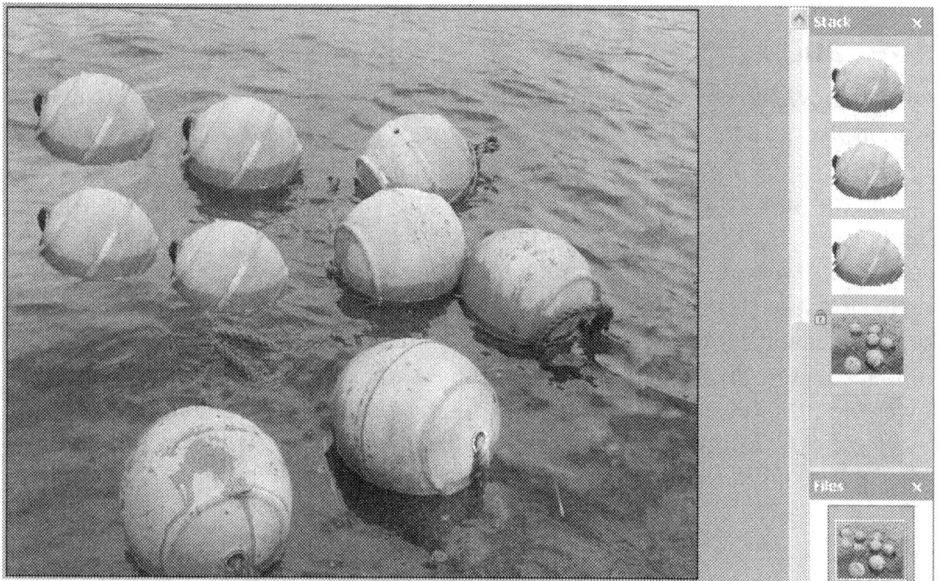

## Insert a Picture to Create an Object Layer

The action of inserting a picture into an image also creates a new object layer for that picture. To insert a picture, select Insert | Picture, and then select a source from the submenu (From the Gallery, From My Computer, and so on). We'll see how to use this feature later in this chapter to combine the contents of two photographs.

# Work with Objects

When you select an object, it appears inside a rectangle with sizing handles and a rotation handle.

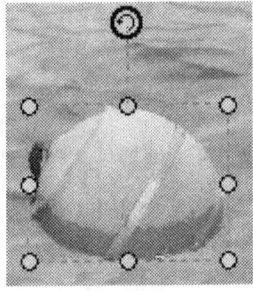

You can modify an object using virtually any of the options under the Format, Touchup, or Effects menus. The options covered later in this chapter (such as adding a shadow) either work with objects only (and shapes— see Chapter 9) or make the most sense when applied to objects. If you do use these options on an object (such as adjusting levels, using the blending brush, or applying the Antique effect), they work just as they do when applied to the entire image. However, if you select multiple objects (as described later in this chapter), the options in the Format, Touchup, and Effects menus are applied to the entire image, *not* to the selected objects.

## Move and Size an Object

You can move the object by clicking inside the rectangle and dragging it to a new location. To move the image in fine increments, you can press one of the four arrow keys to move the object one pixel in the direction of the arrow.

You can size the object by clicking and dragging one of the sizing handles. Clicking and dragging a corner sizing handle resizes the object maintaining the aspect ratio, whereas clicking and dragging one of the side sizing handles enables you to stretch or shrink the object by distorting it. For example, if you click and drag the sizing handle along the right side, you can make the object wider or narrower without affecting the height of the object. To size the image in fine increments, hold down the SHIFT key and press one of the four arrow keys. The left and right arrow keys make the object wider and narrower; the up and down arrow keys make the object taller and shorter.

You can also use the entries in the Format menu to modify an object. Just select the following items:

- **Rotate | Selected Object**   This opens the Rotate task bar so you turn the object left, right, a half-turn, or a custom number of degrees from 0 to 359.

- **Crop | Selected Object**   This opens the Crop task bar so you can click and drag across the selected object to crop it. We used this trick in the example in Chapter 7 where we removed my brother from a picture.

- **Straighten Picture | Selected Object**   This opens the Straighten Picture task bar so you can draw a horizontal or vertical line to indicate how the object should be oriented; then click Done to straighten the object.

- **Flip | Selected Object**   This enables you to flip the object horizontally, vertically, or both.

- **Center Object on Canvas**   This selection moves the object to the center of the canvas.

The Format menu also enables you to resize the object to fit the canvas. Select Format | Resize Object to Fit Canvas, and then choose one of the three options:

- **Crop to Fit**   Either expands or reduces the object to the size of the canvas. It modifies either the length or width of the object (whichever is smaller) to match the canvas. The result is that the larger dimension falls outside the bounds of the canvas and is cropped off.

- **Scale to Fit**   Scales the size of the object to match either the height or the width of the canvas without distorting the shape of the object.

- **Stretch to Fit**   Stretches the object to fit the entire canvas, distorting the shape if necessary.

## Add a Shadow to an Object

You can give an object a more three-dimensional look by adding a shadow to it, making the shadow seem like it was part of the original picture, rather than something you pasted in. To add a shadow to an object, choose the object and select Effects | Shadow to open the Shadow task bar.

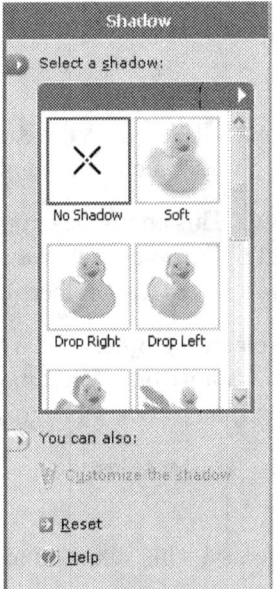

To create a shadow, pick the style from the scrolling list in the Shadow task bar. Variations include different directions, shadow size, and whether the shadow is skewed or not. The following is an example of what a Skewed, Down Right shadow might look like:

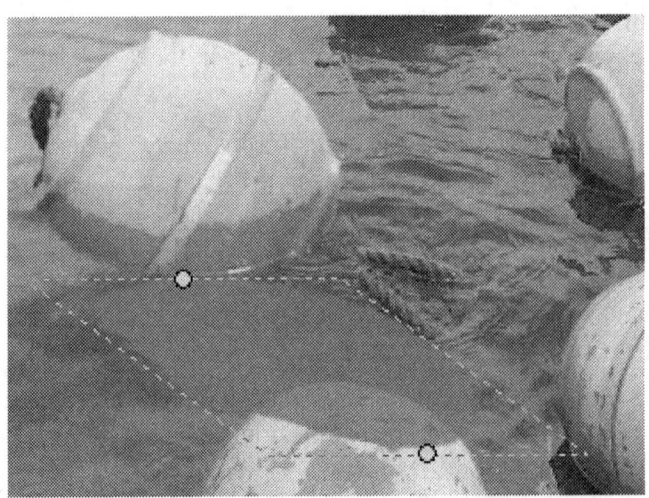

If you wish, you can set the properties of the shadow by clicking Customize the Shadow to open another version of the Shadow task bar.

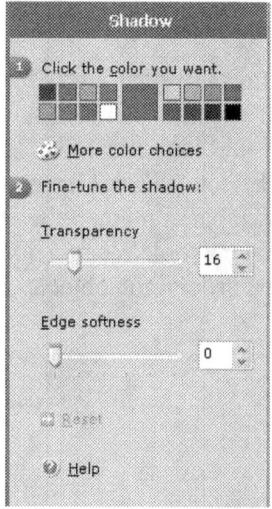

From this new task bar, you can:

- **Choose a shadow color**   Pick a color from the list of colors at the top of the task bar. As with other colors, you can click More Color Choices to choose a custom color.

- **Set the Transparency**   Drag the Transparency slider to change the transparency of the shadow from 0 (fully opaque) to 100 (invisible).

- **Change the Edge Softness**   You can feather the edges of the shadow by dragging the Edge Softness slider from 0 (hard edge) to 100 (very soft edge).

You can also change the size and position of the shadow using the mouse. When you create the shadow (and while the Shadow task bar is still open), Digital Image Pro displays the shadow inside a resizable frame. To move the frame (and the shadow it contains), click inside the frame and drag it to a new position. To change the size of the frame (and the shadow it contains), click and drag one of the sizing handles. You can also skew the shadow by dragging the sizing handles left or right.

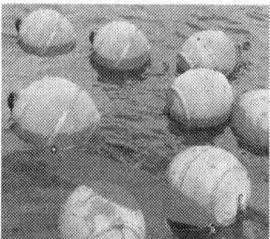

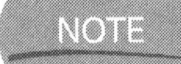 *Once you click Done to create the shadow, the shadow sizing frame disappears. The object layer is resized to hold both the object and its shadow.*

## Skew an Object

Skewing refers to slanting an object in such a way that a rectangle ends up as a parallelogram. For example, if I start with a square shape and skew the image, it would look like this.

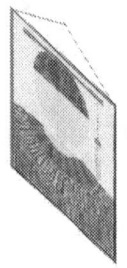

To skew an object, choose Effects | Skew Object to open the Skew task bar. However, this task bar contains little other than instructions on how to use the Skew tool. What is important is that a skewing rectangle appears around the object.

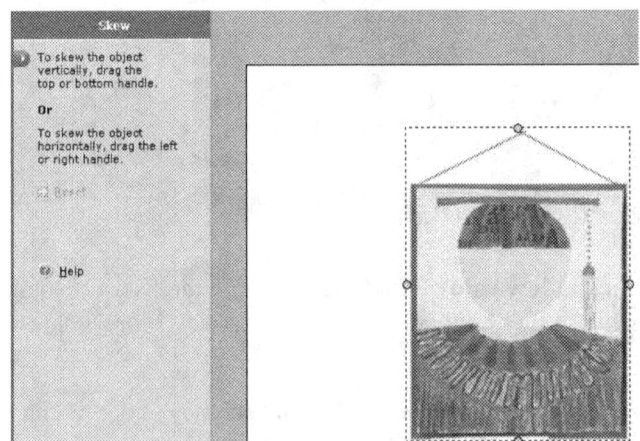

To skew an object horizontally (left or right), click the handle in the middle of the top or bottom side and drag it left or right. To skew an object vertically (up and down), click the handle in the middle of the left or right side and drag it up or down. Here is an example of doing just that.

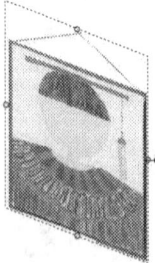

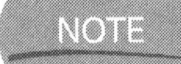 *Don't be confused by the instructions in the Skew task bar—the instructions in the task bar are backwards. Further, when you move your mouse pointer over one of the skew points, the arrow turns into a pointer that points in the wrong direction. For example, when you move the mouse pointer over the skew handle in the top or bottom side, it turns into an up/down arrow, even though you actually drag the side left or right. You can drag the side up or down, but that just stretches the shape, it doesn't skew it.*

## Call Attention to an Object with Emphasis

The Emphasize tool (select Effects | Emphasize) is one of the slickest tools in the Digital Image Pro arsenal. The Emphasize task bar enables you to pick an emphasizing effect, and then applies that effect to everything in an image *except* the selected object(s).

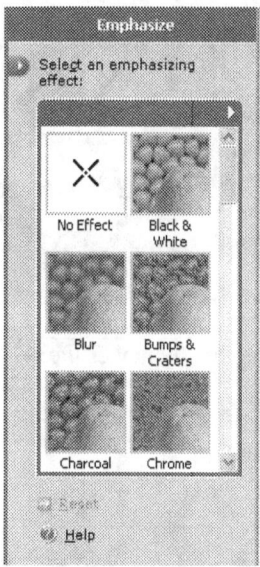

The emphasizing effects are really effective, ranging from Black & White (everything is reduced to shades of gray except the selected object) to media filters such as Charcoal, Watercolor, Fresco, Pastels, Chalk, and Stain Glass. Figure 8-6 shows a sample of what you can do with the Emphasize tool.

## Fill an Object with Color and Use Transparency

In Chapter 7, we worked with selections. You can fill a selection with color, but since the color obliterates the contents of the image, that particular effect is not very useful. What *is* useful is to fill an object with color, and modify the transparency of the object so that part of the original image shows through. This technique is very handy for adding a color tint to an image—for example, to "warm up" a morning photo and make it look like it was taken at sunset. And that is what we are going to do now.

The first step is to select the sky area of the image, as shown in Figure 8-7. The Edge Finder with a little Freehand tool touchup around the intersection between the sky and land did a great job. I also feathered the edges by 5 to soften the transition from sky to ocean.

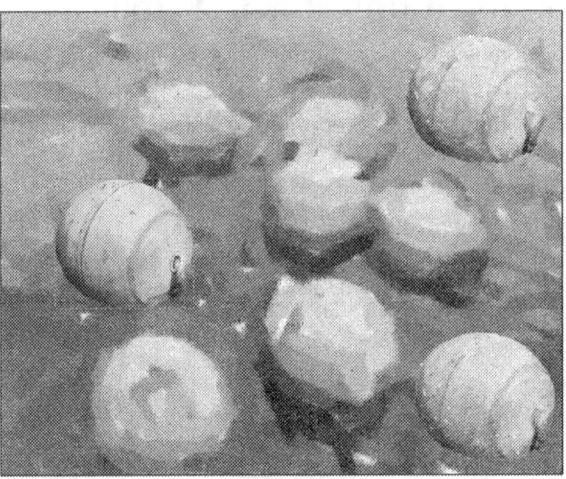

The Emphasize tool really makes the selected objects stand out from the image.

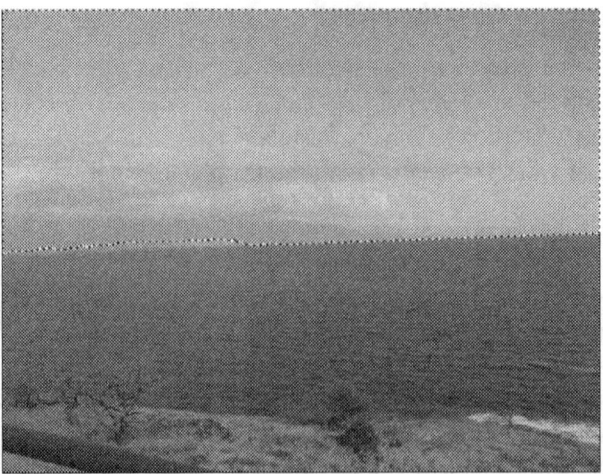

This photo from the Maui coastline will soon look like it was taken at sunset.

The next step is to copy and paste the selected section. This creates the sky on a separate layer where I can work with it. To begin the process of filling the sky with color, click the sky layer and select Effects | Fill with Texture or Color.

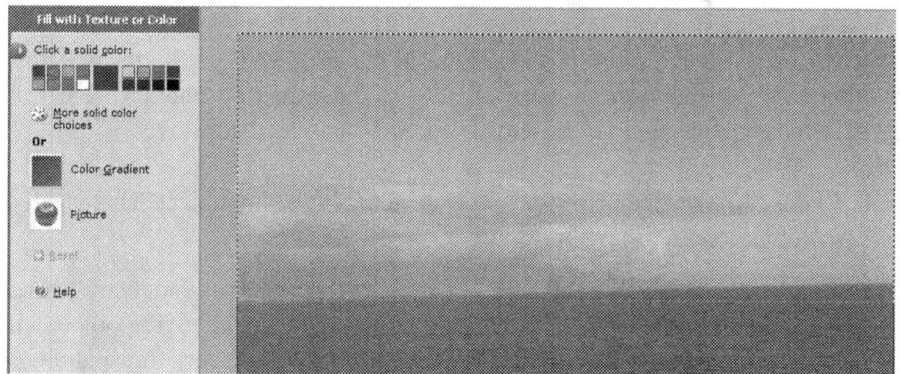

To fill the sky with a color, I could have clicked one of the color squares. However, because I want to use a color gradient, click Color Gradient to open another version of the task bar for choosing a gradient.

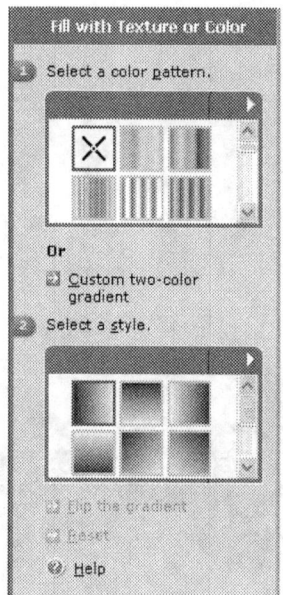

**8**

Pick a color pattern from the first scrolling list. *Fancy Gradient 48* works well for sunsets. Next, pick a gradient style from the second scrolling list. The gradient style in the middle of the top row works well. Figure 8-8 shows what we have so far. Notice that the gradient fill has completely hidden the details of the sky layer. Click Done to return to the image.

Next, the transparency of the layer has to be increased so you can see the background (with the clouds) through the color gradient. To adjust the transparency, select Effects | Transparency. The three items in the submenu are as follows:

- **Even**  Applies the same transparency across an entire object. That is, all of the object has the same transparency.

- **Gradual**  Applies a gradient transparency to an object. A variety of gradients are available. The dark areas of the gradient indicate where the object will be opaque; lighter areas indicate where the object is highly transparent. Gradients are good for shading an effect so that the effect is not too jarring.

- **Transparency Brush**  The Transparency Brush is just what it sounds like—everywhere you paint an object with the brush, the object becomes transparent. Selecting this option opens the Transparency Brush task bar, which enables

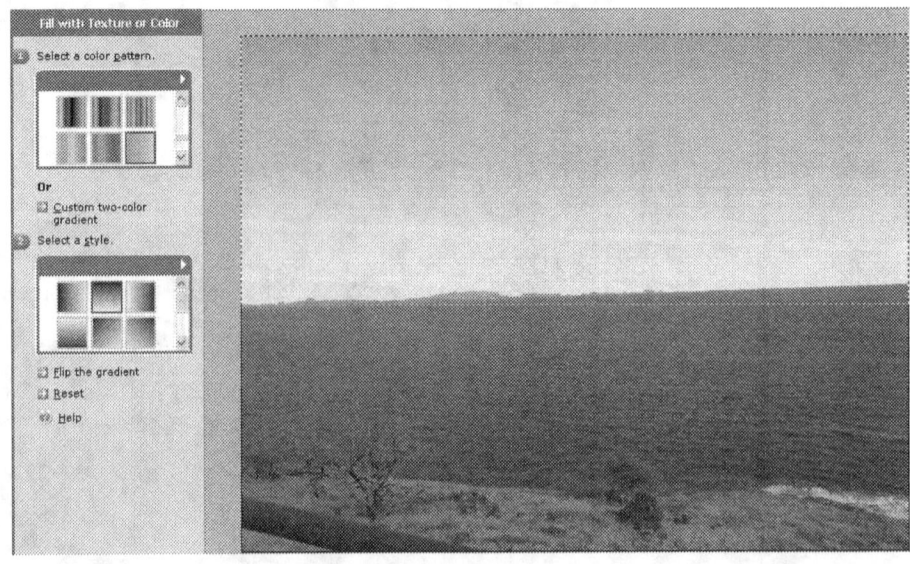

**FIGURE 8-8**    The gradient looks pretty much like sunset, but what happened to all the clouds? They are now hidden.

you to pick a brush size and brush style (hard edge or soft edge), and adjust the paint transparency (drag the slider).

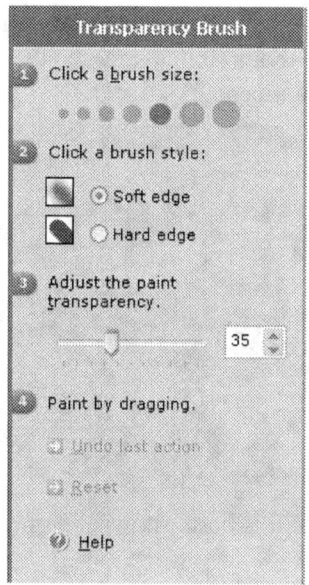

To continue, select Effects | Transparency | Even, and set the transparency to 40. This looks pretty good, but the mountains are almost invisible, so we need to increase the transparency in just that area. We'll do that with the transparency brush, as described earlier. Use a low value (about 15), and be careful not to overlap your strokes, as the transparency increases each time you pass the brush over an area.

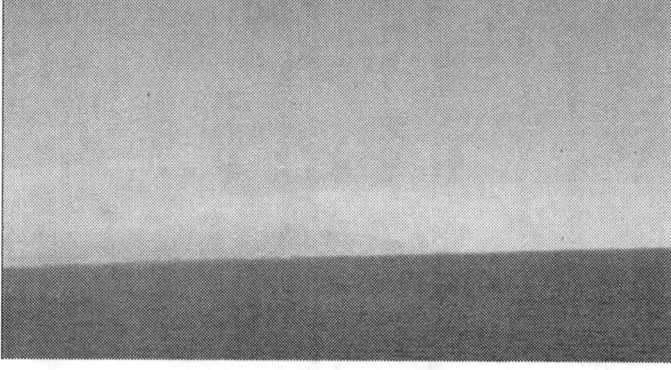

We need to do one last thing. The rest of the landscape does not match the warm coloring of the sky. To change that, we'll select the bottom portion of the image (the ocean and the land in the foreground). Then we'll copy and paste it back into the image, creating a new layer.

Choose the new layer and fill it (Effects | Fill with Texture or Color) with a light orange color. Then select Effects | Transparency | Even, and adjust the transparency of the ocean/land layer up to about 80, leaving just the barest hint of orange and warming the lower half of the image.

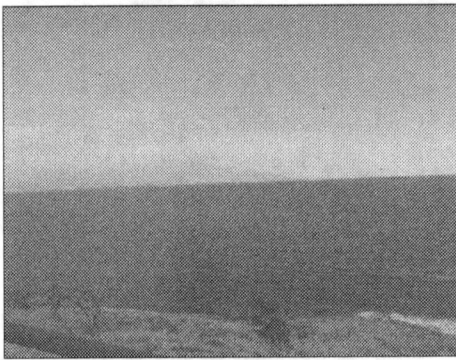

The color insert section of this book shows the progression of this photo so you can clearly see what changed.

## Use Distortion on an Object

You can apply a variety of distortions to an object, leading to some interesting effects. To apply distortion, choose the object and select Effects | Distort to open the Distort task bar.

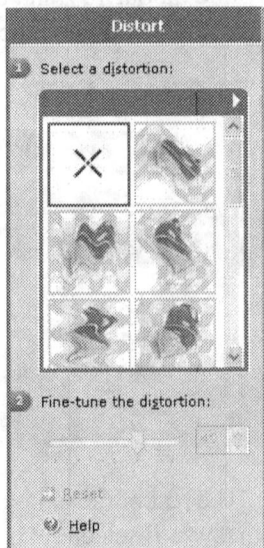

## How to ... Create a Custom Gradient

The gradients supplied with Digital Image Pro are adequate, but I have found that they don't always suit my needs. Fortunately, you can create custom gradients. To do so, choose Effects | Fill with Texture or Color. Then, use the following steps:

1. Click the style of gradient you want to build from the gradient style scrolling list (the second scrolling list).

2. Click Custom Two-Color Gradient to open a new version of the task bar.

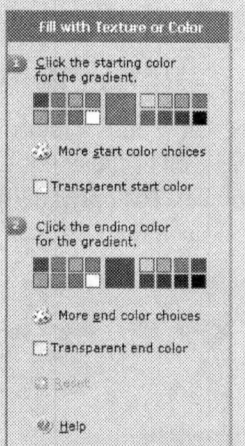

3. Choose the start color from the top set of colors (1). If you don't see the color you want, click More Start Color Choices to pick a color using the color wheel. If you wish, you can make the starting color transparent.

4. Choose the end color from the bottom set of colors (2). You can make the end color transparent as well.

5. Click Done to finish creating the custom gradient.

**NOTE** *If you don't flatten your layers prior to saving your file in a format that doesn't support layers, Digital Image Pro will automatically flatten them for you, after warning you first.*

**8**

Select a distortion from the scrolling list, and set the amount of the distortion to apply by dragging the Fine-tune slider (or using the associated field). For example, here is an object to which I applied Star 1 distortion at a Fine-tune value of 40.

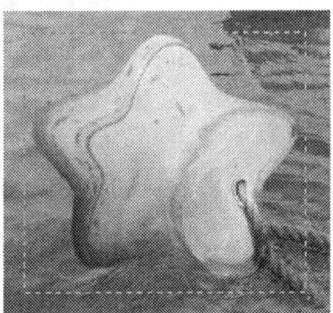

## Add a Diffuse Glow to an Object

Diffuse Glow adds a (surprise!) glow to an object. You can pick the intensity of the effect as well as the color. Used with care, the Diffuse Glow can change the lighting of an object. To apply a Diffuse Glow, choose the object and select Effects | Diffuse Glow to open the Diffuse Glow task bar.

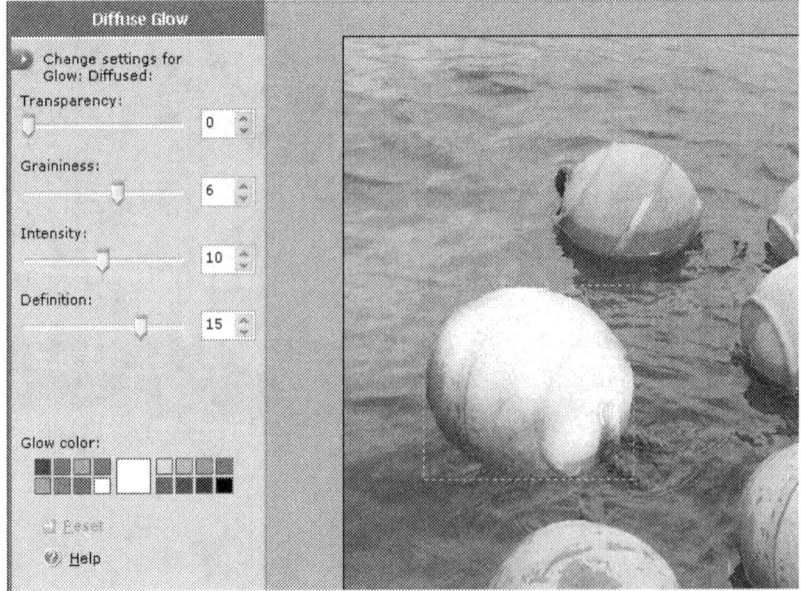

As you can see, the Diffuse Glow filter is applied immediately using the default values of the various parameters. However, you can set these values by using the sliders or associated fields. The parameters are:

■ **Transparency**   The Transparency slider sets the transparency of the filter. At low values, the glow is opaque and very visible, obliterating the details of the object "below" it. At higher values of the transparency, the glow is less pronounced, and you can see the object through the glow. Here is the same glow with a transparency of 70.

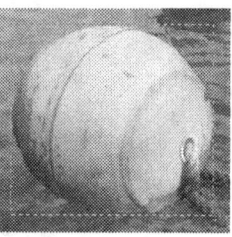

■ **Graininess**   The Graininess slider sets how smoothly the glow is blended with the unmodified portion of the object. The effects of increasing grain are only noticeable around the edges of the glow.

■ **Intensity**   The Intensity slider sets how much glow is present, and over how much of the object the glow is spread. For example, at this very high value of Intensity, the glow covers almost the entire shape.

■ **Definition**   The Definition slider sets the overall size of the glow. You'll need to experiment with different values of Intensity and Definition, as they affect each other—a given value of Definition covers more of the object at higher Intensity levels.

You also have control over the glow color. To choose it, pick one of the color squares near the bottom of the task bar.

# Work with Multiple Objects

Earlier in this chapter, you saw how you can select multiple objects and stretch, move, or rotate them. However, you can also align objects and group them.

## Move, Size, and Rotate Multiple Objects

You can select multiple objects at once, enabling you to move, size, or rotate all the selected objects at once. To select multiple objects in the workspace, click the first object, and then hold down the CTRL key and click the other objects you want to include.

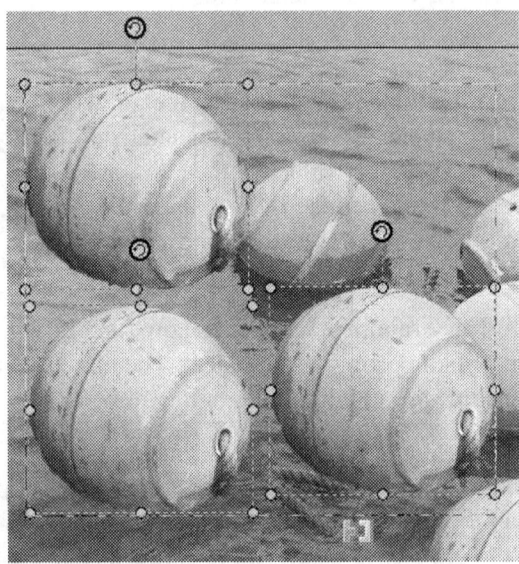

You can also perform this operation in the Stack—click the first layer, and then hold down CTRL and click another layer. Once you've selected multiple objects, you can click a sizing handle of any of the selected objects, and drag to resize the collection of objects. You can also click the rotation handle of any selected object and rotate all the objects in the group. To move the set of objects, click any object in the set and drag the entire set to its new location.

## Align Multiple Objects

To align multiple objects, start by selecting all the objects. One way to do that is to select the first object, and then hold down the CTRL key and click the other objects. Select Format | Align Multiple Objects. Make your alignment choice from the submenu:

- **Left**    Aligns the left edges of all the objects to the left-most object.
- **Right**    Aligns the right edges of all the objects to the right-most object.
- **Top**    Aligns the top edges of all the objects to the top-most object.
- **Bottom**    Aligns the bottom edges of all the objects to the bottom-most object.

- ■ **Center Horizontally**   Aligns the top-to-bottom centers of all the objects and locates them in the center between the left-most object and the right-most object.

- ■ **Center Vertically**   Aligns the left-to-right centers of all the objects and locates them in the center between the top-most object and the bottom-most object.

- ■ **Space Horizontally**   Spaces all the objects evenly from left to right. The boundaries of the area are determined by the left-most object and the right-most object.

- ■ **Space Vertically**   Spaces all the objects evenly from top to bottom. The boundaries of the area are determined by the top-most object and the bottom-most object.

## Group Multiple Objects

8

You can group multiple objects into a single group so you can work with them as a single object. Grouping objects places them on the same layer in the Stack. To group objects, select the objects you want to group and choose Edit | Group or click the Group icon that appears in the workspace when you select multiple objects.

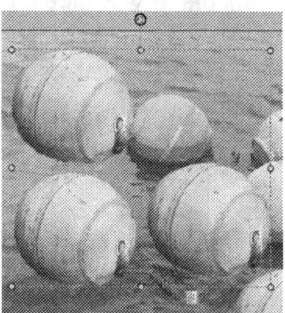

You can ungroup the objects by selecting the group and choosing Edit | Ungroup or clicking the Ungroup icon in the workspace.

## Flatten Object Layers

Objects Layers are very flexible, but you may find that you need to combine several layers into one, a process called "flattening." Object layers use a lot of resources (memory), so if you have a very complex image (with many layers), you may need to flatten the object layers you are done working with. Additionally, none of the image formats (except for Digital Image Pro's native format) support layers, so you'll need to flatten the layers before saving your file as (for example) a JPEG.

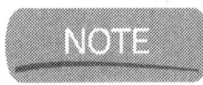

*If you don't flatten your layers prior to saving your file in a format that doesn't support layers, Digital Image Pro will automatically flatten them for you, after warning you first.*

To flatten specific objects, choose the objects and select Edit | Flatten Selected Objects. To flatten all the objects, select Edit | Flatten All Objects.

# Use Objects to Add Something That Wasn't There Before

Because you can create an object out of anything by copying and pasting, it can be fun to add objects and people to photographs that weren't there when the photograph was taken. For example, take a look at the photo in Figure 8-9. Notice that handsome fellow in the tuxedo in the back? That's me, the author. Just one problem—I wasn't born until about 25 years *after* this photo was taken. How do I know? See that cute little baby in the front? That is my *mother* in her grandmother's arms. Those are her parents (my grandparents) behind her, my great-grandfather on her right, and the other children are my maternal aunt and uncles. Clearly, I wasn't there when this photo was taken!

The first step in combining these two photographs was to take the original portrait of me and remove the background. I used the Edge Finder to cut myself out, inverted the selection, and selected Edit | Delete to discard the background, leaving a cutout of just me.

The next step was to make the sharp, color portrait look more like the aging print of my mother's family. To do so, I converted my image to black and white (Effects | Black and White). I then removed some of the sharp focus by selecting Touchup | Sharpen or Blur and chose –11 to blur the image slightly. I adjusted the brightness down to match the muted tones of the old photo (Touchup | Brightness and Contrast). Oh yes—I also resized the image to be the correct size as the portrait (Format | Resize Image). I could have resized the image once I had added it to the family portrait, but the resampling results (to shrink my picture) are better if you resize it before pasting it in.

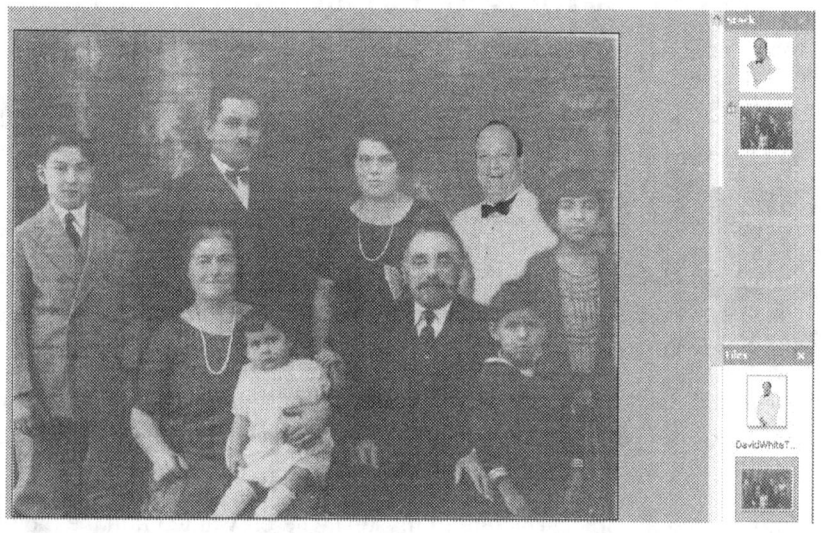

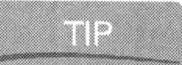 Combining four generations isn't hard when you have a scanner and a copy of Digital Image Pro!

**TIP** *Save your work each step of the way, just in case.*

Once this work was all done, I added myself to the old photo. There are actually two ways to do this—by using the Clone brush and by using the selection tools.

## Use the Clone Brush to Add an Object to a Photo

To use the Clone brush, I copied myself into the photo by opening the image of myself, selecting the portion that contained my picture, copying the selection, and pasting it into the old photo. I then placed the image off the canvas on the right side. I made sure the object (myself!) was selected, and chose the Clone brush (Touchup | Clone Brush). I then carefully painted myself into the picture at the right side of my grandmother. I enlarged the image to exercise extreme care at the point where my picture touched the existing people, such as my great-grandfather's and Aunt Claire's shoulders and my Uncle Lenny's head.

Once I was done with the Clone brush, I switched to the cropping tool (Format | Crop | Selected Object). The object that originally contained my picture had expanded to contain that original picture plus the portion I added with the Clone brush. Using the Crop tool, I cropped off the original picture, leaving just what I had created with the Clone brush. Done!

8

## Use the Selection Tools to Add an Object to a Photo

To use the selection tool to add myself to the photo, I used the following steps:

1. I created an object containing my picture in the old photo by opening the image of myself, selecting the portion that contained my picture, copying the selection, and pasting it into the old photo. Once this was done, I closed the image that contained my picture as I didn't need it anymore.

2. In the old photo, I selected the object (picture of myself), and copied and pasted it to create a duplicate. I needed the duplicate because I ended up throwing one of them away.

3. I selected the duplicate object and made it transparent by selecting Effects | Transparency | Even and setting the transparency level where I could clearly see through the object.

4. I positioned the object (picture of myself) where I wanted it in the old photo.

5. After making sure the old photo was the selected layer (and *not* the transparent picture of myself), I used the Freehand tool to trace around the outline of my partially transparent picture. At the point where I should be behind the other people, I traced along their heads and shoulders, creating a shape that would hold my image.

6. I selected Edit | Cut. This left a hole of exactly the right size in the old photograph.

7. I selected the partially transparent object and discarded it, as I was done with it.

8. I grabbed the original object that contained my picture and dragged it into position in the old photo.

9. Using the Stack, I placed the object *behind* the old photo—and my image then showed through. There were a couple of spots where the match between the hole and my image wasn't perfect, so I used the Clone brush to clean up the edges.

# Add and Configure Shapes

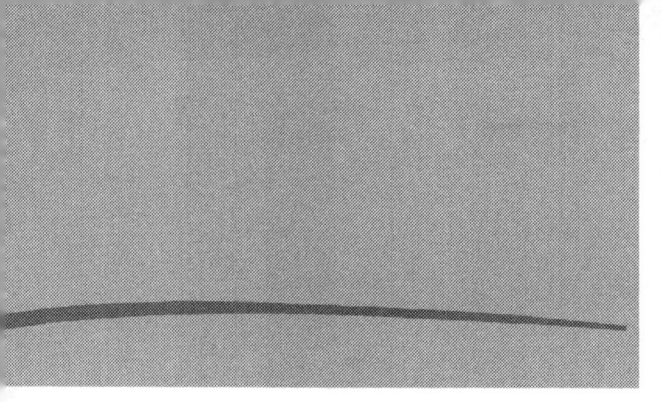

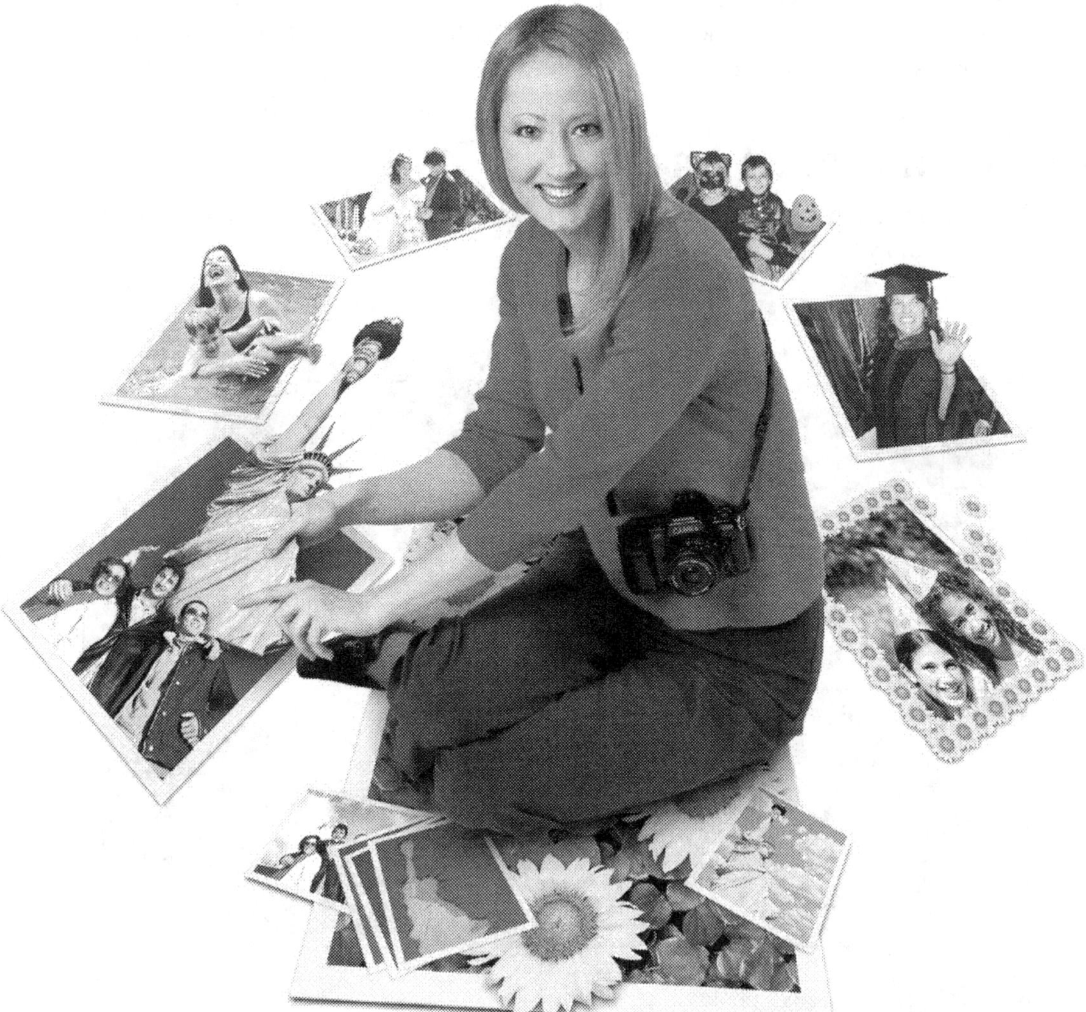

## How to...

- Add a shape to your image
- Move, size, and fill shapes with color
- Configure shapes

You can dress up a photo—especially a photo that is going to be used in a project such as a birthday card—by adding a variety of shapes to the image. Once you do, you can move and size the shapes, fill them with color or a picture, and duplicate the shapes. The result might look like Figure 9-1.

# Add a Shape to an Image

You can add simple shapes from the Insert menu, choose a shape from the Gallery, and even draw freehand shapes and lines.

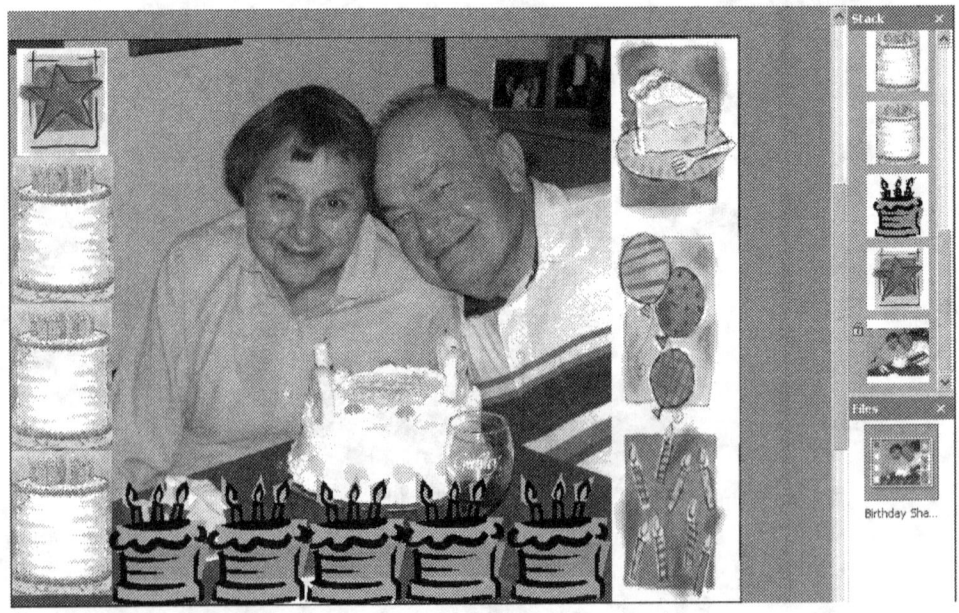

Here is a photo suitable for use as a birthday card. And it only took about 10 minutes to dress it up this way.

## Pick a Shape from the Menu

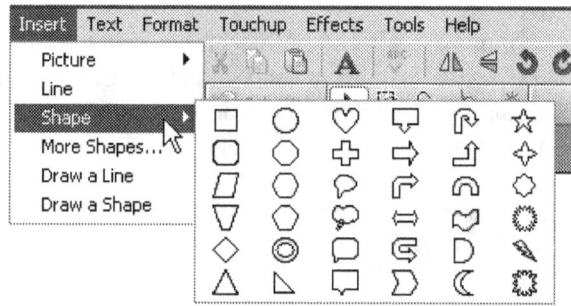

## Add a Shape from the Gallery

Digital Image Pro provides an entire gallery of shapes for you to use. To access
these shapes, select Insert | More Shapes. This opens the Gallery, with Shapes
selected in the Select a Collection scrolling list.

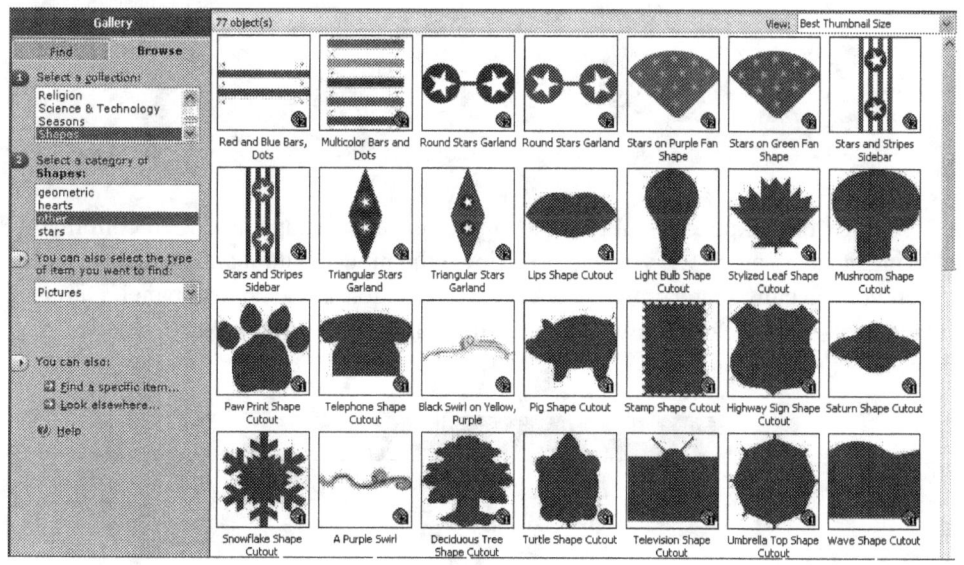

Pick a category of shape from the Select a Category scrolling list and click Open
to display the shape.

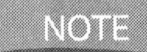 *If you didn't install the Gallery contents, Digital Image Pro prompts you for the CD-ROM that contains the shape.*

You can also click Find a Specific Item to open the Find tab of the Gallery. Using the Find tab, you can type in a search term and find all shapes that match the search criteria. However, note that Digital Image Pro returns *all* Gallery contents that match your search, not just shapes.

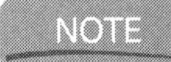 *Some options (discussed later in this chapter) do not work with shapes inserted from the Gallery.*

## Draw a Freehand Shape

You can also draw a shape freehand. To do so, Choose Insert | Draw a Shape. The mouse cursor turns into a crosshair, and a two-button control panel appears.

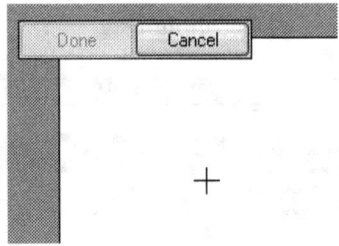

To draw the shape, click at the starting point for the shape, and then continue clicking at each vertex. Or, you can hold down the mouse button and draw the shape. When you have the shape drawn, click the Done button in the control panel. Digital Image Pro automatically draws a line from the last point you clicked to the starting point, closing the shape.

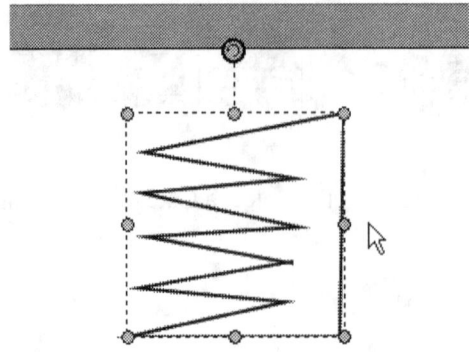

*As you move the mouse over to the Done button, it drags a line with it. But that line is removed when you click the Done button.*

The finished shape displays sizing handles and a rotation handle—moving, sizing, and rotating the shape works exactly the same as with objects (see Chapter 8).

## Add Lines to an Image

To add a simple line (a line with just one segment), select Insert | Line. To draw a line with multiple segments, select Insert | Draw a Line. As with drawing a shape, Digital Image Pro provides the two-button control panel. Draw the line just as you would a shape, clicking Done when you are finished.

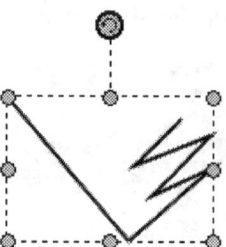

# Customize Your Shapes and Lines

Working with shapes (including drawn lines) is very much like working with objects, as described in Chapter 8. Each shape you insert is placed on its own layer. As a result, you can select a shape—either in the workspace or in the Stack—identically to objects.

## Customize an Inserted Line

You can move an inserted line by clicking and dragging the line anywhere except on the endpoints. To change the length and slope of the line, click and drag one of the endpoints.

You can also change the line thickness and line color. To change the line thickness, right-click the line and choose Change Shape or Line | Line Thickness from the shortcut menu (you can also select Format | Shape or Line | Line Thickness). Digital Image Pro opens the Line Thickness dialog box, where you can pick one of the available thicknesses, or use the *pt* field to specify the line thickness in points.

9

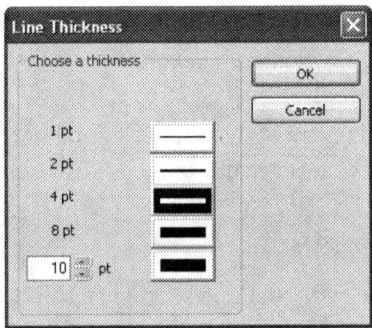

To change the line color, right-click the line and choose Change Shape or Line | Line Color from the shortcut menu (you can also select Format | Shape or Line | Line Color). Digital Image Pro opens the Change Color dialog box.

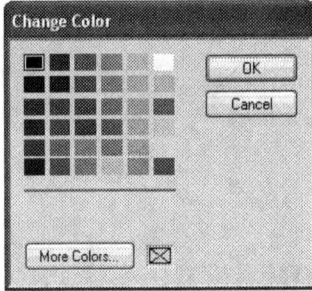

From here, you can pick one of the available colors, or click the More Colors button to open the More Line Colors dialog box.

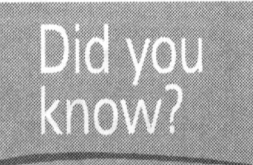

## A Good Point

"Points" is a way of measuring line thickness and font size (see Chapter 10). There are 72 points to an inch.

**9**

> **NOTE** *The More Line Colors dialog box is a standard Windows color picker. You pick the Hue and Saturation by clicking in the large, multicolored square on the right side of the dialog box; then pick the Luminance (brightness) by dragging the slider up and down the column at the extreme right edge of the dialog box. Alternatively, you can type in values for Hue, Saturation (Sat), and Luminance (Lum) or Red, Green, and Blue. To preserve the color you chose, click one of the squares under Custom Colors before you pick the color; then click the Add to Custom Colors button after you pick the color.*

## Customize a Drawn Shape or Line

Once you have built your shape, you can modify it in many ways, including moving, sizing, rotating, and filling it with a color, along with many of the same operations you can perform on objects (discussed in Chapter 8).

### Replace One Shape with Another

If you change your mind about a particular shape, you can delete it (select it and press the DELETE key) or replace it with another shape. To replace a shape, right-click the shape and select Change Shape or Line | Replace Shape from the shortcut menu (or choose Format | Shape or Line | Replace Shape). Digital Image Pro displays the list of shapes in a submenu; simply pick the shape you want to use.

## Change the Line Color and Thickness

To change the line thickness of the shape, right-click the shape and choose
Change Shape or Line | Line Thickness from the shortcut menu (you can also
select Format | Shape or Line | Line Thickness). Digital Image Pro opens the Line
Thickness dialog box, where you can pick one of the available thicknesses, or use
the *pt* field to specify the line thickness in points.

To change the line color of the shape, right-click the shape and choose
Change Shape or Line | Line Color from the shortcut menu (you can also
select Format | Shape or Line | Line Color). Digital Image Pro opens the Change
Color dialog box. Pick one of the available colors, or click the More Colors
button to open the More Line Colors dialog box.

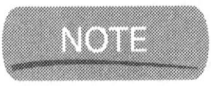 *These options work only for "simple" shapes—those you insert by selecting
Insert | Shape. They are not available for shapes you insert from the Gallery
(Insert | More Shapes).*

## Change the Fill Color

To change the fill color of a shape, right-click the shape and choose Change Shape
or Line | Fill Color from the shortcut menu (you can also select Format | Shape or
Line | Fill Color). Digital Image Pro opens the Change Color dialog box.

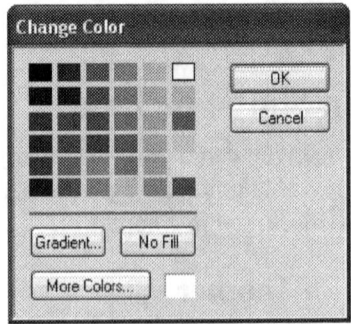

To choose one of the displayed colors, click the color and then click OK. You can
also click the More Colors button to open the More Shape Colors dialog box, which
is identical (except for the title) to the More Line Colors dialog box. Here, you can
specify the exact color you want, and store it in the Custom Colors if you wish.

To fill the shape with a gradient, click the Gradient button in the Change
Color dialog box. This opens the Fill With Gradient task bar, discussed in
Chapter 8. Pick the color pattern and gradient style, and then click Done to
finish. Of course, you can also click Custom Two-Color Gradient to create
a custom gradient to fill your shape.

**NOTE** *These options work only for "simple" shapes—those you insert by selecting Insert | Shape. They are not available for shapes you insert from the Gallery (Insert | More Shapes).*

## Fill a Shape With a Texture or Color

You can fill a shape with a color, gradient, or picture. To start, select Effects | Fill With Texture or Color to open the Fill With Texture or Color task bar. Filling the shape with a solid color or gradient works just as with objects—pick the color or click Color gradient to pick a color pattern and gradient style.

From the Fill With Texture or Color task bar, you can fill a shape with a picture. You could do this with objects, too, but it makes more sense to perform this action with shapes. To fill a shape with a picture, select the Picture button. This opens a new version of the task bar.

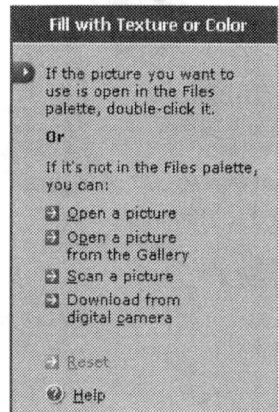

If the picture you want to use is already open in the Files area, double-click the picture. If not, use one of the selections in the task bar to access your picture. Here, I used one of the simple pictures in the gallery to fill a shape. The shape is not visible because the inserted picture is hiding it.

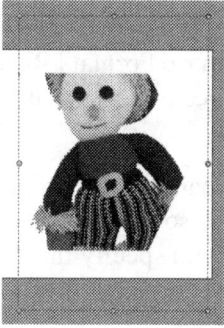

By default, Digital Image Pro scales the picture to fit the shape, cutting off any sections of the picture that fall outside the shape boundaries. However, you can adjust this. The picture is inserted with a set of sizing handles, which you can use to change the size of the picture. Again, if you make the picture larger, more of it will be cut off by the shape boundaries. You can also click and drag inside the sizing rectangle to move the picture relative to the shape. Here, I have made the picture smaller so that it will fit in the shape:

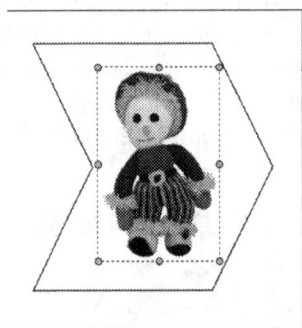

The picture background is also a solid color (usually white), which hides any fill color you may have assigned to the shape.

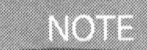 *Clicking Done to insert the picture flattens the shape, so you can no longer modify the line thickness/color, or the fill color with the shape commands.*

## Work With Shapes as Objects

The other things that you can do with shapes are, in most ways, identical to working with objects, covered in Chapter 8. Here is a summary:

- **Move the shape**   To move a shape, click and drag the shape to its new location. You can also choose Format | Center Object on Canvas (to do just that).

- **Size the shape**   You can size a shape by clicking and dragging the sizing handles. You can also choose Format | Resize Object to Fit Canvas, and then choose one of the three options for the resize: Crop to Fit, Scale to Fit, and Stretch to Fit.

- **Rotate the shape**   You can rotate a shape by clicking and dragging the rotation handle. You can also select Format | Rotate | Selected Object to open the Rotate task bar and specify the rotation direction or number of degrees of rotation.

■ **Crop the shape**   To crop a shape, select Format | Crop | Selected Object to open the Crop task bar and specify the size and shape of the cropped section. Cropping flattens the shape; that is, after cropping the shape, you will no longer be able to replace the shape, or change the fill color, line color, or line thickness.

■ **Flip the shape**   To flip a shape, select Format | Flip | Selected Object to open the Flip task bar and specify whether to flip the shape horizontally, vertically, or both.

■ **Change the shape stacking order**   You can change the stacking order of shapes by clicking and dragging them in the Stack, or selecting Format | Move Forward or Backward, and then selecting one of the four options: Bring to Front, Send to Back, Bring Forward, or Send Backward. When you have both objects (see Chapter 8) and shapes in your image, both types of items show up in the Stack. You can interweave objects and shapes by adjusting the stacking order.

■ **Change the shape transparency**   To change the shape transparency, select Effects | Transparency, and pick one of the three options: Even, Gradual, or Transparency Brush. Adjusting the transparency of a shape flattens the shape.

■ **Add a shadow**   To add a shadow to a shape, select Effects | Shadow. This opens the Shadow task bar, where you can add and customize a shadow. Applying a shadow flattens the shape.

■ **Skew the shape**   To skew a shape, select Effects | Skew Object. This opens the Skew task bar so you can skew the shape.

■ **Emphasize the shape**   To emphasize a particular shape, select Effects | Emphasize to open the Emphasize task bar to choose an effect. Other (unflattened) shapes are not affected by Emphasize; the effect is applied to only the background and any flattened shapes.

■ **Distort the shape**   To distort a shape, select Effects | Distort to open the Distortion task bar and apply a distortion (such as *Wave 1*) to the shape. Applying a distortion flattens the shape.

■ **Add a diffuse glow to a shape**   To add a Diffuse Glow to a shape, select Effects | Diffuse Glow to open the task bar and apply the effect. Adding a Diffuse Glow flattens the shape.

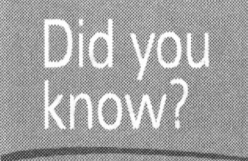

## Change Your Shape

There are many more menu options you can apply to a shape. Although it doesn't often make sense to do so, you can apply any of the options from the Touchup menu and other options from the Effects menu (such as Antique, Black and White, and Negative) to a shape.

# Use Shapes With Photos

You can dress up photographs with shapes, although you don't want to overdo it! The next few sections show some examples of what you can do.

## Dress Up an Image with Thought Bubbles

The most obvious way to dress up photos is to add "thought bubbles," as I did in Figure 9-2. To achieve this effect, follow these steps:

1. Select Insert | Shape and pick the Thought Bubble shape from the submenu.

2. Because I want the thought bubble on the left, I need to flip it horizontally. Select Format | Flip | Selected Object, choose Horizontally in the Flip task bar, and click Done.

3. Click and drag the thought bubble to the correct position, and size it if you wish.

4. I then use the text tool to add my thoughts to the image. This tool is discussed in Chapter 10. Select Text | Insert Text. Notice that inserting the text creates a new layer for it in the Stack.

5. In the resulting text box, type your thoughts.

6. Change the size of the font (it starts out pretty big) and use the sizing rectangle for the text to get the text to fit the thought bubble. You'll probably have to resize the thought bubble as well. If necessary, position the mouse cursor near the edge of the rectangle and drag the text to line up with the thought bubble.

7. If you wish, select both the thought bubble and the text and group them together (select Edit | Group) to make moving them easier.

TIP *Grouping shapes and text not only makes moving them easier, it also makes sizing them easier. Clicking and dragging the sizing handles of the group not only changes the size of the shape, but automatically scales the text font size to match.*

## Build a Custom Sign

As you can tell from Figure 9-2, I was leaning on a sign that indicated I wasn't allowed to go off the trail and into the trees behind me. Of course, this sign didn't work too well for the German tourists we encountered on this trail, who didn't speak English! That gave me the idea to transform the sign into something a little more "international," which resulted in the image you see in Figure 9-3. Here is how I did it:

1. The first step was to cover up the existing sign. I selected Insert | Shape and chose the rectangle, and then dragged it to cover up the sign. I scaled the shape to the size of the sign, and rotated it slightly because the original sign was a little crooked.

9

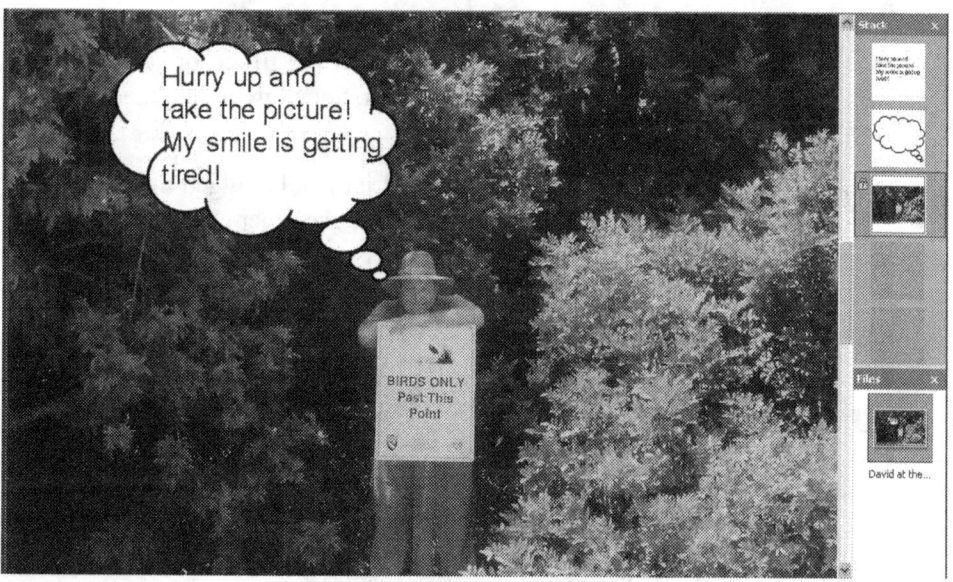

Combine an image, a custom shape, and some text to add personality to a picture.

2. I removed the dark black outline by right-clicking the rectangle and choosing Change Shape or Line | Line Thickness from the shortcut menu. In the Outline Thickness dialog box, I selected None and clicked OK.

3. Because a small portion of the original sign is visible near the top (where my hand is), I needed to change the rectangle color to match. To do so, I selected Effects | Fill With Texture or Color. In the Fill With Texture or Color task bar, I clicked More Solid Color Choices. I then moved the mouse cursor over the picture, where it turned into an eye dropper. I clicked the original sign to pick up the color, and then clicked Done to finish filling the rectangle and return to the image.

4. Because Digital Image Pro doesn't provide the international "not" symbol (circle with a line through it), I had to build one. Here is what I did:

   a. I inserted a circle and set the line color of the circle to a medium gray by right-clicking the circle shape, choosing Change Shape or Line | Line Color, and selecting the color from the Change Color dialog box.

   b. I filled the circle with the same medium gray color by selecting Change Shape or Line | Fill Color from the shortcut menu, and selecting the color from the Change Color dialog box.

   c. I created a second circle and made it slightly smaller than the first one, set its line color to medium gray, but left the fill color set to white. I dragged the second circle inside the first one, giving me the outline of the symbol.

   d. I added a line to the diagram (Insert | Line) and dragged the endpoints of the line until they crossed the inside of the inner circle.

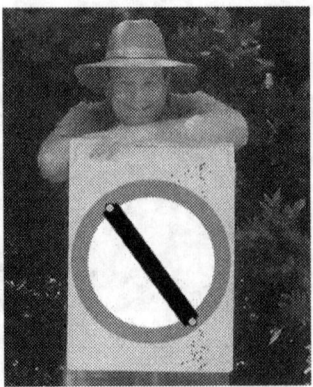

**e.** I set the thickness of the line by selecting Change Shape or Line | Line Color from the shortcut menu, and setting the thickness in the Line Thickness dialog box.

**f.** I set the color of the line to the same medium gray as the circles by selecting Change Shape or Line | Line Color, and choosing the color from the Change Color dialog box.

**g.** I selected the entire set of shapes by clicking and dragging a rectangle around them, and then grouped them by clicking the group icon that appeared below the collection of shapes.

**h.** I adjusted the grouped set of shapes so they fit correctly over the sign rectangle, and scaled them (by dragging the sizing handles) to fit the sign.

**i.** Finally, I made the symbol partially transparent so that the symbols we are going to add next would be visible through the "not" symbol. To do so, I selected Effects | Transparency | Even, dragged the slider to 45, and clicked Done. This flattened the shapes into one shape, but that is okay.

**5.** Digital Image Pro didn't provide a good symbol I could use for the new sign, so I opened another application, and copied and pasted a symbol available there into the image.

**6.** Because the hiker symbol was now on top of the "not" symbol, I rearranged the layers by dragging them in the Stack to place the "not" symbol on top. Because I made it partially transparent, you can see the hiker through it. And that is it!

## Use Gallery Shapes to Build Frames

The Gallery contains a set of shapes designed specifically to be used as frames for images, and this makes it very easy to quickly add a frame. To do so, use the following steps:

**1.** Create an empty image big enough to leave some white space around the edges of the image you want to frame.

**2.** Select Insert | More Shapes to open the Gallery. In the Select a Collection scrolling list, choose Borders and Frames, and then select a category from the second scrolling list. The *Designs and Patterns* category is especially good, containing 150 different items.

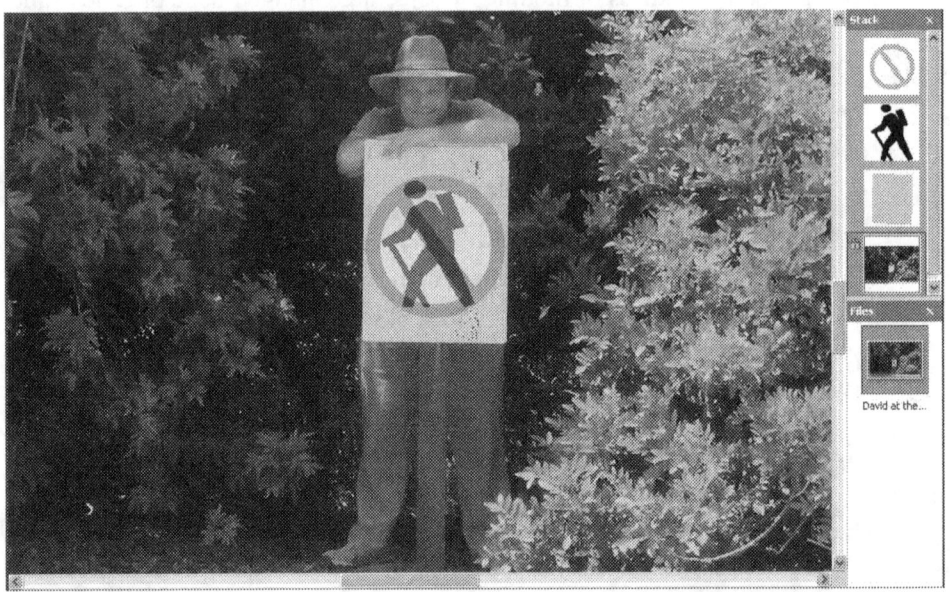

"Don't go off the trail"—understandable in any language.

3. Pick the frame you want to use and click Open to insert that frame into the image as a separate layer.

4. Open the image you want to frame.

5. Select either the entire image or just a portion of it, and copy it to the Clipboard (Edit | Copy).

6. Switch back to the image with the frame and paste the picture into the frame.

7. Drag the pasted image to position it over the frame and use the sizing handles to match the frame size with the image size. You may also have to adjust the size of the canvas. An example of the result is shown in Figure 9-4.

NOTE    *Don't use File | Get Pictures From | Gallery to grab a frame. This creates a separate image with just the frame, which is not what you want.*

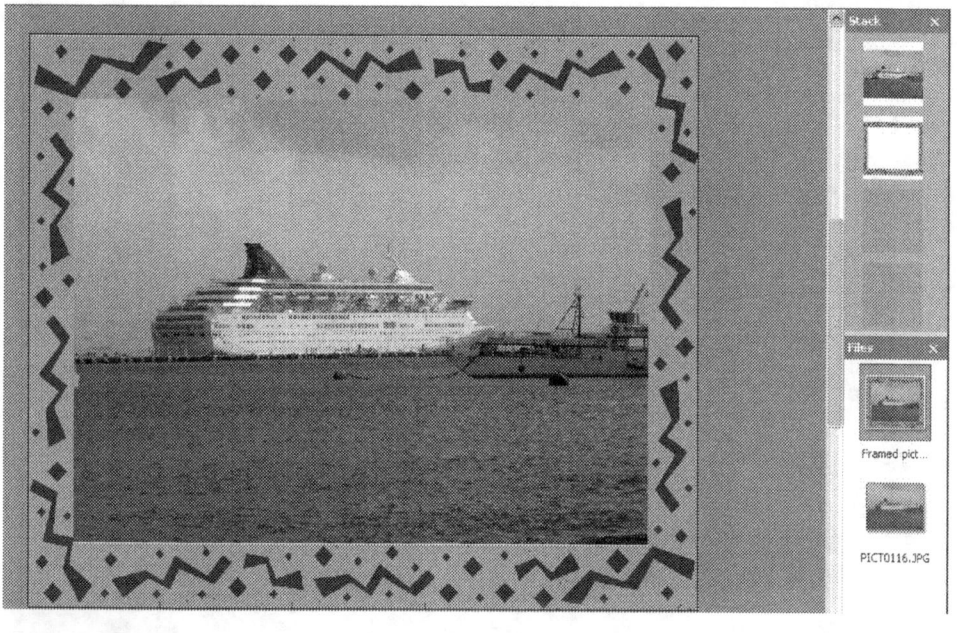

Quickly add a frame from the Gallery Borders and Frames to dress up a photo.

9

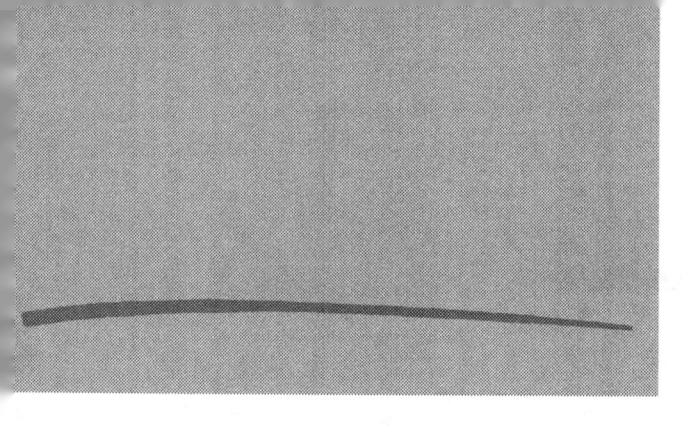

# Use Filters, Text, and Edges to Go Beyond the Darkroom

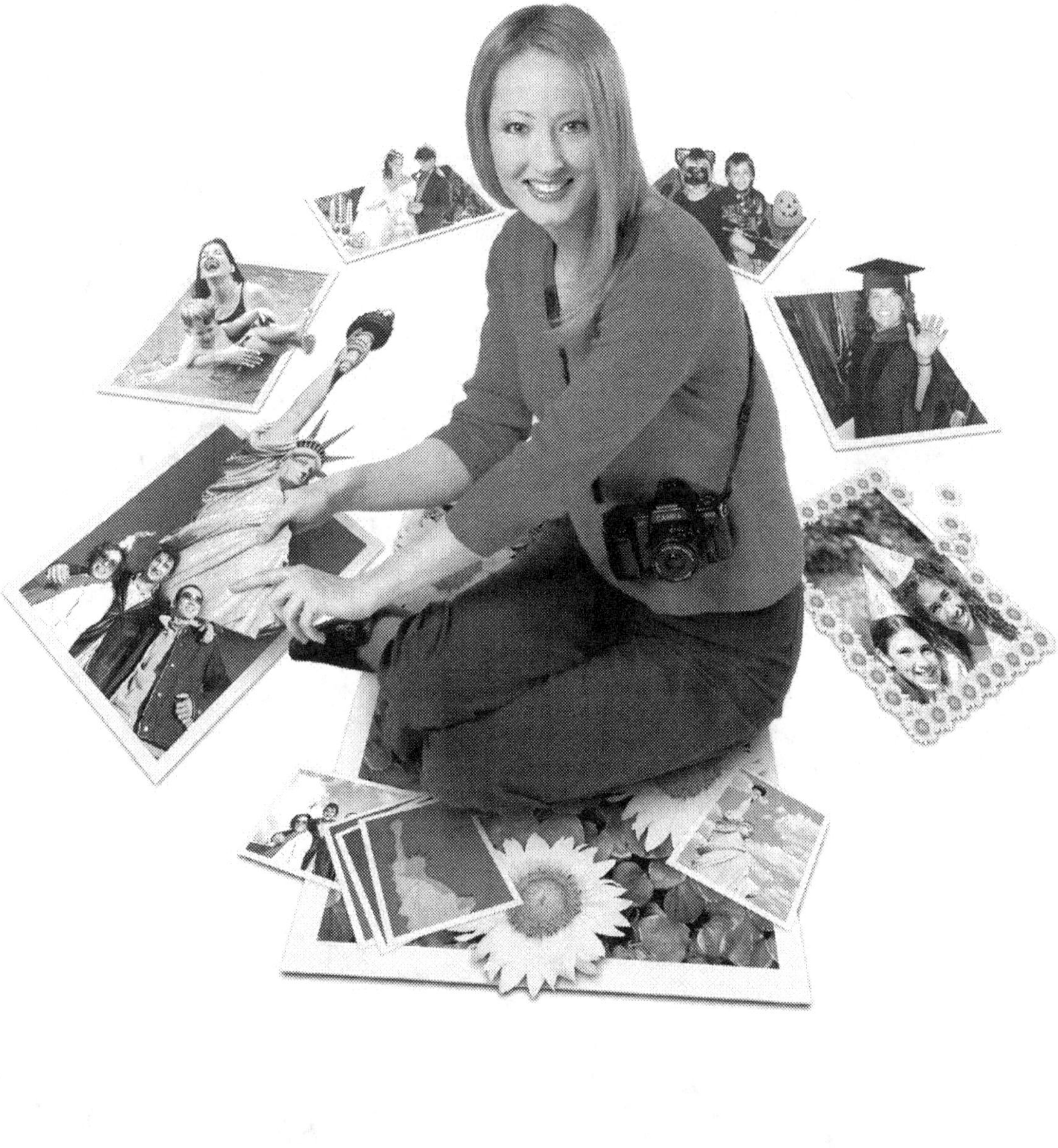

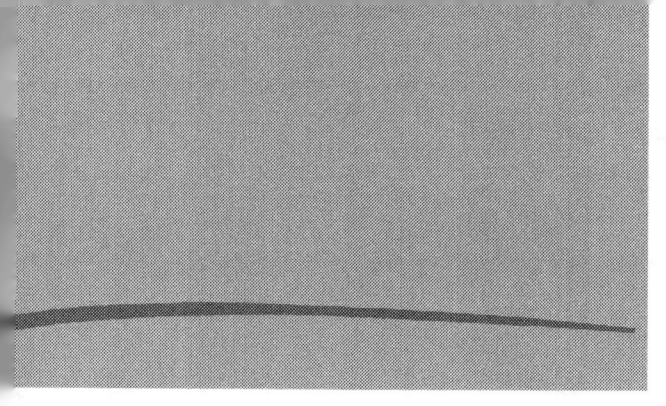

# Add Text to
# Your Image

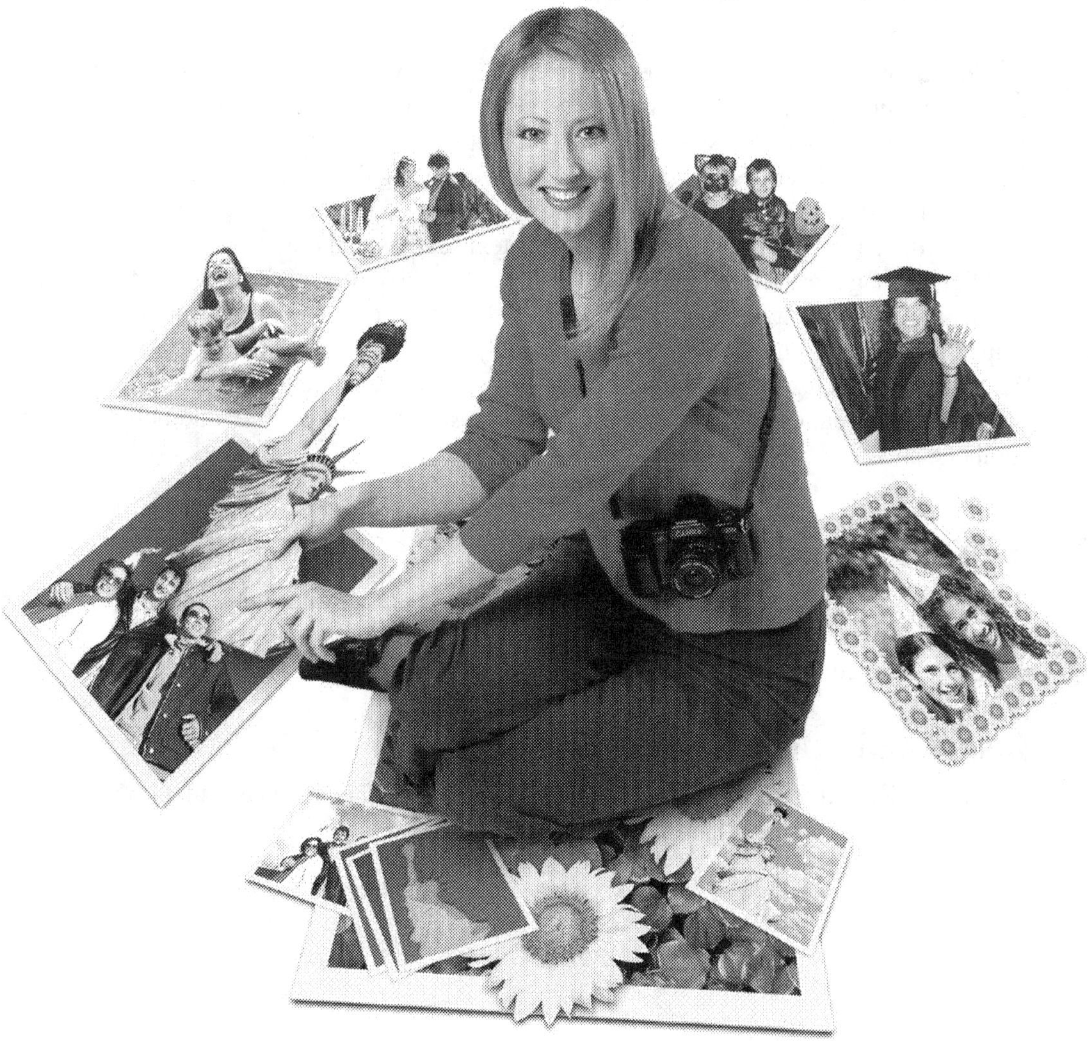

## How to...

- Add standard text to an image
- Add shaped text to an image
- Adjust the font, color, and size of your text
- Add a drop cap and wrap text around objects
- Add shadows, outlines, and fill color to text

Adding text to an image can be very useful. Not only can you label an image to point out important parts, but you can also add titles. How often have you put together a photo album and wished you had a picture to put on the cover that stated the subject of the album? Now you can add titles, choosing the font, size, style, and color of the text. You can also apply fill colors, outlines, shadows, and even gradient fills and filters (see Chapter 12) to make your text really stand out.

Digital Image Pro provides two kinds of text: "regular" text and shaped text. These two kinds of text actually behave quite differently. For example, you can warp shaped text into various shapes (hence the name) and apply outlines and shadows. But all the shaped text must be the same color—whereas each letter in regular text can have a different color if you wish. And unlike shaped text, you can add bullets, numbers, and drop caps to regular text.

# Work with Regular Text

Regular text works much like any word processor you are familiar with—you type and edit the text right in a text box in the image. Like adding a shape or an object, the text is inserted into the image in its own layer, and shows up as such in the Stack.

## Insert and Edit Regular Text

To add regular text to an image, select Text | Insert Text. This displays a text box with the words "Your Text Here."

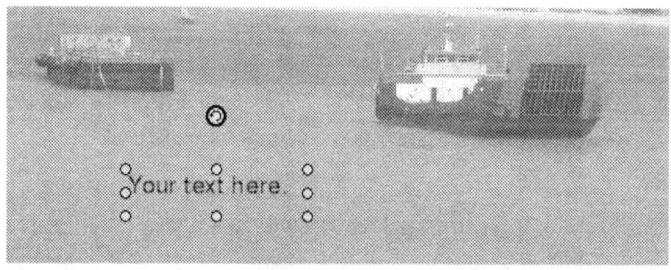

Just as you would with a word processor, click and drag in the text box to select the existing text, then type your text. To begin a new line, press ENTER.

When you select Text | Insert Text, the toolbar changes to display the options available for creating and editing the text, as shown in Figure 10-1.

NOTE    *If you wish, you can set the options prior to creating the text box. If you do, the default text will be in the font, size, and color you selected.*

You can move the insertion point around as you would with a word processor. Use the Left Arrow and the Right Arrow to move the insertion point back and forth in the current line of text, and use the Up Arrow and the Down Arrow keys to move the insertion point to other lines of text. Pressing the BACKSPACE key erases the previous character, and pressing the DELETE key deletes the current character.

To make changes to your text, you must select the portion of the text you want to modify. Digital Image Pro lets you know which text is selected by highlighting the text.

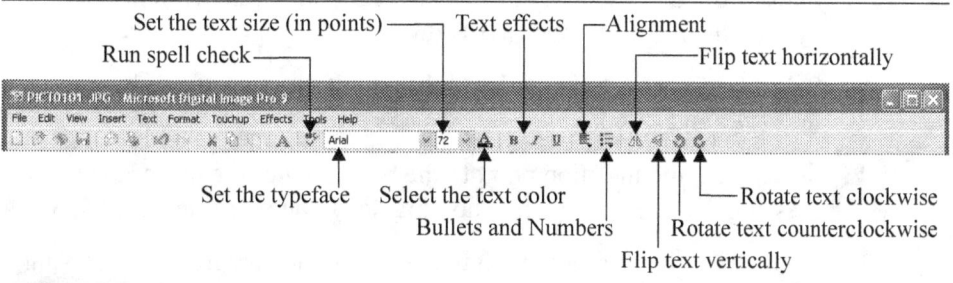

Use the tools in the toolbar to set the text properties.

You can select text using either the mouse or the arrow keys:

- **Select with the text cursor (mouse)**    To select a portion of the text in the text box, click inside the text box and drag to highlight the text you want. In addition, you can:

  - Double-click a word to select the whole word.

  - Click to set the insertion point at the beginning of the selection, and then SHIFT-CLICK at the ending point to select everything between the two points.

- **Select using the arrow keys**    Once you click in the text box, you can select text using the arrow and SHIFT keys, just as you would with a word processor. Simply hold down the SHIFT key and press the arrow key to move the insertion point in the direction you want, selecting text as it moves. For example, to select the three characters to the left of the insertion point, hold down the SHIFT key and press the LEFT ARROW three times. You can also make a quick selection by doing the following:

  - Select from the insertion point to the beginning of the current word by pressing the LEFT ARROW key while holding down the SHIFT and CTRL keys.

  - Select from the insertion point to the end of the current word by pressing the RIGHT ARROW key while holding down the SHIFT and CTRL keys.

  - Select from the insertion point to the beginning of the current line by pressing the SHIFT and HOME keys.

  - Select from the insertion point to the end of the current line by pressing the SHIFT and END keys.

  - Select from the insertion point to the beginning of the paragraph by pressing the UP ARROW while holding down the SHIFT and CTRL keys.

  - Select from the insertion point to the end of the paragraph by pressing the DOWN ARROW while holding down the SHIFT and CTRL keys.

## Spell Check Your Text

Nothing says "amateur" like misspelled text! Digital Image Pro makes it easy to spellcheck the text in a text box. Simply select Text | Spelling or click the Spelling icon in the toolbar. If the spell checker finds an unfamiliar word in any text box in the image, it displays the Check Spelling dialog box, with the word it doesn't recognize in the Not in Dictionary field.

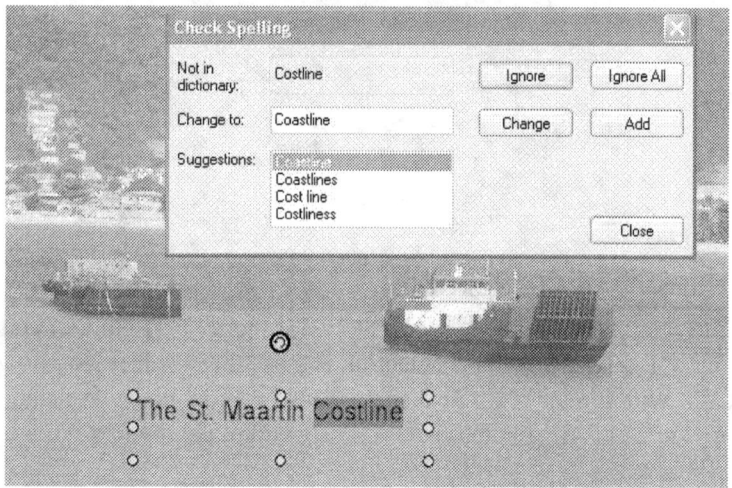

To accept the replacement in the Change to field (if any), click the Change button. To use one of the options in the Suggestions field, click the word you want and then click the Change button. You can also:

■ **Ignore**   Clicking the Ignore button ignores just this instance of the word. If the same word appears again, the spell checker will display it as an error again.

■ **Ignore All**   Clicking the Ignore All button ignores this word everywhere it appears.

■ **Add**   Add the word to the dictionary so it will not be flagged as a misspelling in the future.

## Modify the Text Box

As with objects and shapes, a text box has sizing handles and a rotation handle so you can scale and rotate the text box. Rotating the text box also rotates the contents, as shown here:

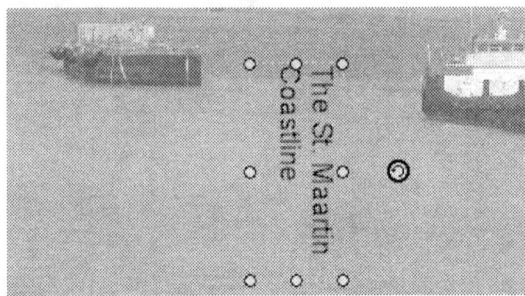

### Change the Size of the Text Box

Changing the size of the text box does not change the font size unless you select Text | Stretch to Fit Text Box. This selection is a toggle so select it again to turn this feature off. With Stretch to Fit Text Box enabled, Digital Image Pro automatically scales the text to fit inside the text box, whether you make the text box bigger or smaller.

### Move the Text Box

Moving the text box is a bit tricky because when you click inside the text box to try and drag it (as you would a shape or object), all you get is the text cursor. Instead, move the mouse cursor to the inside edge of the text box, where it turns into a four-headed arrow. Once it does, you can hold down the left mouse button and drag the text box (and its contents) to a new location.

### Delete a Text Box

Deleting a text box is also a little tricky, because if you click in the text box and press the DELETE key, Digital Image Pro simply deletes the character to the right of the insertion point. Instead, click in the text box and select Delete from either the Edit menu or the shortcut menu. This removes the text box.

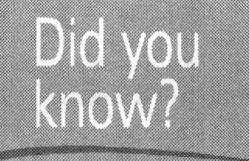

## You Can Manipulate Text Boxes

Except for this idiosyncrasy with moving, text boxes behave like objects and shapes in most other ways. For example, you can change the stacking order of text boxes either on the canvas or from the Stack, group text boxes with each other or with objects and shapes, center a text box on the canvas, crop or flip it (choose the *Selected Object* option), skew it, and resize a text box to fit the canvas. And, as with objects and shapes, you can apply any of the options under the Touchup and Effects menus.

## Modify the Text Properties

Digital Image Pro enables you to change all the text properties after you type the text. You can use the options in the Text menu or click the icons in the text toolbar. Some of the property changes (such as font, size, and color) apply just to the selected text, while others (such as text effects) apply to the entire text box. And still others (such as alignment and indent) apply just to the current paragraph (the paragraph where the insertion point is located).

10

*If you want to quickly select all the text in a text box prior to modifying a text property, select Edit | Select All.*

### Change the Font and Style

To change the typeface (font) of the text, select the text you want to change and click the down arrow alongside the Font drop-down list in the toolbar. This displays a list of typefaces available on your machine. Pick the typeface you want from the list.

You can set the style of the text to Bold, Italic, or Underline by clicking the icon for that effect in the toolbar.

### Change the Text Size

To change the size of the text, click the down arrow alongside the Font Size drop-down list and pick the size you want from the list.

## Change the Text Color

One very good way to dress up your text is to change its color. Try choosing a color that contrasts with the image. You can select each word or letter and give it a separate color if you wish. To change the text color, click the Font Color icon in the toolbar to display a drop-down list of colors.

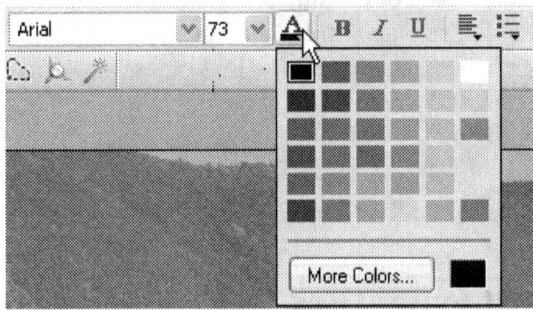

Click the More Colors button to open the standard Windows color dialog box (labeled More Text Font Colors) in which you can pick any color, specify a color in Hue, Sat, and Lum, or specify a color in Red, Green, and Blue.

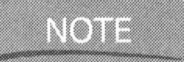 *You can apply a color or a color gradient to regular text as well. Click the text box, select Effects | Fill with Color or Texture, and use the taskbar to add a color or color gradient. The color or color gradient is applied to all the text in the text box, even if you select only part of the text first. In addition, applying a color or gradient this way flattens the text object.*

## Change the Text Alignment

You can change the alignment of the text by clicking the Alignment icon in the toolbar.

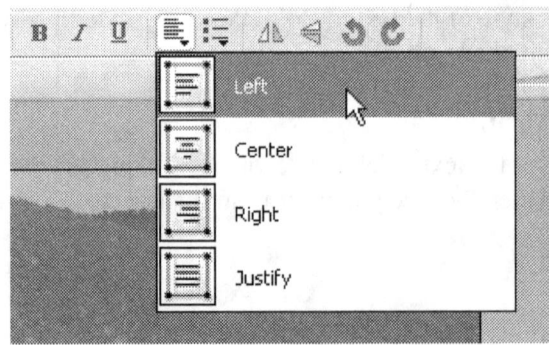

Alignment choices include:

- **Left**   Aligns the text to the left side of the text box. As you type, the text extends to the right and wraps when it reaches the right side.

- **Right**   Aligns the text to the right side of the text box.

- **Center**   Centers the text in the text box.

- **Justify**   Stretches the text evenly across the width of the text box. This effect is only visible on full lines of text; partial lines are aligned left.

You can also choose Text | Alignment and choose the alignment you want from the submenu.

## Add Numbers or Bullets

Numbers and bullets are great for constructing lists. For example, you might want to list the names of the people in a portrait. To add bullets or numbers to a text list, select the text and click the Bullets and Numbers icon in the toolbar. Choose Bullets, Numbers, or None (to remove the bullets or numbers). You can also select Text | Bullets and Numbering, and then choose the option you want from the submenu. Here is a sample of an image with bulleted text:

10

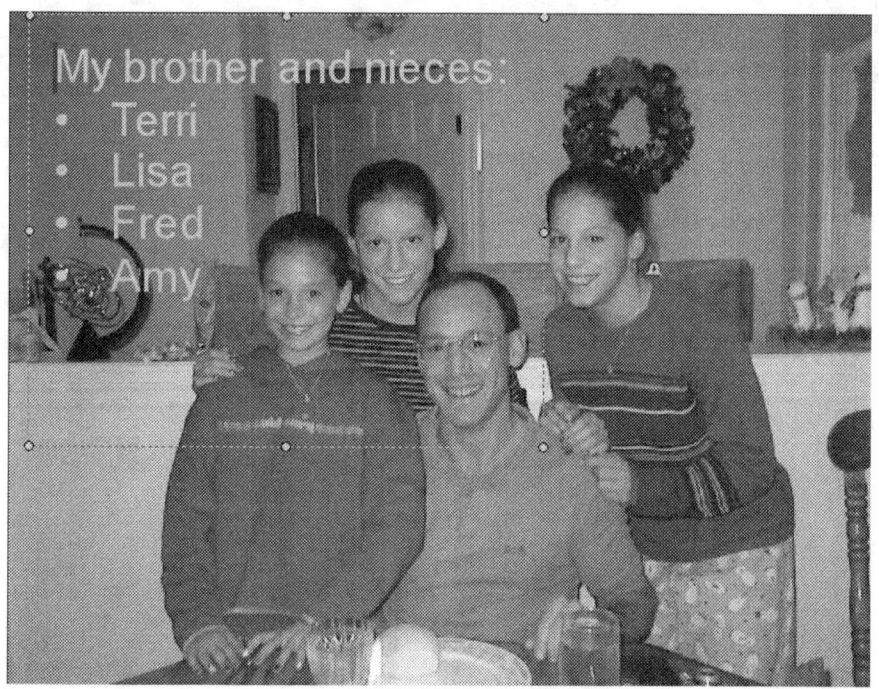

## Change the Line Spacing and Indents

You can choose the spacing between lines by selecting Text | Line Spacing to open the Line Spacing dialog box.

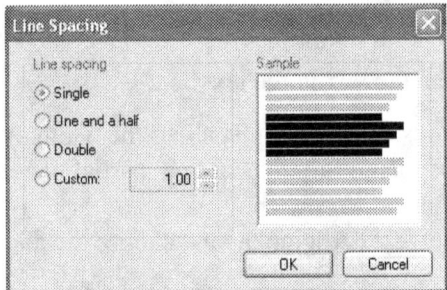

You can choose one of the standard options (Single, One and a Half, or Double spacing) or set a custom spacing by clicking the Custom option and using the field to set the spacing, including using a value less than one, which causes the lines of text to overlap each other.

You can also adjust the amount of indent for each paragraph by selecting Text | Increase Indent or Text | Decrease Indent.

## Flipping and Rotating Your Text

You can flip your text either horizontally or vertically using the icons in the toolbar. The effects are kind of interesting. For example, here I've flipped the contents of the text box horizontally.

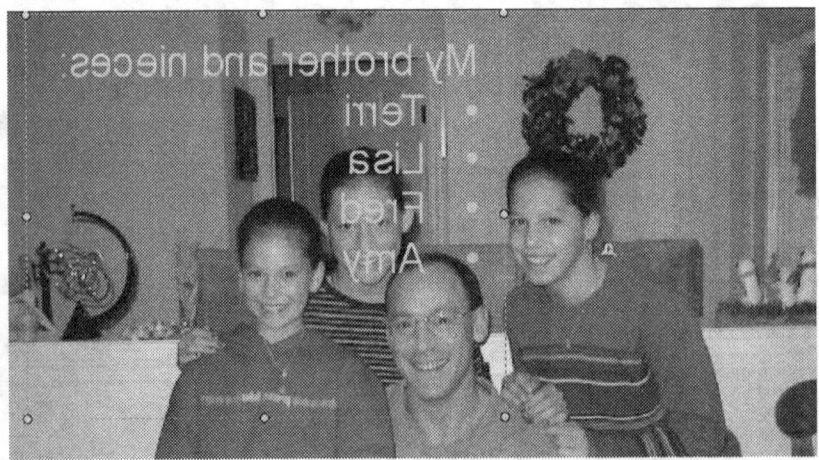

## Did you know?

## Size Matters

The size of the text you see on the screen depends entirely on the image resolution. For example, if you select an image at 72 dots per inch (dpi) and choose a font size of 72 points, you'll see uppercase letters that are approximately 1 inch tall (viewed at 100 percent magnification). However, if the resolution is 300 dpi, the text will appear to be about 4 inches tall! Appearances are deceiving, however. The letter is still only an inch tall when compared against the dimensions of the image. To prove this, turn on the rulers. You'll see that the letter is only an inch tall when compared against the ruler dimensions.

Flipping the text vertically is somewhat more useful. Here, I've used this effect and softened the text using Gaussian Blur to show the text as a "reflection" in the water.

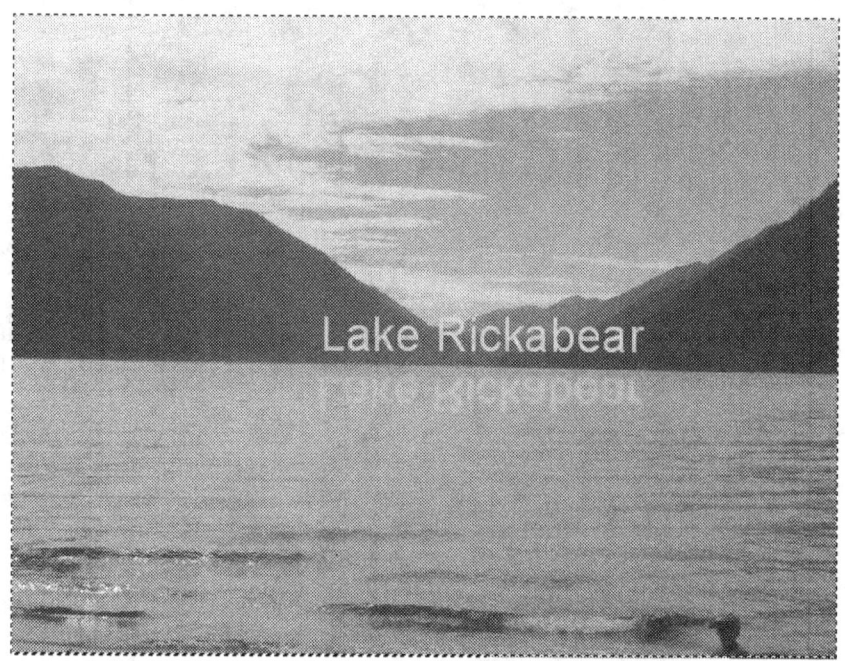

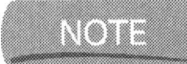 *You can skew the text by selecting Effects | Skew Object and working with the text box just like any other object. Skewing the text box does not flatten it.*

## Use the Font Dialog Box to Modify the Text Properties

Many of the font controls are scattered between the toolbar and the menu. If you'd like to set most of the attributes of your text (including some that are not available elsewhere) from one dialog box, select Text | Font or choose Font from the text shortcut menu to open the Font dialog box:

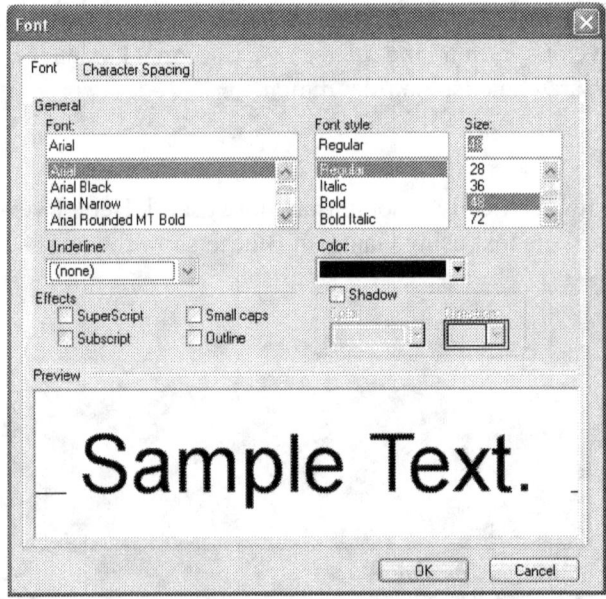

There are two tabs in the Font dialog box. From the Font tab, you can set the following:

- **Font**    Set the typeface you want from the Font scrolling list.

- **Font Style**    Choose the style, such as Regular, Italic, Bold, or Bold Italic from the Font Style scrolling list.

- **Size**    Select the text size from the scrolling list.

- **Underline**    You can pick from a large variety of underline styles from the Underline drop-down list.

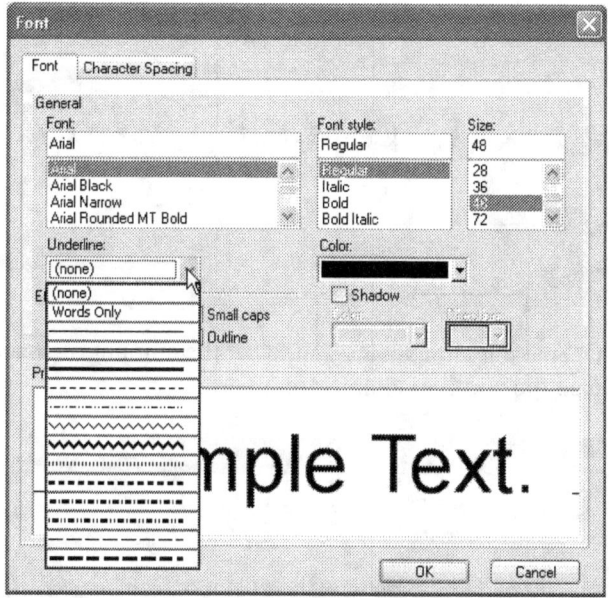

- **Effects**   Select the checkboxes in the Effects section to turn your text into super- or subscript, small caps, or outline text. Outline text "hollows out" the text, leaving just an outline:

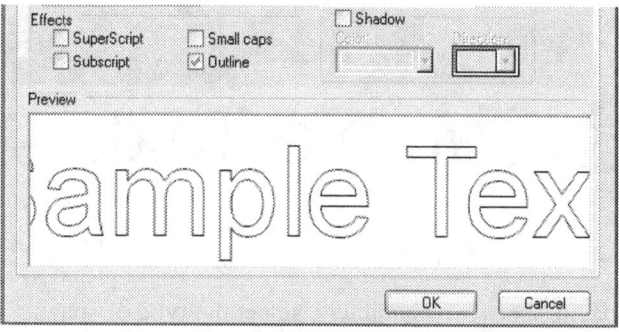

- **Color**   Set the font color from the Color drop-down list.

- **Add a shadow**   Select the Shadow checkbox and choose a color from the Color drop-down list in the Shadow section of the dialog box. You can also pick a direction from the Direction drop-down list. The shadow is applied to each individual letter, and provides a really excellent three-dimensional effect.

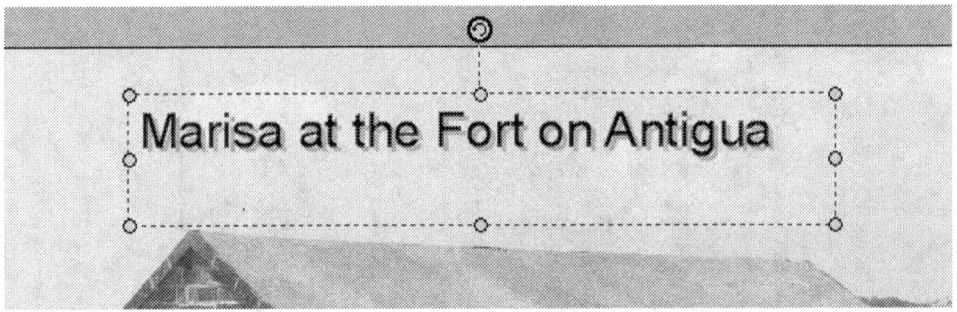

The Character Spacing tab enables you to set the amount of space between characters and scale the width of characters.

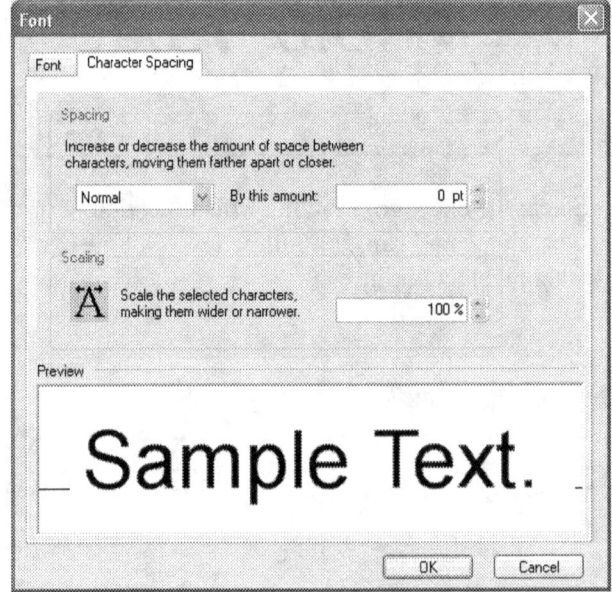

To set the spacing between characters, select the type of spacing adjustment you want to make from the drop-down list:

■ **Expand**    Increasing the value in the By This Amount field increases the spacing between the letters.

■ **Condense**    Increasing the value in the By This Amount field decreases the spacing between the letters. However, you can't decrease the spacing past the point where the letters touch—you can't adjust the spacing so that the letters overlap.

■ **Normal**   Removes the spacing adjustment and returns the spacing to normal.

To set the scaling (width of the characters), use the field in the Scaling section of the dialog box. Here is a sample of text scaled to 150 percent:

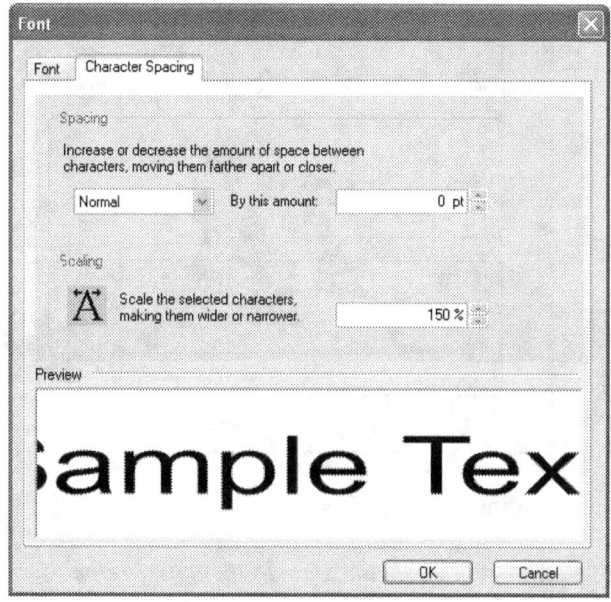

10

## Add a Drop Cap

When the first letter in a paragraph is made large, and the other text in the paragraph wraps around that large letter, it is called a *drop cap*.

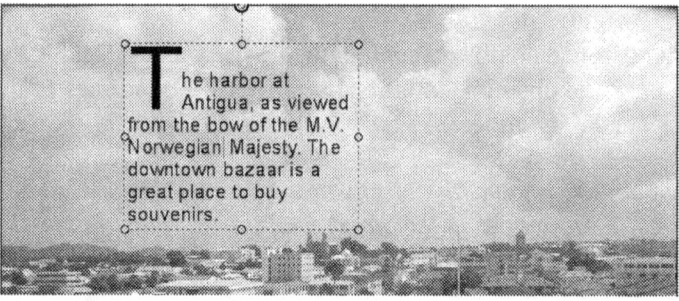

You can add a drop cap to text in Digital Image Pro by placing the insertion point anywhere in the paragraph and selecting Text | Drop Cap. This opens the Drop Cap dialog box, which displays the various styles of drop cap available.

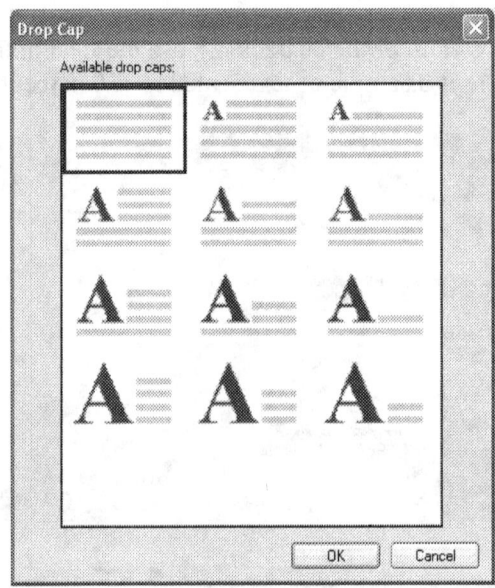

Pick the style you want and click OK.

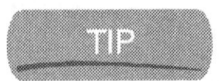
*To remove a drop cap, pick the style in the upper-left corner of the Drop Cap dialog box.*

## Wrap Text Around Objects

You can wrap text around objects, as shown in Figure 10-2. The text moves "out of the way" of the object. This technique can be handy for describing the object the text wraps around.

To wrap text around an object, click in the text box and select Text | Wrap Text Around Object. If the object is not already inside the boundaries of the text box, click the object and drag it there.

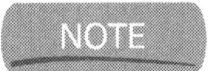
*Wrapping text around an object works consistently only if the object is on a higher level (higher in the Stack) than the text box. If the object appears on a lower level, the text will ignore it and not move out of the way.*

Text in text box          Object on higher level than text box in Stack

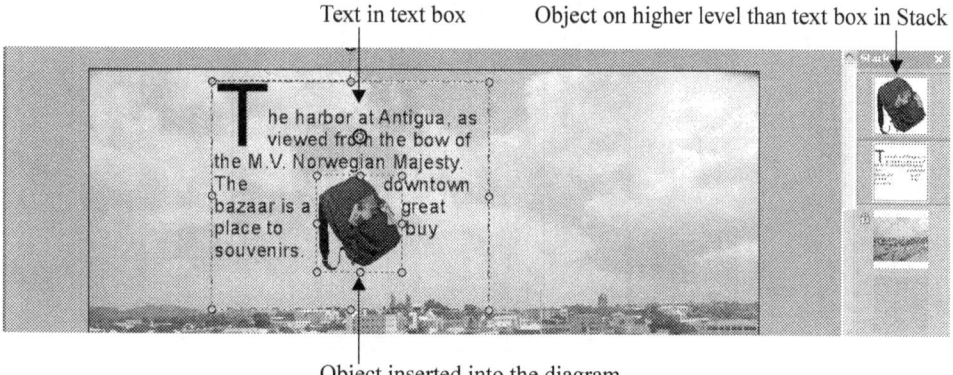

Object inserted into the diagram

Wrapping text around an object gives your image a professional touch.

## Add a Fill Color to the Text Box

You can fill the text box with a color, which can provide a nice contrast to the text. To do so, click in the text box and select Text | Text Box Color to open the Change Color dialog box. Pick the color you want, or click More Colors to open the standard Windows color picker. Click No Fill to remove any existing fill color. Here is a sample of a text box filled with a background color:

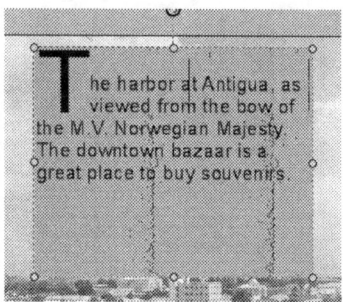

## Add Text Effects

You can apply special fills and text shaping functions by selecting Text | Text Effects to open the Text Effects task bar.

**10**

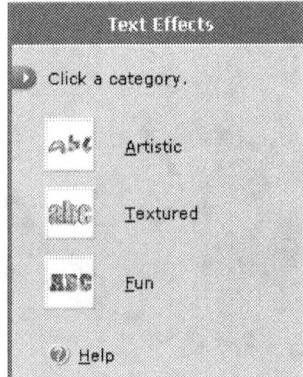

Choose the category of effect you want to apply by clicking one of the category buttons. For example, here I have clicked the Textured button to view a selection of available textured effects.

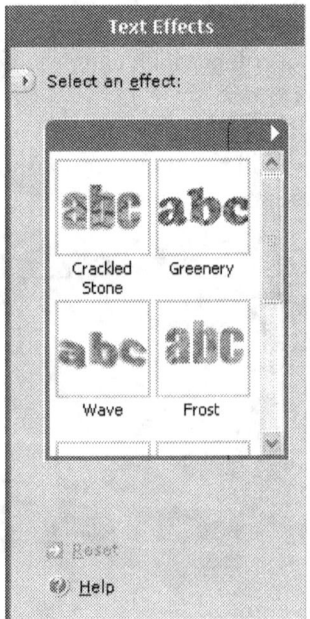

Pick the effect you want and click Done to apply the effect. Adding text effects flattens the text layer.

## How to ... **Smooth Text Edges with Gaussian Blur**

Digital Image Pro does try to do some smoothing of the text edges, but does not offer a function to enable you to anti-alias or smooth the edges of the text yourself so that it blends in better with the background. At high magnification, you can see the jagged edges of the text against a different-colored background:

## souvenirs.

You can fix this, however. To smooth the edges of the text better, click in the text box and select Touchup | Gaussian Blur. Use a low setting—such as .5 or .6—to smooth the edges.

## souvenirs.

**10**

**NOTE** *You should only try this with single-color text because Gaussian blur will blur all the edges in the text. In the case of single-colored text, that is what we want. Also note that using Gaussian Blur will flatten the text layer, so don't try this until you are sure you won't need to edit the text or apply any of the selections in the Text menu. (You can't edit the text content after the text layer has been flattened.)*

# Work with Shaped Text

With "shaped text" you can modify the shape of the text box. For example, here is shaped text that is shorter in the middle than it is at the ends.

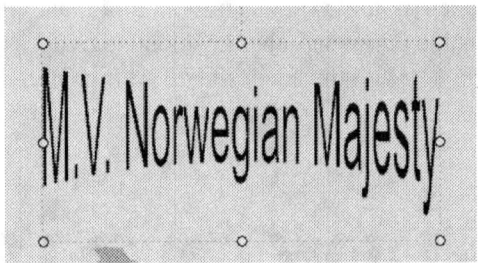

You can also add shadows, outlines, and various fills to shaped text as well. However, shaped text does not have all the editing capabilities of regular text. For example, you cannot add bullets and numbers to shaped text, nor can you apply a drop cap or change the indenting.

## Insert and Edit Shaped Text

To add shaped text to an image, select Text | Shaped Text and select the shape from the submenu.

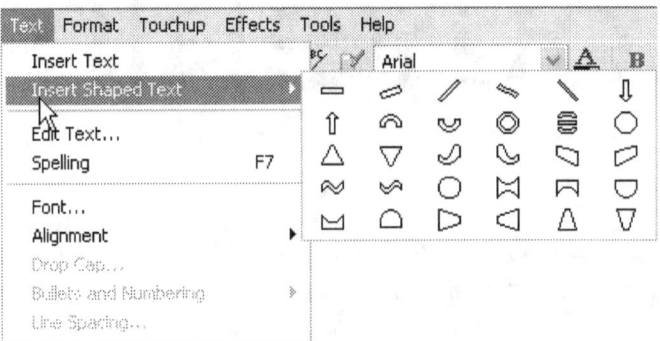

Digital Image Pro places the text box for the shaped text in the image and opens the Edit Shaped Text dialog box. This is where you actually input and edit your text.

Enter the text in the Edit Shaped Text dialog box, pressing CTRL-ENTER to begin a new line of text. When you are done, click OK to insert the text into the text box.

To edit the text later, double-click in the text box, or choose Edit Text from either the Text menu or the shortcut menu.

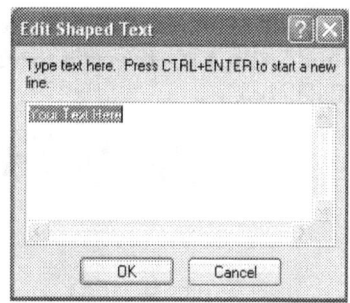

## Modify the Shaped Text Properties

You can modify the shape of the text, as well as the font, and rotate or flip the text. You can also customize the text by adding a shadow or gradient fill, and even modify the transparency of the text.

### Change the Text Box Shape

If you change your mind about the shape of the text box, you can change it. Click the Replace Shape button in the toolbar (to the left of the Flip Horizontal button) to open a drop-down menu of shapes.

All the original shapes are available; simply click the shape you want to use and Digital Image Pro applies it to the shaped text box.

### Change the Look of the Text

As with regular text, you can change the alignment of shaped text within the text box by choosing the option you want from the Alignment buttons in the toolbar (Left, Right, Center, or Justify), or from the Alignment menu option in either the Text menu or the shortcut menu.

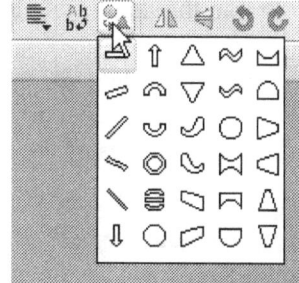

You can change the text color by clicking the Text Color icon in the toolbar and selecting a color from the submenu. Unlike regular text, all the shaped text in a text box is the same color; you can't change the color of only part of the text.

10

Shaped text also has a Font dialog box (select Font from the Text menu or the shortcut menu). However, there are many fewer options than the regular text Font dialog box:

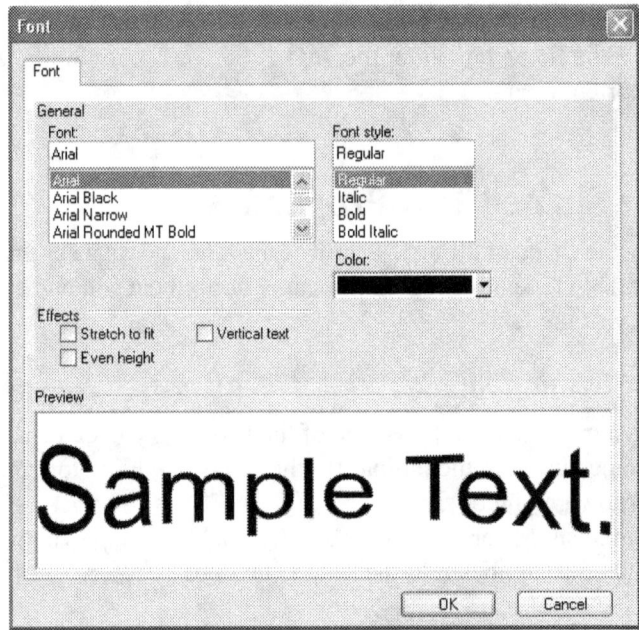

From the shaped text Font dialog box, you can:

■ **Set the Typeface**    Select the typeface you want from the Font scrolling list. All the text in the shaped text box must be the same typeface; unlike regular text, you can't select part of the text and change the typeface for just that text.

■ **Set the Font Style**    Choose the font style from the Font Style list. Choices include Regular, Italic, Bold, and Bold Italic. All the text in a shaped text box must use the same Font style.

■ **Set the Font Color**    Click the down arrow alongside the currently selected color to display a list of available colors (or click More Colors to pick a color from the standard Windows color picker). All the text in a shaped text box must be the same color.

■ **Stretch to Fit**   Click the Stretch to Fit checkbox to stretch the text so that it fills the text box from edge to edge and from top to bottom. Here is a sample of stretched text:

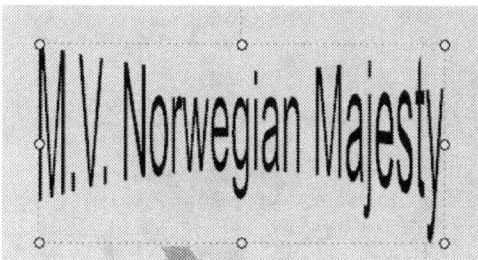

■ **Even Height**   By default, Digital Image Pro makes uppercase letters taller than lowercase letters. However, if you check the Even Height checkbox, all the letters are scaled to be the same size:

10

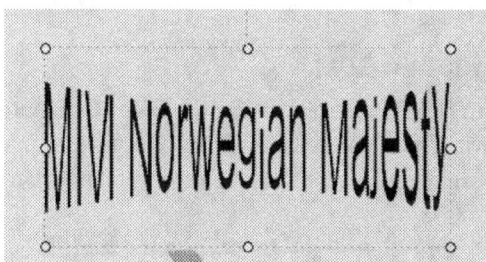

■ **Vertical Text**   Selecting the Vertical Text checkbox turns the shaped text so that it runs from the top of the text box to the bottom, maintaining the originally chosen shape. Here, I've stretched the height so you can see the result better:

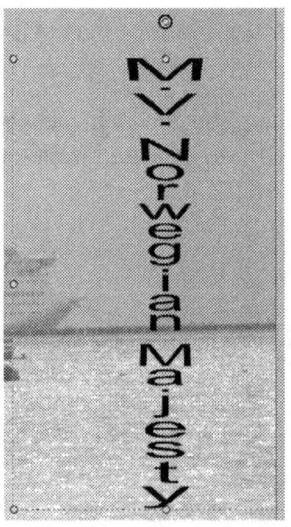

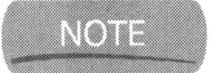 *You can switch the shaped text between the normal horizontal layout and Vertical Text by selecting Text Layout from the shortcut menu or clicking the Change Text Layout button in the toolbar.*

## Rotate and Flip Shaped Text

You can rotate and flip the shaped text using the Flip Horizontally, Flip Vertically, Rotate Counterclockwise, and Rotate Clockwise buttons in the toolbar. For example, here is an example of shaped text that has been rotated counterclockwise:

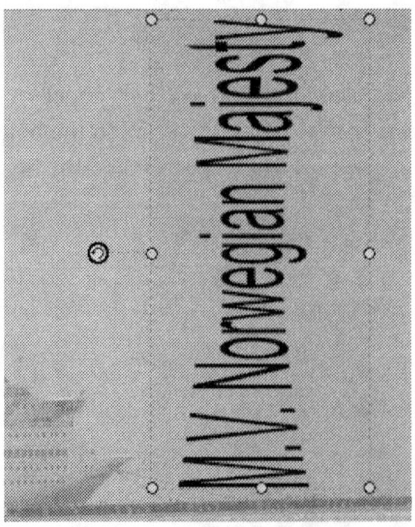

## Add a Shadow

You can add a completely configurable shadow by clicking the Shadow button in the toolbar or choosing Text | Shaped Text | Shadow. This opens the Shadow dialog box:

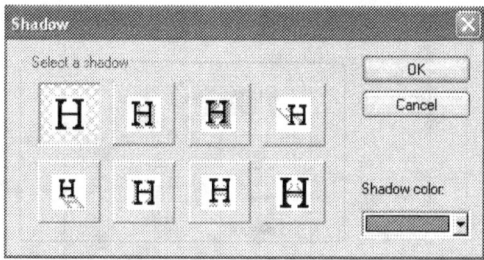

From here, you can pick the style and direction of the shadow. Each letter in the shaped text box gets it own shadow, making for an effective three-dimensional effect. You can also choose the color of the shadow from the Shadow Color dropdown list. When you pick one of the options in the dialog box, you can instantly see the result in the shaped text box.

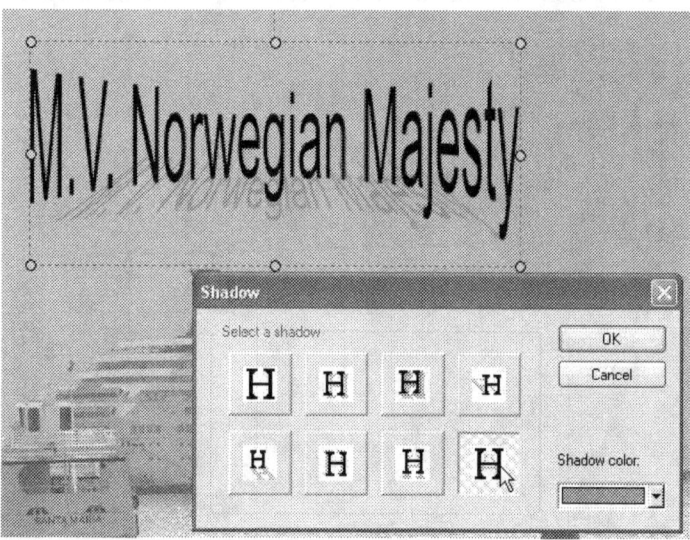

To apply the shadow, click OK.

10

## Add an Outline

To add an outline to the letters, click the Outline button in the toolbar or select
Text | Shaped Text | Outline. This opens the Outline dialog box:

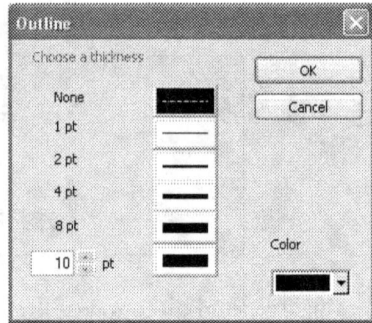

Choose a thickness for the line by clicking one of the preset thickness buttons
in the dialog box, or setting a custom thickness in the last field. You can also choose
the color of the outline from the Color drop-down list. When you pick one of the
options in the dialog box, you can instantly see the result in the shaped text box.

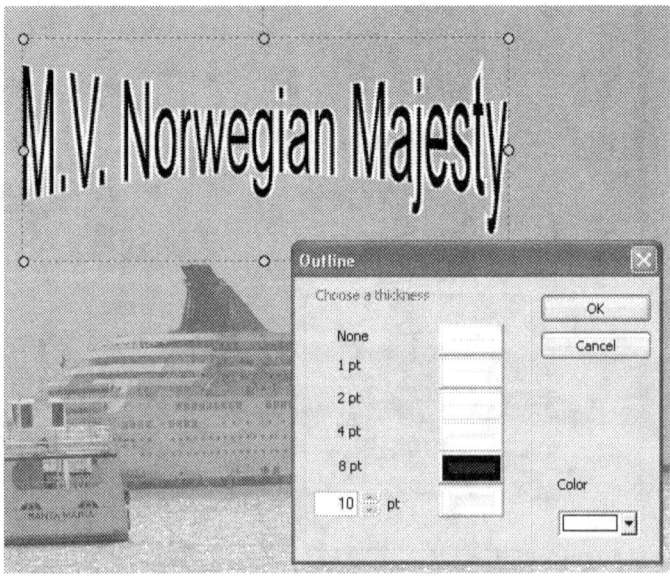

To apply the outline, click OK.

*If you want to create text that only has an outline, set the outline color and set the fill color to white (or whatever the background color is).*

## Add a Gradient

Although there is nothing different about applying a gradient to shaped text than to any other object, the results can be pretty impressive. A brightly colored gradient can really call attention to your text:

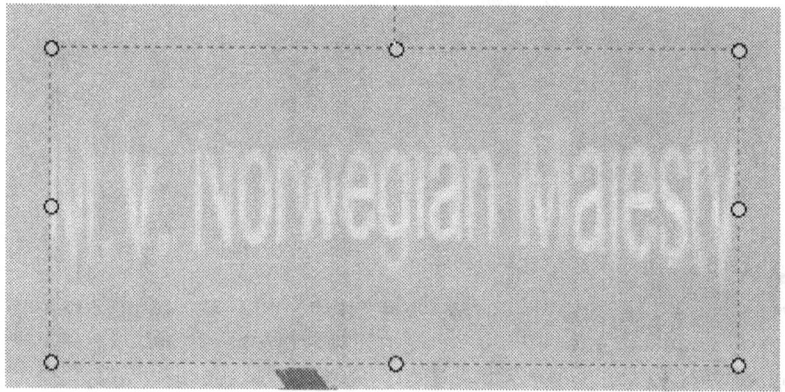

To apply a gradient, select the shaped text box and select Effects | Fill with Texture or Color. Click the Color Gradient button and choose the color pattern and style.

## Skew the Text

You can skew the shaped text box by selecting Effects | Skew Object to open the Skew task bar. Work with the shaped text box just as you would with any other object.

## Apply an Object Shadow

As we've seen already, you can apply a shadow to a shaped text box by clicking the Shadow button in the toolbar or selecting Text | Shaped Text | Shadow. This type of shadow applies individual shadows to the letters. But there is another type of shadow, which you can access by selecting Effects | Shadow to open the Shadow task bar, as discussed in Chapter 8. This type of shadow (which also works with regular text boxes) treats the contents of the text box as a single object, and draws the appropriate shadow when you click Done:

10

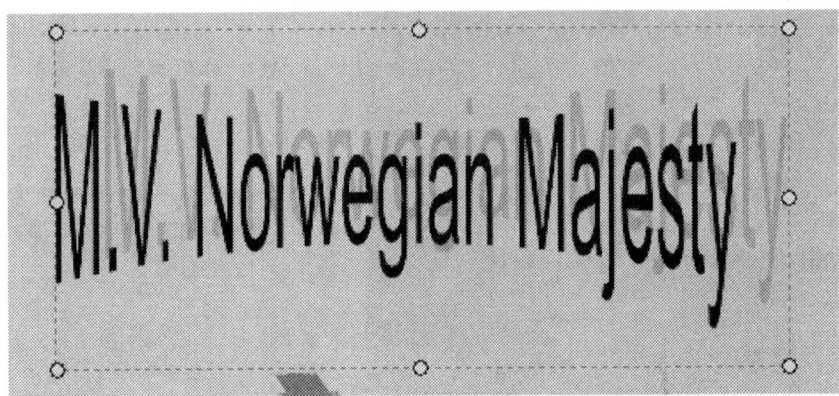

*Applying an object shadow to a text box flattens the text box.*

## Change the Transparency

It can be very useful to see the image underneath your text through the text. You can adjust the transparency of either regular text boxes or shaped text boxes by selecting Effects | Transparency, and then choosing the type of transparency you want (Even, Gradual, or Transparency Brush) from the submenu. Set the transparency and click Done to see the result:

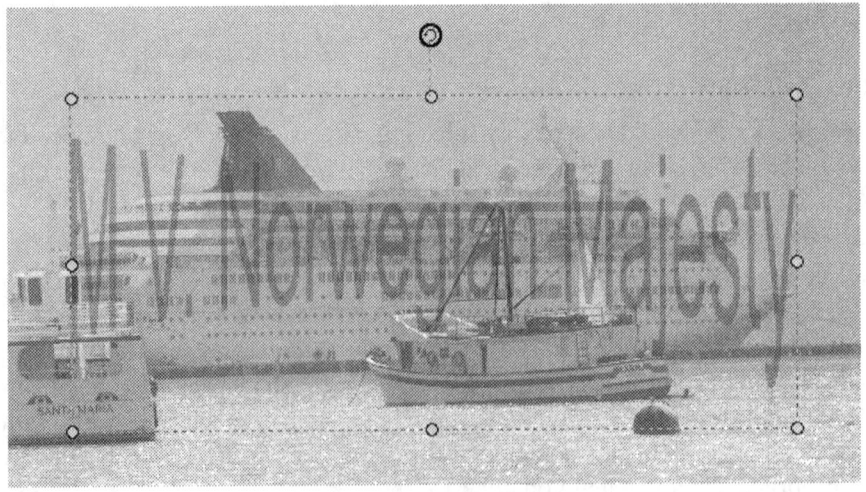

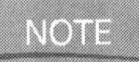 *Making the text transparent flattens the text box.*

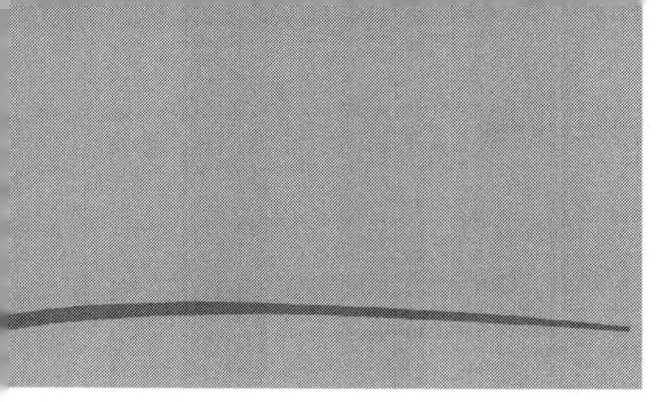

# Apply Edges to Dress Up an Image

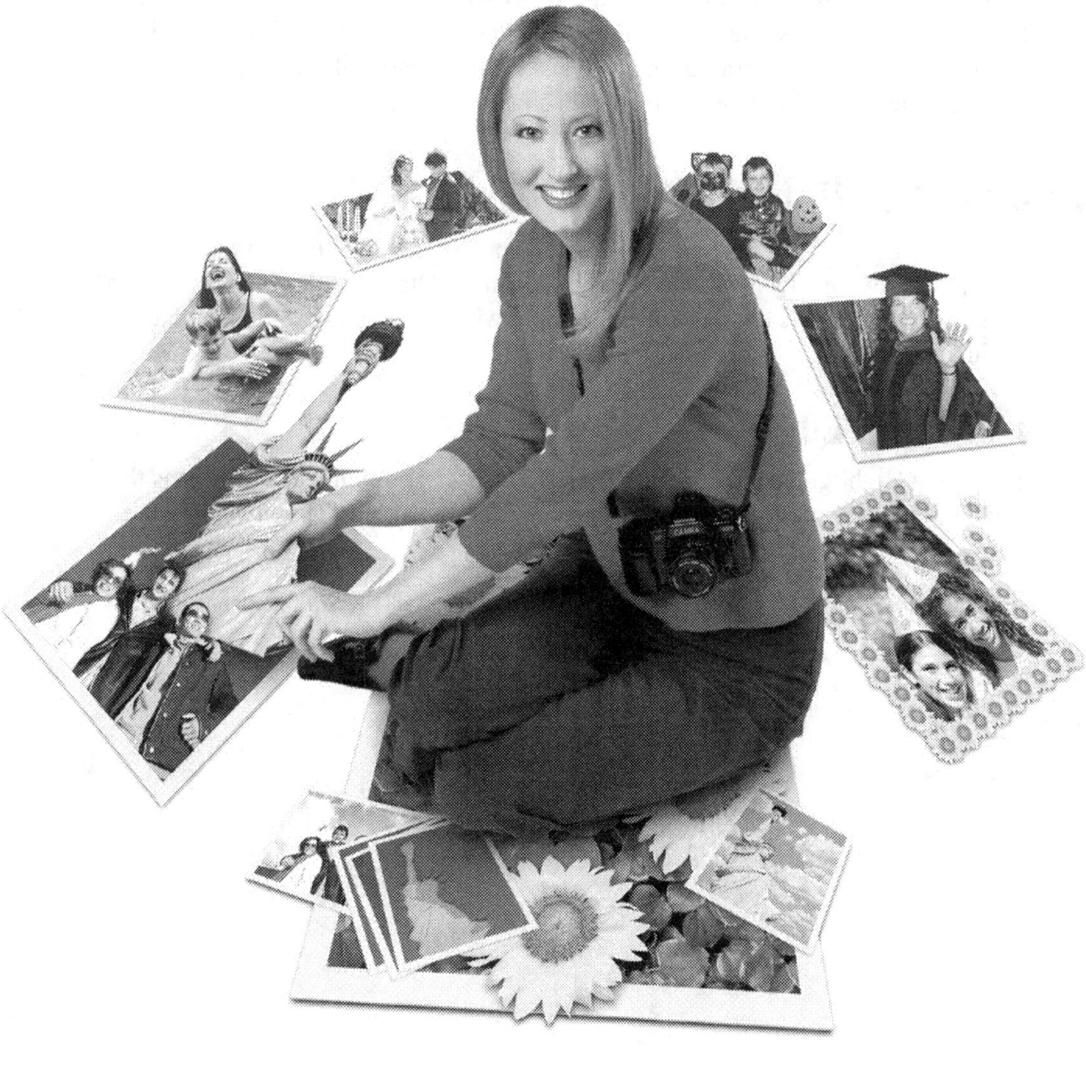

## How to...

- Apply a variety of edges, frames, and mattes to your images
- Vary the width, shape, and color of the edges
- Create your own custom borders for your images

Digital Image Pro makes it possible to apply a wide variety of edges and frames to an image to dress it up and get it ready for printing. Possibilities include highlighted edges, designer edges, Photo Strokes, Art Strokes, and stamped edges. In addition, you can use frames, mattes, and borders. Most of these edges have configurable options so you can further customize the result.

# Apply a Highlighted Edge

Highlighted edges are rendered in a single color that can fade toward the outer boundary, drawing attention effectively to the image. Other options include varying width and whether the edge is drawn partially within the picture, hiding some of the image.

## Choose an Edge

To apply a Highlighted Edge, select Effects | Edges | Highlighted. This opens the Highlighted Edges task bar, where you can select the edge style you want to use:

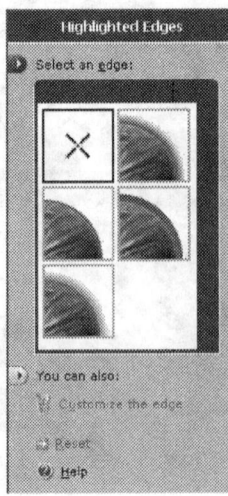

Select the type of highlighted edge by clicking it. This applies the edge with the default options, as shown in Figure 11-1.

*Styles that include the word "over" in their title (such as thin over) modify the image by applying the effect partially within the border of the image. This hides part of the image, so make sure nothing important is hidden by these types of edges.*

A portion of most styles of edges falls outside the boundaries of the canvas. To make sure that the entire edge is included (and thus will print), you'll need to expand the size of the canvas (select Format | Resize Canvas) to include the entire edge.

## Customize the Highlighted Edges

You can customize the Highlighted Edge by clicking Customize the Edge to display a new version of the Highlighted Edges task bar:

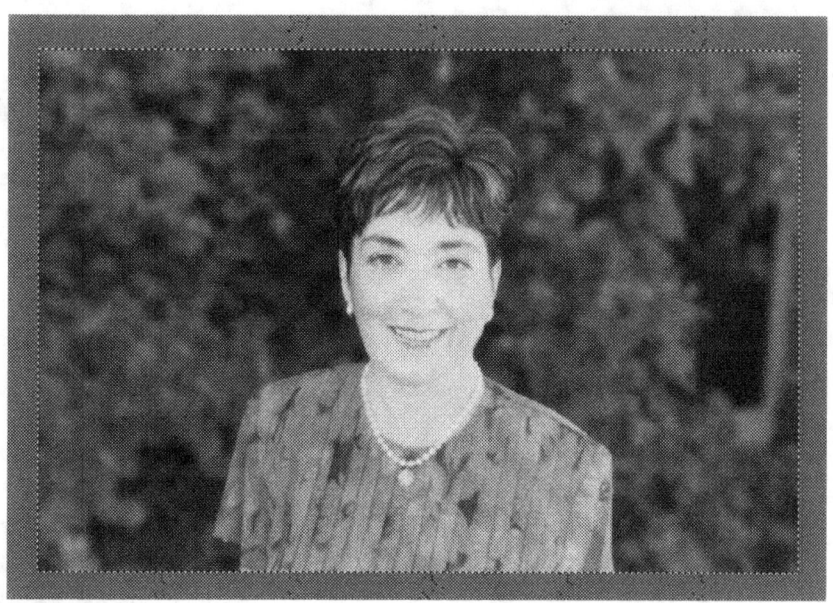

Highlighted Edges can really dress up an image.

11

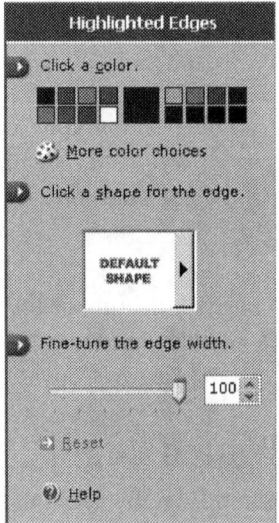

You can customize a highlighted edge in the following ways:

- **Pick a color**    Select the color of the edge by picking it from the color choices in the task bar or clicking More Color Choices to pick a color using the color wheel.

- **Choose the edge shape**    Click the right arrow in the Click a Shape for the Edge field to choose a shape to use. There are solid color shapes as well as shapes with feathered edges. The edge shape you choose also determines the shape of the edge corners. For example, if you select a round shape, the edge corners are rounded, whereas if you choose a square shape, the edge corners are square.

- **Set the edge width**    Use the Fine-Tune the Edge Width slider to set the width of the edge.

# Apply a Designer Edge

Designer edges come in three categories: Artistic, With Text, and With My Own Text. Each of the categories has its own set of options, and in one (With My Own Text), you can even specify the exact text that will be placed around the edges of the photo.

To choose the category of designer edge you want to use, select Effects | Edges | Designer to open the Designer Edges task bar, showing the three available categories:

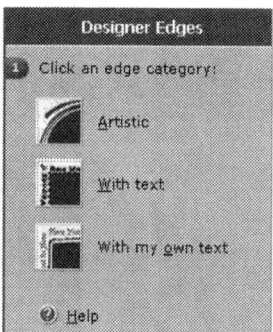

## Configure an Artistic Edge

When you click the Artistic Edge category, a new version of the Designer Edge task bar opens to display the "artistic" options:

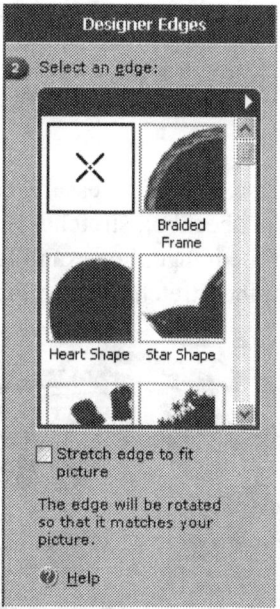

There are quite a few stylized options, including Pop Art, Doilies, Confetti, Paper Clips, Shells, Notebook Paper, and many others. Artistic Edges appear entirely within the border of the picture, so at least some of the image is hidden by an Artistic Edge. For example, Figure 11-2 shows a Whirligig Edge.

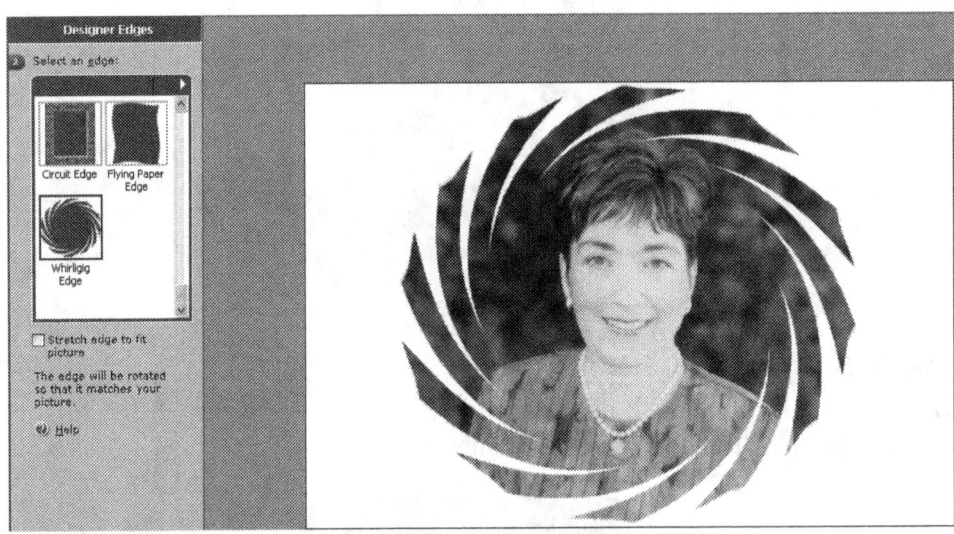

Artistic Edges hide part of the image, so pick your edges carefully.

Pick the edge you want to use, and, if necessary, check the Stretch Edge to Fit Picture checkbox. Checking the checkbox stretches the artistic edge to the borders of the photo, showing more of the image. For example, here is the same edge as shown in Figure 11-2, but with the Stretch Edge to Fit Picture checkbox selected:

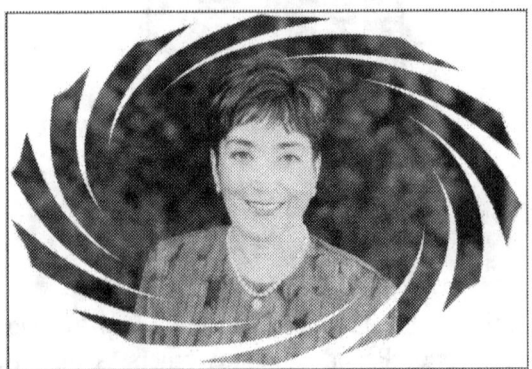

Once you are done picking an Artistic Edge, click Next> to move to the next option. This opens still another version of the Designer Edges task bar:

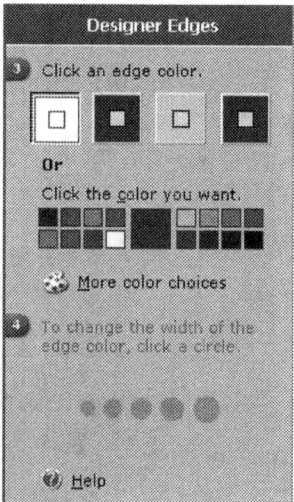

Using this version of the task bar, you can add a colored border to the Artistic Edge. Pick one of the Click an Edge Color buttons, or pick a color from the color boxes. Once you have done so, you can set the width of the colored border by clicking a circle in Step 4 of the task bar. Here is the same image as in Figure 11-2, but it now has a colored border (and is stretched to fit).

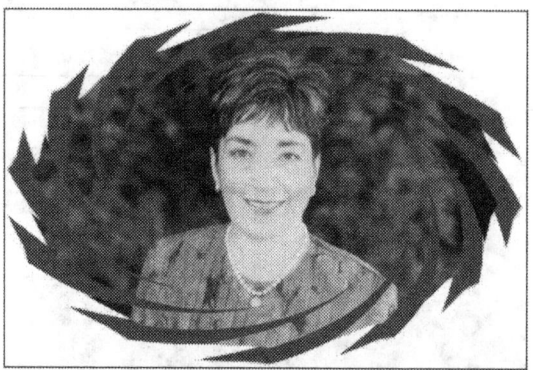

Click Next> to move to the last step. Here you can click and drag the image to place it more advantageously under the Artistic Edge. You can also resize it if you wish, using the standard sizing handles.

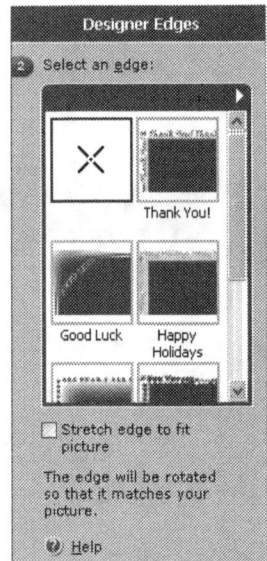

# Configure a "With Text" Edge

When you click the With Text Edge category, a new version of the Designer Edges task bar opens to display the text edge options.

There are quite a few of these text options as well, including "Thank You," "Happy Holidays," "Good Luck," and "Bon Voyage." For example, Figure 11-3 shows the "Happy Holidays" edge. As with Artistic Edges, you can select the Stretch Edge to Fit Picture checkbox to expand the text edge to the borders of the photo.

Click Next> to proceed to the version of the Designer Edges

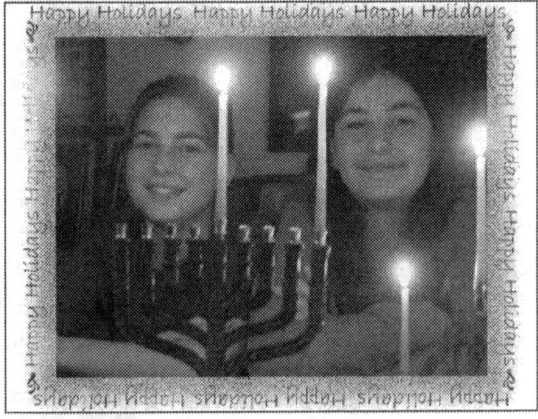

task bar where you can add a colored border to the text edge and set the width of the colored border. Here is the same image as Figure 11-3, but it now has a colored border:

Finally, click Next> to proceed to the last step, where you can move and resize the image.

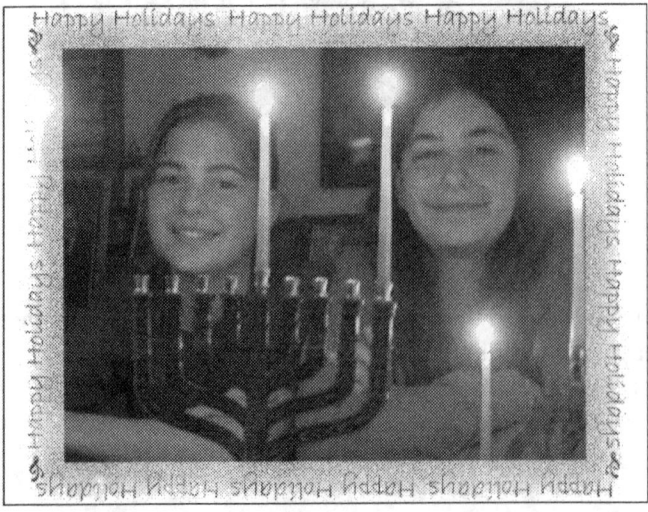

Add a text message to the borders of a photo with a text edge.

## Configure a "With My Own Text" Edge

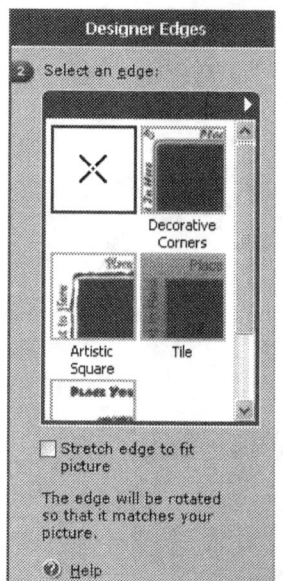

The last of the Designer Edge categories enables you to add your own text to the edge. When you click the With My Own Text category, a new version of the Designer Edges task bar opens to display the varieties of edge types you can select. As with Artistic Edges, you can select the Stretch Edge to Fit Picture checkbox to expand the text edge to the borders of the photo.

Select the type of edge you want and click Next> to proceed to the version of the Designer Edges task bar where you can specify your text.

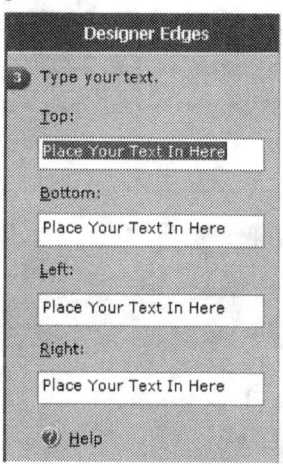

Type the text you want into each of the fields to specify text for the Top, Bottom, Left, and Right sides of the photo. Figure 11-4 shows the Artistic Square edge combined with text.

Finally, click Next> to proceed to the last step, where you can move and resize the image.

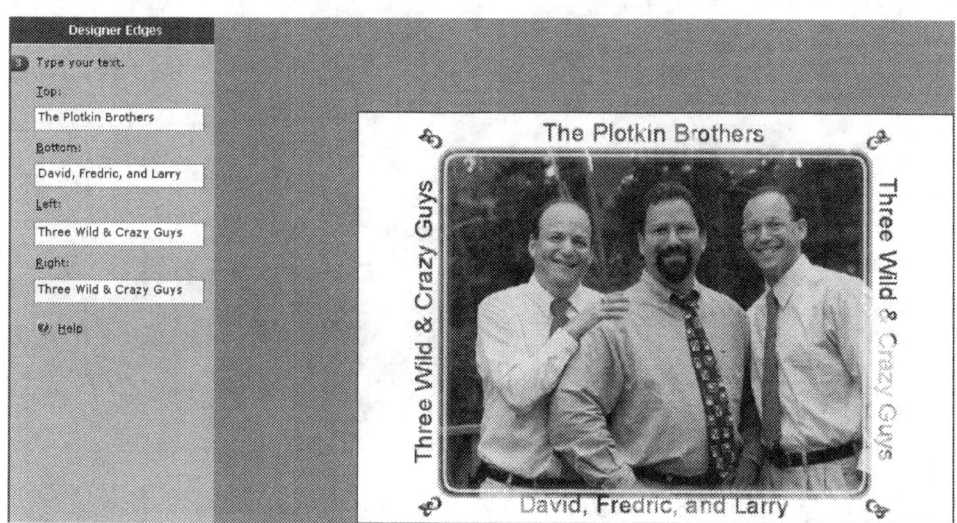

By adding your own text, you can tell what the picture is about.

11

## Apply a Soft Edge

You can feather the edges of an image by selecting Effects | Edges | Soft. This opens the Soft Edges task bar. Simply drag the slider to apply the feathering effect to the image, as shown in Figure 11-5. Higher values of the slider increase the width of the feathered edge.

## Apply an Art Stroke Edge

Art Stroke edges are edges that look like they were created using various media, such as crayon, wet Conte, pencil, pen, markers, and others (see Figure 11-6). To create

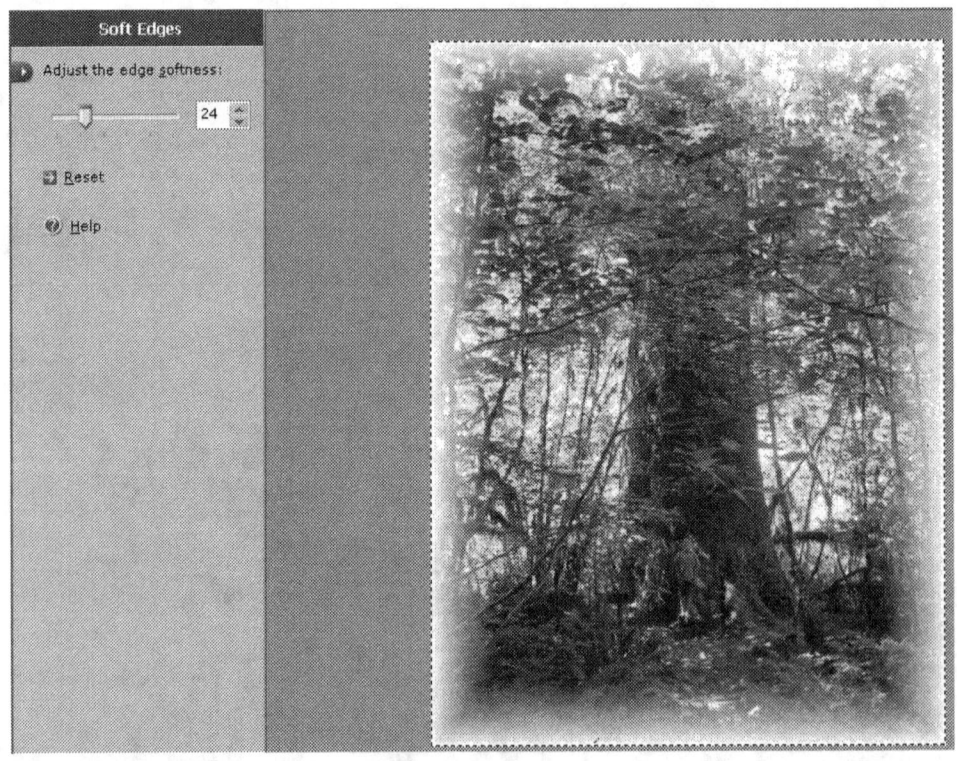

Add a soft fading effect to the borders of a photo with Soft Edges.

an Art Stroke edge, select Effects | Edges | Art Stroke. This opens the Art Stroke Edges task bar:

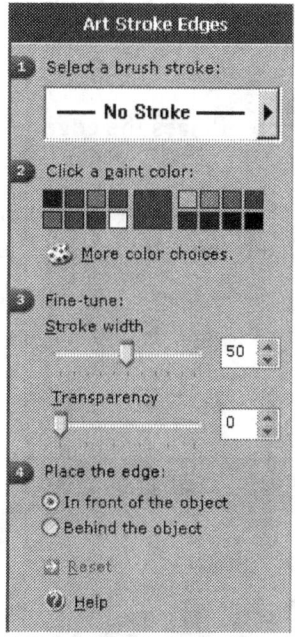

The first step is to choose the brush stroke you want to use. Click the right arrow under Select a Brush Stroke to view the many options and pick the one you want:

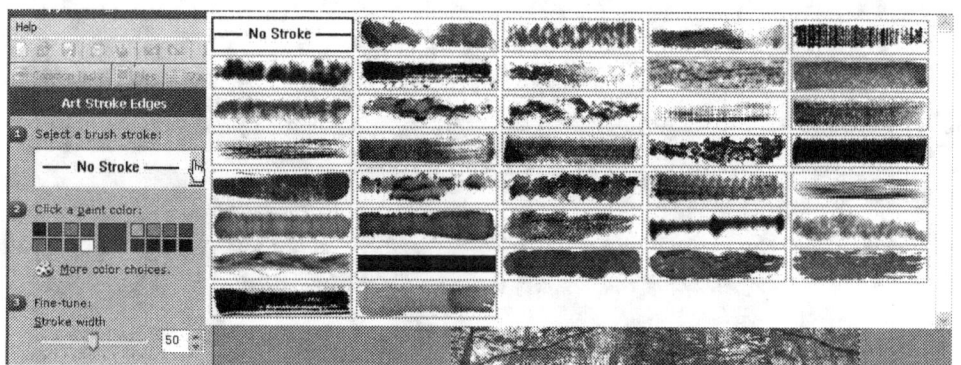

Once you have picked a brush stroke, select the border color from the color square or click More Color Choices to select a color using the color wheel. Under Fine-Tune (Step 3 in the task bar), use the sliders to adjust stroke width and transparency (higher values increase the transparency). Finally, choose one of the options for placing the edge:

- **In Front of the Object**   Places the edge in front of the image, hiding part of it.

- **Behind the Object**   Places the edge behind the image, so the only portion of the edge that is visible is the part that is located outside the boundaries of the picture.

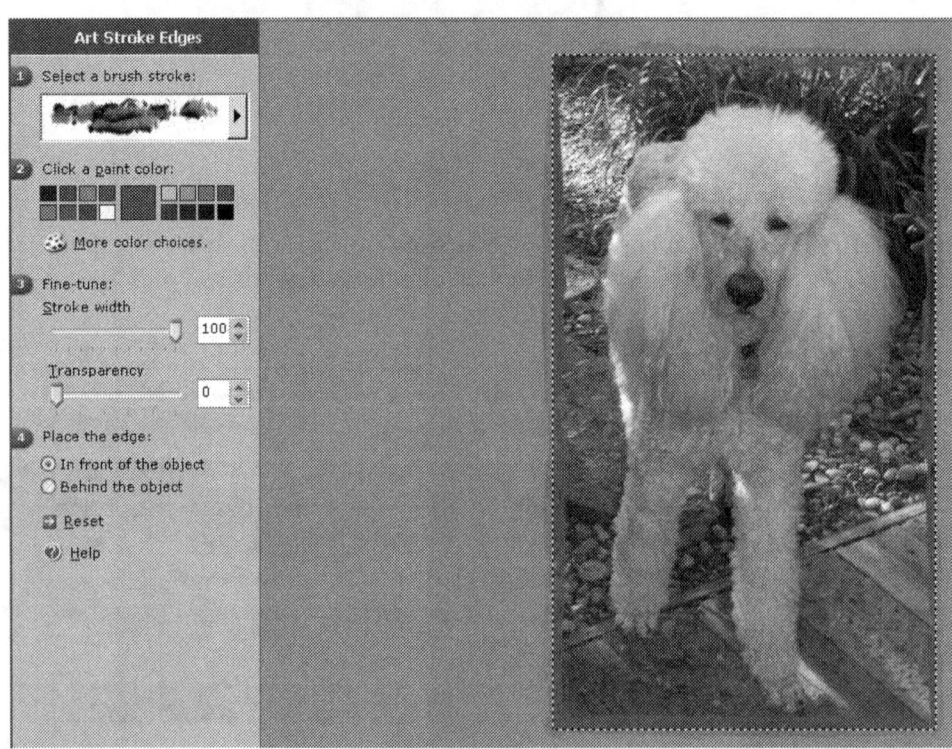

An Art Stroke edge gives an artistic feel to an image.

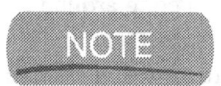 *Part of the resulting edge is off the edge of the canvas. To correct this, unlock the image (choose Unlock from the shortcut menu). This displays the sizing handles. Use the sizing handles to resize the image to fit onto the canvas including the edges. It is best to click and drag a corner sizing handle to maintain the aspect ratio.*

## Apply a Photo Stroke Edge

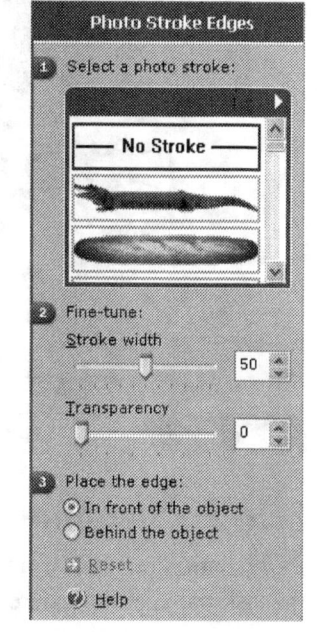

Photo Stroke edges apply edges that look like they were created from small photographs, such as bread, bamboo, Eight-balls, rope, and even chili peppers (see Figure 11-7). To create a Photo Stroke edge, select Effects | Edges | Photo Stroke. This opens the Photo Stroke Edges task bar:

Choose the Photo Stroke you want to use from the Select a Photo Stroke scrolling list. Under Fine-Tune (Step 2 in the task bar), use the sliders to adjust stroke width and transparency (higher values increase the transparency). Finally, choose one of the options for placing the edge:

■ **In Front of the Object**   Places the edge in front of the image, hiding part of it.

■ **Behind the Object**   Places the edge behind the image, so the only portion of the edge that is visible is the part that is located outside the boundaries of the picture.

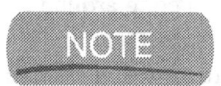 *As with the Art Stroke edge, you'll need to adjust the image size to fit the canvas.*

## Apply a Stamped Edge

A stamped edge is a border made up of stamps—the same stamps discussed in Chapter 5. To add a stamped edge to a photo, select Effects | Edges | Stamps to open the Stamped Edges task bar.

From here, you'll need to make some choices to set up the stamped edge.

**11**

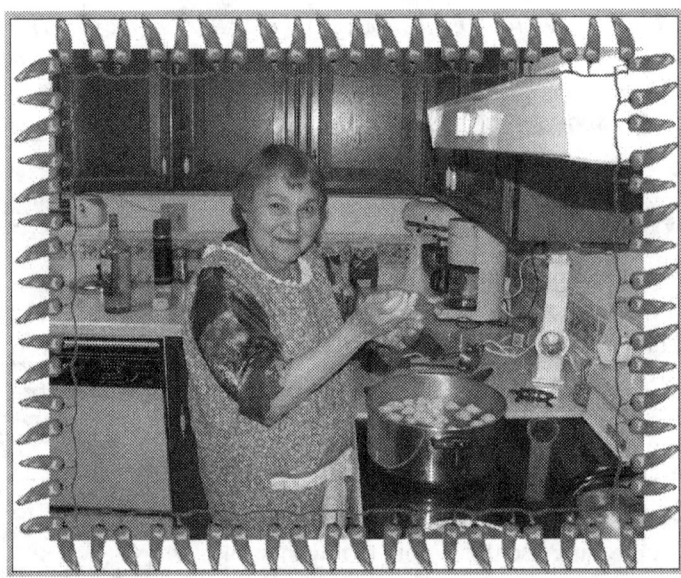

Spice up an image by adding an edge made up of small photographs!

## Select a Stamping Style

Pick a stamping style from the Select a Stamping Style scrolling list in Step 1 in the task bar. The styles are as follows:

- **Stamps Over**    Places the stamps edge to edge around the perimeter of the image. About half the stamp object is off the edge of the image; the other half overlaps the image itself, as shown in Figure 11-8.

- **Stamps Under**    Places the stamps edge to edge around the perimeter of the image. The placement is similar to *Stamps Over*, but the stamps are placed behind the image so that none of the image is hidden by the stamps.

- **Overlapping Stamps**    Overlaps the stamps around the edge of the image (see Figure 11-9). Like the *Stamps Over* style, the stamps hide a portion of the image around the edges.

- **Shapes**    Creates an edge using a selection of simple shapes, selected from the Select a Stamp field (discussed in the text that follows).

- **Erase Stamps**    Creates an edge using one of the simple shapes. Anywhere the shape is dark, the border area is opaque and white; anywhere the shape is dark, you can see through the border to the image underneath (see Figure 11-10).

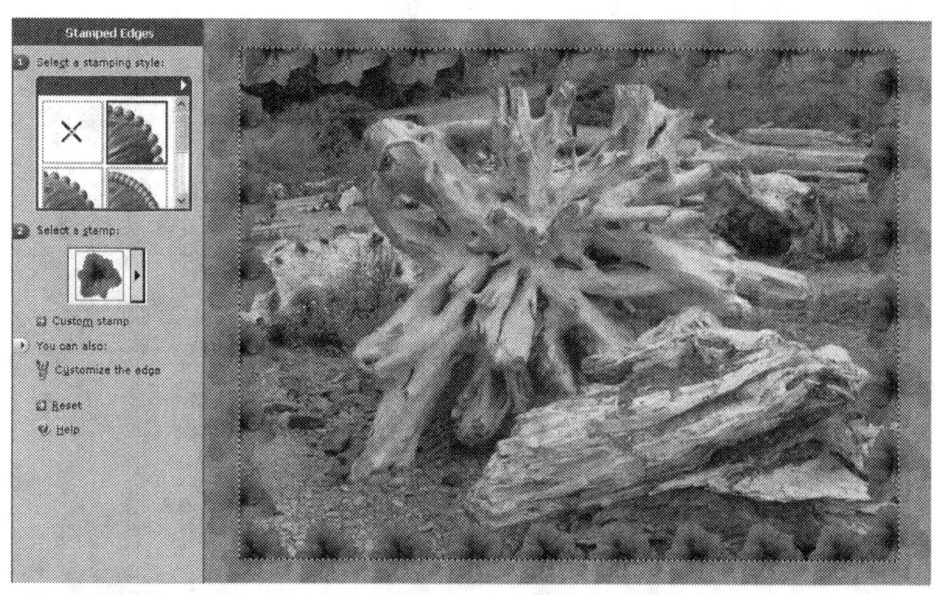

Stamps Over places the stamps edge to edge, and hides part of the image with the stamps.

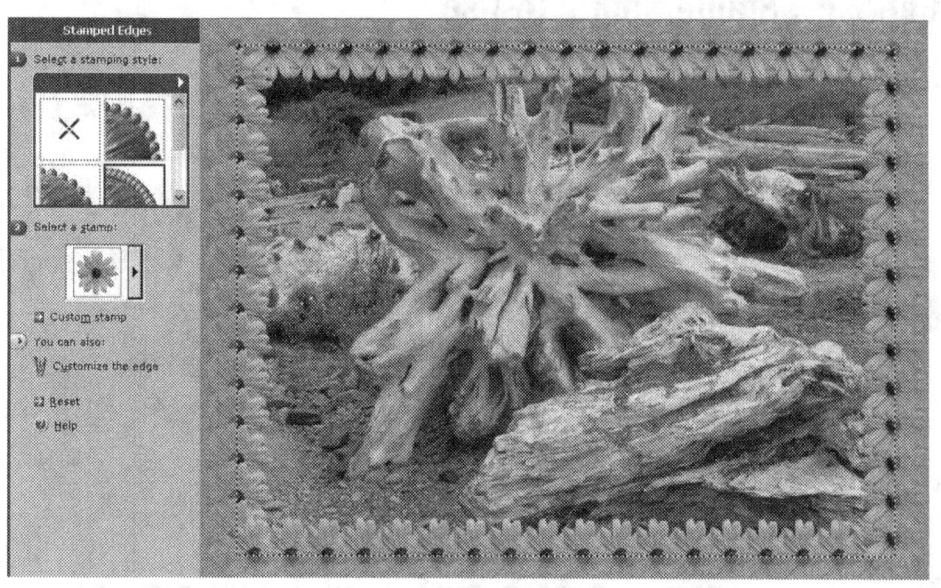

Overlapping Stamps places the stamps in an overlapping pattern.

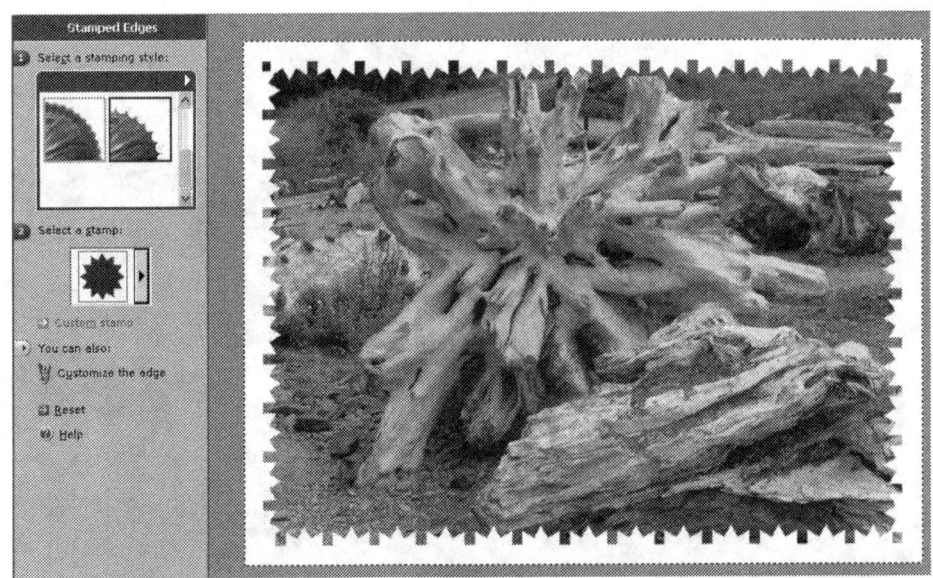

Erase Stamps displays the dark part of the shape in white, and the white part of the shape as transparent.

## Choose a Stamp Shape to Use

Use the Select a Stamp field to choose the stamp you want to use. For Stamps Over, Stamps Under, and Overlapping Stamps, the selection of stamps is fairly complex, and includes various balls, magnets, question marks, jacks, and dice:

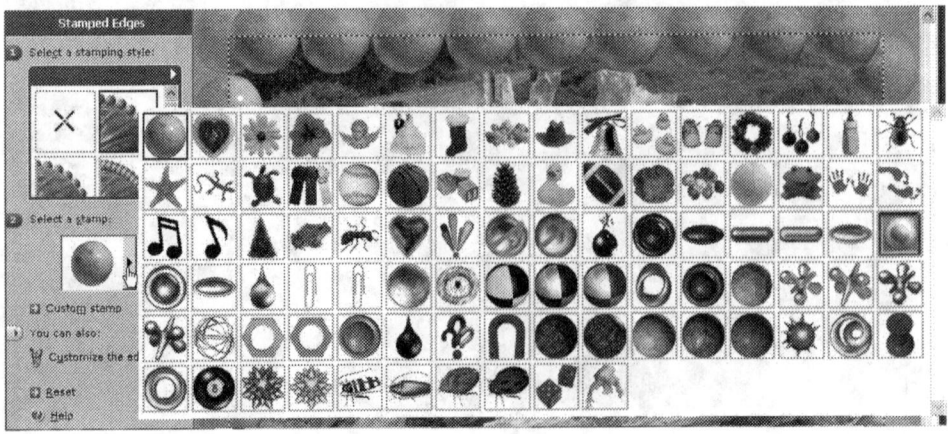

For Shapes and Erase Stamps, Digital Image Pro provides a small selection of simple shapes:

You can also create a custom stamp. To do so, click Custom Stamp to display a version of the Custom Stamp task bar from which you can pick a picture by looking in the Gallery, opening a picture, scanning in a picture, or downloading a picture from a digital camera.

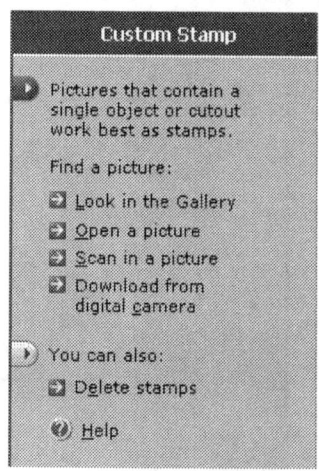

## Customize the Stamp

Click Customize the Edge to open another version of the Stamped Edges task bar in which you adjust the size of the stamps using a slider. If the stamping style you selected was *Shapes*, you can set the color of the stamps by clicking one of the color choices in Step 2, or by clicking More Color Choices to select a color from the color wheel.

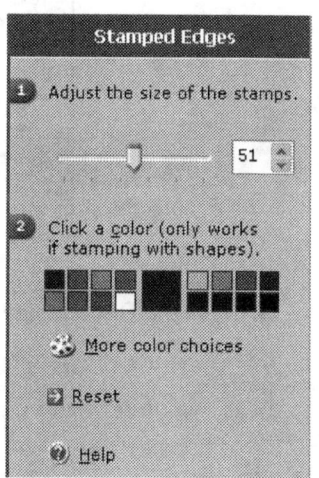

# Add a Border to Your Image

You can add a variety of borders to your photos—from staid business themes to some wild and crazy ones. To add a border, select Effects | Edges | Borders. This opens the Borders dialog box.

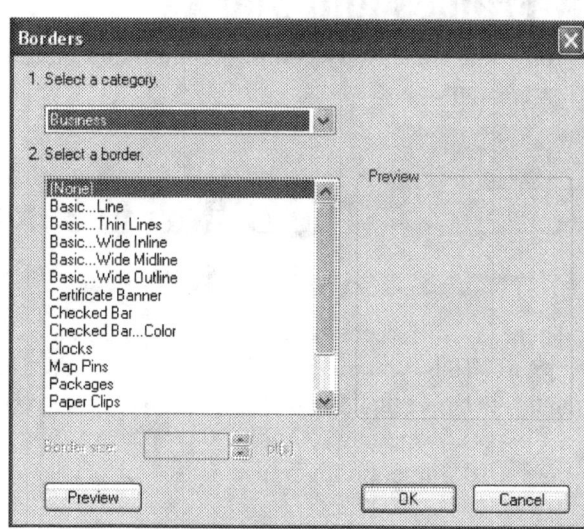

11

To specify a border, use the following steps:

1. Select a category from the Select a Category drop-down list.

2. Pick a border from the Select a Border scrolling list. Digital Image Pro shows a preview in the Preview area.

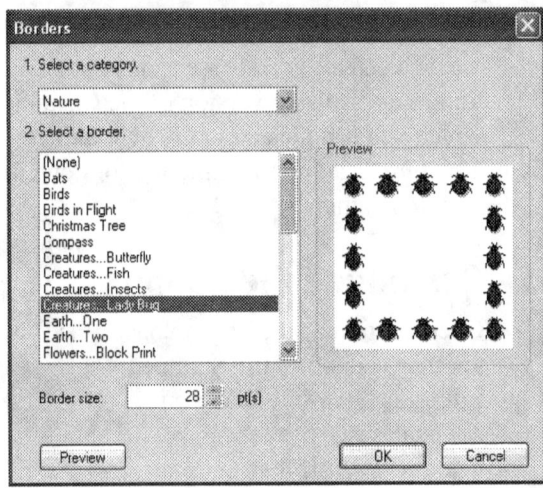

3. Use the Border Size field to specify the size of the border.

4. Click the Preview button to preview the border on the actual photo.

5. If you like what you see, click OK to add the border to the image.

## Apply Frames and Mattes

If you want some pretty complex frames and mattes for your image, select Effects | Edges | Frames and Mats.

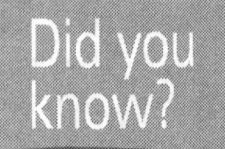

# The Difference Between Frames and Mattes

There is a difference between frames and mattes. A frame is the same size as a picture. Thus, you use a 5 x 7 frame to hold a 5 x 7 picture. A matte, on the other hand, is larger than the picture it holds. Thus, you might use an 8 x 10 matte with a 5 x 7 opening to hold a 5 x 7 picture. You could put the 8 x 10 matte in an 8 x 10 frame, giving a nice artistic effect.

## Build a Frame or Matte Using Supplied Designs

Digital Image Pro supplies a large number of frames and mattes, ready for you to use. To add one of these to your photo, pick one of the themes from the Theme scrolling list, and then select one of the designs that appears to the right of the task bar.

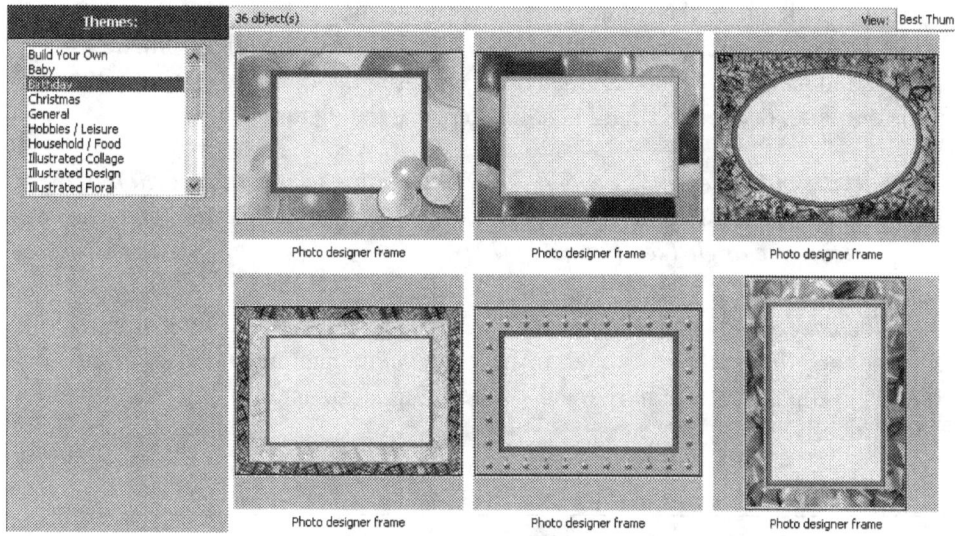

If you want to preview the design in a larger size, click the Preview button to open the Preview Design dialog box. You may be asked for one of the Digital Image Pro CDs if you didn't load all the art when you installed the package.

11

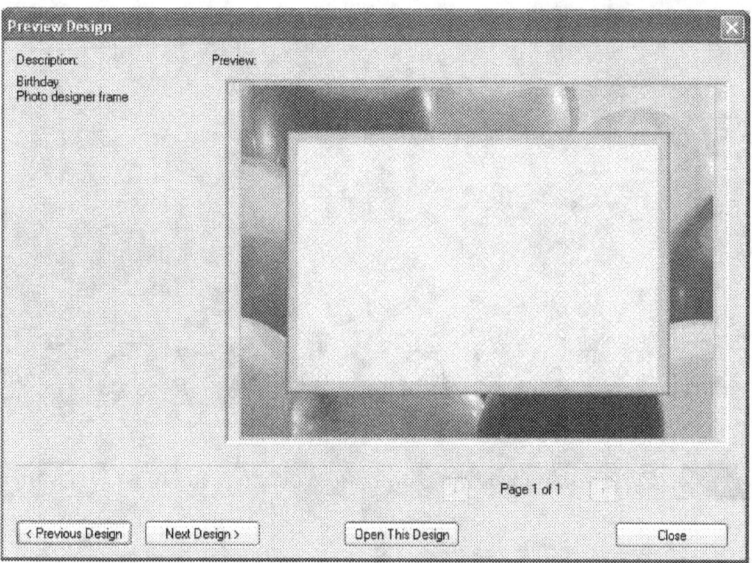

To select the frame or matte, click Open from the Themes task bar or Open This Design from the Preview Design dialog box. Digital Image Pro places the frame or matte in the work area. However, it is still empty—all you have is the frame, as shown in Figure 11-11. The empty sizing rectangle is the active area of the frame or matte— where the frame or matte design expects the image to go.

To add a picture to the frame or matte, you can drag it from the File palette, open a new picture, scan in a picture, or download it from a digital camera, as described in Chapter 3. You can then click and drag the image to position it in the frame or matte, or use the sizing handles to resize the picture.

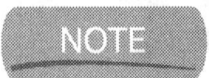 *If the picture extends beyond the bounds of the frame, that portion of the picture is not visible. You can, however, see the outline of the picture's sizing rectangle (see Figure 11-12).*

If you dragged the picture from the Files palette, click Next> to continue to the last task bar, which prompts you to resize or move the picture and also provides controls to flip the picture horizontally (click Flip Horizontally) or vertically (click Flip Vertically).

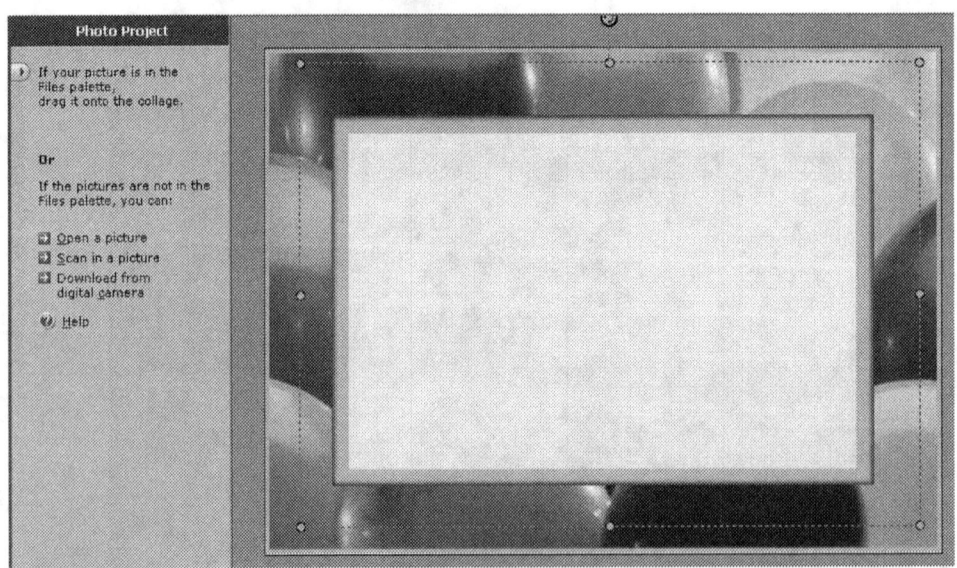

Once you pick a frame or matte, you are ready to add your image to it.

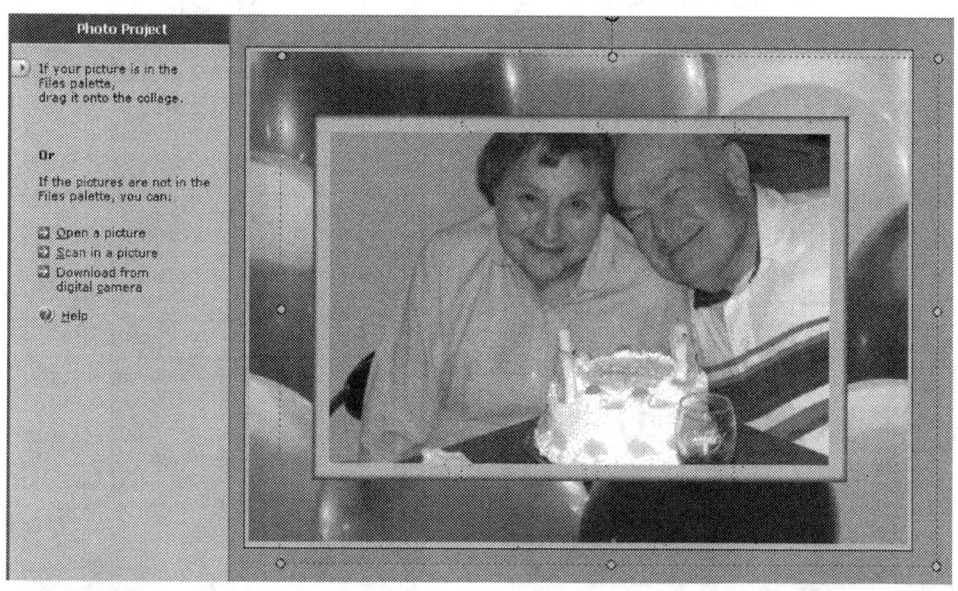

Any portion of the picture that falls outside the frame is not visible.

Click Done to add the frame or matte to the image. In this final version, the image is cropped to fit the open area of the frame or matte:

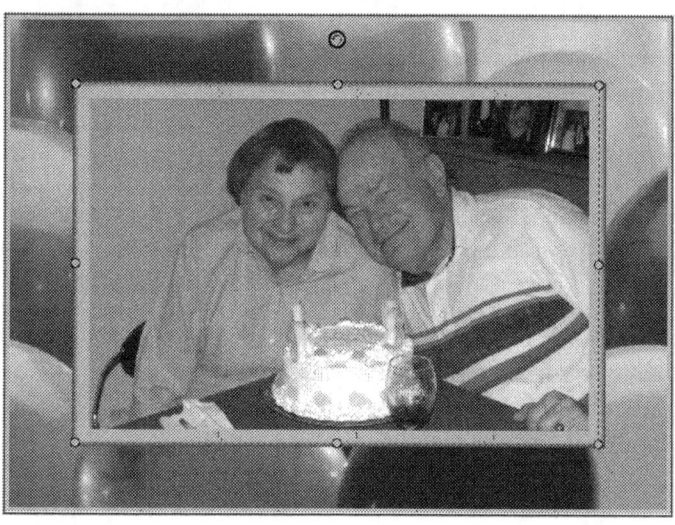

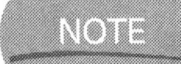 *Frames and Mattes is an example of a Digital Image Pro project. I will cover projects in more depth in Chapter 13.*

## Build Your Own Frame or Matte

If you don't find a frame or matte you like in the vast collection supplied with Digital Image Pro, you can build your own. To do so, choose Build Your Own from the list of themes in the Themes task bar scrolling list. This presents you with two options: Photo simple frame and Photo simple matte:

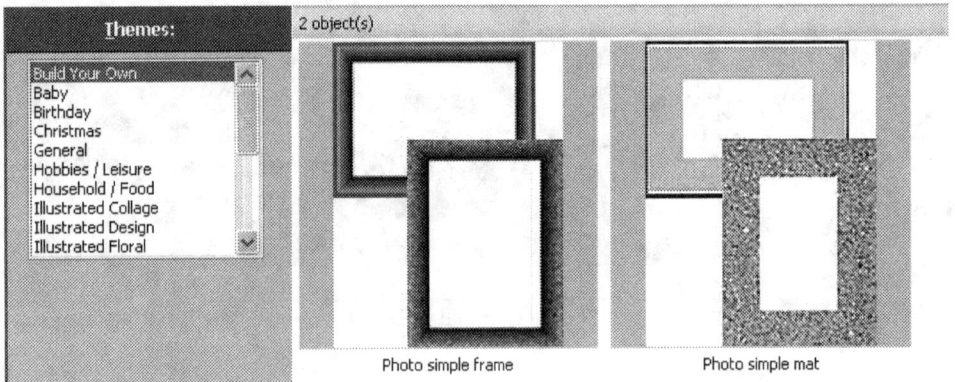

Photo simple frame          Photo simple mat

Pick the option you want, click the Open button, and continue using the following steps:

1. If the picture you want is already in the File palette, click the file to select it, and then click Next> to continue. If the file is not in the File palette, use the options in the Simple Mat or Simple Frame task bar to open a picture, scan in a picture, or download a picture from a camera.

2. The Gallery opens. Use the Browse tab or the Find tab to locate the object you want to use to build the frame or matte, as described in Chapter 3. Select the object and click Open.

3. The next version of the Simple Mat or Simple Frame task bar enables you to pick the width of the frame or matte you want to apply. Click the option you want to see a preview of the result, as shown in Figure 11-13. Click Next> when you're done admiring your work.

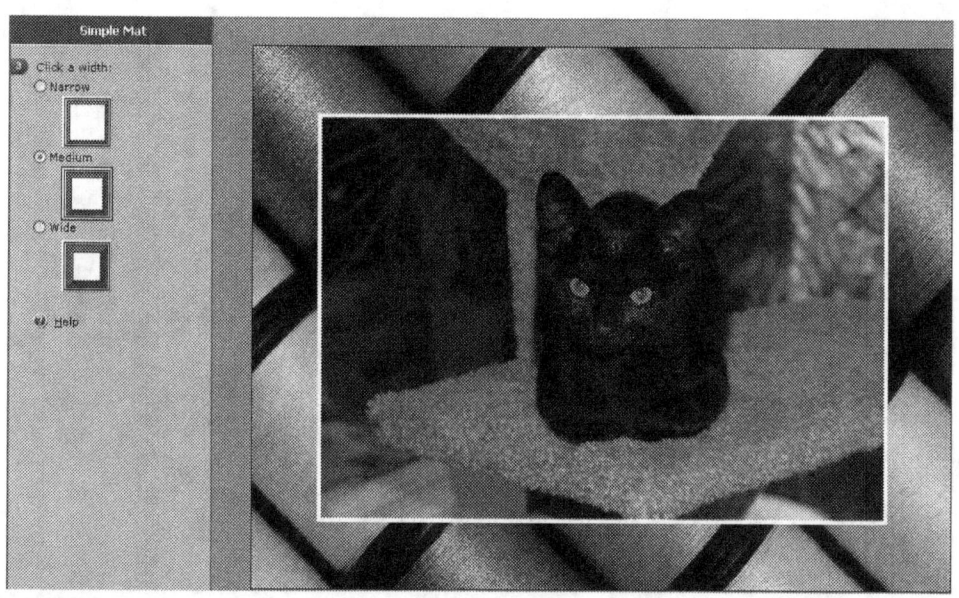

Choosing the frame or matte width shows you how the picture will look in that frame or matte.

**11**

4.  If you are creating a matte, the next frame enables you to pick a simple shape as the outline of the picture. Once you pick one of the shapes, you can see a preview of the result (see Figure 11-14). This step is skipped if you are building a frame. Click Next> to proceed.

5.  Use the next version of the task bar to change the color of the matte either by picking one of the preset colors at the top of the task bar or by clicking Choose Your Own Color to pick a color from the color wheel. Click Next> to continue.

6.  Use the sizing rectangle and sizing handles to move or resize the image within the frame or matte.

7.  Click Done to complete the work.

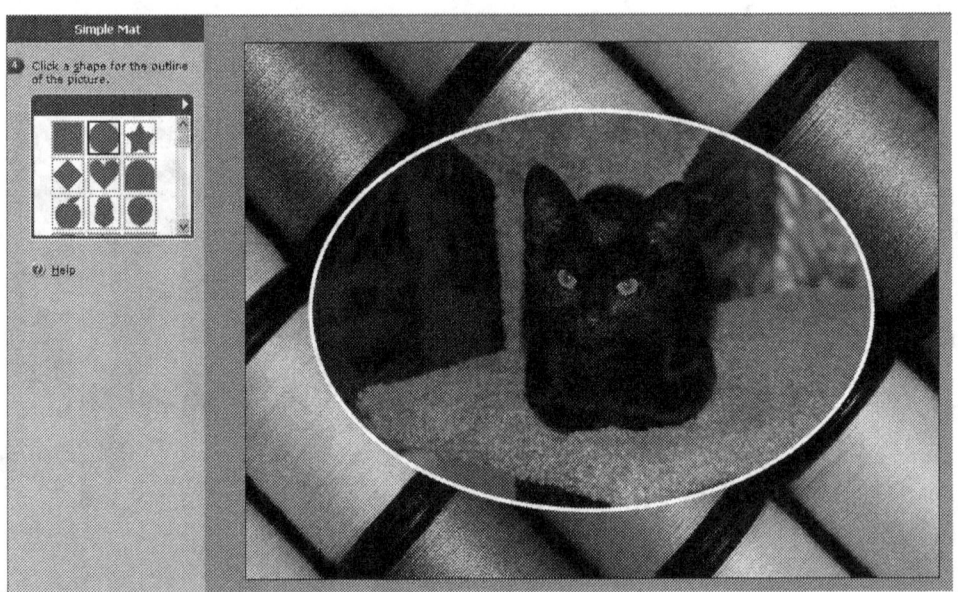

Select a shape to use as a matte, and see the result right away.

The task bars in the previous steps were labeled "Simple Mat" because I used the example of building a matte. If you choose to build a frame, the task bars are identical with the exception of the title. As mentioned, the task bar in Step 4 does not appear for frames.

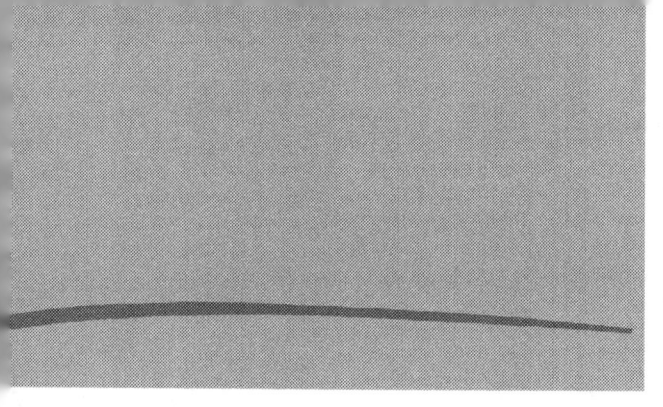

# Apply Filters
# to Customize
# Your Picture

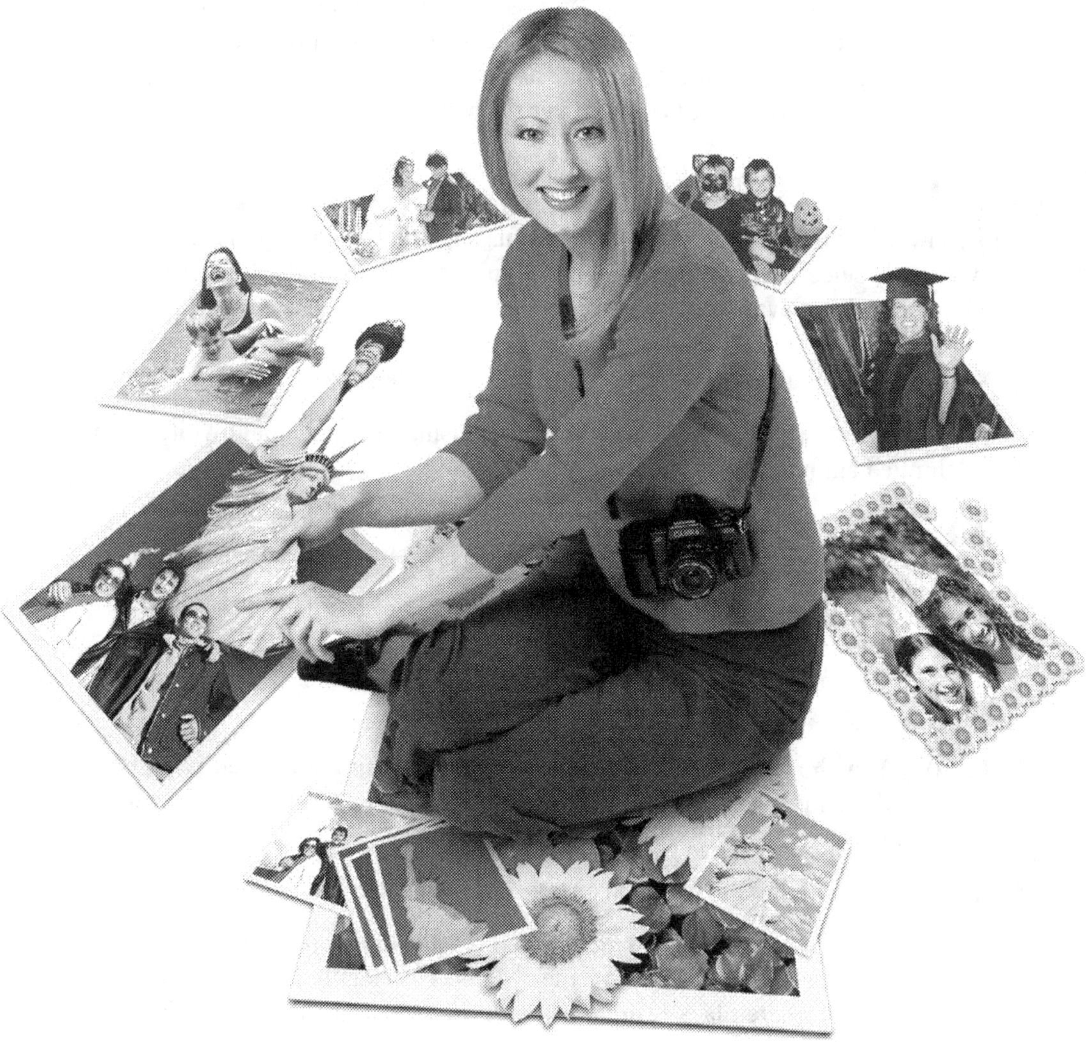

## How to…

- Apply quick filters
- Use standard filters
- Modify filter settings to get the effect you want

I've never been the kind of artist who could create a watercolor painting or a drawing. But that hasn't kept me from wanting to create, draw, and paint—it was just that the results were atrocious. But using Digital Image Pro's filters, I can convert my photographs (which I happen to think are mostly pretty good!) into crayon drawings, pastels, watercolor, line art, and more. And by fine-tuning the filter parameters, I have a lot of control over the results.

# Apply a Quick Filter

If all you want to do is apply a filter without fussing with settings, you can do so easily. Simply select Effects | Filters, and then pick the name of the filter from the submenu. The filters available are as follows:

- **Chalk**   Simulates drawing in coarse colored chalk strokes (see Figure 12-1).

- **Charcoal**   Draws the image in charcoal, using only black and white, with limited amounts of gray.

- **Chrome**   Renders the image in shades of reflective chrome, using only black and white and some gray. The result is pretty much unrecognizable from the original photo.

- **Colored Pencil**   Renders the image in colored pencil. The similarity to the strokes made by someone drawing in this medium is uncanny (see Figure 12-2).

- **Dry Brush**   Simulates the image in "paints" using a limited palette of colors and a dry brush. Quite a lot of detail is preserved, however (see Figure 12-3).

- **Emboss**   Shows the image in a very sharp-edged style with lots of contrast.

- **Film Grain**   Reduces the palette of colors and simulates missing colors by dithering (mixing colors together). This is especially noticeable in the dark areas, where black is mixed in with the predominant color to simulate shadows (see Figure 12-4).

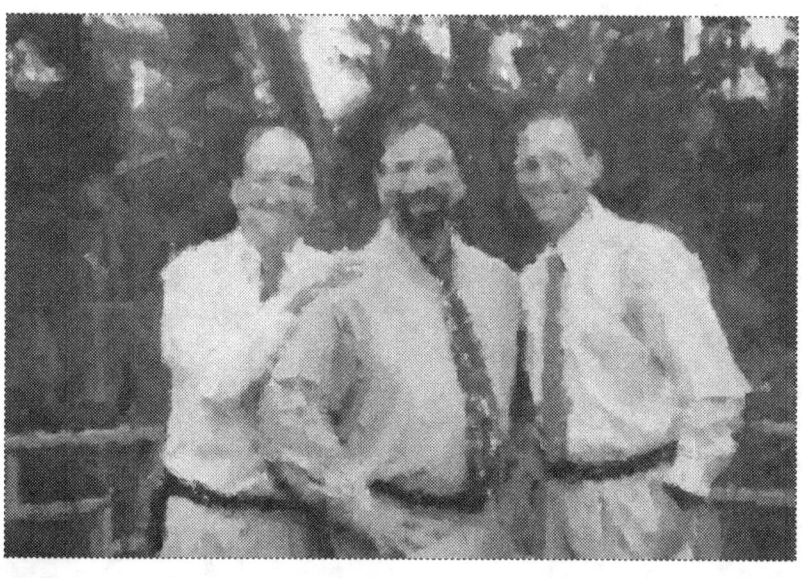

Coarse, colored chalk gives an abstract look to an image.

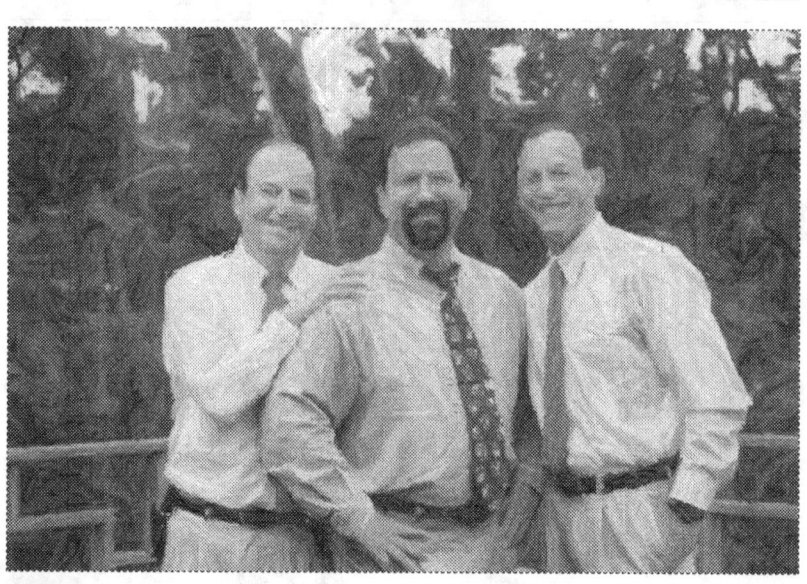

Colored pencil preserves most of the details but gives the image a very artistic look.

12

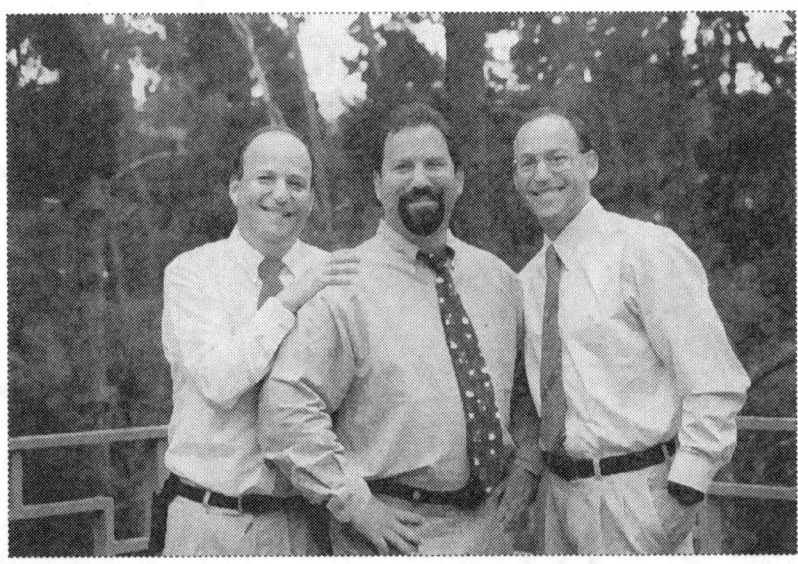

You say you can't paint? Well, you'd never know it with the Dry Brush filter.

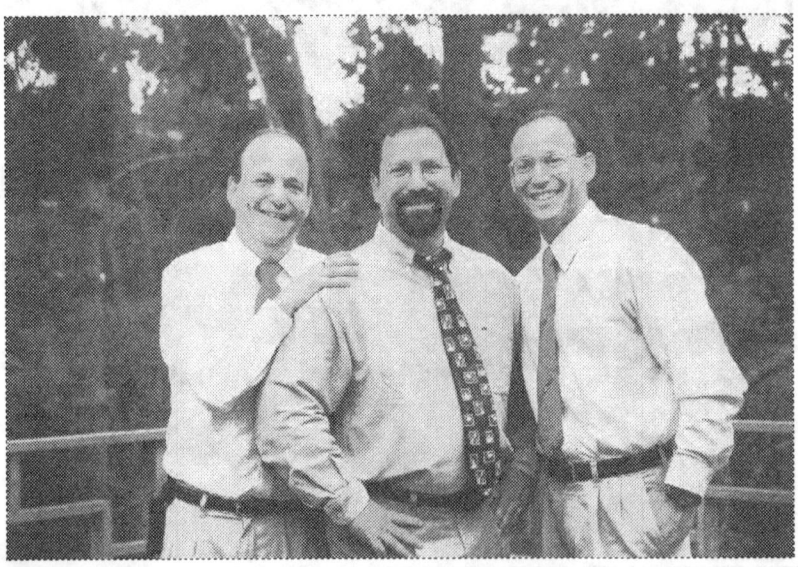

Film Grain dithers a limited palette of colors to produce this effect.

- **Glowing Edges**   Makes the entire image dark, except for brightly colored lines where the edges were.

- **Mosaic**   Shows the image as a set of tiles.

- **Stained Glass**   Displays the image as blocks of stained glass. The rendering is so coarse that the result really isn't usable for much.

- **Water Color**   Similar to Dry Brush, Water Color displays how the image would look if painted.

# Apply Interactive Filters

Digital Image Pro comes with a huge assortment of filters, divided up into categories. Many of these filters aren't particularly useful for digital photographs, but many of them are. You have just about every conceivable media available, including colored pencils, chalk, charcoal, Conte crayons, water colors, oil paints, ink, markers, and pencil. You can paint on almost any surface, including burlap, lattice, mosaic tile, cloth, and even concrete! You can change many of the parameters to customize each filter.

To start working with the interactive filters, select Effects | Filters | All Filters to open the Filters task bar.

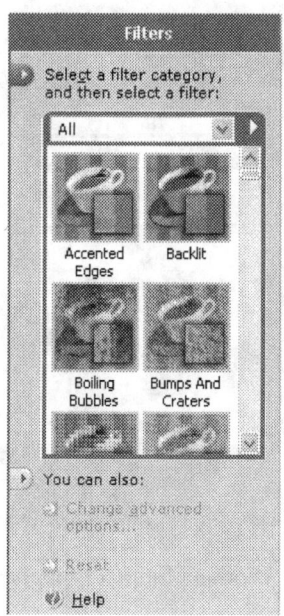

## Choose a Filter Category

You can choose a filter category from the drop-down list. When you do, the list of filters for that category appears in the scrolling list below the category drop-down list. You can also click the right arrow to the right of the category drop-down list. This displays the list of filters in a submenu—you won't have to scroll through the list to see what filters are available. Here is the list for the Arts & Crafts category:

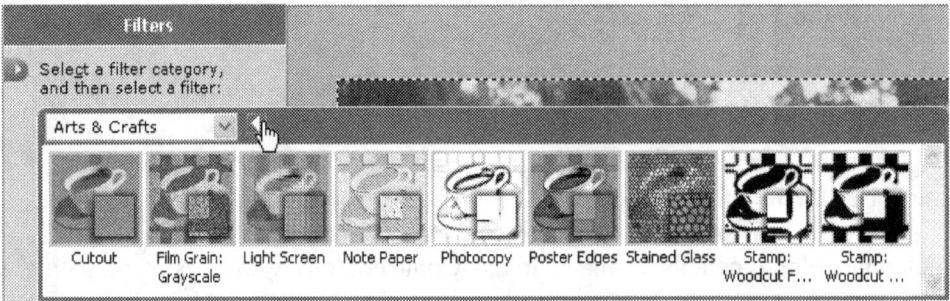

To "retract" the list, click the left arrow to the right of the category drop-down list.

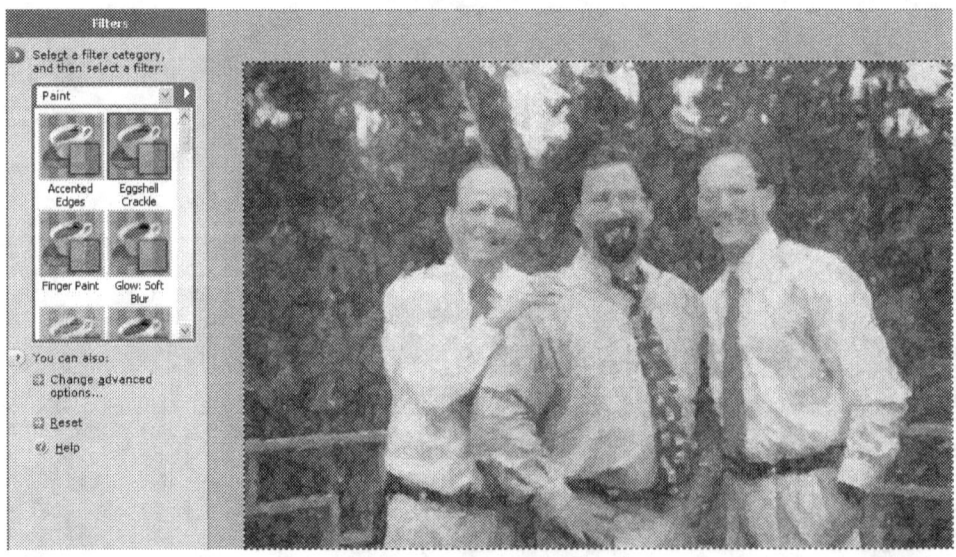

When you first choose a filter, it is applied to the image with the default parameters.

## Choose a Filter

Pick a filter from either the scrolling list or from the submenu. Once you do, the filter is applied to the image with the default settings, as shown in Figure 12-5.

## Change the Filter Settings

All the filters have various settings you can use to customize the filter results. To access these settings, click Change Advanced Options in the Filters task bar. The parameters vary from filter to filter, and you change the settings using the sliders or the associated fields. To change the field values, type in a value or use the spinners.

For many filters, you can set the type of brush by clicking the right arrow alongside the Brush field.

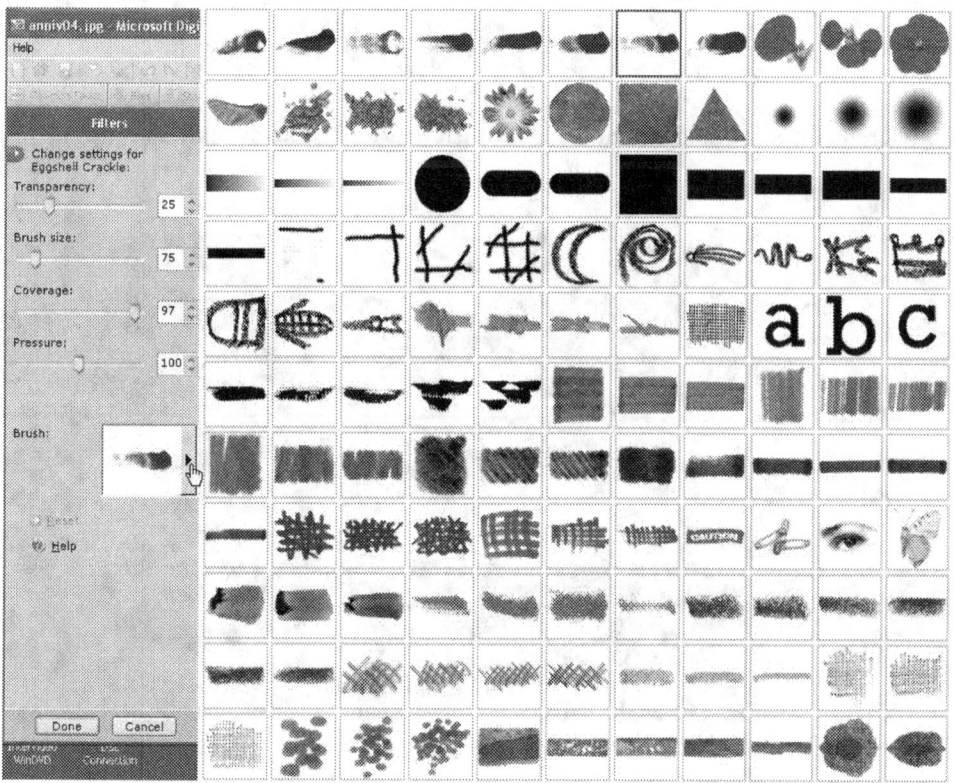

Changing the brush has a significant effect on the filter. For example, here is a portion of a watercolor filter using a short, stubby brush stroke:

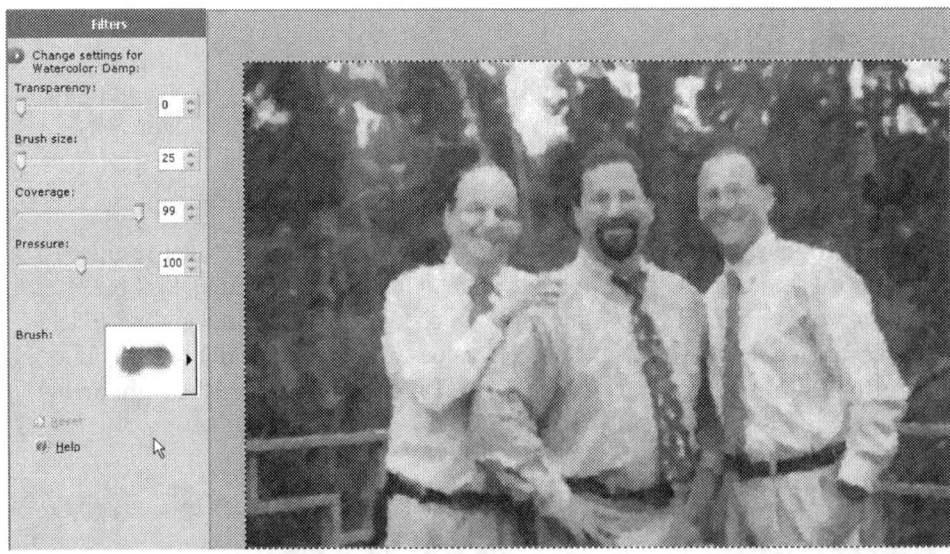

Here is the same image, but using a brush that looks like a small insect.

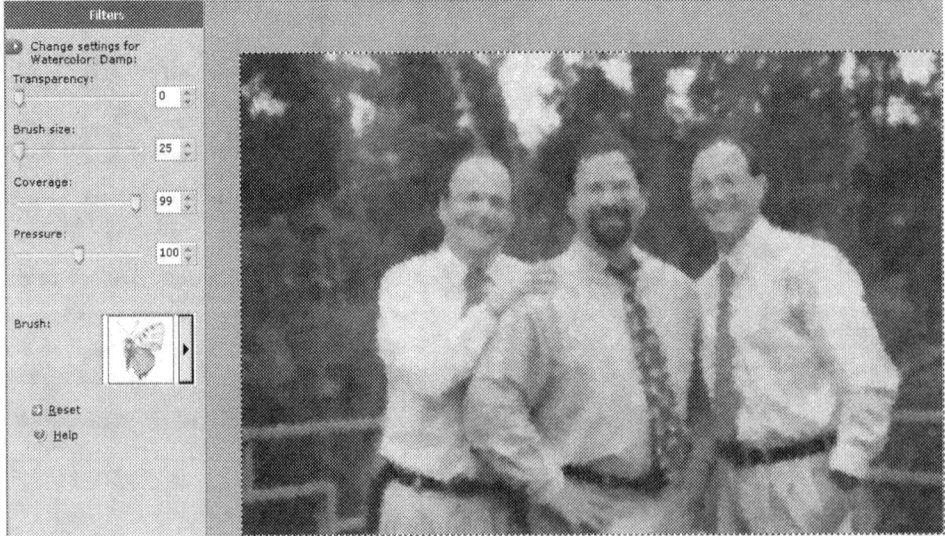

# Understand Some Useful Filters

There are far too many filters available for this book to cover them all. Instead, I have chosen some of my favorite effects, and focused on those that are most useful with digital photographs. Many of the filters produce a result that is unrecognizable from the original photo, and we won't cover those.

# Use the Arts & Crafts Filters

The Arts & Crafts category uses a variety of different arts and crafts materials to render the image, including colored paper, film, embossing, and woodcut. This category is one of my favorites because it preserves much of the original detail while still giving lots of variation in the filtered result.

## Use the Arts & Crafts Cutout Filter

The Cutout filter produces a result that looks like it was built up from pieces of colored paper (see Figure 12-6). The settings are as follows:

- **Transparency**   The transparency setting determines how much of the original image shows through the filtered result. Setting a high value of transparency enables a lot of the original image to show through.

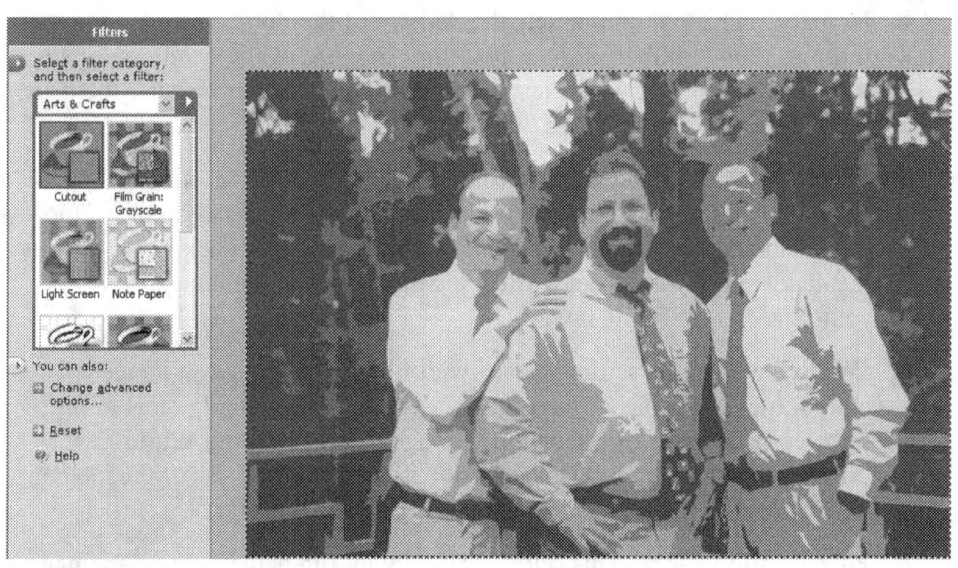

12

The Cutout filter produces a result that looks like it was created from pieces of colored paper.

- **Number of Levels**  This sets the number of levels of colored paper you use—the more levels, the more colors are available in the image. Thus, increasing the number of levels provides more colors and more detail in the final image.

- **Edge Simplicity**  Determines how closely the edges of the sheets of "colored paper" match the original edges in the image. A low value matches the original edges closely. This setting tunes the edges at a coarse level; use Edge Fidelity to make more subtle changes to the edges.

- **Edge Fidelity**  This setting has little effect at low values of Edge Simplicity; at high values, it modifies the edges in the filtered result to more closely match the details of the edges in the original image.

## Use the Arts & Crafts Film Grain: Grayscale Filter

This filter (see Figure 12-7) reduces the image to two colors, and combines the light and dark colors in fine dot patterns (called *dithering*) to simulate the texture and color of the original image. The settings are as follows:

- **Transparency**  Discussed previously.

- **Density**  This parameter sets the density of the dots. At high settings, there is a low number of dots, resulting in more of the bright color (or white), whereas at low settings the image is much darker because there are more dots/grids in the image.

- **Black Level**  This setting is used with filters that reduce an image to two colors. It changes the amount of black (or the background color) in the dark-colored areas of the original image. Increasing the Black Level darkens the dark areas. This does not affect the light areas of the image, which is controlled by the White Level.

- **White Level**  This setting is used with filters that reduce an image to two colors. It changes the amount of white (or the foreground color) in the light-colored areas of the original image. Increasing the White Level brightens the light areas. This does not affect the dark areas of the image, which are controlled by the Black Level.

- **Foreground Color**  This setting is used with filters that reduce an image to two colors. Pick the foreground color from the color squares. The foreground color is used for the lighter areas of the image.

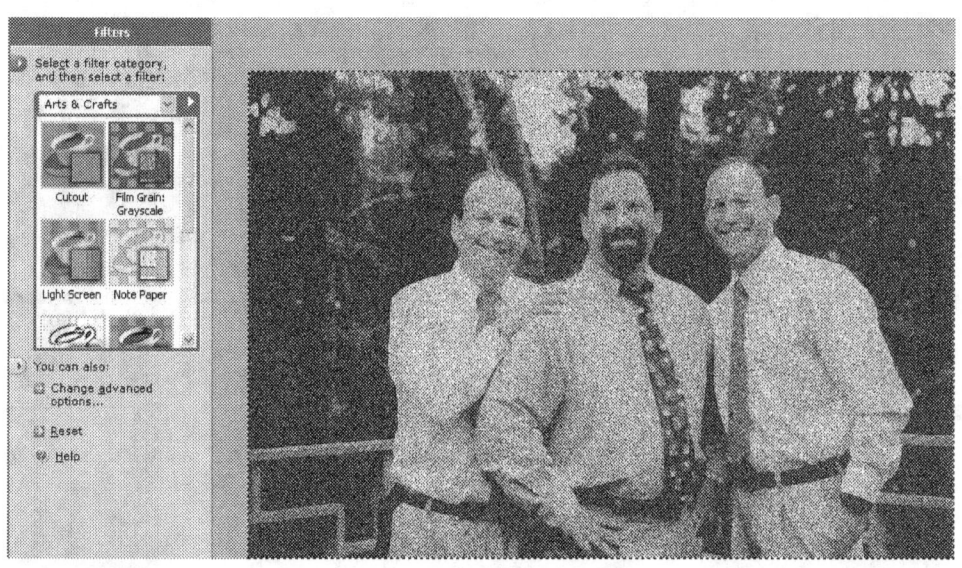

Two colors is all you need with the Film Grain filter.

- **Background Color**   This setting is used with filters that reduce an image to two colors. Pick the background color from the color squares. The background color is used for the darker areas of the image.

## Use the Arts & Crafts Light Screen Filter

This filter produces a result that looks like it was built from small square tiles (see Figure 12-8). The tiles are three-dimensional: light-colored tiles stick out of the image, dark-colored tiles are recessed. The settings are as follows:

- **Transparency**   Discussed previously.

- **Square Size**   This sets the size of the squares. A small square size preserves more of the detail of the image.

- **Relief**   This setting increases or decreases the difference between the high (light colors) and the low (dark colors) areas.

12

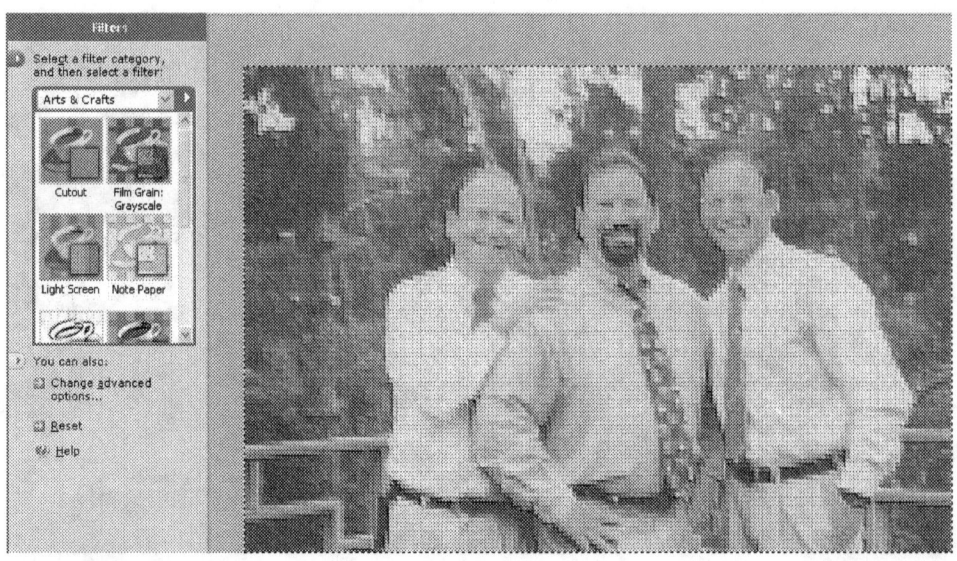

Build an image out of tiles with the Light Screen Filter.

## Use the Arts & Crafts Note Paper Filter

This filter reduces the image to two colors and renders it as embossing on paper (see Figure 12-9). You can control the details of the embossing, as well as the color used. The settings are as follows:

- **Transparency**   Discussed previously.

- **Image Balance**   This setting establishes the balance between the light and dark areas of the filtered image. A high value of Image Balance darkens more of the light areas, while low values lighten more of the dark areas.

- **Graininess**   This setting sets the fineness of the grain. At low values, the grain is very fine—almost to the point of being invisible. At high levels, you can clearly see the coarse grain.

- **Relief**   Discussed previously.

- **Paper Color**   Sets the color used for the dark area of the image. Choose the paper color from the color squares.

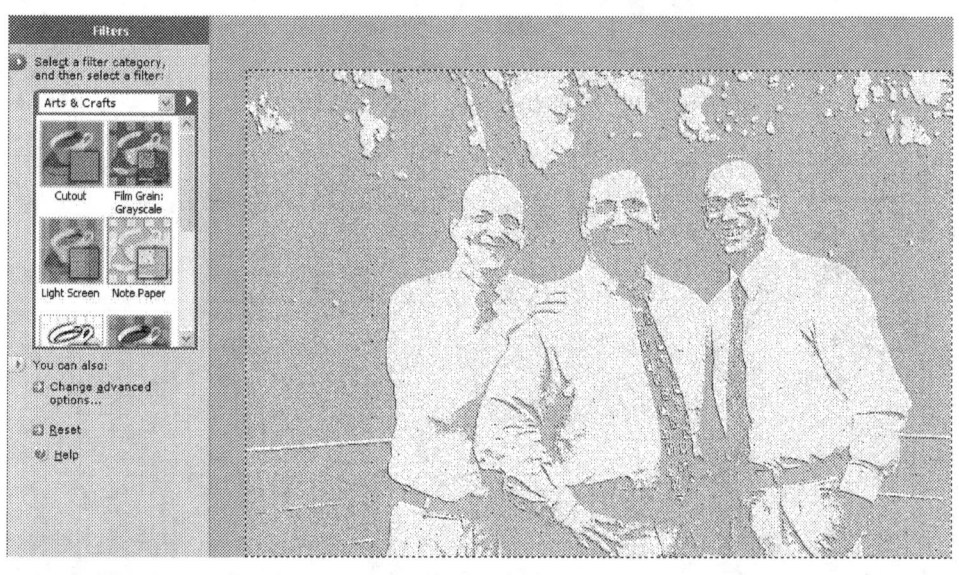

Emboss your image on colored (or white) notepaper.

- **Emboss Color**   This color is used for the lighter areas of the image. Choose embossing color from the color squares.

## Use the Arts & Crafts Photocopy Filter

This is another filter that reduces an image to two colors, but it highlights the original edges by drawing them with heavy black lines (see Figure 12-10). The settings are as follows:

- **Transparency**   Discussed previously.
- **Detail**   High values of Detail preserve more of the details from the original image.
- **Darkness**   Specifies how dark (and how wide) the edges are drawn in the filtered result. Higher values increase the darkness at the edges.

12

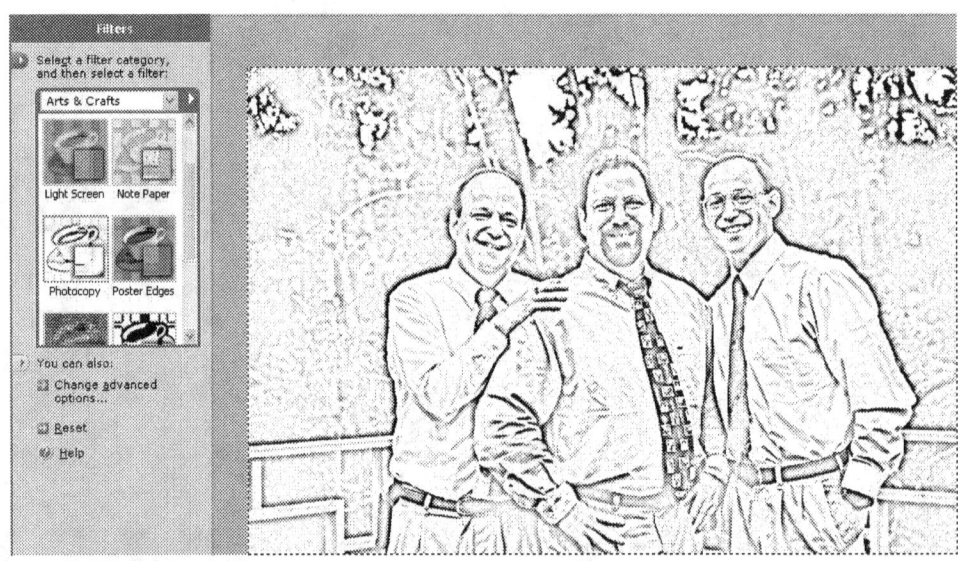

A two-color photocopier might produce the same result.

## Use the Arts & Crafts Poster Edges Filter

This filter applies *posterization* to the image. The result is an image with a smaller color palette, and areas of the original image that had subtle color changes are now drawn all in one color, resulting in some "patchiness" (see Figure 12-11). The settings are as follows:

- **Transparency**  Discussed previously.

- **Edge Thickness**  Increasing this setting increases the width of the edges.

- **Edge Intensity**  Increasing this setting adds more dark coloring around the edges to make them more noticeable.

- **Posterization**  Increasing this setting increases the number of colors used in the palette, reducing the posterization effect.

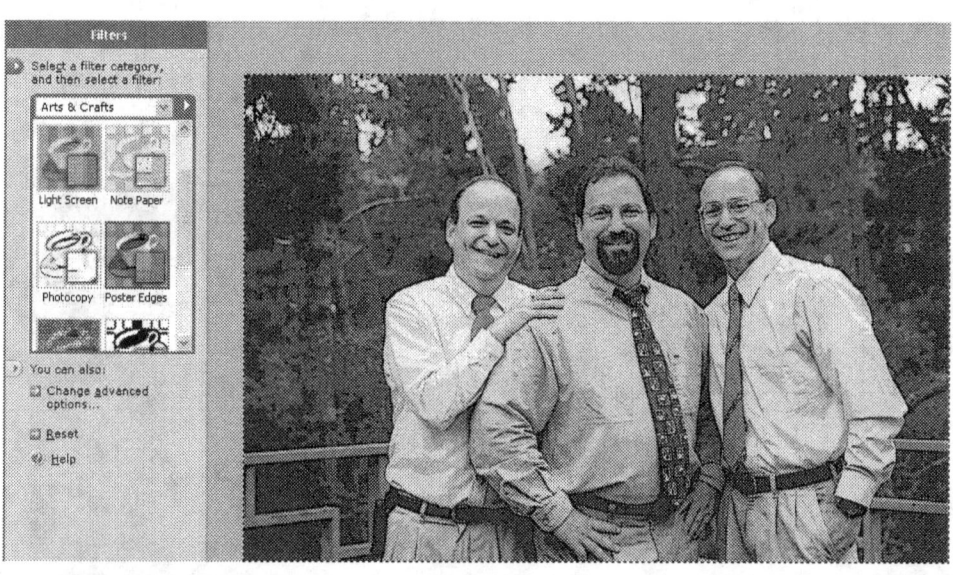

Posterization reduces the number of colors in the image and introduces some patches of color in the final result.

## Use the Arts & Crafts Stained Glass Filter

This filter renders the image as stained glass (see Figure 12-12). You need to use very small pieces of glass to preserve any of the details. The settings are as follows:

- **Transparency**   Discussed previously.

- **Cell Size**   Sets the size of the glass cells. Use a small value to preserve the detail of the original image.

- **Border thickness**   Sets the width of the border between the glass cells.

- **Light Intensity**   Sets the intensity of the light shining through the glass. In other words, this parameter controls the brightness of the image.

- **Border Color**   Sets the color of the border between the glass cells. Use a lighter color to have a less noticeable effect. Choose the color from the color square.

12

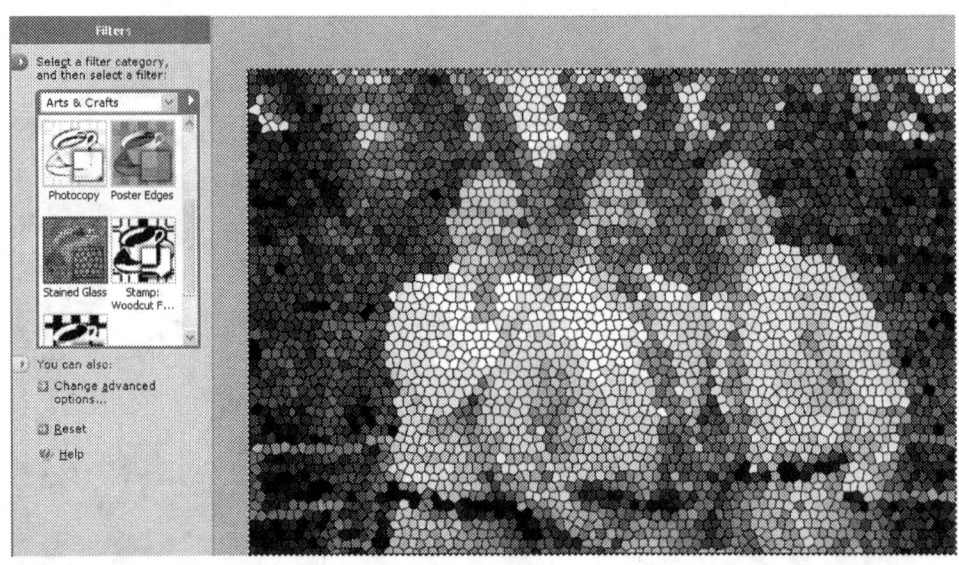

Transform your image into stained glass—but you probably wouldn't put it up in a church!

## Use the Chalk Filters

The Chalk category provides a variety of results that look like they were drawn in (what else?) chalk—either colored chalk or black chalk. All the filters have the same set of parameters, which are as follows:

- **Transparency** Discussed previously.

- **Brush Size** For paint-type filters, this setting determines the size of the brush used—and thus the amount of detail possible. A small brush size preserves a lot of the original detail; large values degenerate to unrecognizable swatches.

- **Coverage** Determines how much of the canvas is covered with paint (or other media). A low value leaves large dark areas. You might not think this would be useful, but if you raise the transparency, a low coverage has the effect of just adding a few touches of paint (or marker, or pencil, and so on) to a photograph.

- **Pressure** Sets the pressure used to apply the filter media. A low pressure creates a barely visible result, whereas high pressure creates the full effect.

■   **Brush**   Choose the shape and size of the brush from the Brush field (discussed earlier in this chapter).

### Use the Chalk Chalk: Medium Filter

This filter draws the image in chalk at a medium level of detail (see Figure 12-13). As mentioned earlier in this chapter, which brush you choose makes a significant difference in how the image looks.

### Use the Chalk Chalk: Opaque Filter

This filter provides more of the original image detail and fills in all the areas in colored chalk (see Figure 12-14).

## Use the Charcoal Filters

The Charcoal filters are similar to chalk, except they tend to use rougher strokes, especially on the diagonal. The parameters are the same as the Chalk Filters.

### Use the Charcoal Charcoal: Drawing Filter

This filter gives a result with clearly visible strokes, especially in the dark areas (see Figure 12-15).

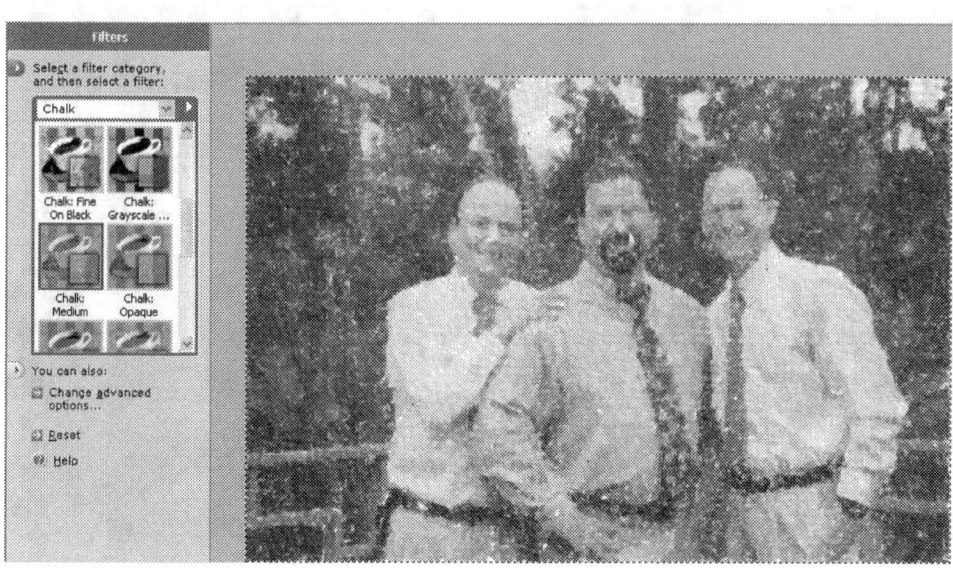

12

Chalk Chalk: Medium Filter

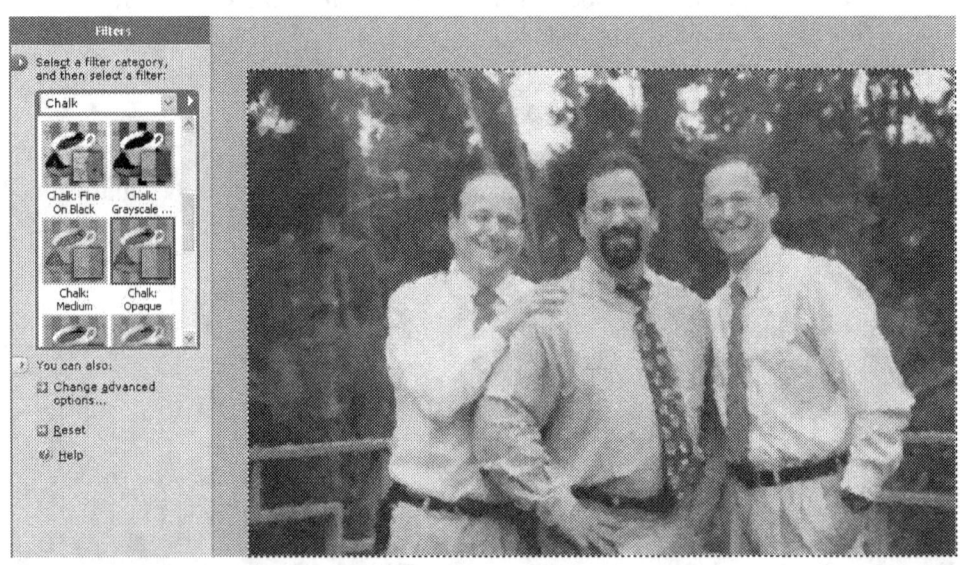

Chalk Chalk: Opaque Filter

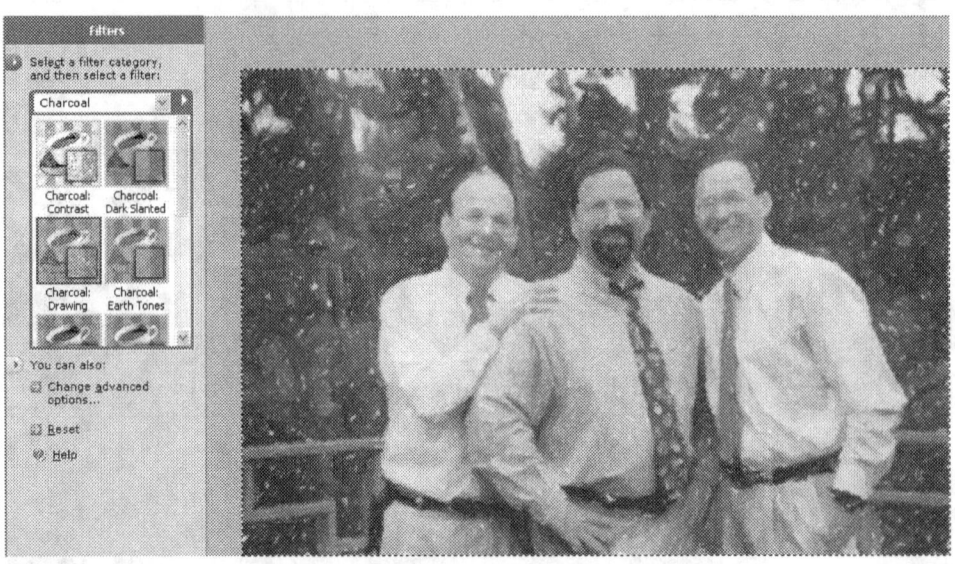

Charcoal Charcoal: Drawing Filter

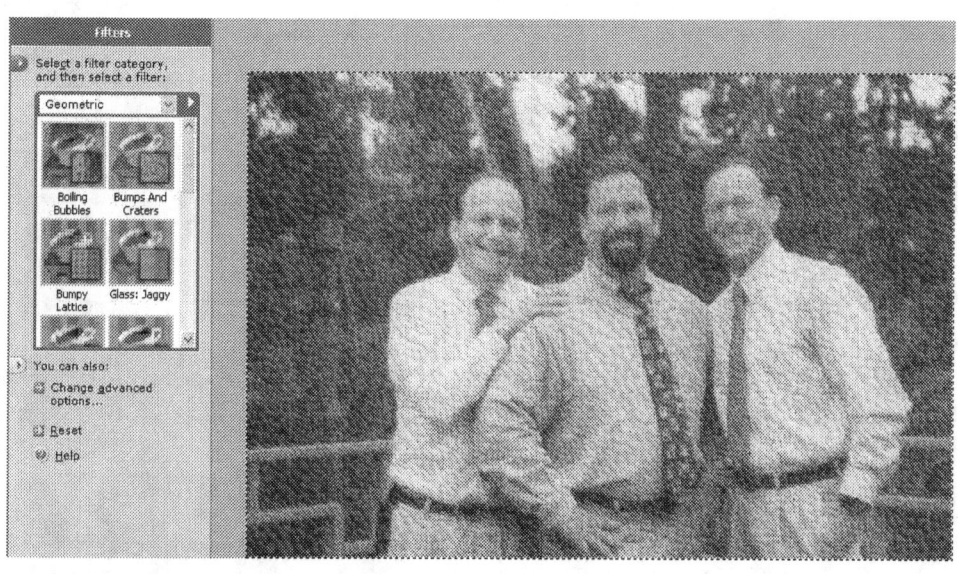

Geometric Bumps and Craters Filter

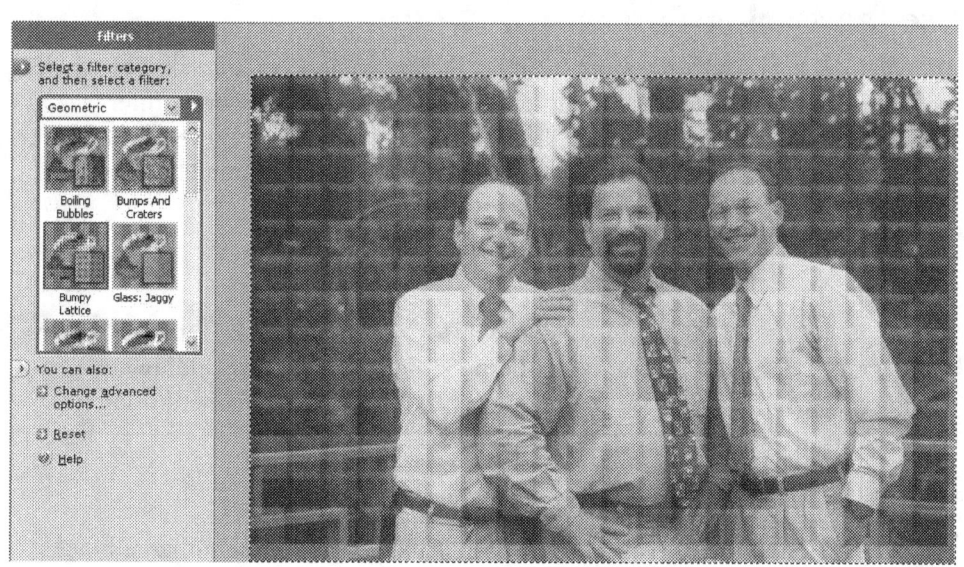

Geometric Bumpy Lattice Filter

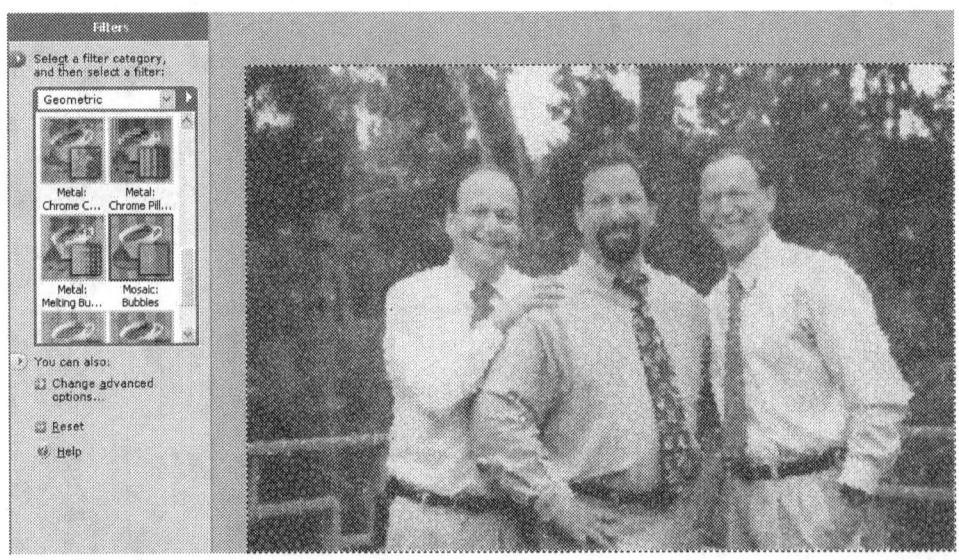

Geometric Mosaic: Bubble Filter

## Use the Marker Filters

The Marker filters render the image as if it were drawn in magic marker. The results tend to be pretty coarse because markers have big tips, but the Burlap filter (see Figure 12-21) is interesting because the result not only preserves much of the detail, but is drawn on burlap, so you can see the cloth pattern. The parameters are the same as for chalk.

## Use the Natural Filters

The biggest puzzle about the Natural filters is why they are called "natural." They apply a range of effects, including building an image from foil, adding a gauze underlay, and simulating cave painting (huh?). The parameters are the same as for chalk.

### Use the Natural Impressionist: Green Herbal Filter

The Impressionist filter gives a mottled look to the image, making large blocks of color look like they were painted, but preserving most of the fine detail (see Figure 12-22).

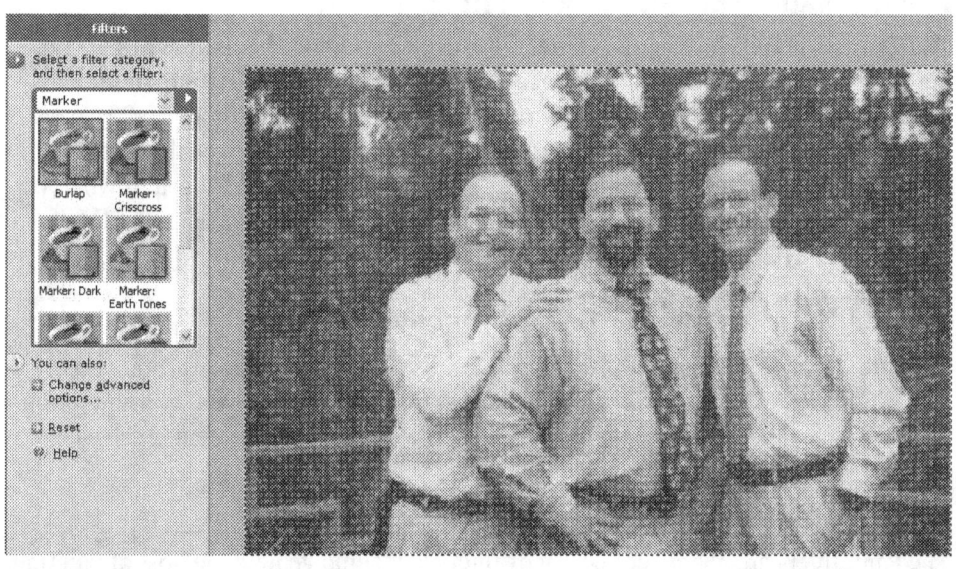

Marker Burlap Filter

12

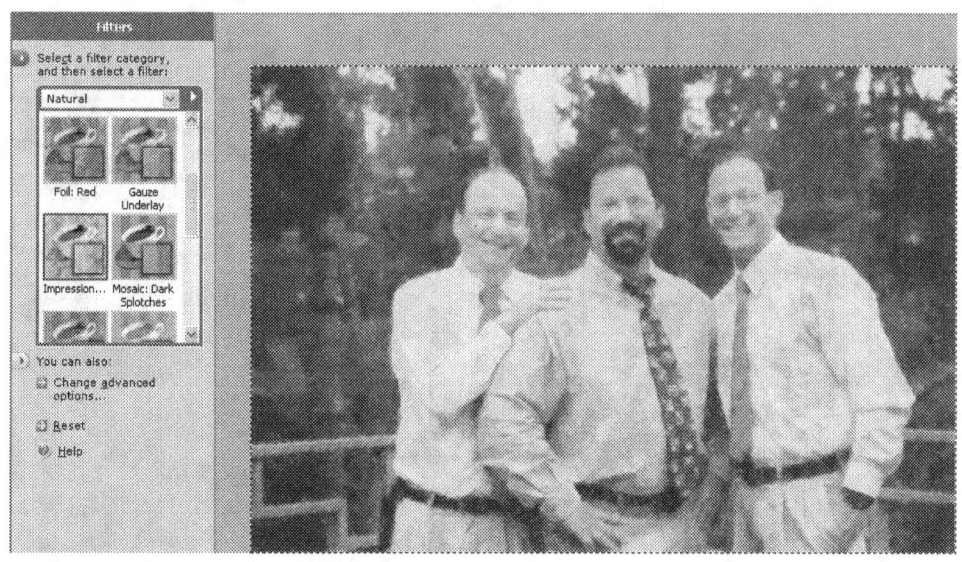

Natural Impressionist: Green Herbal Filter

### Use the Natural Quilt: Smooth Filter

The Quilt: Smooth filter applies a default square pattern to the image. In general, the squares aren't disruptive, but occasionally a square will be dumped into a detailed area (such as a face), with a rather jarring effect (see Figure 12-23). You can control this by setting the brush size: smaller brush sizes minimize these strangely placed squares. Changing the type of brush changes the square pattern to whatever you choose for the brush, giving you a great deal of control over what the final product looks like.

### Use the Natural Mosaic: Dark Splotches Filter

This filter makes the image look like it is being viewed through bathroom glass (see Figure 12-24). You can change the amount of detail preserved by minimizing the brush size, and change the glass pattern by switching to a different brush shape.

## Use the Paint Filters

The Paint filters are a large collection of filters that simulate a whole host of painting styles, including finger painting, pointillist, painting on eggshells, daubing, dry brush, fresco, and various impressionist styles. The differences between some of the filters are fairly subtle.

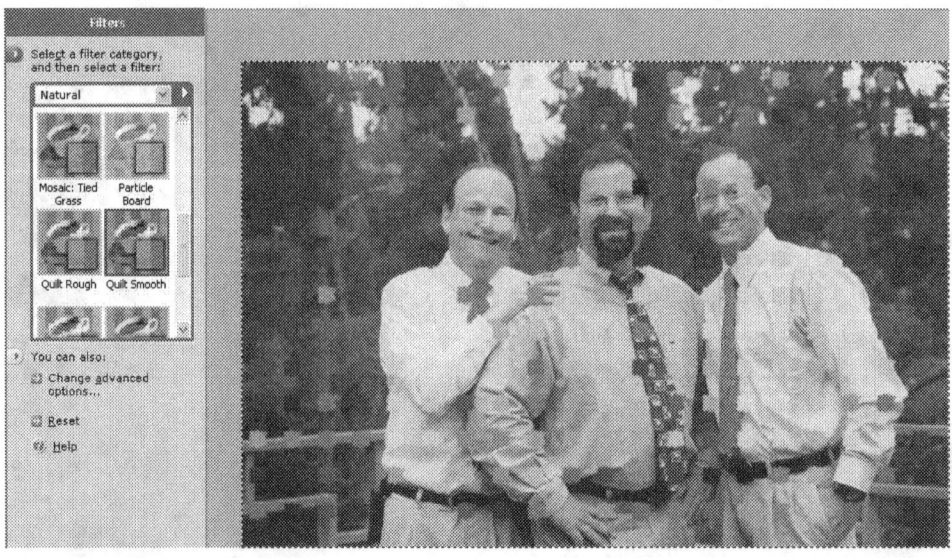

Natural Quilt: Smooth Filter with a square brush

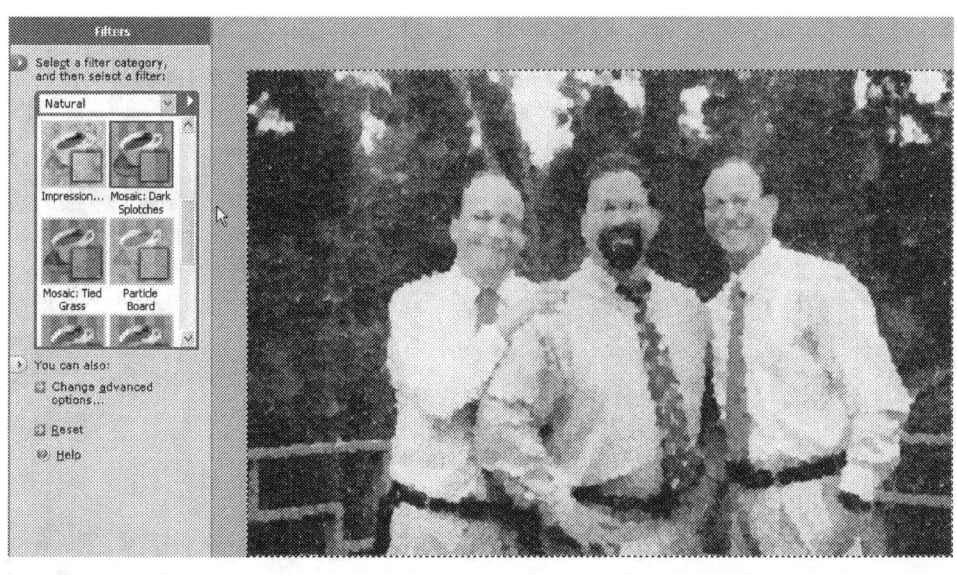

Natural Mosaic: Dark Splotches Filter

## Use the Paint Eggshell Crackle Filter

The Eggshell Crackle filter simulates painting the image onto a bed of crushed eggshells (see Figure 12-25). It sounds kind of strange, but the effect is interesting, as there are subtle shadings and borders between the pieces (the black and white image in Figure 12-25 really doesn't do it justice). You can change the basic shape of the shells by changing the brush shape.

## Use the Paint Old Paper Filter

The Old Paper Filter mutes the colors of the image and adds a texture to simulate printing the image on rough paper (see Figure 12-26). You can vary the texture by changing the brush shape, and make the texture less noticeable by reducing the transparency.

## Use the Paint Paint: Dark Freehand Filter

If you'd like your image to have the classic "oil painting" look, this is the filter to use. It works (in my opinion) better for this effect than any of the other paint filters (see Figure 12-27).

12

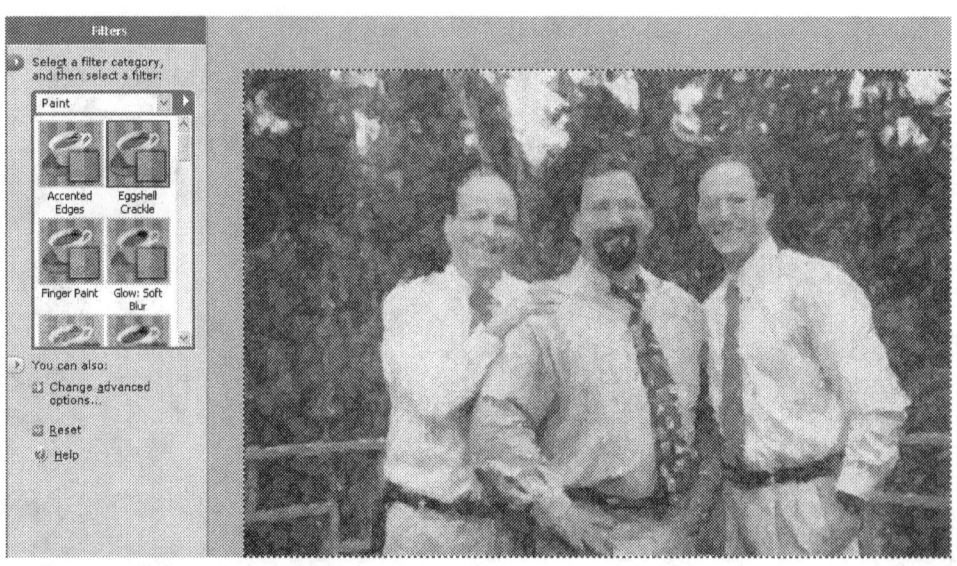

Paint Eggshell Crackle Filter

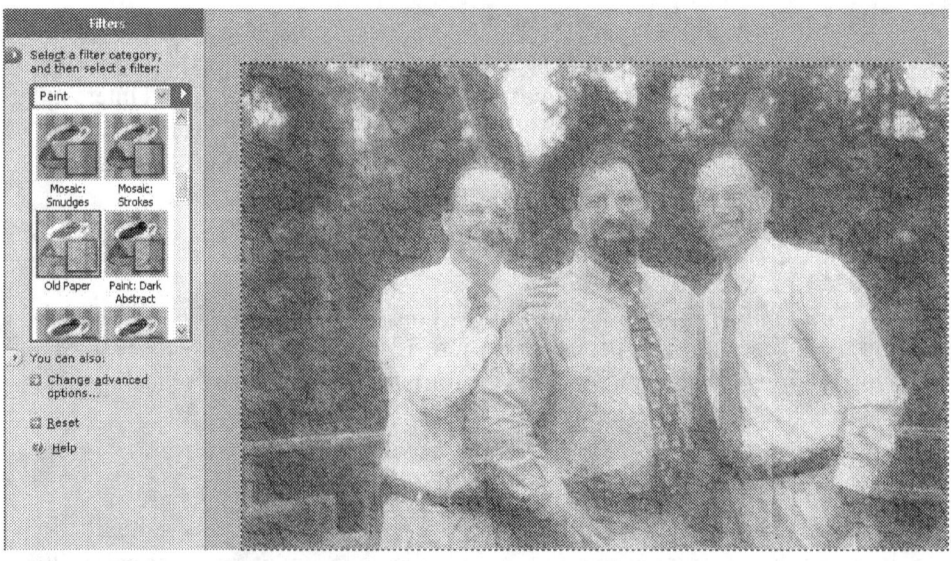

Paint Old Paper Filter

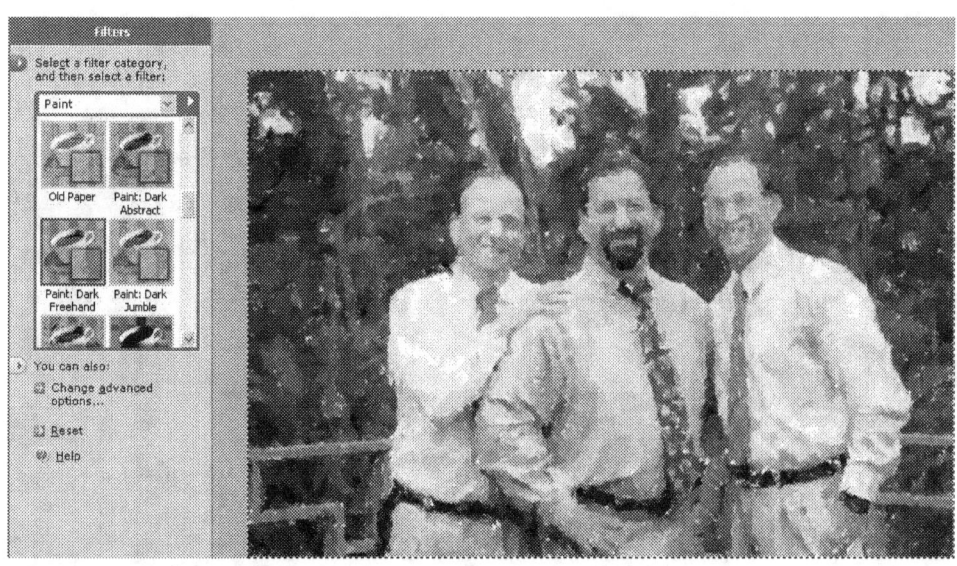

Paint Paint: Dark Freehand Filter

### Use the Paint Paint: Dry Brush Filter

The Paint: Dry Brush filter is another filter that is effective at giving the "painted" look to your image (see Figure 12-28). The paint daubs are quite visible (because of the use of a dry brush) but the different-colored areas blend together well.

### Use the Paint Paint: Slanted Filter

This is yet another effective paint filter, which renders the image in short diagonal strokes (see Figure 12-29). These strokes simulate the brush marks well, and yet preserve most of the detail of the original image.

## Use the Pencil Filters

The Pencil filters render the image as it might look if it had been drawn in pencil. Variations include different sketch patterns, paper, and the hardness of the pencil lead. The parameters are the same as for Chalk.

### Use the Pencil Crisscross: Pencil Filter

The Crisscross: Pencil filter adds pencil texture to the image (see Figure 12-30). This texture is most noticeable in the shadow areas and at interfaces between widely varying colors.

12

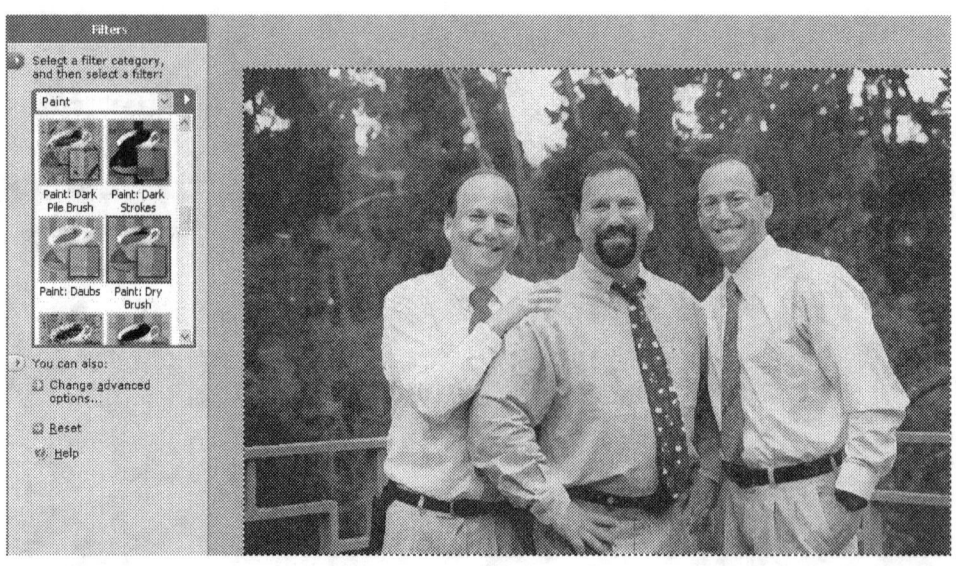

Paint Paint: Dry Brush Filter

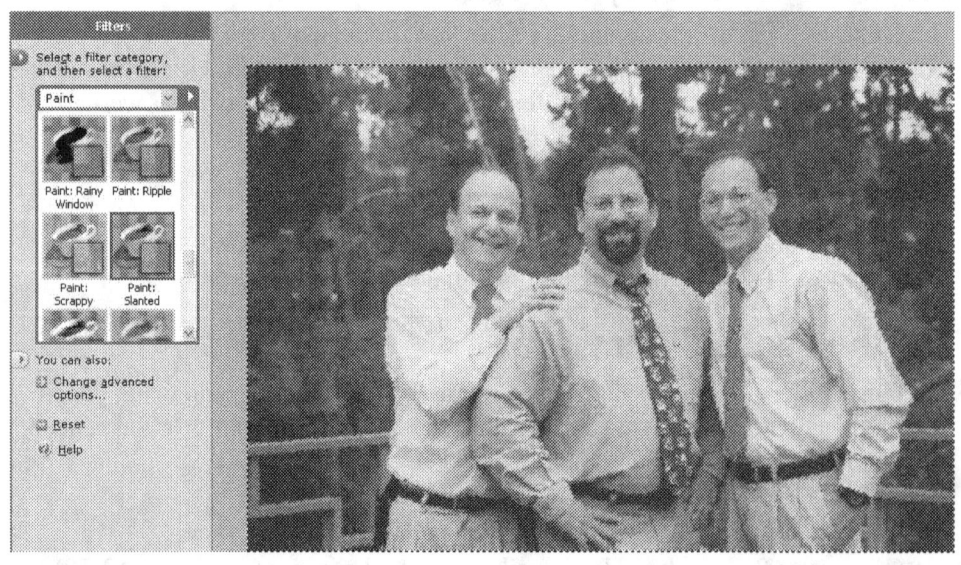

Paint Paint: Slanted Filter

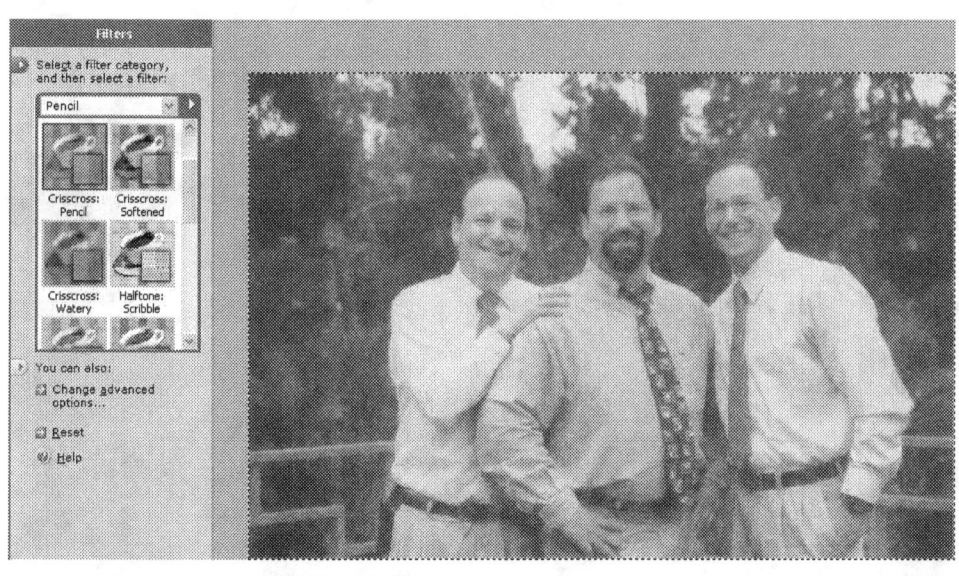

Pencil Crisscross: Pencil Filter

### Use the Pencil Pencil: Detailed Sketch Filter

This filter renders the image using a blunt-tipped pencil (see Figure 12-31). Broad areas of color are colored in, but edges are plainly visible as a pencil stroke of another color.

### Use the Pencil Pencil: Soft Sketch Filter

This filter uses vertical strokes that are clearly visible to render the image, yet it manages to preserve enough of the detail to keep the result recognizable (see Figure 12-32).

## Use the Photographic Filters

The photographic filters apply some limited photographic effects to the image. For example, you can apply the Sepia filter to change a color photograph into a sepia-tone image.

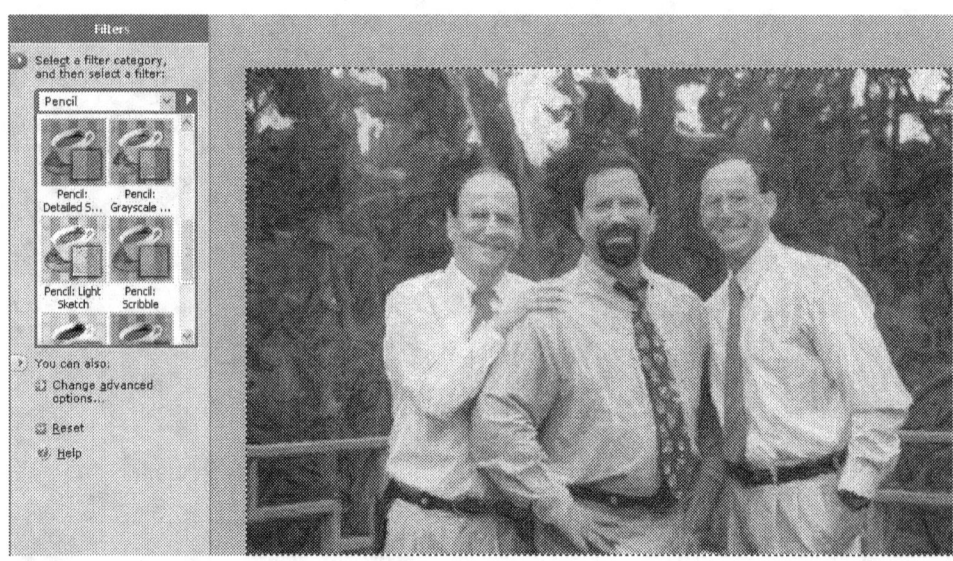

Pencil Pencil: Detailed Sketch Filter

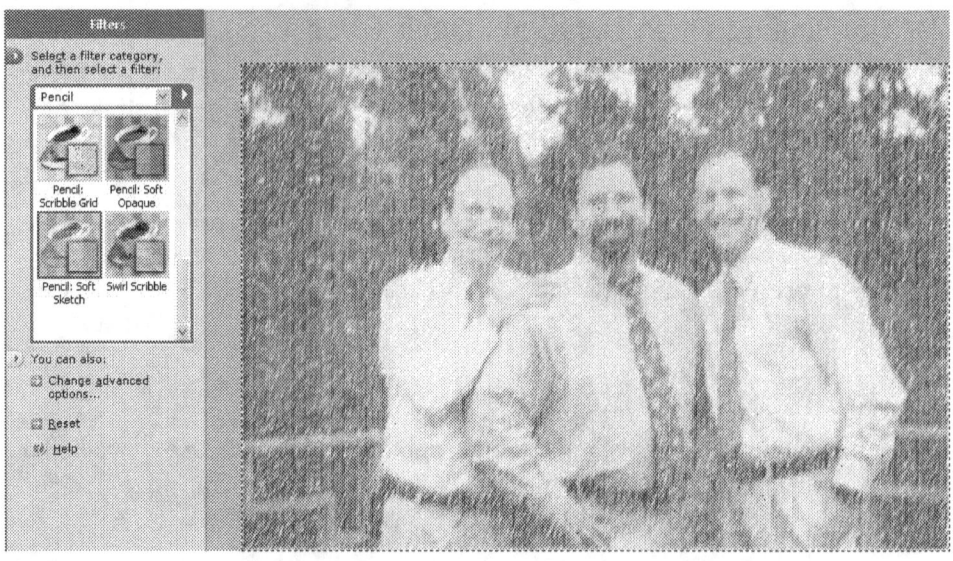

Pencil Pencil: Soft Sketch Filter

## Use the Photographic Film Grain: Rough Filter

The Film Grain: Rough filter applies grain to the image, almost like you used a very high-speed film or push-processed a lower speed film to get more sensitivity out of it (see Figure 12-33).

The parameters are as follows:

- **Transparency**    Discussed previously.

- **Graininess**    Controls the amount of grain applied to the photo. Lower values of this slider really do look a lot like high-speed film.

- **Grain Type**    Controls the pattern of the grain applied to the image. Choose the grain type from the Grain Type drop-down list.

- **Contrast**    Sets the overall contrast of the photograph.

- **Foreground Color and Background Color**    You can select either the foreground color or the background color by clicking one of the color boxes, but they seem to have little effect on the image.

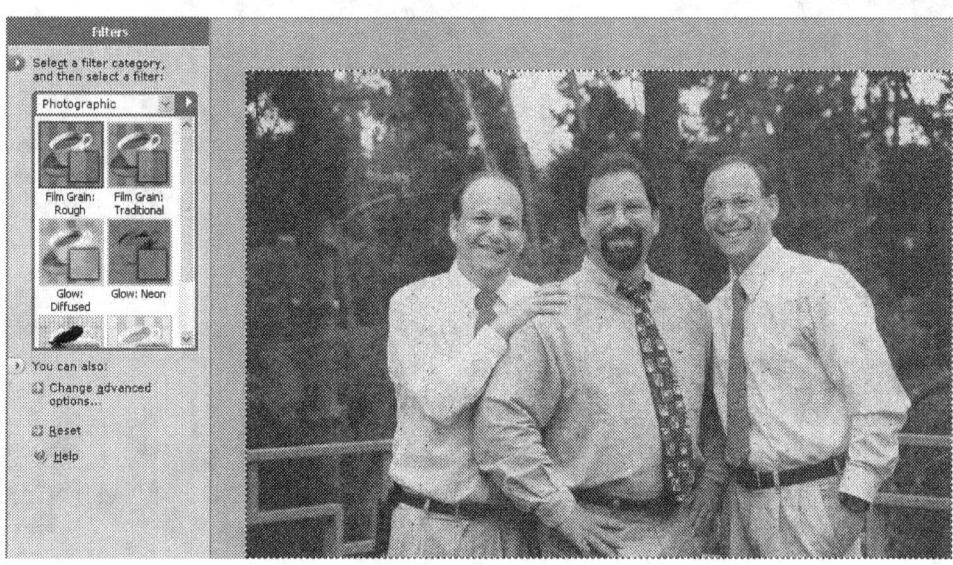

12

Photographic Film Grain: Rough Filter

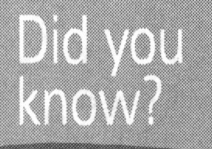

## Increase Your Speed

You can force a film to a higher "speed" (sensitivity to light) by leaving it in the development chemicals longer. This might be necessary when all you have is a low-speed film (for example, ISO 100) and encounter low-light conditions for which you really should have had a higher speed film. There are limits to how much you can increase the speed, and doing so degrades the quality of the image and introduces visible grain. This technique is called "push processing."

### Use the Photographic Halftone: Screen Filter

The Halftone: Screen filter converts the image to black and white, and applies a screen pattern to the image (see Figure 12-34). This screen pattern is only visible in the lighter areas of the image.

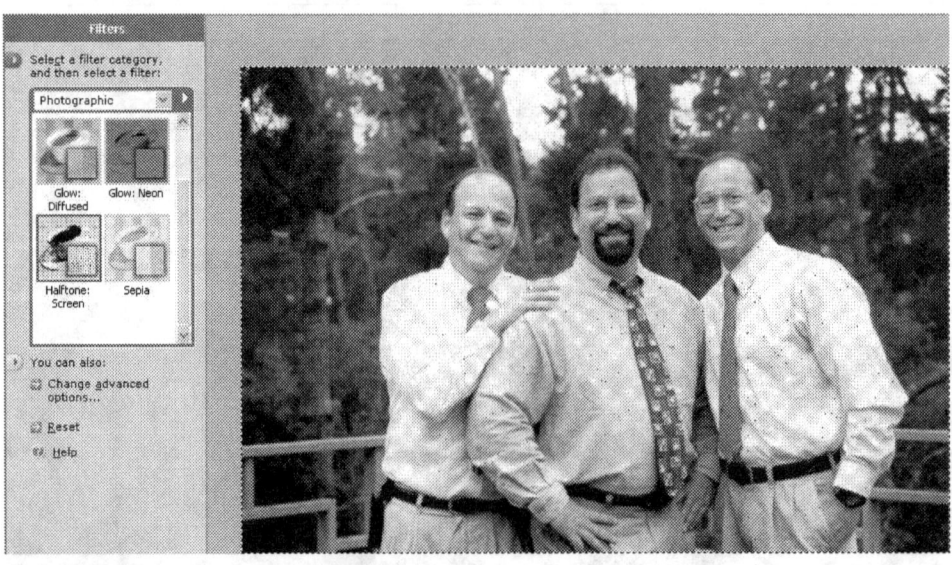

Photographic Halftone: Screen Filter

The parameters are as follows:

- **Transparency**    Discussed previously.

- **Size**    Sets the size of the "dots" in the screen pattern. Keep this small unless you want to obliterate your picture with the screen pattern.

- **Screen Type**    Sets the type of element (dots, lines, or circles) used to create the screen pattern. Choose the type from the drop-down list. Except for "dots," however, these options do not lead to an attractive result.

- **Contrast**    Sets the overall contrast of the photograph.

- **Foreground Color and Background Color**    You can select either the foreground color or the background color by clicking one of the color boxes, but they seem to have little effect on the image.

## Use the Pointillist Filters

The Pointillist filters (named after a short-lived painting technique) reduce the image to a set of points. The amount of detail preserved depends entirely on the size of the points, which is controlled only through the brush shape parameter. The only filter in this set that I use is the Pointillist: Sparse, shown in Figure 12-35.

## Use the Sketch Filters

The Sketch Filters render your image using various simulated media (chalk, charcoal, pen, pencil) with a variety of techniques, such as crisscross. For example, Figure 12-36 shows the Pencil: Canvas filter, which simulates using a sketching pencil on canvas. The parameters are as follows:

- **Texture**    Choose the texture of the canvas from the Texture field.

- **Light Position**    The position of the light has a big impact on how the texture looks. Choose the light position (such as *Top Right*) from the Light Position drop-down list.

- **Scaling**    Sets the size of the elements in the texture. A small size leaves a very fine-grained texture; a larger size is rougher.

- **Relief**    Sets the depth of the texture. Higher relief makes the texture visible in more areas of the image. For example, if you set the relief to a low value, the texture is not visible in the dark areas. If you set the relief to a high value, however, the text *is* visible in the dark areas.

12

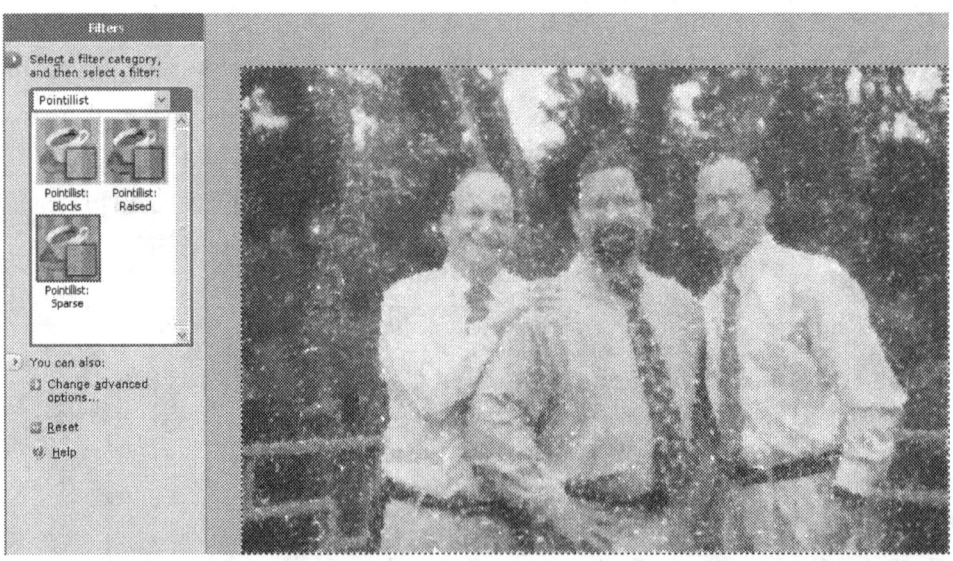

Pointillist Pointillist: Sparse Filter

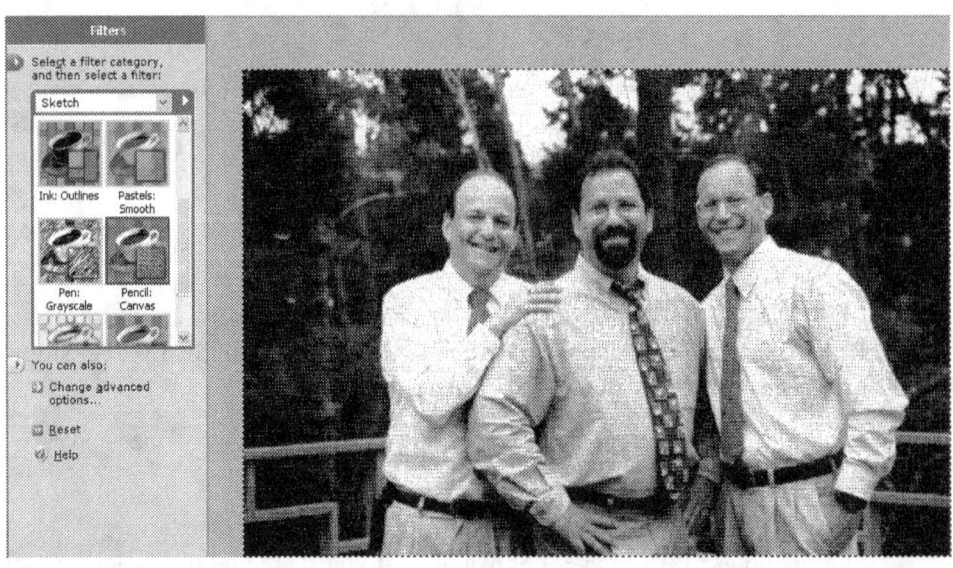

Sketch Pencil: Canvas Filter

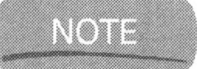 *You can invert the texture by selecting the Invert checkbox. The effect is to essentially reverse the texture pattern.*

# Use the Stamp Filters

The Stamp filters combine a variety of different media effects into one category. These include embossing, impressionist, mural, painting (with sponges, no less), and even torn scraps. The parameters are the same as for Chalk.

## Use the Stamp Paint: Dry Rag Filter

This filter simulates painting the image using a dry rag (hence the name). Dark backgrounds are especially effective in this filter. See Figure 12-37 for a sample.

## Use the Stamp Mural Filter

The Mural filter uses a large brush on a rough surface to render your image as a mural. See Figure 12-38 for a sample.

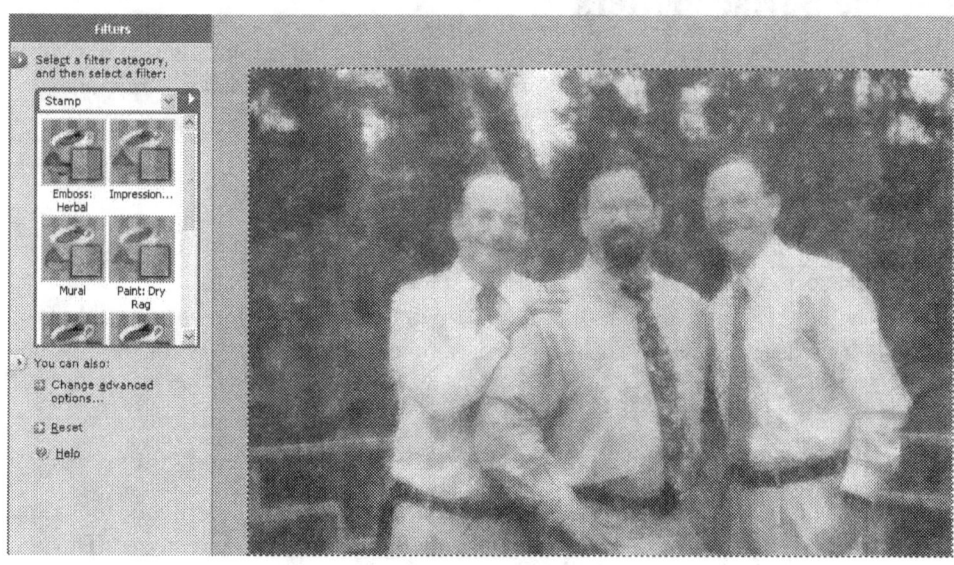

Stamp Paint: Dry Rag Filter

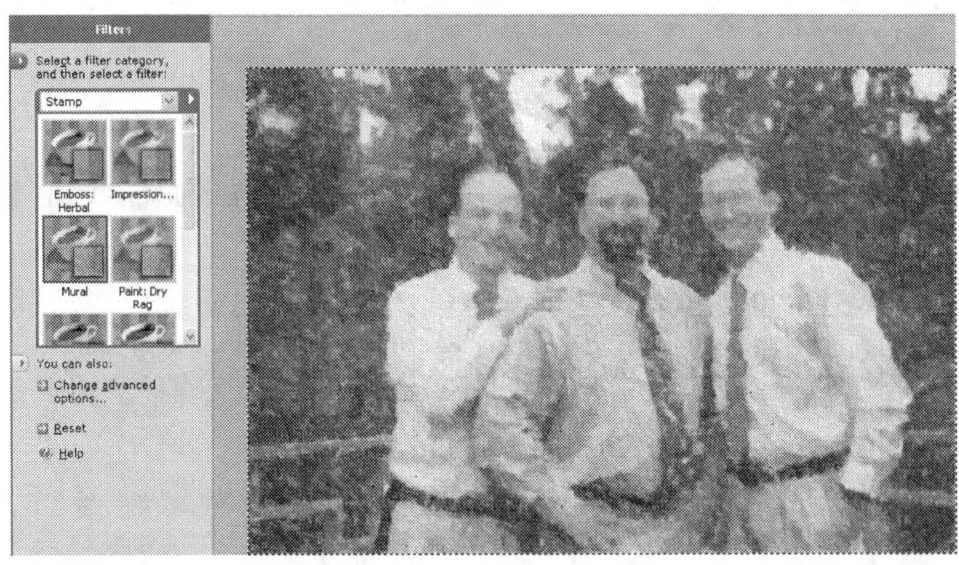

Stamp Mural Filter

## Use the Surface Filters

The Surface filters group effects from other categories that render the image on a variety of surfaces, such as cement, embossing, glass, plaster, plastic wrap, and water ripple.

## Use the Texture Filters

The Texture filters apply textures to an image. Some of the textures are quite strange—like the Maze and the Fossil texture. The most useful of these filters is the *Texturizer*. This filter (as you can guess) applies a texture to the image that is most visible in the lighter areas (see Figure 12-39). The parameters are the same as for the Sketch filter described previously.

## Use the Watercolor Filters

The Watercolor filters provide a collection of (surprise!) watercolor effects, including using damp paper and different techniques (spatter, grid, wash, and so on). The parameters are the same as for Chalk. Figure 12-40 shows a sample of the Watercolor: Traditional filter.

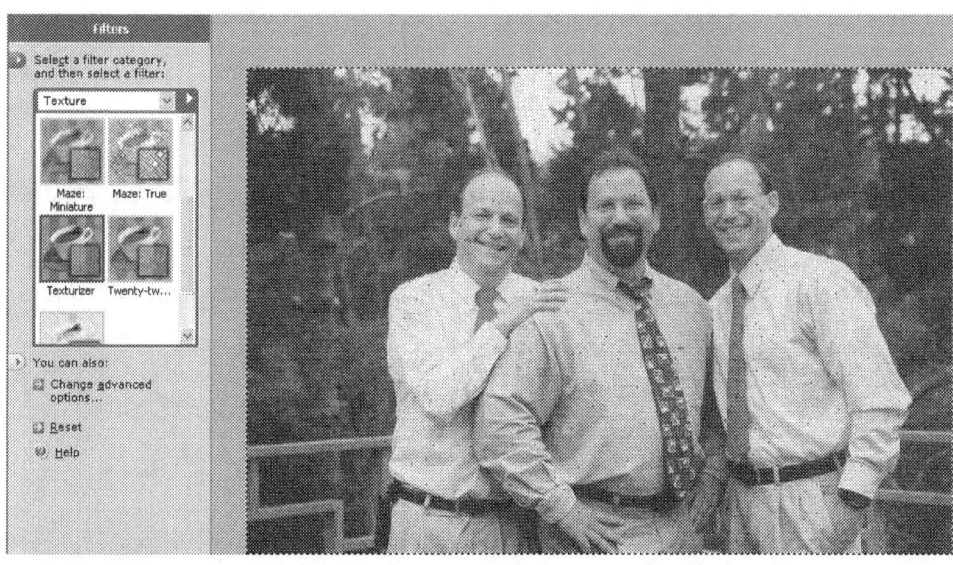

Texture Texturizer Filter

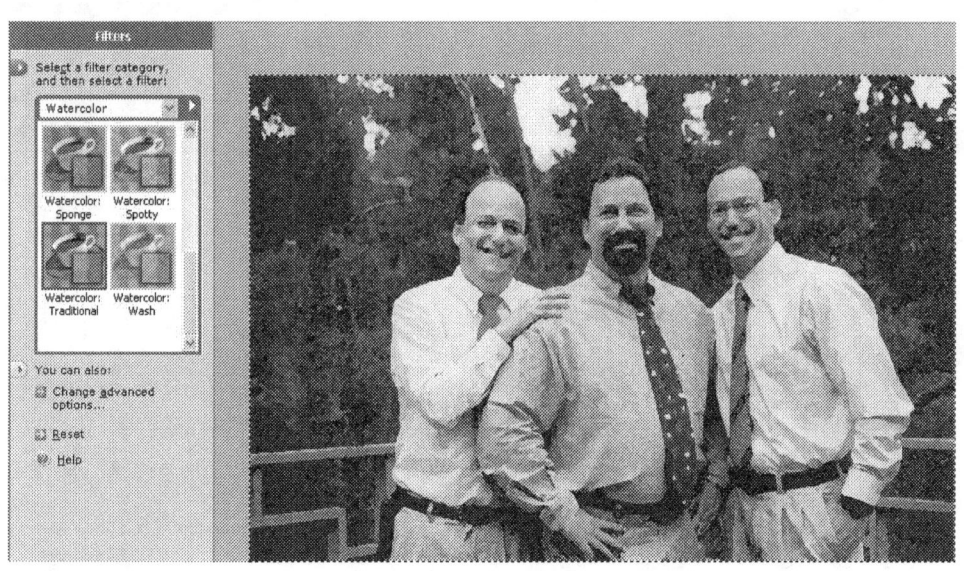

Watercolor Watercolor: Traditional Filter

# Use Your Photos in a Project

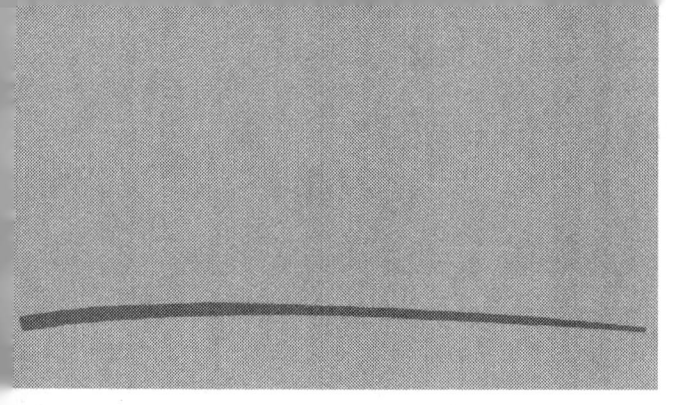

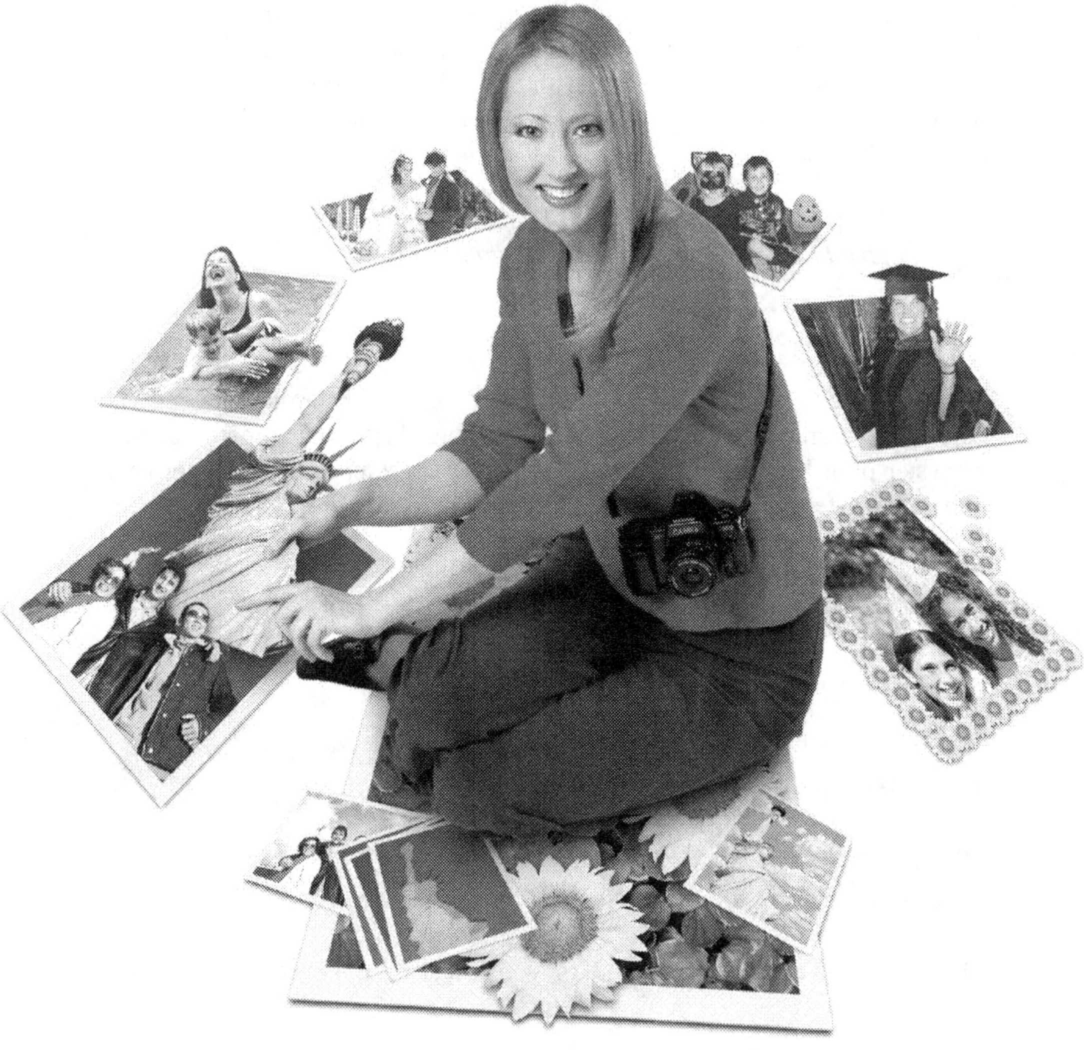

## How to...

■ Build Cards, labels, awards, and other projects

■ Place your pictures in projects

■ Add text to the project

■ Customize the result to get just what you want

Once you have your photos looking the way you want, what can you do with them? Well, if you're using Digital Image Pro, you can use your images in *projects*. Digital Image Pro makes it easy to build albums, awards, business or address cards, calendars, cards, flyers and brochures, and postcards. You can even order gifts online that use your photos as part of the design.

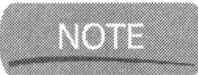 *You've already seen an example of a project. We built frames and mattes in Chapter 11, so we won't cover them again here.*

## How Do You Build a Project?

In general, the steps you follow to build a project are similar for the different types of projects, but there are some differences. In Chapter 11, a matte project required the extra step of picking the matte shape, a step that was skipped in a frame project.

The general steps for building a project are as follows:

1. Pick a project design.

2. Pick a subcategory (for some types of projects only).

3. Choose a Theme.

4. Pick the item to create.

5. Insert your picture(s) when required.

6. If you inserted picture(s), position and size the picture(s).

7. Customize the result (modify text, customize additional pages, and so forth).

These steps are discussed in the next few sections. To get started, select File | Create a Project.

*You may want to load the files you are going to use in the project prior to starting the project. Although you are given the opportunity to load files while constructing the project, it is quicker and easier to have them already available in the Files palette.*

## Pick a Project Design

The first screen you see enables you to pick the type of project you want to create (as shown in Figure 13-1). Except for MSN E-cards (covered later in this chapter), pick the type of project design you want from the top portion of the screen.

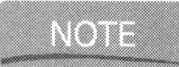
*As you move the mouse over a design, samples of the design appear on the screen to help you understand the purpose of the design.*

The project designs are as follows:

■ **Albums**   Build photo albums with the tools offered here, including a collection of different types of album pages (Album Sets), collages, scrapbook pages (Scrapbooks), and dividers to insert between sections (Tab Dividers). To build an entire photo album, you must build multiple projects—each project consists of a single page, collage, scrapbook page, or tab divider.

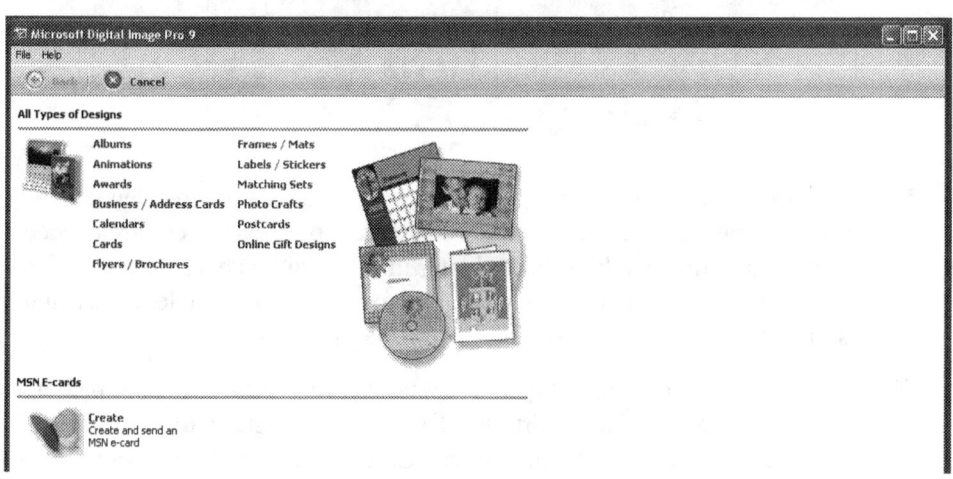

Pick the design of the project from the top of the first Project screen.

13

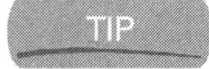 *Save each project for an album into the same directory so that your pages are all grouped together. Also, add a number to the filename (for example, 1BabyPhotoAlbum.png) so that the files are listed in the same order as pages in the album.*

- **Animations**   Create either a flipbook animation or a web animation by using multiple files in the File area. You can set the order of the files, size of the animated result, the type of background, and the length of the animation. Because animations are quite different from the other projects, I'll cover them in more detail later in this chapter.

- **Awards**   Build awards and certificates in many categories, such as business, community, family, and school. Most awards include a picture, but some do not.

- **Business / Address Cards**   Create business cards with this design. The designs include some cards with photos, various fonts, and both horizontal and vertical layouts. The cards are sized to fit commercial business card stock, and the Avery label number is included in the description, so you know what stock to buy in order to print the cards.

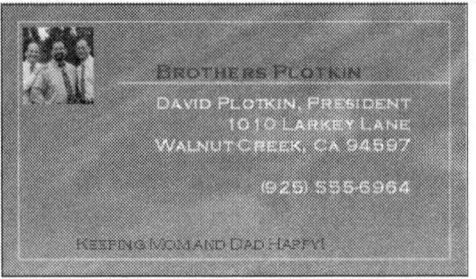

- **Calendars**   Build one month, one week, yearly, or 12-month calendars. Most calendar designs have space for a picture. Some extra steps are needed for the12-month calendar (covered later in this chapter) because the project finishes after you have inserted a picture into only one month, leaving you to insert pictures into the rest of the months manually.

- **Cards**   This design enables you to create greeting cards. You can pick a subcategory, such as Baby, Birthday, Christmas, Congratulations, Father's Day, Valentine's Day, and many others. Cards are available in various sizes, such as Quarter side-fold, Half side-fold, Half top-fold, and so on. Once the project is done, Digital Image Pro provides some additional help in customizing the multiple pages in the card (as you'll see later in this chapter).

■ **Brochures / Flyers**   Create multipage brochures and single-page flyers. Once the project is done, Digital Image Pro provides some additional help in customizing the multiple pages in the brochure.

■ **Frames / Mats**   Build frames and mattes for photographs, as discussed in Chapter 11. You can use the supplied designs, or build your own from scratch.

■ **Labels / Stickers**   Build address labels, CD-DVD labels, food labels, shipping labels, and stickers. The labels are sized to fit commercial label stock, and the Avery label number is included in the description, so you know what stock to buy in order to print the labels.

■ **Matching Sets**   This project groups sets of designs together to make them easier to choose and build. For example, Figure 13-2 shows a "garden" motif, with CD-DVD labels, awards, business cards, flyers, and greeting cards. You have to pick and build each design individually, but having them grouped together makes that operation easier.

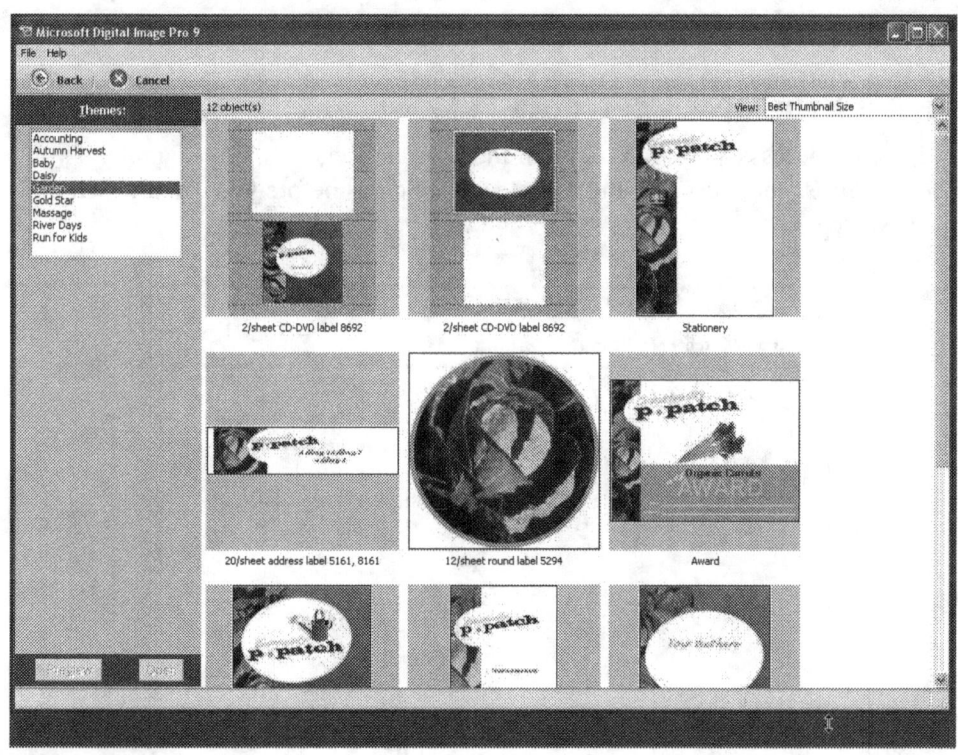

Matching Sets brings together all the projects for a given design in one place.

■ **Photo Crafts** Build garlands, IDs for kids, magazine covers, ornaments, playing cards, and trading cards, and even put your head on someone else's body. Unfortunately, the magazine covers don't include real ones, such as *Newsweek* or *Time,* but you can put your own title on the magazine cover.

■ **Postcards** Build your own postcards in a variety of themes. The postcards are sized to fit commercial label stock, and the Avery label number is included in the description, so you know what stock to buy in order to print the postcards.

■ **Online Gift Designs** Put your photos and text on clothing, mouse pads, posters and canvas prints, and photo puzzles. Although these designs work pretty much like any other, you must print them professionally online when you are done to actually get the product made and sent to you. Printing professionally online is covered in detail in Chapter 16.

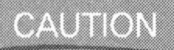 *Make sure to remove the print instructions from the project before printing an online gift design. Otherwise, the print instructions will show up in the finished product!*

## Pick a Project Subcategory

This step is necessary for only a few of the project categories. For example, if you choose *Cards*, you must pick the subcategory of cards before you can proceed to the next step.

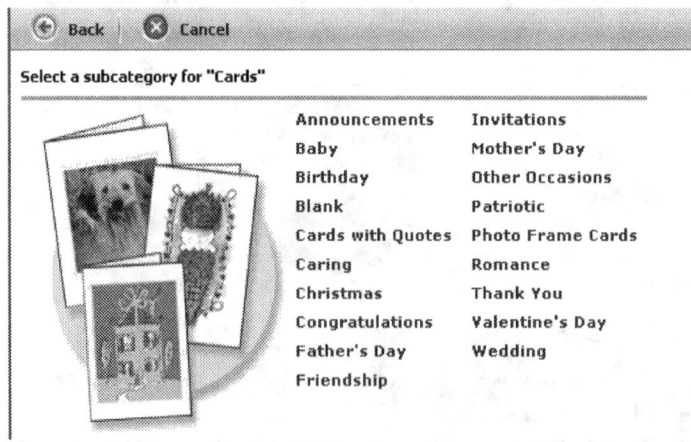

Choosing one of the subcategories moves to the next step.

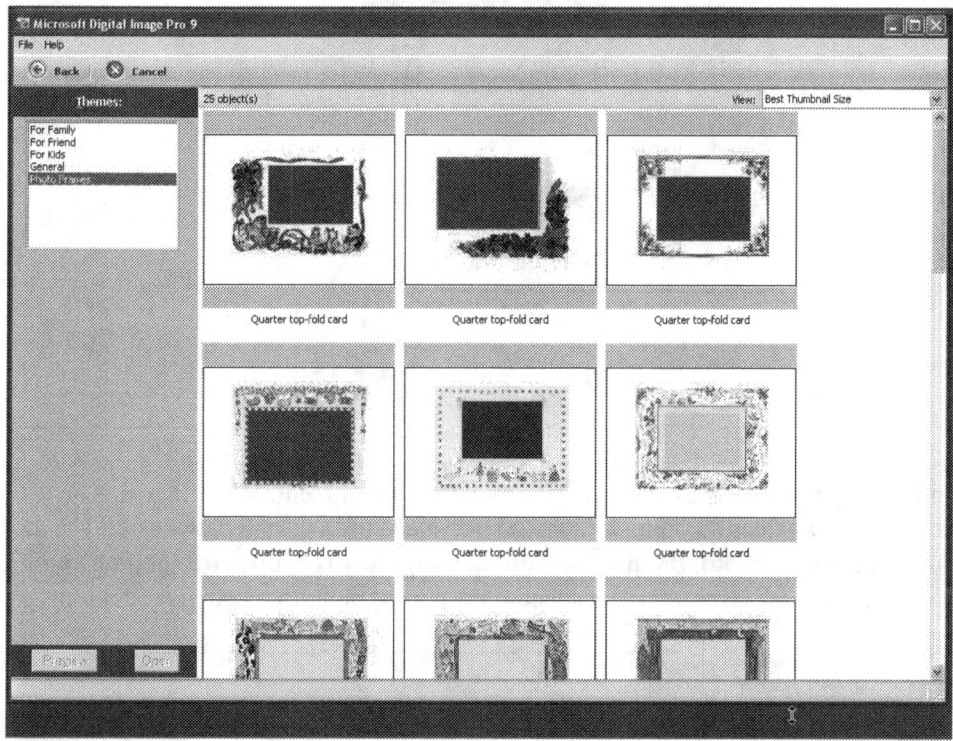

Choose a theme from the list and view the items in that theme.

## Pick a Theme

Choose a theme for the project from the list in the Themes task bar, as shown in Figure 13-3. Once you do, the available projects are displayed in the large window on the right side of the screen. For example, Figure 13-3 shows the choices for Christmas cards with a theme of *Photo Frame*.

## Pick the Item and Create It

Choose the item you want to create from the right side of the window. If the item (such as a Christmas card) has textual sentiments on any of the pages, the Message box appears to display the sentiment. You can't edit the sentiments at this point, although you will be able to later in the process.

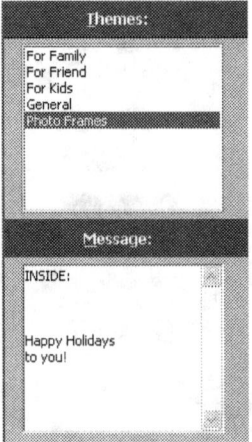

Either click the item and then click the Open button, or double-click the item. Either way opens the design, ready for you to customize it. What happens next depends on whether the item you picked has space for a photograph or not. If you need to insert a photo, the next screen (see Figure 13-4) provides guidance to complete the task. If there is no space for a photograph, the next screen simply

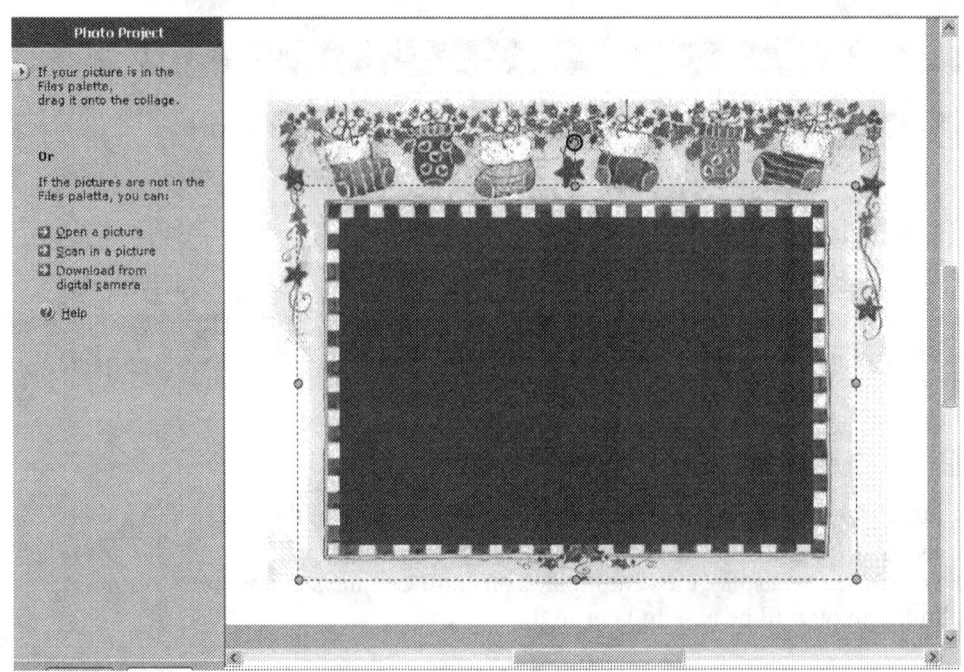

Insert a photograph into the project using this screen.

displays the results of the project in Digital Image Pro, ready for you to customize it further (see Figure 13-5).

NOTE *Do you see the small window at the lower-left side of the window in Figure 13-5? This window helps you view the different pages in the card you created. To see another page, click the icon for the page you want to see. For example, to see the inside of the card, click the icon in the middle.*

## Place the Picture

If the project requires a picture (has a picture area), Digital Image Pro refers to it as a *photo project*. The next screen enables you to place the picture in the project (as shown in Figure 13-4, shown previously). Either drag the picture from the Files palette (and then click Next>), or use the Photo Project task bar to open a picture, scan in a picture, or download the picture from a digital camera. Figure 13-6 shows what the result might look like with a picture.

In the last panel, use the sizing handles and rotation handle to size and rotate the picture. You can also click inside the picture and drag it to move it so it lines up better with the project's photo opening. You can also click Flip Horizontally or Flip Vertically in the task bar to flip the image.

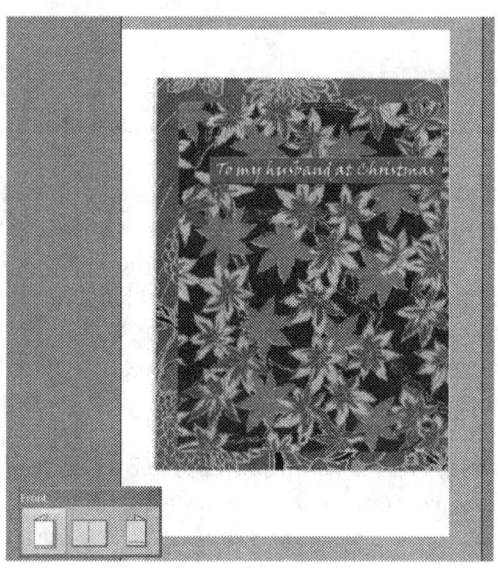

13

If no photograph is necessary, the project is done, and you can customize it as described later in this chapter.

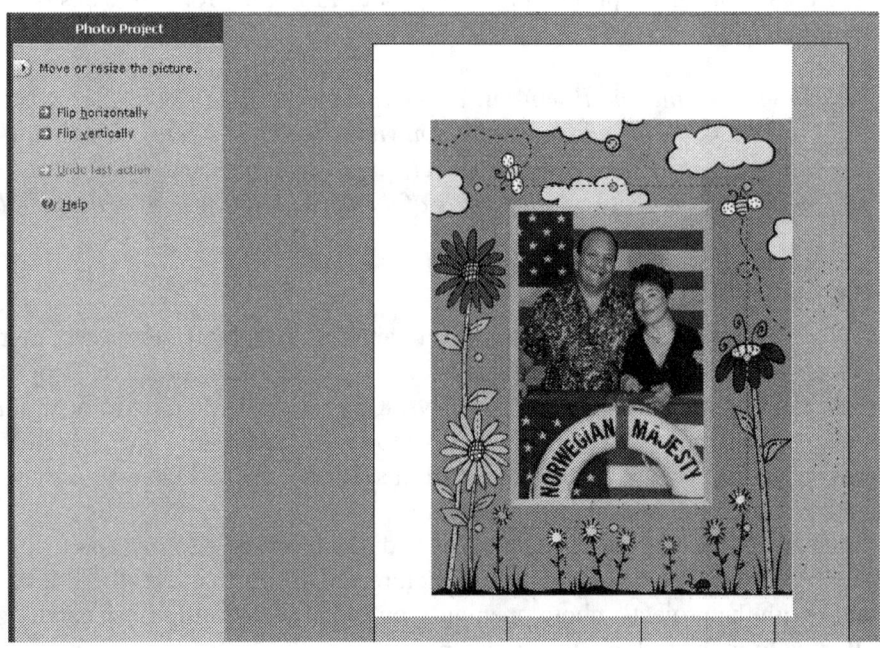

Place the picture to personalize the card.

## Customize the Result

Once you click Done, you are returned to the main Digital Image Pro screen, as shown in Figure 13-7. If there is any text in your project, you can now select that text and customize it, as described in Chapter 10. Each block of text is on its own layer. If you look carefully in Figure 13-7, you can see the text layers in the Stack. As with any other object, you can select the text either by clicking the text block in the project or by clicking the layer in the Stack. In all cases, the text is regular text, not shaped text. Thus, you can change the font, size, color, and effects for each letter, as well as move, resize, and rotate the text box by using the sizing handles and the rotate handle.

NOTE    *In many cases, the text is white so that it shows up well against a dark background. However, white text shows up as a blank layer in the Stack (white text on a white Stack background), so you have no clue as to which Stack layer represents which text block. To work around this, click the text block in the project!*

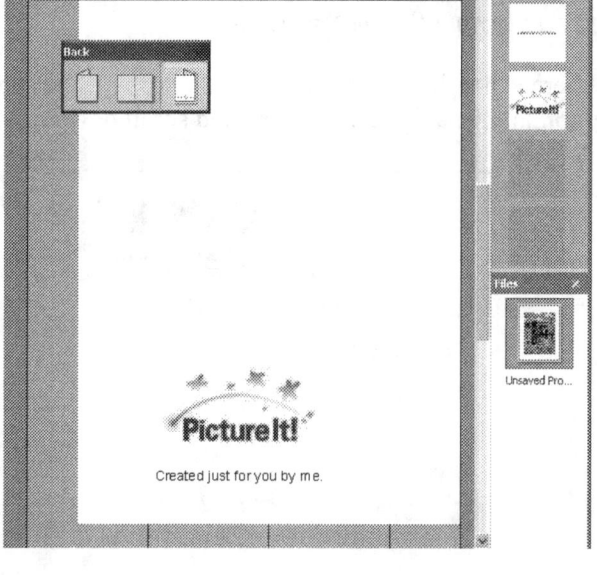

Customize the project text to get your message across.

# Build Some Useful Projects

As mentioned, most of the projects are built using similar steps and options. The next few sections build some representative projects, highlighting the types of projects that have significant differences from the "standard."

## Build a Greeting Card

Greeting cards are among the most-used projects, and illustrate most of the common steps needed to build a project. To build a greeting card, use the following steps:

1. Select File | Create a Project, click Cards, and pick a subcategory (I chose *Birthday* for this example).

2. From the Theme task bar, choose a theme. I chose *For Family* for this example.

3. Select the card you want to build from the thumbnails on the right side of the screen. I chose the one with the photograph of the two babies on it (on my screen, it is in the fourth row of thumbnails). Click Open.

13

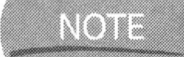 *If the card you choose uses a photograph, drag it into the appropriate spot in the card at this point, and then use the sizing and rotation handles to move, size, and rotate the photograph to fit.*

4. Because there is nothing to customize on the front of the card, click the center option in the navigation window and scroll down to the sentiment:

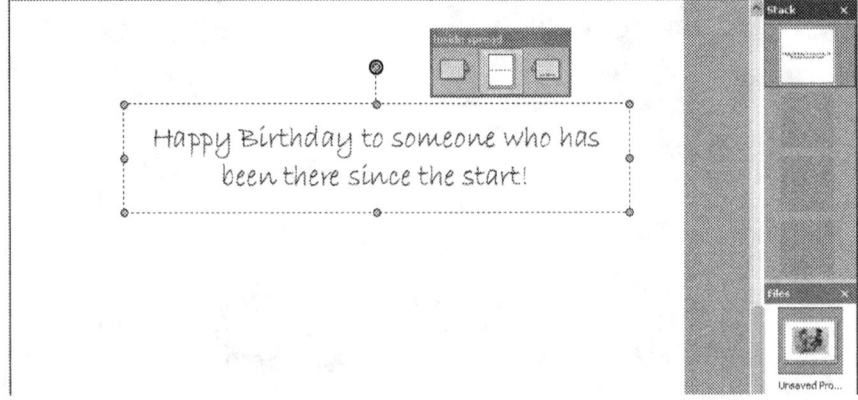

5. Select Text | Insert Text.

6. Click near the edge of the new text box and drag it below the sentiment.

7. Select the text and customize it to "sign" your card. Choose an appropriate color and font. I chose Bickley Script, 24 point, magenta for this example:

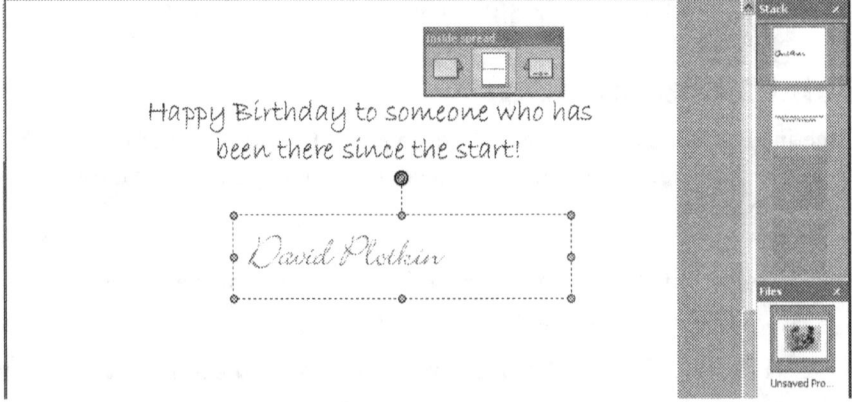

8. Click the back of the card in the navigation window. Click the image on the back.

9.  The image on the back is a grouping of a graphic and two lines of text. Ungroup these items by clicking the ungroup item that appears.

10. If you wish, customize the text (perhaps to insert your own name) and replace the graphic.

## Build a Flipbook Animation Project

To build a project that rapidly "flips through" still frames to create an animation, use the following steps:

1.  Open all the files you want to use in the animation. To keep from getting confused, make sure to open them in the same order you want the files in for the animation.

2.  Select File | Create a Project, and then choose Animations.

3.  In the Theme panel, choose the Flipbook theme.

4.  Double-click the Photo flipbook icon to get started on the animation.

5.  In the Flipbook task bar, you are informed that all the Files in the File area will be turned into an animated picture. You can use the options in the task bar to open another picture, scan in a picture, download a picture from a digital camera, or close the current picture. If you choose to open, scan, or download a picture, it is added to the Files area at the end of the list, and will be the last frame in the animation. You can continue retrieving pictures this way, so if you forgot to load the pictures into the File area before starting, you can do it now.

13

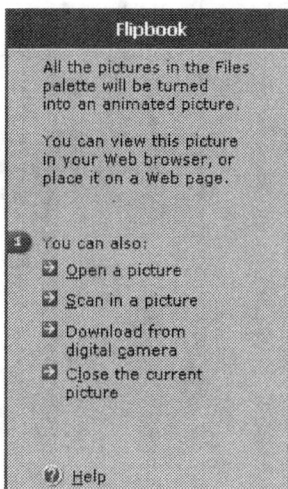

NOTE *If you choose to close the current picture, Digital Image Pro closes the image you are viewing. To select a different picture to view, double-click the picture in the Files area.*

6. Click Next> to continue. Choose the type of background you will be using on your web page. You can select either a patterned background or a solid color background. You can also pick a color from the color squares available in the task bar, or click More Color Choices to pick a color from the color wheel.

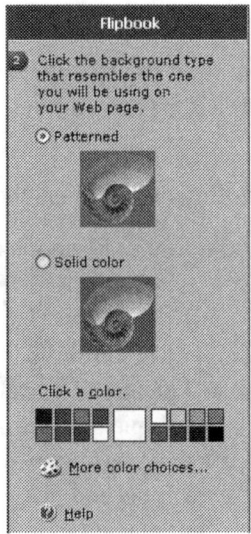

7. Click Next> to continue. In the next task bar, pick the size of the flipbook from the Select a Picture Book drop-down list. If you choose *Custom*, you can input the Width and Height in the appropriate fields. If you want to avoid distorting the images, check the Maintain Proportions checkbox.

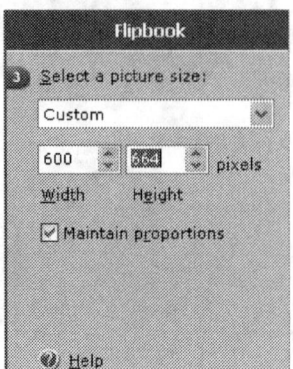

8. Click Next> to continue. In the next task bar, use the Set the Length of the Animation field to set the number of seconds that it will take for the animation to play. You can also use the Set the Play Style for the Animation options to set the animation to play once, continuously, or to specify the number of times it will play.

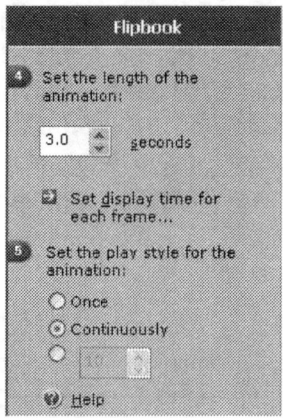

9. Click Next> to continue. Digital Image Pro constructs the Flipbook and displays the result in the workspace.

10. Click Save As in the task bar and provide a filename to save the animation. Then click Done.

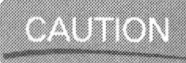 *If you click Done before you save the animation, the results of your work will be lost.*

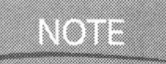 *The result is saved as an animated GIF. Because a GIF file can contain only 256 colors, the number of colors will be reduced to 256 if you are animating photographs that contain more colors than the GIF can handle.*

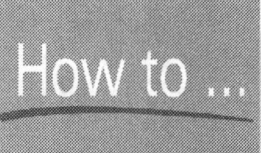 **Set the Animation Time for Each Frame**

In step 8, you set the time for the entire animation to play. The way this works is that Digital Image Pro takes the total time, divides it by the number of frames, and shows each frame for the same amount of time. But what if you want certain frames to be displayed longer?

13

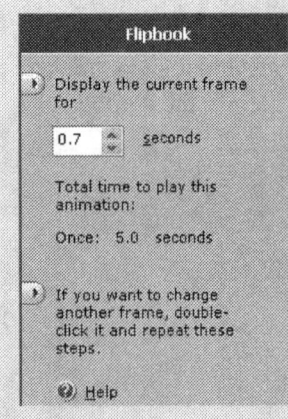

To accomplish that, click Set Display Time for Each Frame to open a new version of the Flipbook task bar.

Use the Display the Current Frame for field to specify the number of seconds to display the current frame. To set the display time for another frame, double-click the frame in the Files area to view that frame, and use the field to set the display time for that frame. Repeat this process for each frame. Digital Image Pro displays the time to display the complete animation just below the field.

## Build a Web Animation

A web animation is different from a flipbook animation—it uses a single image, and animates it by moving and rotating the image. To build a web animation, follow these steps:

1. Choose File | Create a Project, and click Animations. In the Theme taskbar, select Web Animations, and double-click the *Photo Animation* object.

2. To use the picture in the workspace, just click Next> to continue. If you want to use a different file from the Files palette, double-click the file to open it. You can also use the options in the task bar to open another picture, scan in a picture, or download a picture from a digital camera. Then click Next>.

3. If the image contains multiple objects, you can choose to animate just one of them by clicking that object in the Stack and then clicking Next>. Or, click Animate the Whole Project to animate the entire image, including all the objects.

4. In the next task bar, select the animation effect you want to use from the Select an Animation scrolling list. A sample of the animation is displayed in the window immediately below the list.

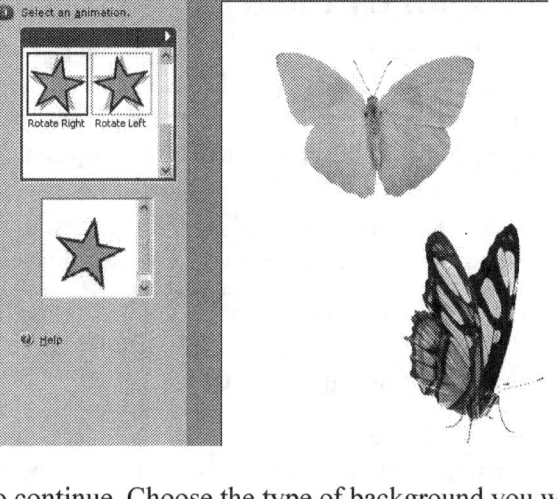

5.  Click Next> to continue. Choose the type of background you will be using on your web page. You can select either a patterned background or a solid color background. You can also pick a color from the color squares available in the task bar, or click More Color Choices to pick a color from the color wheel.

6.  Click Next> to continue. In the next task bar, pick the size of the flipbook from the Select a Picture Book drop-down list. If you choose *Custom*, you can input the Width and Height in the appropriate fields. If you want to avoid distorting the images, check the Maintain Proportions checkbox.

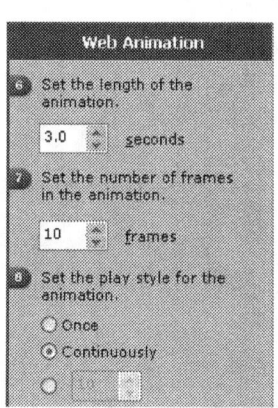

7.  Click Next> to continue. In the next task bar, use the Set the Length of the Animation field to set the total length of the animation in seconds. Choose the number of frames from which to create the animation using the Set the Number of Frames in the Animation field. Using more frames gives you smoother animation but results in a larger file. You can also use the Set the Play Style for the Animation options to set the animation to play once, continuously, or to specify the number of times it will play.

8.  Click Next> to continue. Digital Image Pro constructs the Flipbook and displays the result in the workspace.

9.  Click Save As in the task bar and provide a filename to save the animation. Then click Done. The result is saved as an animated GIF file, suitable for use in a web page.

13

# Build a 12-Month Calendar

When you build a single month calendar, the steps you use are the same as any other single-page project, such as a flyer. But a 12-month calendar requires more steps because you need to work with each of the 12 pages (one for each month) that make up the calendar. To create a yearly calendar, use the following steps:

1. Choose File | Create a Project, and click Calendars. In the Subcategory panel, select Calendars, and select the Twelve Month subcategory.

2. Choose one of the two themes in the Theme task bar (I used *General*), and then double-click the calendar style you want. I chose the second one from the left on the top row—it has a "To do" list in it.

3. In the next panel, select the year for the calendar and choose which day the week begins on from the Begin Weeks On field. The day you pick appears in the far-left column of the calendar.

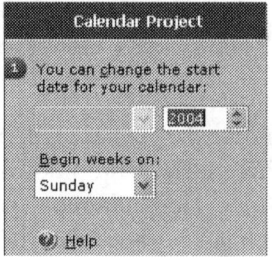

4. Click Next> to continue. In the next panel, you can drag an image from the File area into the calendar page for January, or use the options in the task bar to open a picture, scan a picture, or download a picture from a digital camera.

5. Click Next> to continue. Use the sizing and rotation handles to move, size, and rotate the image to fit.

6. Click Done. The "finished" product is shown in Figure 13-8. Of course, it's not finished at all. We still have quite a bit of work to do.

7. If you want to customize anything (such as the text in the January calendar page), click the object in the Stack to select it and make your changes. Realize that anything you customize in January will have to be customized in the other months as well.

Choose the month you want to work
on from this navigation window.

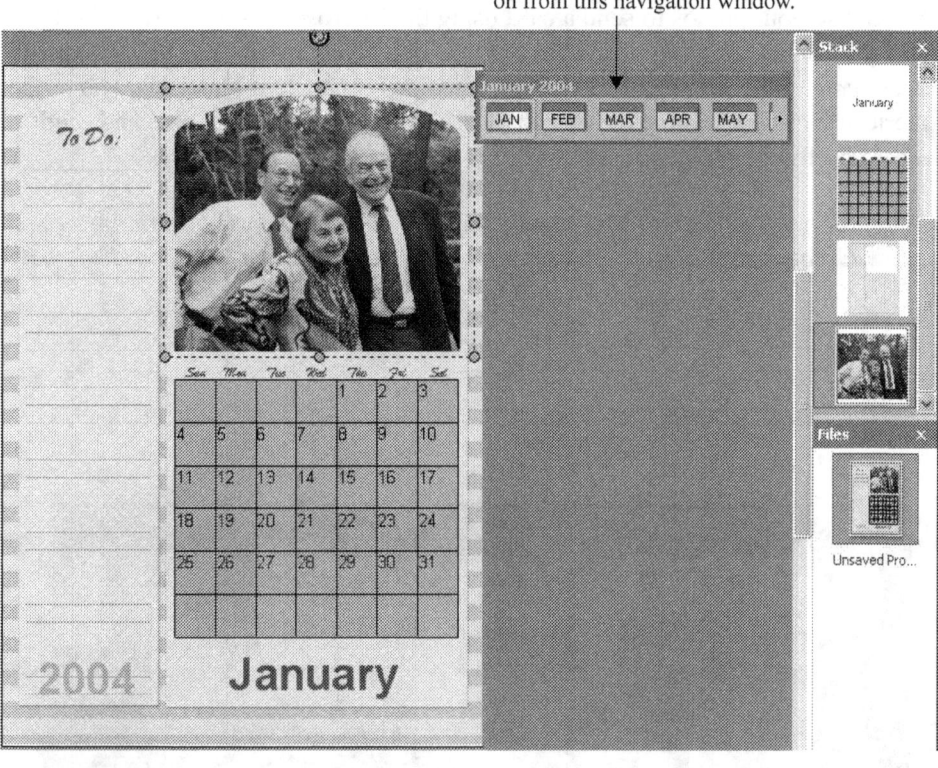

**13**

8. Once you are done making any changes to January, click the next month
   you want to work on (say, February?) in the navigation window.

> **NOTE**   *You can click and drag the title bar of the navigation window to move it.
> If the month you want to work on isn't visible, you can scroll the contents
> of the navigation window back and forth using the small right or left arrows
> that appear at the edges of the window if there is more content in that
> direction.*

9. Continue customizing by choosing each month from the navigation window
   and making your changes.

10. Save your work when you are done.

## Build an MSN E-card

You can use your photos to send a card using the Microsoft Network (MSN). To do so, you'll have to be connected to the Internet. Select File | Create a Project and click *Create* in the MSN E-card section of the project screen. This takes you to the American Greetings Web page (see Figure 13-9) where you can create and send the card by following the prompts.

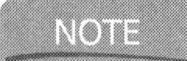

*Many of the card themes require that you be a paid member of the American Greetings service. If you're not, you can still send one of the cards in the free section, such as a Friendship or a Love and Dating card.*

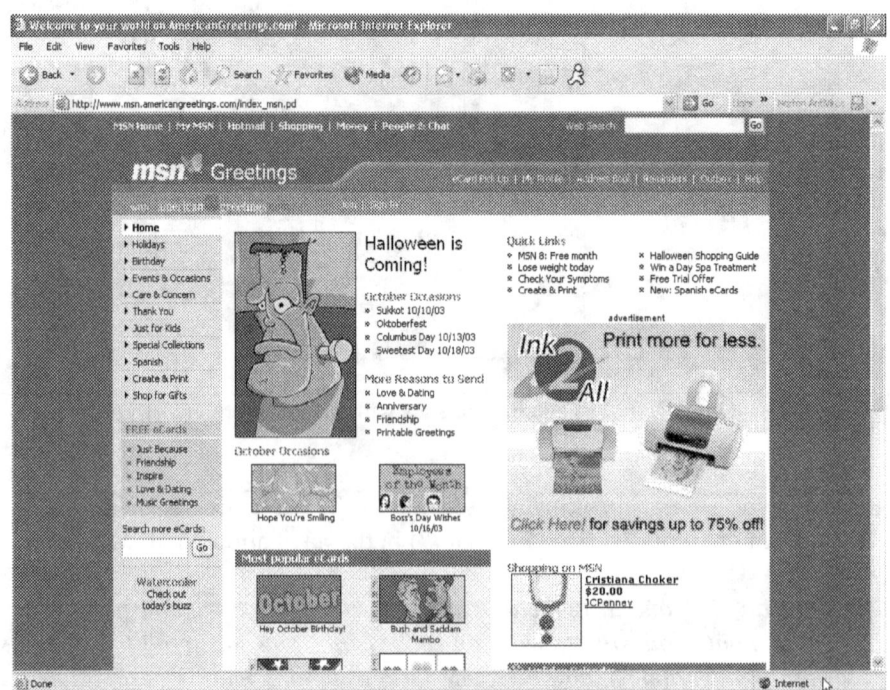

Build and send a card online with MSN E-card.

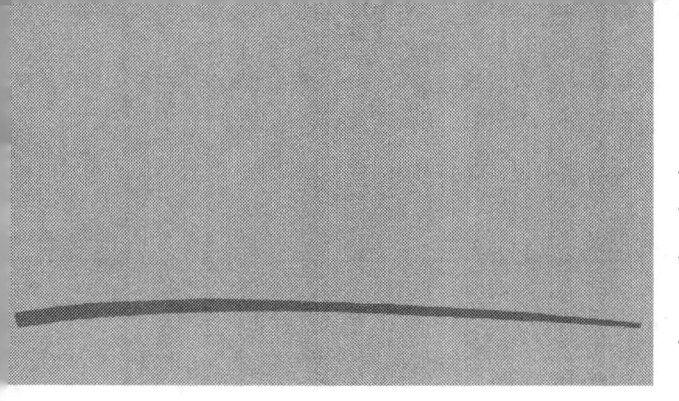

# Modify Multiple Photos in the Mini Lab

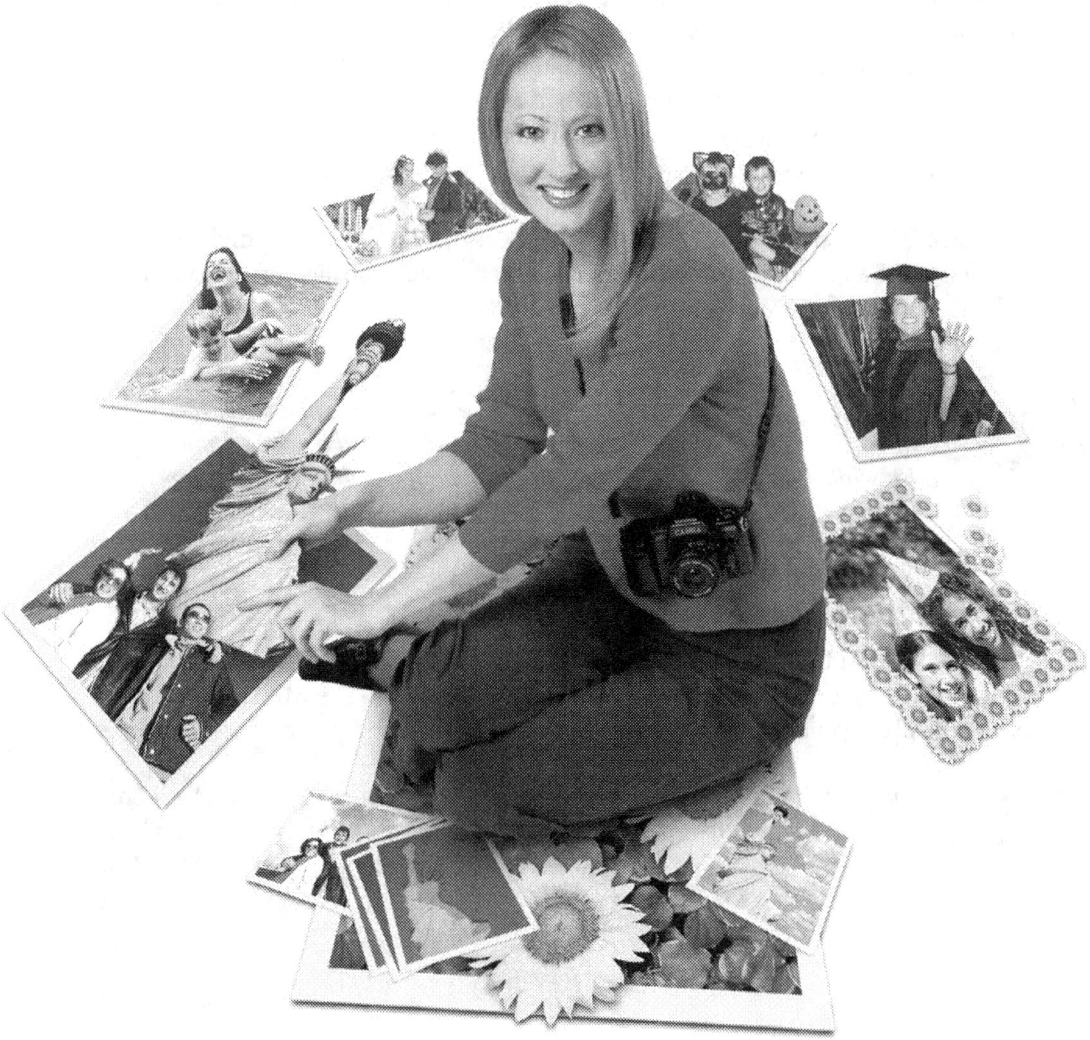

## How to…

■ Make the same changes to multiple photos at once

■ Choose the editing options for your photos

■ Save your changes

I recently took an entire roll of film of images that included large expanses of water and sky. Each of the images had the same problem—muddy mid-tones made it difficult to see most of the interesting parts of the images! After I had worked on the first couple of the photos, I realized that they all needed pretty much the same fix. The Mini Lab in Digital Image Pro makes it possible to apply adjustment —such as Levels, Brightness and Contrast, and tint adjustment—to a whole batch of photos at once, which is quicker and easier than making the same corrections on individual photos.

You can also open a set of photos and apply corrections to them individually. In addition to the adjustments just mentioned, you can rotate, crop, and fix red eye in the Mini Lab. This "batch edit" capability enables you to treat editing a set of photos as a single task.

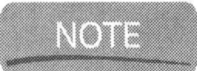
*Opening multiple pictures at once can be very memory intensive. If you find that your machine has gotten very slow and your hard drive is running quite a bit while you edit the pictures, you may want to edit fewer pictures at one time.*

# Open Files in the Mini Lab

To open the Mini Lab and start working with it, select Touchup | Batch Edit in Mini Lab. This opens the Mini Lab screen, shown in Figure 14-1. The Mini Lab task bar clearly displays your options.

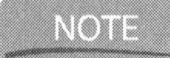
*If any files are already open in the File palette when you start the Mini Lab, those files automatically appear as thumbnails in the work area (as shown in Figure 14-1). If you want to open more files after starting the Mini Lab, click Open More Files in step (1) of the task bar and choose the files to open.*

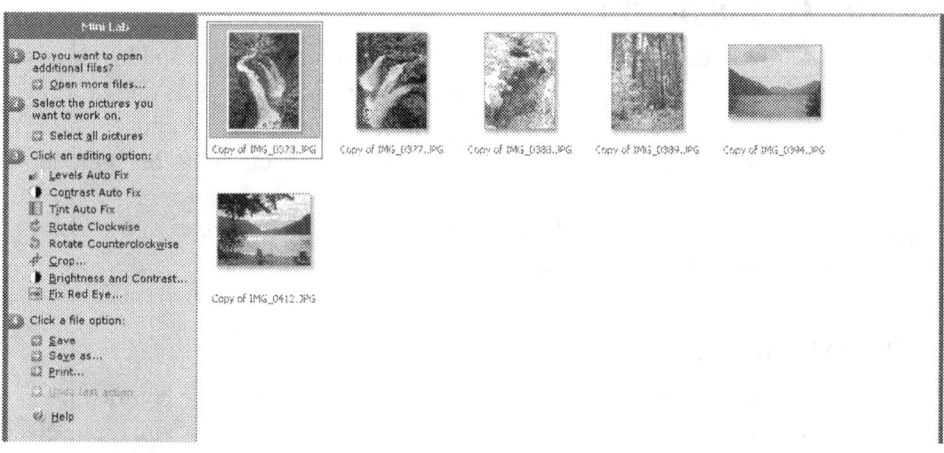

Use the Mini Lab to edit a batch of photos at one time.

# Make Corrections in the Mini Lab

The basics of working with the Mini Lab are pretty simple: pick the picture(s) to work with, choose the correction to apply, apply the correction, and save the result. However, some of the corrections work differently than others, primarily because some corrections (such as cropping) require input from you for each image, while others (such as Levels Auto Fix) can be applied to all the selected pictures without further input.

## Select the Picture(s) to Work With

The open pictures are displayed in the work area of the Mini Lab. Pictures you have selected to work with display a blue border; unselected pictures do not display this border.

To select a single picture, click the picture. Clicking a different picture selects the second picture and deselects the first picture. To select more than one picture, click the first picture, hold down the CTRL key, and click the other pictures. To unselect a single picture, click it again while still holding down the CTRL key. You can also select a set of contiguous images by clicking an image, holding down the SHIFT key, and clicking another image. All pictures between the first one and the last one will be selected.

To select *all* of the pictures, click Select All Pictures.

14

## Use the Levels Auto Fix

The Levels Auto Fix corrects the picture histogram, fixing contrast and brightness problems, as described in Chapter 4. To apply the Levels Auto Fix to one or more images, select the images and click Levels Auto Fix. Other than a pause while the images are corrected, there is no feedback that the correction has been made.

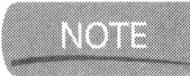 *Well, this isn't quite true. If you look closely at the thumbnails, you'll see some differences. But you have to look close.*

## Contrast Auto Fix

The Contrast Auto Fix applies an automatic correction to the image contrast, as described in Chapter 4. To apply the Contrast Auto Fix to one or more images, select the images and click Contrast Auto Fix. Other than a pause while the images are corrected, there is no feedback that the correction has been made.

## Tint Auto Fix

The Tint Auto Fix applies an automatic correction to the tint of the image, as described in Chapter 4. To apply the Tint Auto Fix to one or more images, select the images and click Tint Auto Fix. If the tint change is large enough, you'll see the color change in the thumbnail.

## Rotate Clockwise and Rotate Counterclockwise

You can rotate one or more images either clockwise or counterclockwise. This is handy when an image is lying on its side or is upside down. To rotate one or more images, select the images and click either Rotate Clockwise or Rotate Counterclockwise. You'll see the thumbnails rotate to indicate the new orientation.

## Crop Your Images

You can crop multiple images in the Mini Lab. To do so, select the pictures you want to crop and click Crop. Digital Image Pro displays the first image, along with the Crop task bar. Crop the image as described in Chapter 4. When you are done with the image, either click Next> to move to the next image or Done if it was the last selected image.

## Fix the Brightness and Contrast

You can adjust the brightness and contrast settings for multiple images in the Mini Lab. To do so, select the pictures you want to adjust and click Brightness and Contrast. Digital Image Pro displays the first image, along with the Brightness and Contrast task bar. Make the adjustments using the sliders, as described in Chapter 4.

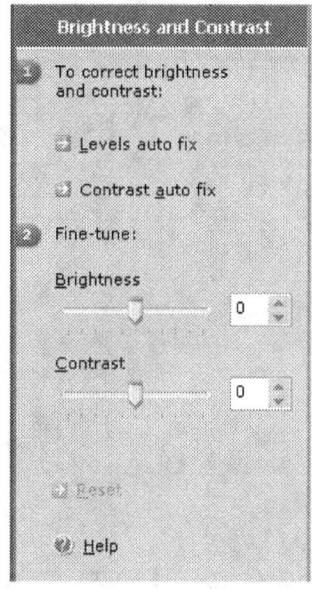

When you are done with the image, either click Next> to move to the next image or Done if it was the last selected image.

## Correct Red Eye

You can correct the red eye for multiple images in the Mini Lab. To do so, select the pictures you need to work on and click Fix Red Eye. Digital Image Pro displays the first image, along with the Fix Red Eye task bar. Make the corrections by clicking the red part of the eye and then click Red-Eye Auto Fix. When you are done with the image, either click Next> to move to the next image or Done if it was the last selected image.

14

# Save the Results

After to going to all this "trouble," you need to make sure you save your results. Select the files you want to save, and then click either Save or Save As. If you click Save, the modified files are saved over the originals. However, if you click Save As, Digital Image Pro opens the Batch Save dialog box.

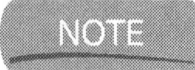

*The Batch Save dialog box only appears if you have more than one file selected (the normal case). If you have only one file selected, Digital Image Pro opens the Save As dialog box.*

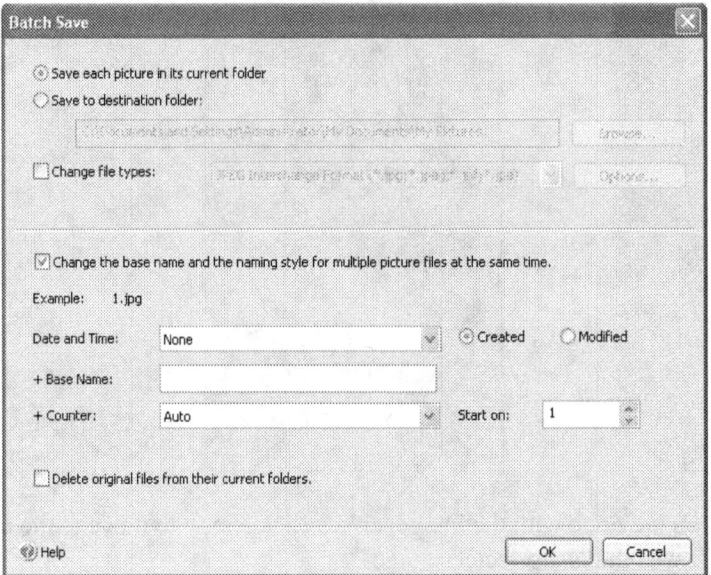

Using the Batch Save dialog box, you can:

- **Choose a destination folder for the image(s)** To leave the images in their current folders, click the Save Each Picture in Its Current Folder option. To direct the image to a different folder, click the Save to Destination Folder option and either type in a path or use the Browse button to choose the destination folder. All the selected files must go into the same folder.

- **Change the type of file** You can convert the file(s) to another type—for example, converting JPEGs to TIFFs. To do so, check the Change File Types checkbox and choose the file type from the drop-down list. For the selected file type, click the Options button to set the available options—such as the quality level for JPEG images. The options are the same as those discussed in Chapter 3.

**TIP**  *If all the original images are of the same type (such as JPEG), you can use the Options button to adjust the options for that file type when you save the files. For example, you could reduce the quality level of JPEGs to create smaller files prior to saving the images. Just check the Change File Types checkbox and click the Options button to open the Save As Options dialog box.*

You can also rename the files by applying an algorithm to generate a name using the options in the lower half of the Batch Save dialog box. To generate a new filename, check the Change the Base Name and the Naming Style for Multiple Picture Files at the Same Time checkbox. Then build the new name for the file using the following options:

■ **Add the date and time**    Add either the Created date and time or the Modified date and time to the name by choosing either the Created option or the Modified option. Select the format of the date and time from the Date and Time drop-down list.

- **Add a base name**   To add a text string to the filename, type the text into the Base Name field. Make sure to avoid characters that are not allowed in filenames.

- **Set the counter**   To configure the numeric counter at the end of the filename, choose the number of digits from the Counter drop-down list, or leave it set at *Auto* to allow as many digits as necessary. You can specify the number at which the counter starts by using the Start On field. This is handy if you want to save several batches of files with the same base name.

NOTE   *You can get rid of the original files by checking the Delete Original Files from Their Current Folders checkbox. I do not recommend this until you've checked the results of your batch edit. You have been warned...*

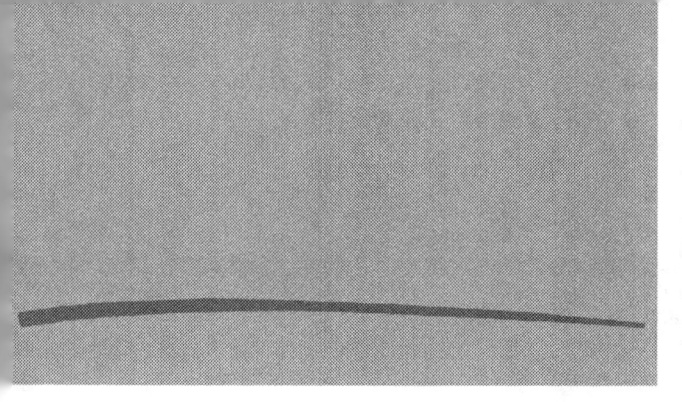

# Publishing and Sharing Your Photos

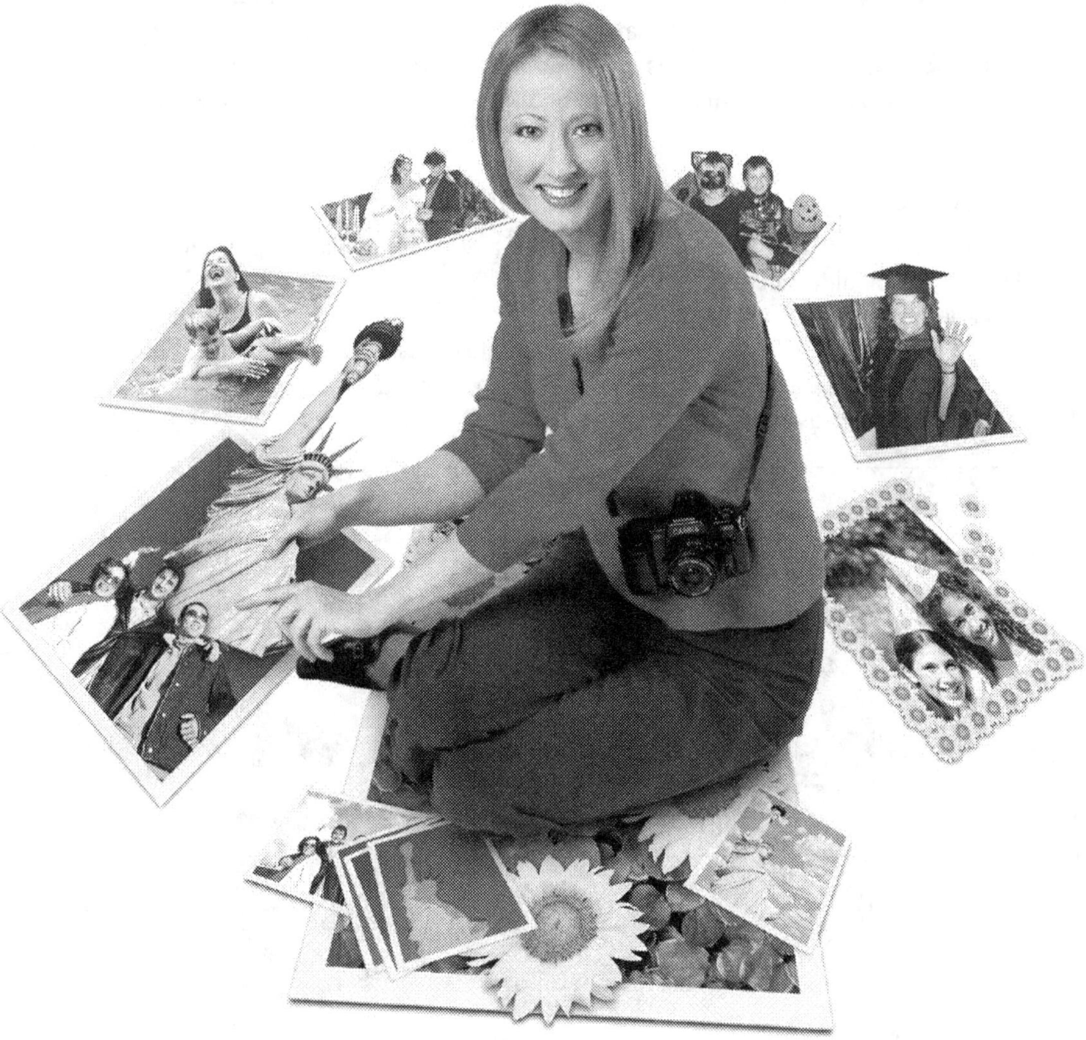

## How to…

- Save your photos for special devices
- Make your photos Web-ready
- Share your photos via e-mail

It's all very well to clean up your photos and store them or print them out. But in this day of the Internet, mobile devices, and e-mail, that seems kind of limiting. Digital Image Pro enables you to save special versions of your files for various purposes, create optimized copies suitable for displaying on devices such as Palm handheld units, and even e-mail a set of photos to someone from within the program.

# Save a Photo as Wallpaper

In Windows, *wallpaper* refers to the image (if any) that appears on your desktop. This image shouldn't be too "busy" or you may have trouble seeing your icons and other desktop appurtenances. To save an image as wallpaper, select File | Save a Copy For | Save As Wallpaper. When this operation has completed, you'll find that your picture has replaced your previous wallpaper. For example, Figure 15-1 shows my desktop after saving an image as wallpaper.

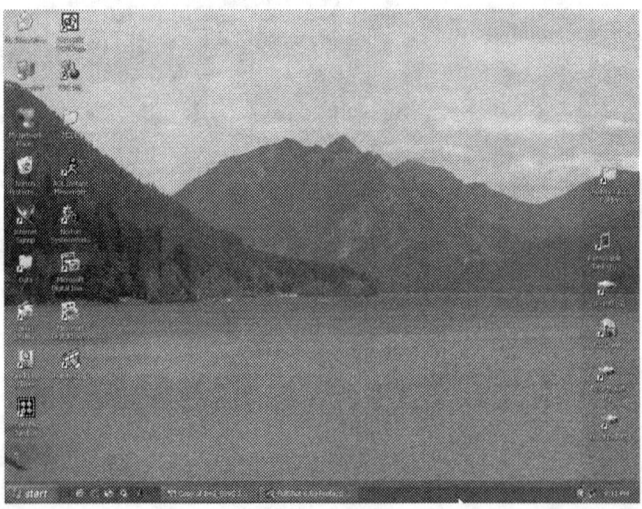

With just a few clicks, your image is now your wallpaper!

If you choose another image and save it as wallpaper, your previous image is replaced because Digital Image Pro creates a single "slot" in your list of available wallpapers, which it calls *Picture It! Wallpaper*. Each time you save an image as wallpaper, the image in that slot is replaced by the new image. You can see this if you look at your desktop properties dialog box. To do so, right-click the desktop and choose Properties. Then click the Desktop tab to view it.

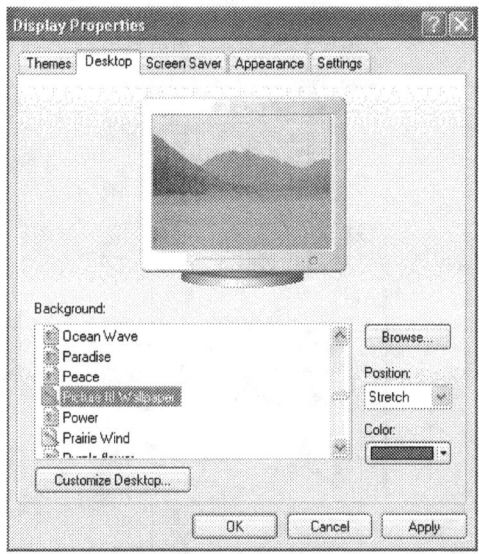

To pick a different wallpaper (or None), select it from this list. To return to using your image, choose Picture It! Wallpaper from the list.

# Save an Image for the Web or E-mail

One of the first things you learn about digital photography is to take (and store) pictures at the highest possible resolution to preserve as much of the original quality as possible. Because disk space (and increasingly, flash memory space) keeps getting cheaper, it really doesn't cost much to store the large files. Furthermore, earlier in this book (Chapter 3), I advised you to preserve the quality of your files as you worked on them by choosing high quality (least compression)—or even storing the files in a format that doesn't compress them at all.

However, there *are* situations for which you don't want really big files—when you or someone else must access the image via the Internet or a download. Viewing the image on a web site or downloading it as an attachment to an e-mail can be

15

painfully slow for big files. Further, if someone is just viewing the file on a web site, you don't need the high resolution necessary when you want to print the image.

Of course, it helps to know how long it is going to take to receive or view a file, and that is where Digital Image Pro can help. To get started, select File | Save a Copy For | Save for E-mail or Web. This opens the Save for E-mail or Web task bar. This task bar tells you the picture size, file size, estimated transfer (upload/download) times, and at what size the image will produce a quality print.

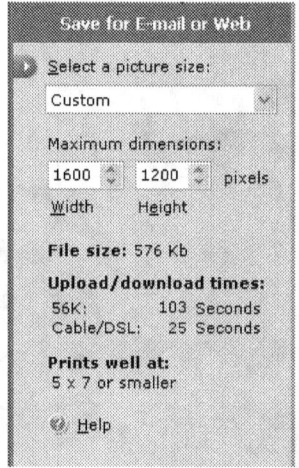

Clearly, you wouldn't want to be the poor person who has to download the picture in this example, especially if you don't have a cable modem or DSL. To modify the image to a form that is more reasonable for use with e-mail or the Web, click the Save As button. This opens the standard Save As dialog box where you can name the file, change the file type, and set important options such as the quality (click the Options button).

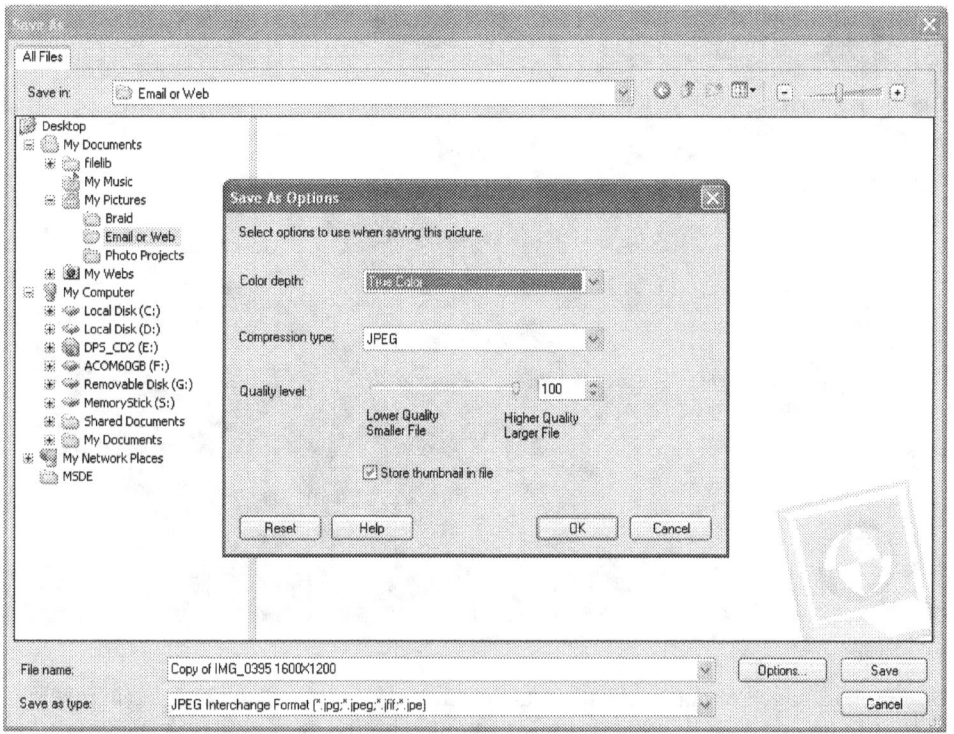

# Save an Image for a Device

There are more and more portable devices being marketed to which you can send an image. People are carrying around Palm and Pocket PC handheld computers and even telephones that can receive pictures. However, you wouldn't want to send a full-blown image to one of these devices! Not only would it take a LOOOONG time to be received (infrared and cellular phone networks are even slower than dial-up connections, in most cases), but the device wouldn't be able to render the image properly. For example, many Palm devices use a 160 x 160 pixel screen. What would it do with a 1,536 x 1,024 image?

You can scale your image to make it compatible with a range of wireless devices and cellular telephones. To do so, select File | Save a Copy For | Save For Device. This opens the Save For Device task bar. From the Select a Device drop-down list, choose the device for which you want to size your image (for example, a Pocket PC).

15

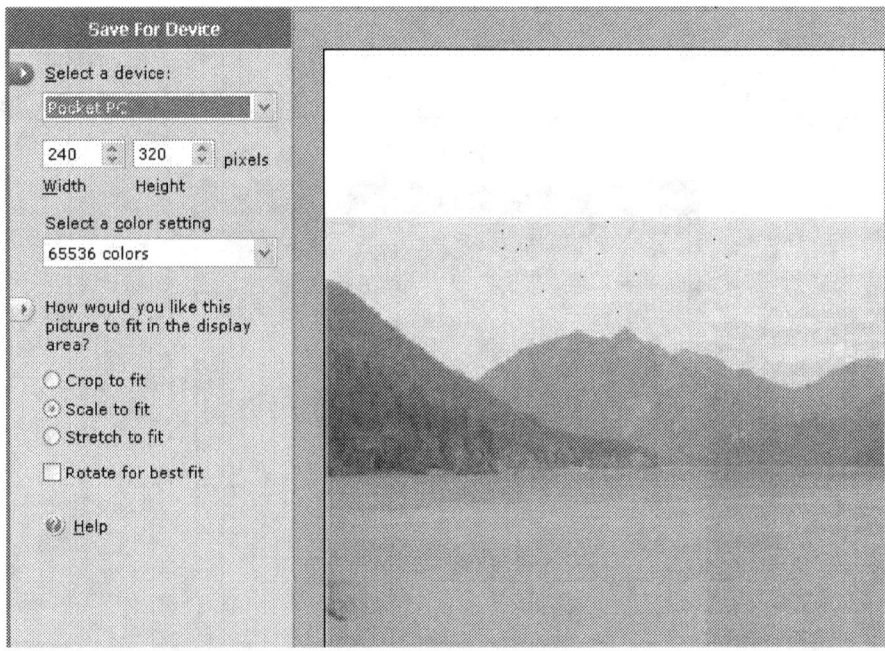

Digital Image Pro automatically sets the value of the Width and Height (in pixels) fields for the device and sets the number of colors in the Select a Color Setting drop-down list. If the image won't fit the device screen exactly, you can select an option to specify how to fit the image to the device screen. The options are as follows:

- **Crop to Fit** Either expands or reduces the object to the size of the canvas. It matches either the length or width of the object (whichever is smaller) to the canvas. The result is that the larger dimension falls outside the bounds of the canvas and is cropped off.

- **Scale to Fit** Scales the size of the object to match either the height or the width of the canvas without distorting the shape of the object.

- **Stretch to Fit** Stretches the object to fit the entire canvas, distorting the shape if necessary.

You can also select the Rotate for Best Fit checkbox to turn the image to fit the device screen. This is handy because the screens of most devices are not square. Selecting the checkbox will turn the image so that the long side of the image corresponds to the long side of the device. This may require that you rotate the device to see the image correctly. Figure 15-2 shows how the image might look on a Pocket PC screen when it is rotated to fit.

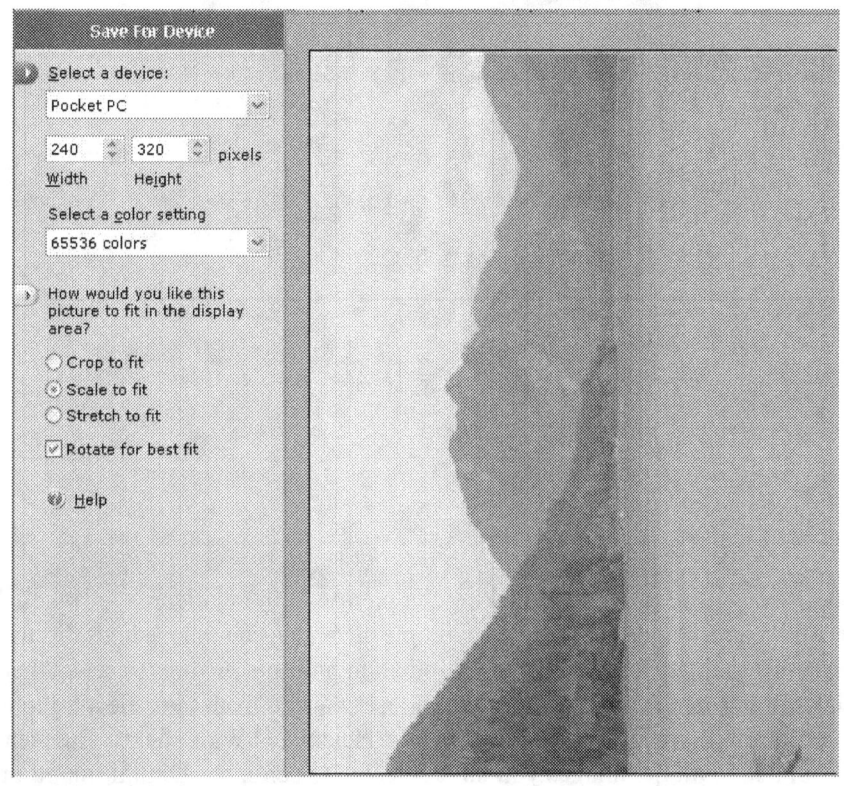

It's a little blocky, but you can see how your picture will look on a low resolution portable device.

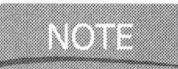
*You can choose Custom in the Select a Device drop-down list and set the Width, Height, and number of colors yourself.*

Once you have specified the parameters of the image for the specified device, click Save As to open the Save As dialog box and save the file.

# Send a Photo By E-mail

One of the easiest ways to send a photo to someone is to attach it to an e-mail. And Digital Image Pro makes it even easier by automating the whole process. To send someone an e-mail with a picture attached, select File | Send in E-mail. This opens the Send in E-mail task bar.

15

Copy of IMG_0395.JPG

Choose a picture to send by clicking the picture in the work area, or by clicking Select All Pictures. You can also select multiple pictures using the methods discussed earlier in this chapter (for example, CTRL-clicking multiple pictures to select them).

Pick the size of the picture by either choosing a size from the Select a Picture Size drop-down list, or by typing values into the Height and Width fields. The picture size is applied to all the images you have selected to send, but Digital Image Pro won't stretch the images to make them bigger (which degrades the picture quality big time). That is why the dimensions are listed as "maximum dimensions."

> **TIP** *If you just want to send the pictures at their actual size, choose Actual Size from the Select a Picture Size drop-down list.*

Click Send to create an e-mail in your e-mail program.

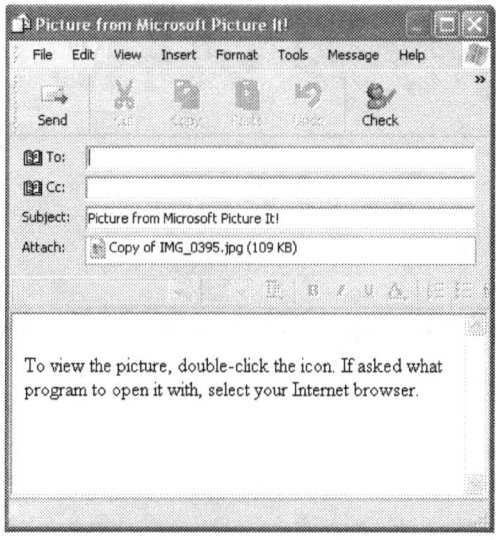

Fill in the e-mail addresses of the recipients, change the subject line and text if you wish, and click Send to send the missive on its way.

NOTE    *If, for some reason, you don't want to use your default e-mail program, click Change E-mail Program and pick a different e-mail program from the list.*

15

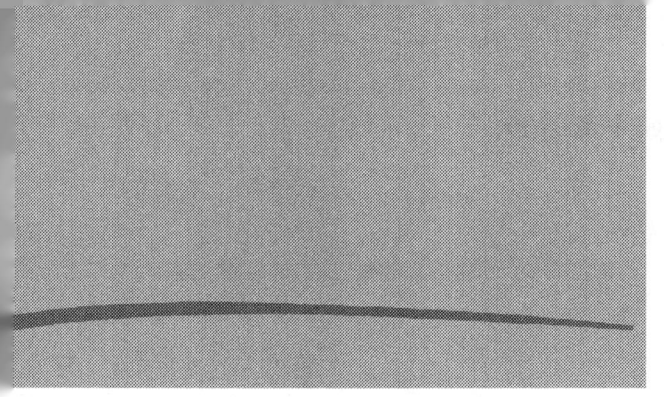

# Print Your Images

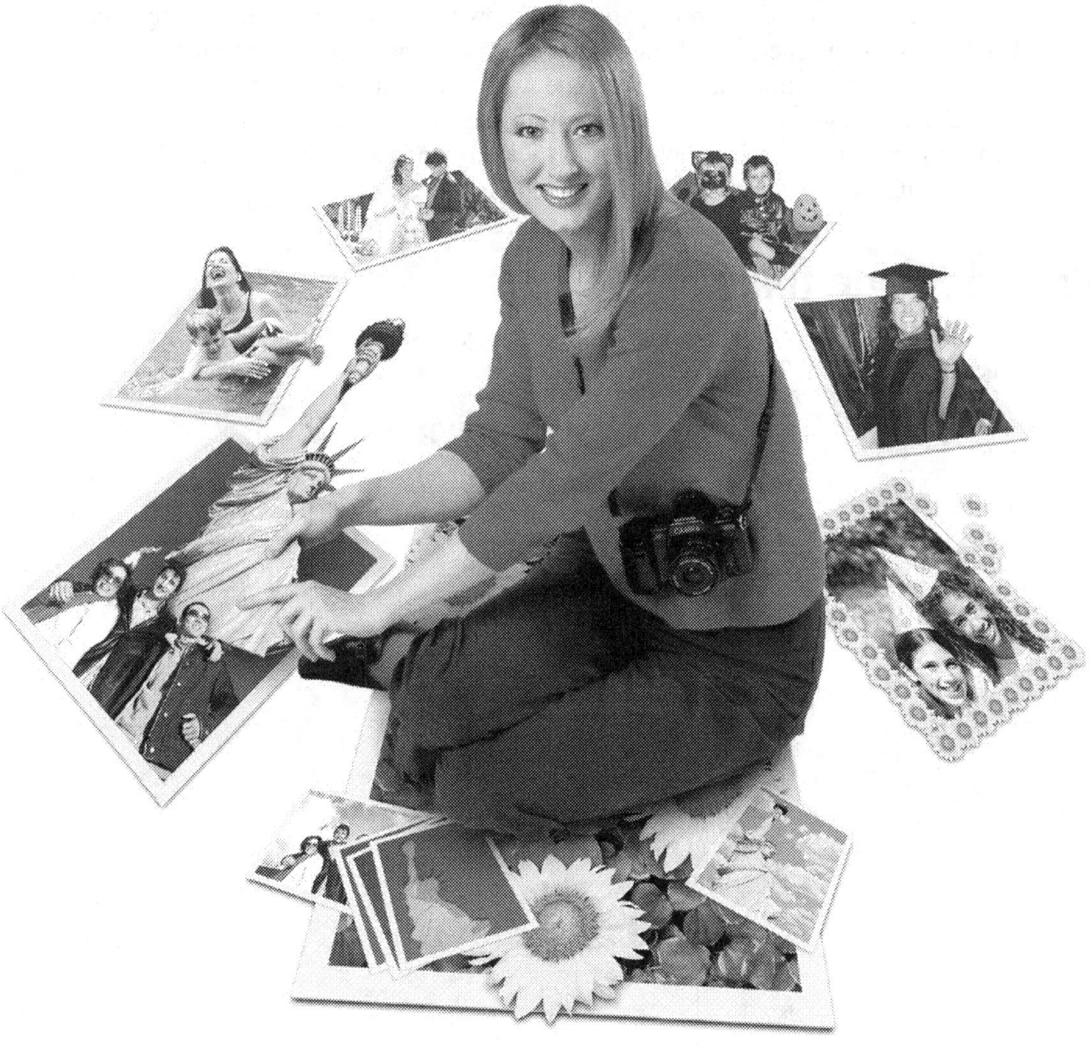

## How to...

- Print an image
- Use layouts to print multiple images
- Print your images professionally online
- Build photo gifts from your photos

If you've read most of this book, you now know how to clean up your photos, fix problems, apply filters, use your photos in projects, and even send a photo to someone via e-mail. But what most people want to do with their pictures is print them. Digital Image Pro makes it easy to print single photos, combine photos into a collage to use that expensive photo paper efficiently, and create professional photos and gifts online.

# Print a Single Image

As with virtually every other Windows program, you start the printing process by selecting File | Print. This opens the Print task bar:

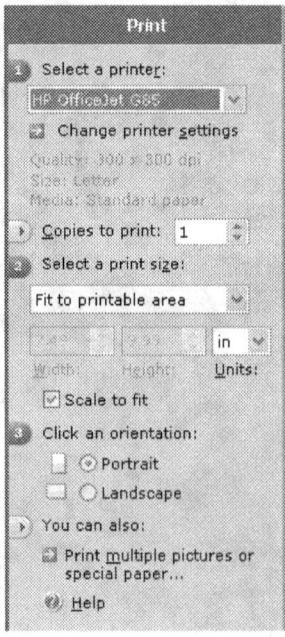

To print the single image in the workspace, set the following options in the Print task bar:

■ **Select a Printer**   Use this drop-down list to choose the printer you want to use. All the printers for which you have installed drivers appear in the list.

■ **Change Printer Settings**   Click Change Printer Settings to open the printer configuration dialog box for the selected printer. What you can do in this dialog box depends on your printer driver. In my case, I can change the print layout and select the type of paper, the quality of the printout, and whether the image prints in black and white or color.

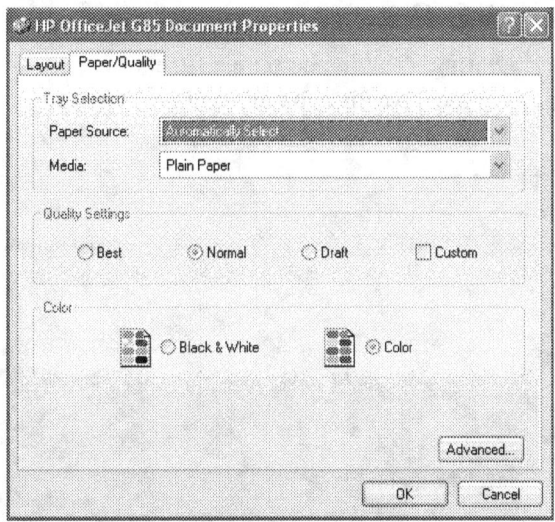

■ **Copies to Print**   Use this field to set the number of copies to print.

■ **Print Size**   Use the Select a Print Size drop-down list to choose the print size. The list contains standard photo sizes (8 x 10, 5 x 7, wallet, and so on) as well as the following three options:

■ **Exact Size**   Prints the photo at the exact size of the image.

■ **Fit to Printable Area**   Stretches or shrinks the photo to fit the printable area of the paper you selected with Change Printer Settings.

■ **Custom**   Choose Custom and fill in a size in the Width and Height fields. You can also select the units of measure (in, cm, or mm) in the Units field.

16

■ **Scale to Fit**   Select the Scale to Fit checkbox to ensure that the image fits on the paper. If you clear this checkbox, you can pick a size that will cause the image to exceed the size of the paper.

■ **Set the Orientation**   Choose either Portrait or Landscape to set the orientation of the image. Digital Image Pro does a good job (based on the size of the image and the size of the paper) at "guessing" which orientation will work best.

To finish the process, click the Print button at the bottom of the task bar. Out comes your photo, ready to share!

# Print Photos Using a Layout

You aren't limited to printing a single photo on a sheet of paper. That is a good thing because photo paper is expensive and you are going to want to fill the paper with

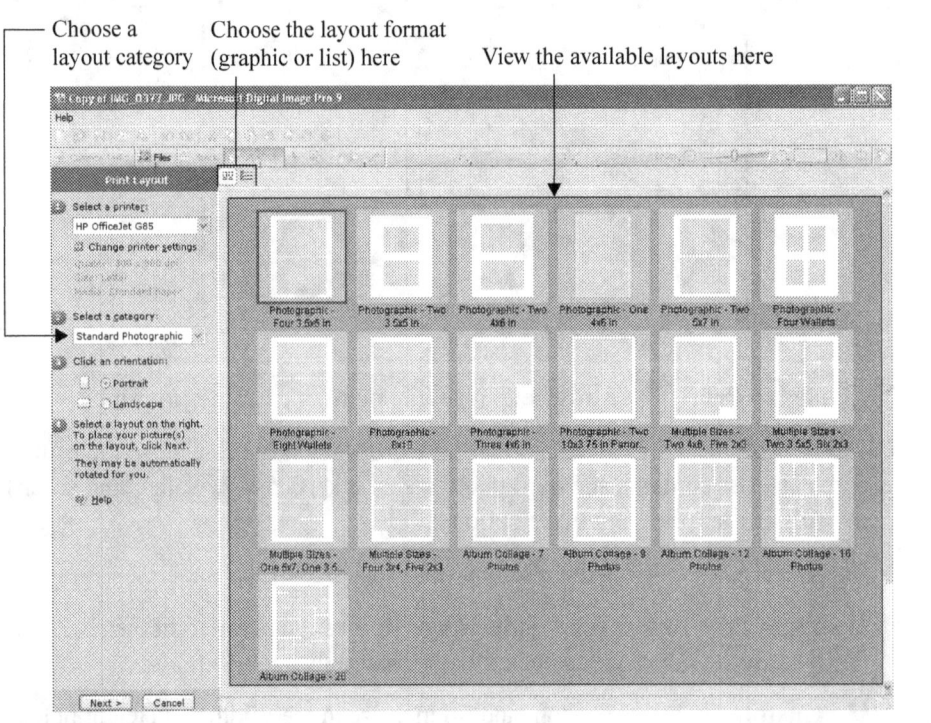

Use the Print Layout task bar and the layout templates to pick the photo layout you want to create.

as many photos as will fit—either multiple copies of the same picture or copies of many different pictures.

To print multiple images on a page, Digital Image Pro uses a *layout*. Each layout provides a template for placing photographs on the page prior to printing. To get started, click Print Multiple Pictures or Special Paper in the Print task bar. This opens the Print Layout task bar, shown in Figure 16-1. At the top of this task bar, you can choose a printer and change the printer settings. Figure 16-1 also shows the workspace, which contains the layouts for the currently chosen category (more on this shortly).

## Select a Layout Category

The Select a Category drop-down list provides a list of the available layout categories.

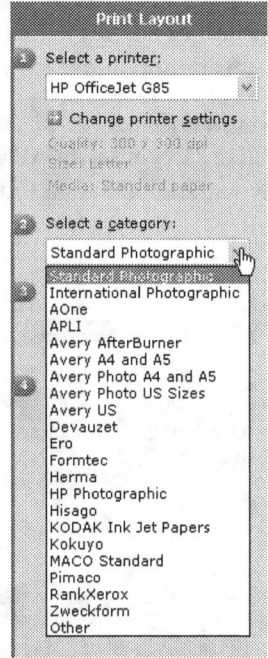

These categories include not only standard photographic page sizes, but a variety of different commercial offerings, such as Avery Photo sizes. For the vendor offerings, the layouts display the item number to make it easy to purchase the supplies you need.

You can also orient the layouts either vertically or horizontally by clicking the Portrait or the Landscape options.

## Pick and Populate a Layout

Once you pick a category, the workspace displays the available layouts for that category. Select the layout you want to use and click Next> to proceed.

### Place Images in the Layout

The next step is to place images in the layout. Each light-blue rectangle (with a white border) represents a "spot" where you can place an image. There are three ways to add images to the layout:

- **Fill the Layout with the selected picture**    To fill the layout with a single picture, select the image in the Files area and click Fill the Layout with the Selected Picture. Digital Image Pro places a copy of the selected image into each spot in the layout, rotating images where necessary to make them fit. Figure 16-2 shows how this option might look.

- **Fill the Layout with all open pictures**    If you have multiple images open in the Files area, click Fill the Layout with All Open Pictures to place all the open pictures into the layout. Digital Image Pro does a good job of arranging

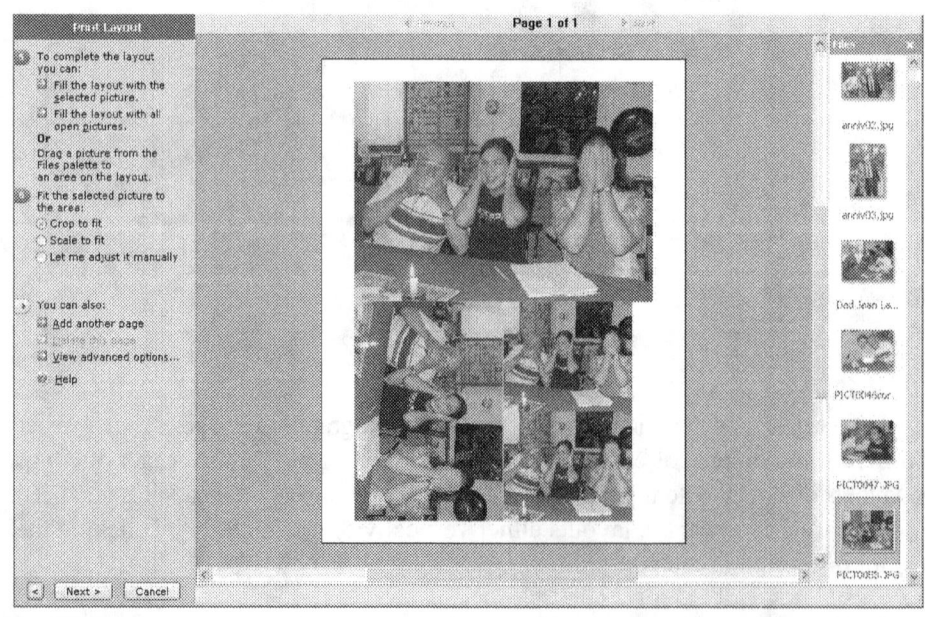

Populate all the slots in the layout with the selected picture to get many copies of that image.

the images, again rotating them when necessary. Figure 16-3 shows how this option might look.

**NOTE**   *If there are too many pictures to fit them all in the slots of the selected layout, Digital Image Pro automatically adds another page with the same layout and adds the remaining pictures into the new page. Scroll through the multiple pages using the <Previous and Next> buttons at the top of the work area (visible in Figure 16-3).*

■   **Add pictures to the layout manually**   You can click an image in the Files area and drag it into an empty spot in the layout. You can also click and drag an image in the layout into a different slot provided that the target slot is empty. To remove an image from a slot, click the image in the slot and press the DELETE key or choose Delete from the shortcut menu.

## Configure the Way Images Are Added to the Layout

It is actually rare that an image fits into a slot on a layout exactly. If the image isn't quite the right size, you need to tell Digital Image Pro how to make the image fit. There are two automatic options, or you can size the image to fit manually.

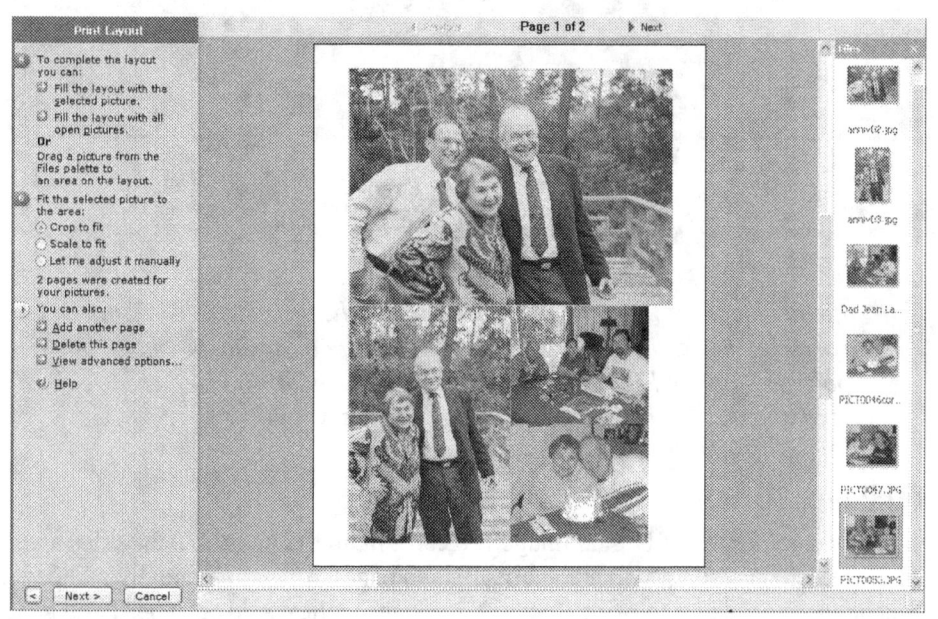

Use all the images in the Files area to populate the slots in a layout.

16

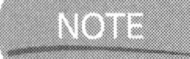 *You can set the sizing options individually for each image. To do so, click the image in the layout and choose the sizing option you want. Then proceed to the next image and repeat the process.*

The first automatic option is Crop to Fit. This option tells Digital Image Pro to fit the shorter dimension to the slot and crop off any part of the long dimension that falls outside the slot boundary. The second automatic option is Scale to Fit. This option tells Digital Image Pro to shrink the image so that it all fits into the slot. This usually means that there will be white space around the edges of the short dimension.

To size the image manually, click the Let Me Adjust It Manually option. When you click the image in the layout, it is displayed with the sizing handles and rotation handle. You can click and drag the image, size it with the sizing handles, or rotate it with the rotation handle, just like an object or a shape.

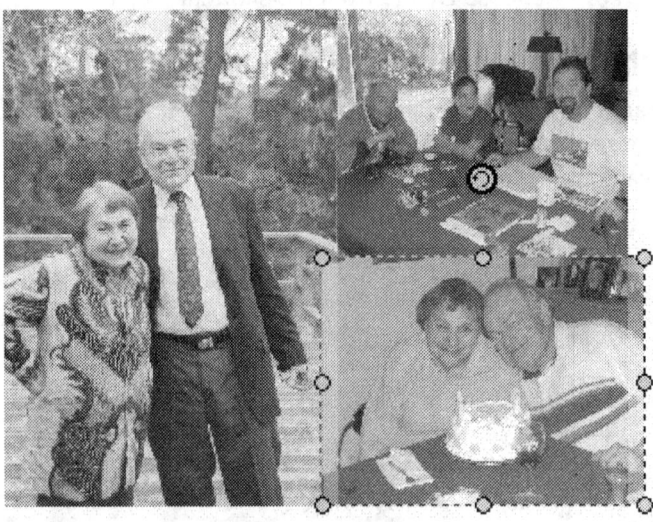

*If you placed an image in the layout manually, it may not be oriented correctly. For example, you may want to place a landscape image into a portrait slot. To do so, drag the image into the slot, choose Let Me Adjust It Manually, and rotate the image 90 degrees.*

## Add Pages to Your Layout

I mentioned earlier that if Digital Image Pro can't fit all the images in the Files area into the selected layout, it will automatically add pages. You can manually add pages to queue up more pages to print. To add more pages, click Add Another Page to display the Add Page dialog box.

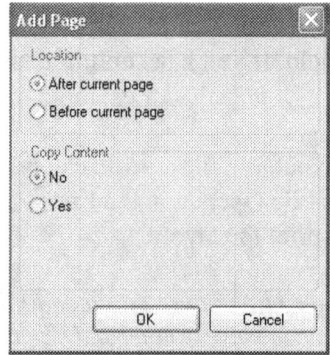

Using the Add Page dialog box, you can choose where you want the new page inserted (before or after the current page) and whether to copy the contents of the current page into the new page (handy if you want to make only minor adjustments to the layout of the new page). Click OK to close the dialog box and add the new page. You can fill the new page with content (or adjust the content) as described in the last few sections.

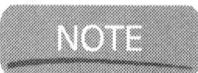 *To remove a page, navigate to the page you want to get rid of, and click Delete This Page.*

### Print the Layout

Once you're done creating layouts and adding pictures to them, click Next> to print the page. This opens a new version of the Print Layout task bar.

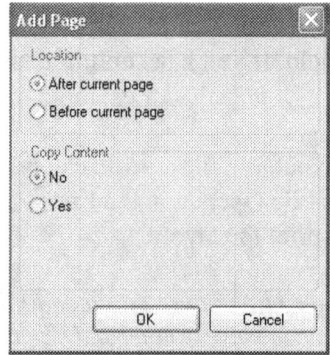

**16**

This version of the task bar enables you to set the number of copies you want to print using the appropriate field. If you have multiple layout pages, the number of copies applies to all of them—you can't, for example, print one copy of page 1 and three copies of page 2.

If you want to save the layout as a file (so you can print it again later), select the checkbox labeled Keep This File Opened in the Files Palette so I Can Save It.

Click the Print button to print the layout.

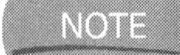 *The images in the saved layout are saved as individual objects (each on its own layer). Thus, you can move, rotate, and size the images just as you would any other objects. However, once you finish creating the layout, the handy guides disappear.*

## Set the Advanced Printing Options

You can set some advanced options, such as adjusting the bleed and setting the position of the images on the paper. To adjust these parameters, click View Advanced Options in the Print Layout task bar. This opens a new version of the task bar.

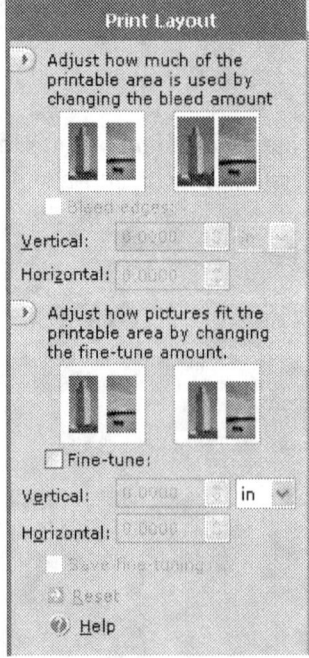

## Set the Bleed

Under normal circumstances, a printer will leave a white border around the edges of the paper and between the images. If your printer supports it (and not all of them do), you can suppress the border and print all the way out to the edges of the paper. This is called "setting the bleed" because when the printing extends all the way to the edges, it is called "full bleed."

To modify the bleed, select the Bleed Edges checkbox and set the amount to extend the edges using the Vertical and Horizontal fields. As you increase the size of these fields, the edges shrink until they disappear completely ("full bleed").

## Fine-Tune the Picture Position in the Layout

You can fine-tune the set of pictures on a layout to position them precisely. This can be important, for example, when you need a set of labels to align with the label stock. To fine-tune the position, select the Fine-tune checkbox and enter a value in the Vertical and/or Horizontal fields. If you enter a positive number, the set of pictures is shifted to the right (Vertical) and down (Horizontal); entering negative numbers shifts the pictures left and up. If you want to save the fine-tune settings, select the Save Fine-Tuning checkbox before clicking the < button at the bottom of the screen. Clicking that button returns you to the previous task bar where you can then click Next> to set the number of copies and print the layout.

# Print an Index Sheet of Your Photos

You can print an index sheet that shows thumbnails of a collection of your photos. These photos can be either in the Files palette or in a directory on your computer. Figure 16-4 shows an example of an index sheet.

To get started creating an index sheet, select File | Print Index sheet. This opens the Print Index Sheet task bar.

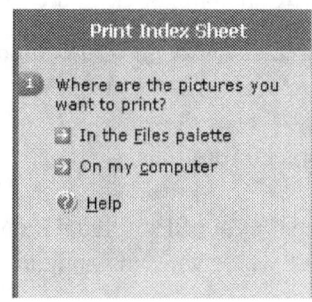

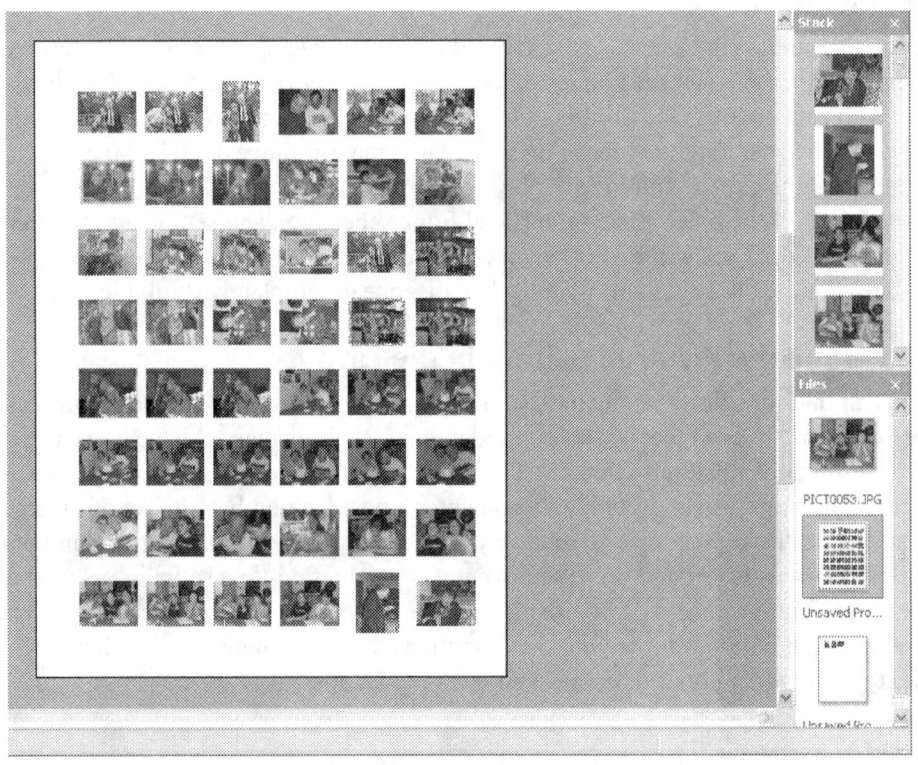

Use an index sheet to help identify your photos.

The first step is to select the pictures to include on the index sheet. You have two choices:

- If the files are in the Files palette, click In the Files Palette.
- If the files are located in a directory on your computer, click On My Computer. This opens the File Browser where you can pick the files. The files must all be in the same directory. You can't pick files from one folder and then navigate to another folder and pick more files.

Once you choose the source for your files, Digital Image Pro opens another version of the Print Index Sheet task bar, where you can configure the parameters for printing.

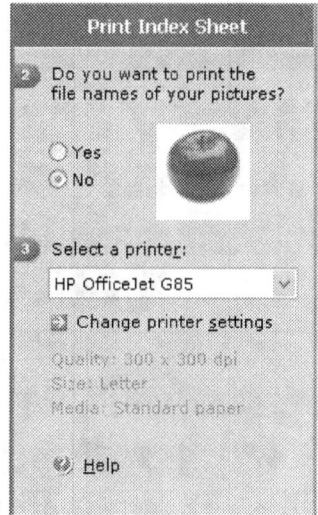

If you want to print the filenames for the images, click *Yes* near the top of the task bar. Then select the printer from the Select a Printer drop-down list, and (if you wish), click Change Printer Settings to configure your printer. Once you are done, click Next> to continue.

At this point, Digital Image Pro displays the index sheet and the task bar (see Figure 16-5) to allow you to specify the number of copies you want and choose to keep the file open after printing so you can save the index sheet to reuse later. Then click Print to print the index sheet.

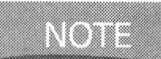 *If you specify more images than will fit on the index sheet, Digital Image Pro automatically creates multiple index sheets. Each sheet appears in a separate project in the Files palette. When you print, all of the index sheets are printed automatically.*

# Print Your Photos Professionally

16

Inkjet printer prices have been falling steadily, so it is now possible to purchase an inexpensive printer that can do a good job printing digital photographs. But such printers are still fairly slow, and the cost of photo-quality paper and the ink can drive the cost of printing a 4 x 6 inch print to $.50 or higher. If you have a lot of photos to print, or don't want to bother with the complexities of printing the images yourself, you can have them professionally printed over the Internet and sent to you.

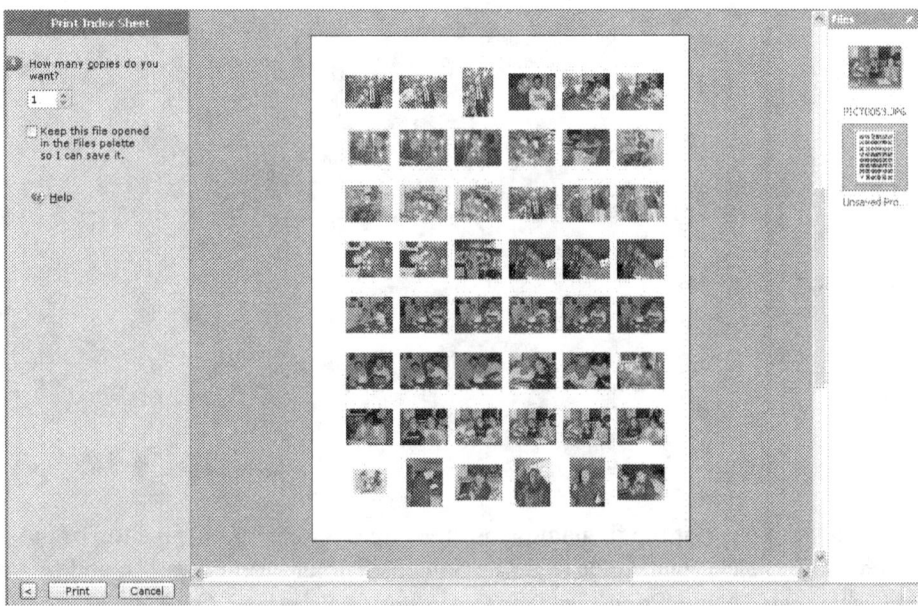

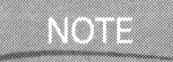 View the index sheet, choose the number of copies, and print it!

There are many other things you can do with your images, including creating "photo gifts" that feature your photos. These include coffee mugs, apparel, teddy bears, mouse pads, and more. Digital Image Pro makes it possible to upload your photos, choose and design a gift, and have it sent to you.

**NOTE** *The photo printing service and photo gift service that you access from within Digital Image Pro (via the Internet) are convenient for you to use, but they are certainly not the only companies that provide these services. By doing a little shopping around, you may find that you can save money and get better quality results from a competitor.*

## Print Photos Online

To print your photos online, you'll need to be connected to the Internet. Select File | Print Professionally Online | Prints and Enlargements. This opens the Prints and Enlargements task bar.

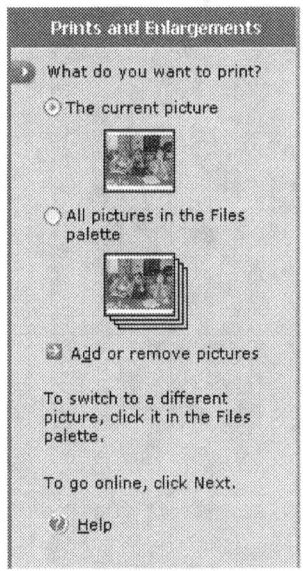

Use the options in the task bar to select whether to print just The Current Picture, or All Pictures in the Files Palette. If you need to, click Add or Remove Pictures to add more pictures to Files palette so they can be printed. Click Next> to proceed to the next step.

At this point, Digital Image links to the price sheet for ordering prints at Fujicolor. Click the Order Prints button to proceed. If you choose to print all the files in the Files palette, a new screen opens to confirm you want to print all the pictures (see Figure 16-6). Select the checkbox in the upper-left corner for each image you want to print; clear the checkbox for any you don't want to print. Then click Continue to proceed to the next screen.

**NOTE**   *The first time you order prints during any session, you'll need to log in with your .Net ID. You can, if you wish, configure your computer to log you in automatically by selecting the Sign Me in Automatically checkbox on the log-in screen.*

At this point, your browser opens and the photos you selected are uploaded to the Web site.

The screen you see next is shown in Figure 16-7. From here, you can choose the quantity of each size of print you want, and the Web site will show a running total of your order. If a small exclamation point is shown alongside a size, that size is not recommended for printing because the photo is not of a high enough resolution to print at that size.

16

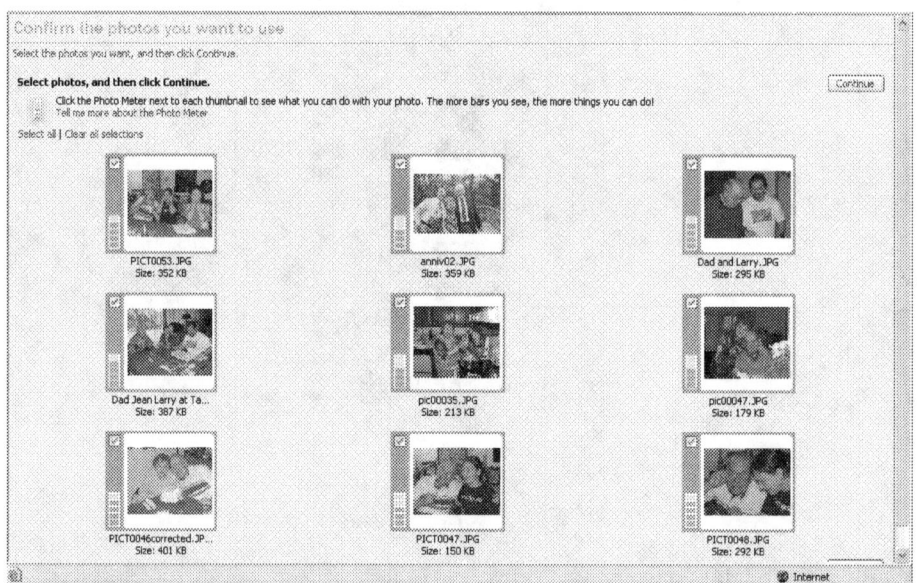

Choose the pictures you want to print by checking the checkbox.

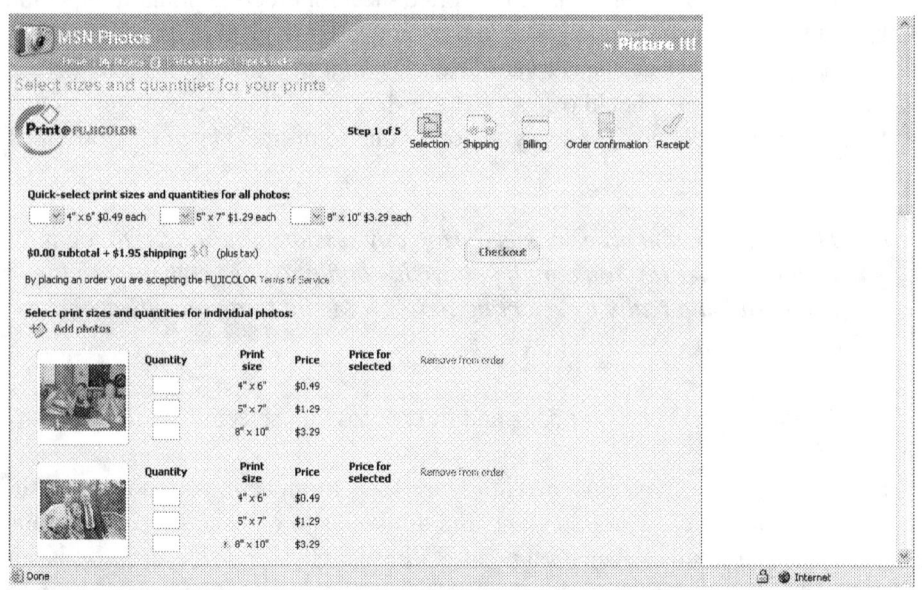

Specify the quantity and size of each print you want.

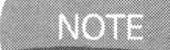 *You can choose to upload more photos by clicking Add Photos. The first time you use this link, you'll have to allow the Web site to upload and install a small application to enable uploading of your images.*

Once you're done selecting the pictures you want to print, click the Checkout button. The Web site will walk you through the payment process. You'll need a .Net ID (such as a Hotmail account) or an MSN account, and you'll have to allow the site to create and configure an *MSN Wallet*. You can only use an MSN Wallet to pay for the prints.

## Create Photo Gifts Online

To create a photo gift and have it sent to you, select File | Print Professionally Online | Photo Gifts. The process starts out the same way as ordering prints: pick whether to use just the current picture or all the pictures in the Files palette.

*Just choose one image. If you choose more than one, you'll be asked later in the process to pick just the one image you want to use.*

Once you click Next>, Digital Image Pro displays the main page for Browse Gifts & Prints (see Figure 16-8). You can pick one of the items on this page (such as T-shirts or Magnets), and proceed.

Most of the good stuff, however, is under the Photo Gifts entry in the list on the left side of the working area. Click Photo Gifts to see a nice selection of gifts, including mugs, mouse pads, Post-it cubes, magnets, clocks, and tote bags (see Figure 16-9).

*The* Clothing *entry enables you to create ties, caps, sweatshirts, various baby wear, boxer shorts, and aprons.*

To choose an item to build, click the icon or select the item from the list on the left side of the work area. This presents a sample image of a finished product and tells you the price for the item. Click the Order button to proceed. If you ignored the previous tip and chose more than one photo, you'll have to select the photo to use at this point.

The steps you follow from this point to customize your photo gift vary slightly, depending on the gift. For example, if you order boxer shorts, you'll have to pick whether to put the image on the right leg or the left leg. Once these small differences are out of the way, you can customize the design using the application running in the

16

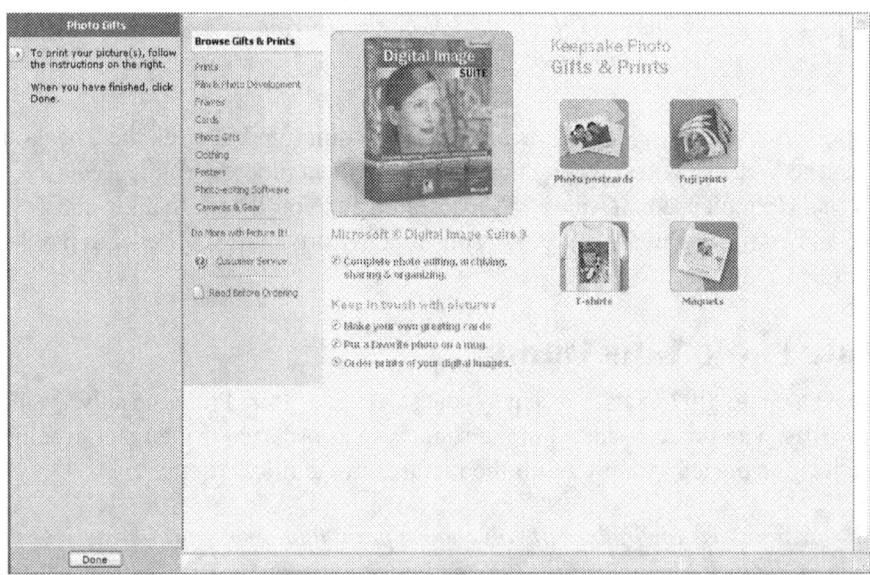

The first page for choosing photo gifts has only a limited selection.

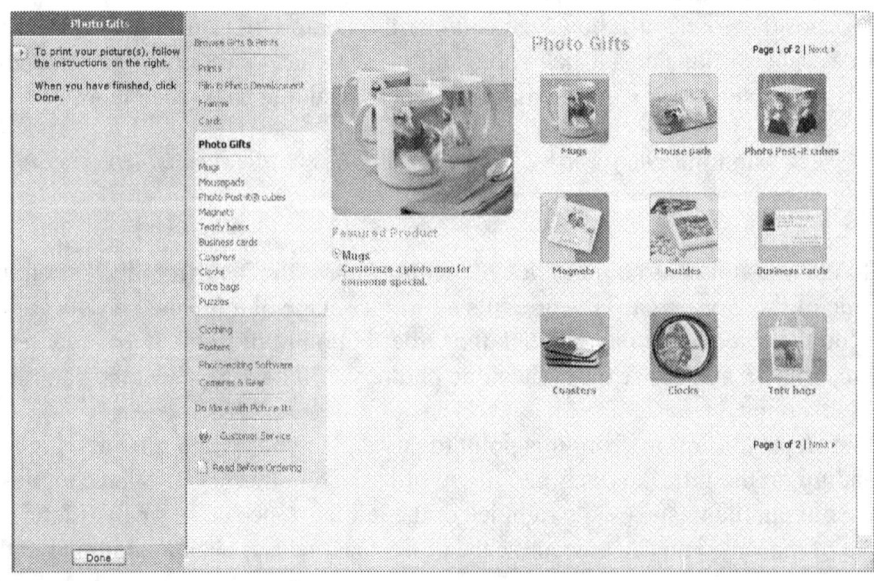

These photo gifts correspond to the designs available when you build a Photo Gift Project.

Web browser. Figure 16-10 shows a sample of the application you use to build your gift. Simply click a button and follow the onscreen prompts. In each screen, you can make choices, click the Update button to see how it looks, and click OK (to keep your changes and proceed) or Cancel to back out your changes. As you build the design, the Web browser displays a preview.

The customization options are as follows:

- **Text**   Most designs allow one or more lines of text. Clicking the Text button enables you to specify the text content and (in most designs) add more lines of text if you wish.

- **Graphic**   You can replace the graphic (photo) with another image from a library of images, with a photo from your hard drive, or from a Web site (you specify the URL that specifies an image on a Web site—good luck!). You can also remove the graphic or add an extra graphic to the design.

- **Colors**   You can change the color of any text block in the design. Either choose the color name from the drop-down list or click View Color Samples to view sample color swatches. To choose a color, simply click the swatch.

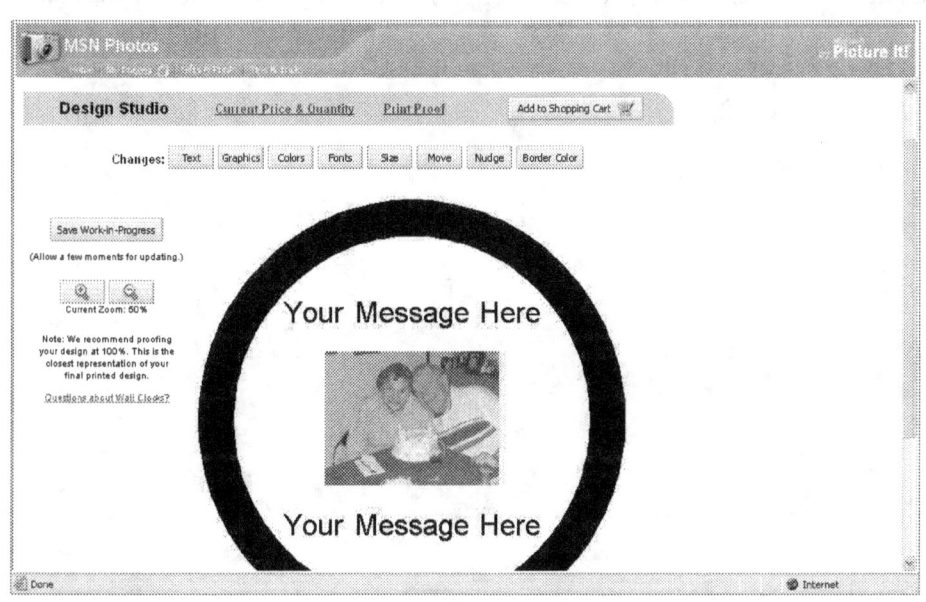

Build your gift using your Web browser.

■ **Fonts**   Change the font and effects (Bold, Italic) for any text block in the design. Pick the font from the drop-down list, or click View Font Samples to see samples of the available fonts. Choose a font by clicking it.

■ **Size**   You can change the size of the text blocks or the graphic. Choose the item you want to change, and then pick the amount of the change (in points) and whether to make the item smaller or larger.

■ **Move**   You can move the text blocks or the graphic. You can move the items horizontally to the Left, Center, or Right; and vertically to the Top, Middle, or Bottom.

■ **Nudge**   This screen enables you to make small adjustments to the position of the text blocks and graphics. Select the item to move from the Change Field(s) drop-down list. Then select the amount to move the item and click one of the direction buttons (Up, Down, Left, or Right) to move the object in that direction. You can repeatedly nudge an item until you have the position exactly right.

Once you are done creating your design, it's time to add the item to your shopping cart and proceed to checkout. Unfortunately, because photo gifts are handled by a different company than the professionally printed photos, you'll need to set up an account for photo gifts as well. After the first time, of course, you can just sign into your account to access the shipping and billing information to pay for your photo gifts.

# Index

## INTERNATIONAL CONTACT INFORMATION

**AUSTRALIA**
McGraw-Hill Book Company
Australia Pty. Ltd.
TEL +61-2-9900-1800
FAX +61-2-9878-8881
http://www.mcgraw-hill.com.au
books-it_sydney@mcgraw-hill.com

**CANADA**
McGraw-Hill Ryerson Ltd.
TEL +905-430-5000
FAX +905-430-5020
http://www.mcgraw-hill.ca

**GREECE, MIDDLE EAST, & AFRICA**
**(Excluding South Africa)**
McGraw-Hill Hellas
TEL +30-210-6560-990
TEL +30-210-6560-993
TEL +30-210-6560-994
FAX +30-210-6545-525

**MEXICO (Also serving Latin America)**
McGraw-Hill Interamericana Editores
S.A. de C.V.
TEL +525-1500-5108
FAX +525-117-1589
http://www.mcgraw-hill.com.mx
carlos_ruiz@mcgraw-hill.com

**SINGAPORE (Serving Asia)**
McGraw-Hill Book Company
TEL +65-6863-1580
FAX +65-6862-3354
http://www.mcgraw-hill.com.sg
mghasia@mcgraw-hill.com

**SOUTH AFRICA**
McGraw-Hill South Africa
TEL +27-11-622-7512
FAX +27-11-622-9045
robyn_swanepoel@mcgraw-hill.com

**SPAIN**
McGraw-Hill/
Interamericana de España, S.A.U.
TEL +34-91-180-3000
FAX +34-91-372-8513
http://www.mcgraw-hill.es
professional@mcgraw-hill.es

**UNITED KINGDOM, NORTHERN,**
**EASTERN, & CENTRAL EUROPE**
McGraw-Hill Education Europe
TEL +44-1-628-502500
FAX +44-1-628-770224
http://www.mcgraw-hill.co.uk
emea_queries@mcgraw-hill.com

**ALL OTHER INQUIRIES Contact:**
McGraw-Hill/Osborne
TEL +1-510-420-7700
FAX +1-510-420-7703
http://www.osborne.com
omg_international@mcgraw-hill.com

# Sound Off!

Visit us at **www.osborne.com/bookregistration** and let us know what you thought of this book. While you're online you'll have the opportunity to register for newsletters and special offers from McGraw-Hill/Osborne.

*We want to hear from you!*

# Sneak Peek

Visit us today at **www.betabooks.com** and see what's coming from McGraw-Hill/Osborne tomorrow!

Based on the successful software paradigm, Bet@Books™ allows computing professionals to view partial and sometimes complete text versions of selected titles online. Bet@Books™ viewing is free, invites comments and feedback, and allows you to "test drive" books in progress on the subjects that interest you the most.

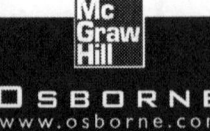

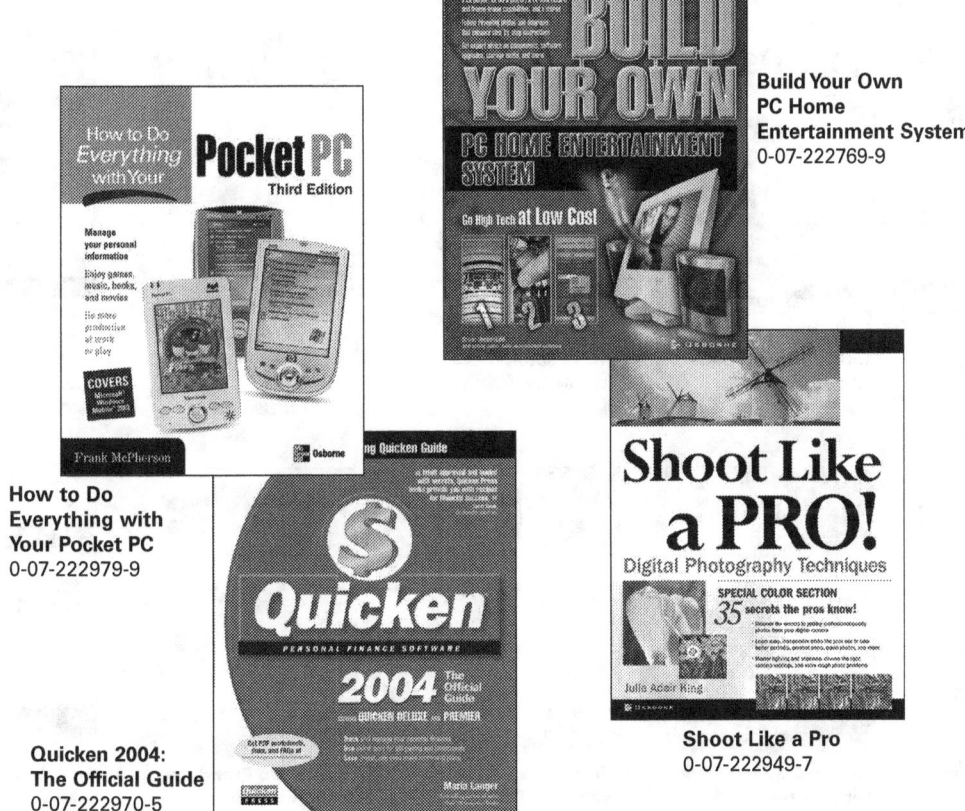
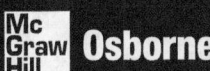

# Know How

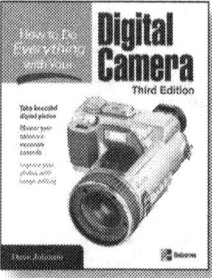

**How to Do Everything with Your Digital Camera**
**Third Edition**
ISBN: 0-07-223081-9

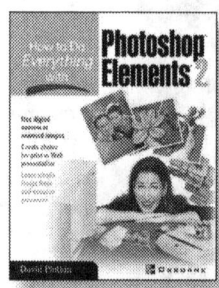

**How to Do Everything with Photoshop Elements 2**
ISBN: 0-07-222638-2

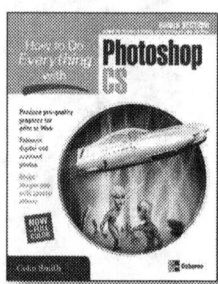

**How to Do Everything with Photoshop CS**
ISBN: 0-07-223143-2
4-color

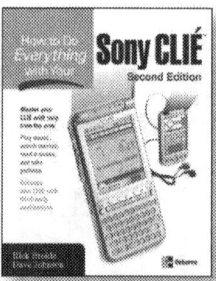

**How to Do Everything with Your Sony CLIÉ**
**Second Edition**
ISBN: 0-07-223074-6

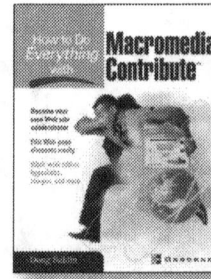

**How to Do Everything with Macromedia Contribute**
0-07-222892-X

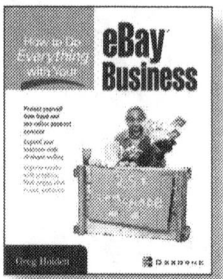

**How to Do Everything with Your eBay Business**
0-07-222948-9

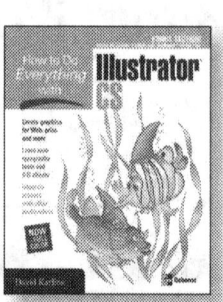

**How to Do Everything with Illustrator CS**
ISBN: 0-07-223092-4
4-color

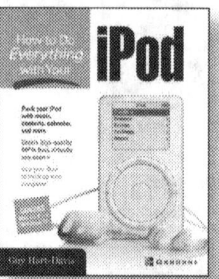

**How to Do Everything with Your iPod**
ISBN: 0-07-222700-1

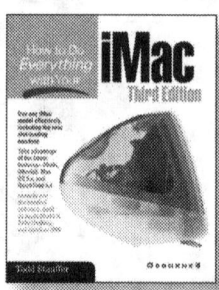

**How to Do Everything with Your iMac,**
**Third Edition**
ISBN: 0-07-213172-1

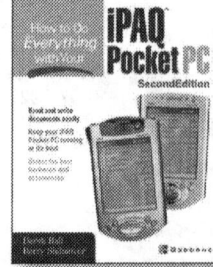

**How to Do Everything with Your iPAQ Pocket**
**Second Edition**
ISBN: 0-07-222950-0

www.ingramcontent.com/pod-product-compliance
Lightning Source LLC
Chambersburg PA
CBHW081139180526
45170CB00006B/1856